Myths and Memories of the Nation

ANTHONY D. SMITH

OXFORD
UNIVERSITY PRESS

OXFORD
UNIVERSITY PRESS

Great Clarendon Street, Oxford OX2 6DP

Oxford University Press is a department of the University of Oxford.
It furthers the University's objective of excellence in research, scholarship,
and education by publishing worldwide in

Oxford New York

Athens Auckland Bangkok Bogotá Buenos Aires Calcutta
Cape Town Chennai Dar es Salaam Delhi Florence Hong Kong Istanbul
Karachi Kuala Lumpur Madrid Melbourne Mexico City Mumbai
Nairobi Paris São Paulo Singapore Taipei Tokyo Toronto Warsaw

and associated companies in Berlin Ibadan

Oxford is a registered trade mark of Oxford University Press
in the UK and certain other countries

Published in the United States
by Oxford University Press Inc., New York

British Library Cataloguing in Publication Data

Data available

Library of Congress Cataloging in Publication Data

Smith, Anthony D.
Myths and memories of the nation / Anthony D. Smith.
Includes bibliographical references.
1. Nationalism. 2. Ethnicity—Political aspects. I. Title.
JC312.S55 1999 320.54—dc21 99–36963
ISBN 0–19–829534–0.
ISBN 0–19–829684–3 (pbk.)

1 3 5 7 9 10 8 6 4 2

Typeset by Graphicraft Limited, Hong Kong
Printed in Great Britain
on acid-free paper by
Biddles Ltd.
Guildford and King's Lynn

PREFACE

This book seeks to explore issues of nations and nationalism from the perspective of 'historical ethno-symbolism', focusing on the historical and popular context of nations, and the central role of myths, memories, symbols, and traditions. It therefore attempts to bring together the previously (and still, to a large extent) separated fields and literatures of 'ethnicity' and 'nations and nationalism'; and to show how they can be mutually beneficial for a broader understanding of some of the problems common to both.

The newly written Introduction provides an extended theoretical statement of my approach, and the chapters that follow illustrate it with empirical applications from mainly pre-modern (Part I) and modern (Part II) epochs. With the exception of the second chapter, which serves as an early preview (1984) of the ethno-symbolic approach, I have chosen journal articles over a recent five-year period from 1992, which demonstrate the nature, scope, and themes of this kind of approach to nations and nationalism.

I have selected the articles for their empirical variety as well as their theoretical interest. They cover such diverse topics as national identity in the ancient and medieval worlds, chosen peoples, nation and ethnoscape, the role of nationalists, the plight of ethnic minorities, diaspora nationalisms, European cultural identity, and the current resurgence of ethnic nationalism. These issues are all viewed through the same lens, and can, I think, be illuminated by an ethno-symbolic approach.

I am grateful to Dominic Byatt and Oxford University Press for their support for this project which aims to bring together essays that are scattered across a variety of academic journals. I should add that responsibility for any errors and omissions is mine alone.

A. D. S.

CONTENTS

PART I

Ethno-history and National Identity

Introduction

'Ethno-symbolism' and the Study of Nationalism

This book seeks to explore one of the central issues of our epoch, the rise of nations and the world-wide appeal of nationalism. The late twentieth century has witnessed an unexpected resurgence of ethnic conflict, and nationalism has once again become the central fact of contemporary politics. Why is it that so many people remain so deeply attached to their ethnic communities and nations at the close of the second millennium? Why do the myths, memories, and symbols of the nation command such widespread loyalty and devotion? And why are so many people still prepared to make considerable sacrifices, even of life and limb, for their nations and cultures?

As might be expected, these questions have been addressed in a variety of ways and from very different standpoints. But most of the answers have fallen into four main categories of explanation: the primordialist, the perennialist, the modernist, and the ethno-symbolic. To date, these form the major paradigms of explanation of the nature, power, and incidence of nations and nationalism. The chapters in this book exemplify the last of these paradigms, and seek to explore its many facets in a variety of thematic contexts. But, since the main concerns and aims of 'ethno-symbolism' emerged as a response to problems raised by the other major paradigms, we must first outline the theoretical context in which they emerged. I shall begin, therefore, with a brief statement of the main features and problems of the primordialist, perennialist and modernist paradigms.[1]

PRIMORDIALISM AND PERENNIALISM

Early explanations of nationalism tended to be greatly influenced by organic varieties of nationalism. Nations were seen as the natural and primordial divisions of humanity, and nationalism was thought to be ubiquitous and universal. What is now termed *primordialism* emerged from these widely accepted assumptions. For the primordialists, the key to the nature, power, and incidence of nations and nationalism lies in the root-edness of the nation in kinship, ethnicity, and the genetic bases of human existence. There are, in fact, several kinds of *primordialism*, and I shall briefly outline three of them.

The first is popular, and, as we saw, nationalist. It sees nations as ele-ments of nature, or the divine plan, not just of history. Nations, as the Abbé Sièyes put it, 'exist in the state of nature', and as such are the ulti-mate source of power, will, and law. They are like natural organisms, sub-ject to the laws of nature, forgotten and silent perhaps, but continuing to exist beneath the debris of history until the moment of their rebirth. The trouble with this nationalist view of nations and nationalism is that it offers no independent evidence of the existence of nations outside the affirma-tions of the nationalists, nor does it confront the incidence and consequences of migration, colonization, and intermarriage for the composition of modern nations. It also fails to explain how and why, nations were for-gotten, why they were so often, in Ernest Gellner's phrase, 'determined slum-berers', why only some of them 'awoke', and why the nationalist awakeners emerged when and where they did.[2]

A second variety of primordialism stems from the recent revival of socio-biology. Van den Berghe (1978, 1995), for example, argues that nations and ethnic communities are really extensions of kinship units and are built up from the same nepotistic drives of *inclusive fitness* as smaller clans and families. At root, they are all attenuated collective extensions of individual genetic reproductive drives, and this is attested by our choice of cultural signs (colour, language, religion) indicating biological affinity. Thus, for van den Berghe, myths of shared descent largely correspond to real bio-logical ancestry, because of the need for at least some generations of endo-gamy to forge ethnic identity. But, as Walker Connor (1994) points out, such *myths* rarely correspond to what we know of real biological descent; even apparently endogamous ethnic communities have often had mixed ancestral origins and some degree of intermarriage with other peoples in the past. Besides, it is very difficult to demonstrate that the genetic pools of families and clans can be extended through nepotism to much larger population groups such as ethnic and national communities.[3]

Finally, there is the familiar cultural variety of primordialism, associ-ated with Edward Shils and Clifford Geertz. Geertz (1963), in particular, while dismissing the political significance of biological descent groups, spoke of the overwhelming power of the *primordial tie* attributed to the *givens* of human existence, namely, congruities of blood, speech, custom, religion, and territory, *givens* that threatened to dissolve the *civil ties* of the modern state. It is important to note that Geertz speaks of *attribution* by human beings of overriding efficacy; it is *we* who feel this ineffable power and endow it with life-enhancing primordiality. Nevertheless, while the cultural approach reveals what we may well call the 'participants' primordialism 'of the community's membership—the members' own sense of the immemorial nature of their nation—as well as the centrality of symbolism in the study of ethnicity and nationalism, it does little to advance the cause of explanation. Primordialism vividly identifies the problem, but is unable to provide any solutions. (Brass 1991, chs. 1–2; cf. Grosby 1994)[4]

A similar charge can be brought against the second major paradigm, the *perennialist*. This term denotes those who hold that nations (if not nationalism) have existed throughout recorded history, but are not part of the natural order. An older generation of historians, many of them influenced by an organic version of nationalism, tended to see *nations* everywhere in the historical record, from the ancient Egyptians and Babylonians to the modern French and British, and to explain the history of humanity in terms of national alignments and conflicts. Nations, in other words, were perennial collective actors but not *natural* or *primordial*. (Walek-Czernecki 1929; Levi 1965)

Actually we need to distinguish two kinds of perennialism. The first we may call *continuous perennialism*, because it claims that particular nations have existed for centuries, if not millennia. Thus, for many earlier scholars, nations like the French, Greeks and Egyptians are immemorial or *perennial*, whereas others in Africa and Asia are more recent. The second kind of perennialism is about nations-in-general. It claims that nations come and go, emerge and dissolve, only to reappear continually in different periods and continents; and here, we may speak of a *recurrent perennialism*.[5]

Now, while it is quite possible to demonstrate in some cases a continuity of national identity going back beyond the Reformation, at least for their élites—as Adrian Hastings (1997) has done for the English, Irish, Scots and other Western nations—there is always the danger of imposing a *retrospective nationalism* onto communities and cultures whose identities and loyalties were local, regional, and religious, but barely national. This is the burden of Susan Reynolds' (1984, ch. 8) critique of the rather teleological approach of Hugh Seton-Watson (1977). While it might be possible, as a result of consistent definition and open-ended empirical investigation, to categorize certain communities in antiquity and the Middle Ages as nations (for example, the Jews, the Armenians, the Swiss, and the Japanese), this

would hardly suffice to allow us to claim that nations were recurrent phenomena of history, since the nationalist ideologies and the vast majority
of nations can be shown to be of much more recent vintage, including all
those *nations of design* (Tilly 1975, Conclusion) created by nationalists or
by pragmatic politicians through international treaties in the aftermath of
prolonged wars like the Napoleonic or First World War. (See Kohn 1967;
Tipton 1972; Johnson 1995)[6]

MODERNISM

It is just these historical and theoretical observations that form the starting-
point of modernism, the dominant scholarly paradigm today. Modernists
regard both primordialist and perennialist approaches as expressions of
nationalism itself, or at least as heavily influenced by its assumptions, and
therefore fatally flawed. For modernists like Eric Hobsbawm and Ernest
Gellner, the nation is not only recent, it is also novel, and a product
of the processes of modernization. They regard the era of the French
Revolution as marking the moment when nationalism was introduced
into the movement of world history. It was then that the ideal of the
sovereignty of the people was fused with the drive to cultural homogeneity, to forge self-determining nations of co-cultural citizens. Hence,
nations as well as nationalism are purely modern phenomena, without roots
in the past. (Gellner 1983; Hobsbawm 1990)

There are several varieties of modernism. The socio-economic version
regards nations and nationalism as products of the uneven development
of capitalism and of disparities in regional resources. Both Tom Nairn (1977)
and Michael Hechter (1975), operating from a post-marxist base, argued
that economic and political cores continually exploit the resources of the
periphery, breeding a nationalist reaction to imperialism or to internal colonialism on the part of peripheral élites, notably their intelligentsias.

Ernest Gellner (1964, ch. 7; 1983), on the other hand, proposed a socio-
cultural version of this model. He argued that nations and nationalism
were exclusively modern phenomena; pre-modern societies and cultures
had neither use nor room for nations.

The great tidal wave of modernization, as it swept outwards from
the West, eroded traditional societies and cultures, uprooting masses of
people and proletarianizing them in the anonymous city. Here, the sole
means of communication was through a shared linguistic education, provided by a state-run, standardized, and public education system. Hence,

the drive to cultural homogeneity in a specialist, literate, state-supported *high culture* was built into the requirements of modernity. But the unevenness of the waves of modernization also generated conflicts over resources between the old inhabitants of the city and the newly urbanized ex-peasants. Such conflicts created the possibility and incentive for ethnic secession wherever social conflict was reinforced by cultural markers such as colour, language, and religion.[7]

But it can be argued that these rather abstract, materialist schemata are overly deterministic. They regard nations and nationalism as functional for industrial or capitalist modernity, and leave little room for collective choices. As a result, they appear to make detailed historical investigation of élite or collective actions irrelevant. Besides, Gellner fails to explain why so many pre-existing *low* (non-specialist and non-literate) cultures turned themselves into *high* cultures and managed to eject the former high culture of the rulers, as occurred in Bohemia and Finland.[8]

This failure to consider the pre-modern roots of modern nations also appears in the political versions of modernism. John Breuilly (1993), for example, claims that nationalism is a spurious historicist solution to the alienation brought on by the split between the absolutist state and civil society. Nationalism must be seen as an exclusively modern, and a strictly political argument and movement, rather than a sentiment of cultural identity. Nationalist ideologies and intellectuals, symbols and ceremonies, are not without importance, but only insofar as they are able to mobilize, co-ordinate, and legitimize the various sub-élites who seek power through control of the modern state. Here too the modernist failure to come to grips with cultural identity (and in this case, ideology) renders its explanation partial and one-sided.

Breuilly's rather narrowly defined, state-centred modernism, like that of Anthony Giddens and Michael Mann, suffers from an excessive emphasis on the role of political institutions, and is too dismissive of the legacies of pre-modern ethnic and cultural ties.[9]

Ideology, on the other hand, forms the key to Elie Kedourie's (1960) path-breaking approach. He is equally insistent on the modernity, and indeed the European philosophical provenance, of nationalism, but he accords a primary role to disaffected intellectuals who purvey nationalist ideology through philology, folklore, and the rediscovery of ethnic history and culture—first in Germany and then in Eastern Europe and the Balkans—in their pursuit of Enlightenment meliorism. In his later work, Kedourie (1971) traced modern nationalism, as a doctrine of the collective will and a quest for unattainable perfection on earth, to antinomian medieval

Christian millennial doctrines, whose influence he saw extending, through the ravages of European imperialism, to the violent messianic nationalisms of Asia and Africa, with their cults of the *dark* gods. Kedourie does not, however, ask why the nationalist message of the *marginal men* in Africa and Asia should continually fall on such receptive ears, nor how an ideology like nationalism can have such profoundly disturbing effects in so many parts of the world. There is also a world of difference between the pessimistic, world-negating visions of Christian apocalyptic millennialism, and the often earth-bound, auto-emancipatory optimism of even the most romantic nationalisms.[10]

A similar kind of cultural diffusionism can also be found in Benedict Anderson's influential account (1991) of the origins and spread of nationalism. But here it is allied to a species of post-modernist constructionism. Nationalism, for Anderson, is a modern cultural artefact. Its object, the nation, is defined as an *imagined political community*—imagined as sovereign, finite, and horizontal. In a world characterized by a basic linguistic diversity, and a widespread desire to transcend mortality, it was only the revolution of print-capitalism—the conjunction of the invention of printing with the capitalist diffusion of its products, books; and later newspapers, in the vernacular languages—that made it possible for people to imagine the nation, once a social space had been created by the decline of sacred monarchies and religious script communities. This in turn required a new conception of linear time, one that allowed people to see themselves as members of linguistic communities moving inexorably forwards through empty, homogeneous time. But, once created, the ideal of the nation could, like any other cultural artefact and construct, be pirated by others in different parts of the world, according to their historical circumstances, to produce different kinds of nationalism—creole, vernacular, official, communist and the like. Anderson is sensitive to these varied circumstances, yet he fails to explain how nationalism can have such a profound popular emotional appeal, how the possibility of *imagining* the *nation* turns into the moral imperative of a mass *dying for the nation*, and why imagined print communities should become prime candidates for nationhood and mass self-sacrifice.[11]

THE ETHNO-SYMBOLIC ALTERNATIVE

This brings us to the central problem of every kind of modernist analysis, whether of Gellner, Breuilly, Kedourie or Anderson. I refer to their systematic failure to accord any weight to the pre-existing cultures and ethnic ties of the nations that emerged in the modern epoch, thereby precluding any understanding of the popular roots and widespread appeal of nationalism. This failure stems from serious inadequacies in the social constructionism and instrumentalism that underpin their modernism, in providing convincing accounts of cultural and political phenomena like nations and nationalism. These limitations include:

(1) a failure to distinguish genuine constructs from long-term processes and structures in which successive generations have been socialized;
(2) a concentration on élite actions at the expense of popular beliefs and actions; and
(3) a neglect of the powerful affective dimensions of nations and nationalism.

Historical ethno-symbolism emerges from the theoretical critique of modernist approaches, as well as from a different reading of the historical record. For ethno-symbolists, what gives nationalism its power are the myths, memories, traditions, and symbols of ethnic heritages and the ways in which a popular *living past* has been, and can be, rediscovered and reinterpreted by modern nationalist intelligentsias. It is from these elements of myth, memory, symbol, and tradition that modern national identities are reconstituted in each generation, as the nation becomes more inclusive and as its members cope with new challenges.

These cultural and historical elements also form the basis of competing claims to territory, patrimony and resources. Where there are clashing interpretations of ancestral homelands, and cultural heritages—as for example in Macedonia, Kashmir, Nagorno-Karabagh, and Palestine—normal conflicts of interest are turned into cultural wars, and moral and political crusades replace everyday politics. History and culture provide the motives for conflict as well as solidarity. They are not simply pretexts, by which the *atavistic emotions* of the masses, in Kedourie's words, are manipulated, nor are they simply *invented traditions* designed, as Eric Hobsbawm claims, to channel and control the energies of the newly mobilized and enfranchised masses. History and culture form integral parts of the fabric of popular visions, and of the social structures and processes in which the designated populations are embedded and through which their élites must forge their strategies. (Kedourie 1971, Introduction; Hobsbawm and Ranger 1983, Introduction and ch. 7)[12]

These are some of the considerations which have led scholars like John Armstrong, John Hutchinson, and myself to consider alternative approaches to an understanding of the continuing power of nationalism and the nation in the modern world. These approaches have much in common and I have found it useful to term them *historical ethno-symbolism*. They seek to overcome the limitations of modernism, while acknowledging its insights, as well as those of the other major paradigms. In what follows, I shall outline the main features of these approaches, thereby highlighting the themes that unite the chapters in this book.[13]

The *ethno-symbolic* approaches make a number of claims, which constitute a set of basic themes or motifs.

1. La Longue Durée

The first theme is the claim that, if we want to grasp the power and understand the shape of modern nations and nationalisms, we must trace the origins and formation of nations, as well as their possible future course, over long periods of time (*la longue durée*), and not tie their existence and formation to a particular period of history or to the processes of modernization. Nations are historical phenomena, not only in the generic sense that they are embedded in particular collective pasts and emerge, sometimes over long time-spans, through specific historical processes, but also because, by definition, they embody shared memories, traditions, and hopes of the populations designated as parts of the nation. Indeed, a central theme of historical ethno-symbolism is the relationship of shared memories to collective cultural identities: memory, almost by definition, is integral to cultural identity, and the cultivation of shared memories is essential to the survival and destiny of such collective identities. That is why, as the first chapter on *Nationalism and the Historians* makes clear, historians have played so central a role in the delineation of the nation and in the rediscovery, transmission, and analysis of its ethnic heritage. It may also be the reason why historians dominated causal enquiry into the nature, course and appeal of nations and nationalism, at least in the earlier stages.

Historical enquiry, while it may demystify and dispel fictions, can also reinforce the shared memories and aspirations of members, their *ethno-history*, by providing material or documentary evidence for events and personages held in reverence by the community. At the same time, it may reveal the long-term processes in which the rise of nations and the spread of nationalism are embedded. For historical ethno-symbolism, this double historicity of nations and nationalism—their rootedness in shared long-term memories or *ethno-history*, and the resulting need to analyse them over long historical time-spans—constitutes an underlying methodological postulate. (See Llobera 1994, ch. 1; A. D. Smith 1986, chs. 1–2)

2. National past, present, and future

This long-term relationship between national past, present, and future constitutes a second major theme, and it can be examined under three headings: recurrence, continuity, and reappropriation.

Recurrence: For perennialists, the nation is a recurrent form of social organization and nationalism a perennial mode of cultural belonging. But this is to read the history of earlier epochs in the light of the nationalist present. The empirical evidence of such past ages presents a much more problematic picture. Chapter Three, *The Problem of National Identity: Ancient, Medieval and Modern?*, explores some of the historical evidence which may support perennialist or modernist arguments, and concludes that, on the whole, the concept of the nation, like the ideology of nationalism, is largely modern, as are most nations. There may well be exceptions like the Jews and Armenians (perhaps also the medieval Japanese and Ethiopian Amhara), and much depends on the tightness of the definition of the nation employed. Using my own definition of the nation—*as a named human population sharing an historic territory, common myths and historical memories, a mass, public culture, a common economy and common legal rights and duties for all members* (admittedly a fairly modernist definition)—it is clear that the majority of nations, and nationalisms emerged in the modern world inaugurated by the French and American Revolutions. At the same time, as we saw, there may be some nations that predate modernity, and there are certainly some widely diffused ethnic elements that recur throughout recorded history: these include ethnic origin myths, beliefs in ethnic election, the development of ethnoscapes, the territorialization of memory, and the vernacular mobilization of communities. All of which suggests that *modern* nations may have *pre-modern* precursors and can form around recurrent ethnic antecedents.[14]

Continuity: Under this heading falls the vexed question of the 'date of commencement of nations' (Hastings 1997, ch. 1)—or how far back in time it is possible to trace the origins of particular nations. If the first heading signalled the recurring components or potential *building-blocks* of nations-in-general, the rubric of continuity points to the persistence of cultural components of particular nations, for example, elements that have been handed down through the generations—names, symbols, languages, customs, territories and rituals of national identity. Some of these continuities are explored in Chapters Two and Four, on *National Identity and Myths of Ethnic Descent* and on the myths of *Chosen Peoples*, and again more theoretically and in connection with nationalist ideology, in Chapter Six, *Gastronomy or Geology?* Clearly, much more work needs to be done on identifying the links between earlier ethnic components and modern national cultures, a point made forcefully and critically by John Breuilly (1996).

However, with ideas of ethnic election and their secular transformations, as with memories of golden ages, a start has been made in establishing important cultural continuities, despite the breaks often introduced by conquest, colonization, migration, and assimilation. (See also A. D. Smith 1993) This should help to counteract what John Peel has called the *blocking presentism*, and constructionism of so much current work on ethnicity, which views our understanding of the ethnic past as social construction based on present needs and reflecting the interests and preoccupations of present generations. (Peel 1989)[15]

Reappropriation: If continuity signifies the forward reach of the ethnic past to the national present, the rubric of *reappropriation* represents the converse movement, a reaching back into the ethnic past to obtain the *authentic* materials, and ethos for a distinct modern nation. This is the subject of Chapter Six, *Gastronomy or Geology?*, which depicts nationalist intelligentsias as *political archaeologists* who aim, not to return to the past, but to recover its pristine ethos and reconstruct a modern nation in the image of the past *ethnie*. Hence, the quest for rediscovery, authentication, and reappropriation of the ethnic past by philologists, historians, archaeologists and ethnologists. Despite many instances of self-delusion and manipulation, it is necessary to treat these activities of nationalist intellectuals as an essential element of the complex interrelationship between national present (and future) and ethnic past. (See A. D. Smith 1981, chs. 5–6; Pinard and Hamilton 1984; Anderson 1991, ch. 5)[16]

3. The ethnic basis of nations

The third fundamental theme, and claim, of ethno-symbolism concerns the ethnic foundations of nations and nationalism. The ubiquity of ethnicity is its starting-point. Ethnic groupings can be found in every epoch and continent, wherever human beings feel that they share common ancestry and culture. Such groupings come in various forms and display varying degrees of organisation and self-awareness. As a first step, we may distinguish *ethnic categories* from *ethnic communities*, with other organizational forms such as ethnic associations in between. *Ethnic categories* are populations distinguished by outsiders as possessing the attributes of a common name or emblem, a shared cultural element (usually language or religion), and a link with a particular territory. *Ethnic communities* or *ethnies* (to use the French term) are human populations distinguished by both members and outsiders as possessing the attributes of:

1. an identifying name or emblem;
2. a *myth* of common ancestry;
3. shared historical memories and traditions;
4. one or more elements of common culture;
5. a link with an historic territory or 'homeland';
6. a measure of solidarity, at least among the élites.

This allows us to define an *ethnie* as *a named human population with myths of common ancestry, shared historical memories and one or more common elements of culture, including an association with a homeland, and some degree of solidarity, at least among the élites.* (A. D. Smith 1986, ch. 2; cf. Horowitz 1985, chs. 1–2)

There is, in most cases, a more or less powerful link between modern nations and pre-existing, and often pre-modern, *ethnies*. Ethno-symbolism claims that most nations, including the earliest, were based on ethnic ties and sentiments and on popular ethnic traditions, which have provided the cultural resources for later nation-formation; and that even those new *state-nations* in Africa and Asia that sought to turn ex-colonies into territorial nations must forge a cultural unity and identity of myth, symbol, value, and memory that can match that of nations built on pre-existing ethnic ties, if they are to survive and flourish as nations. It is this *ethnic model* of the nation that has proved the most influential, with its emphasis on genealogical descent, vernacular codes, popular mobilization and historical nativism in a *homeland*. Most nations, including the first nations in the West (if we leave aside the earlier cases of the Jews, Armenians and Ethiopian Amhara), have been formed around *ethnic cores*—dominant populations united by presumed ties of shared ancestry and vernacular culture—and have gradually expanded their social depth, territory, and geopolitical range around this dominant ethnic core and presumed descent group, to include other ethnic populations, as was the case with the English, the French and the Castilians. This is the burden of the second chapter, on *National Identity and Myths of Ethnic Descent*, which represents an early statement of some theoretical aspects of historical ethno-symbolism, and especially of its emphasis on the role of one or more ethnic myths of descent in the formation of nations and national identity. (See also A. D. Smith 1989)[17]

A crucial part of this third theme is the popular basis of nations and nationalism. Nations may have emerged around élite groups, but even in these early stages, élites were repeatedly forced to take the cultures and interests of wider strata into account. These vernacular cultures and interests were often popular and ethnic in character; they assumed ties of affinity based on presumed common origins and shared customs, linked to *regna* or kingdoms, as Susan Reynolds has argued for early medieval Europe. Even a modernist like Eric Hobsbawm admits the importance of pre-existing (and often pre-modern) *proto-national* communities of language, religion, and region, though he refuses to allow any linkage between them and the rise of a modern, state-creating nationalism. (Reynolds 1983; Hobsbawm 1990, ch. 2))

4. *The cultural components of ethnies*

The fourth major claim of ethno-symbolism is that the pre-existing components and long-term continuities of ethnic communities and nations are cultural and symbolic rather than demographic. The *differentia specifica* of *ethnies* and nations, as well as their continuities, appear in the myths, memories, symbols, values, and traditions of an ethnic community which regards itself as ancestrally related, culturally distinct, and linked to a particular historic homeland. For John Armstrong, following Fredrik Barth, the contents of the *myth-symbol complex* communicated by vernacular linguistic codes, tend to differentiate *ethnies* and guard the cultural border of the community against outsiders. (Armstrong 1982, ch. 1) For myself, this differentiating function needs to be complemented by an analysis of the unifying role of a whole range of cultural and symbolic components—myths and symbols, but also values, memories, rituals, customs, and traditions. Distinctive clusters of these components mark out the boundaries of various *ethnies*, but they also serve to unite the members of each *ethnie* and structure their relations and activities. Hence, although in one sense the major symbolic and cultural elements of an ethno-symbolic approach are *subjective*, in that they focus on the perceptions, memories, beliefs, and values of individuals and communities, their long-term patterning produces a *structure* of relations and processes that is independent of those beliefs and perceptions, one which can provide a framework for the socialization of successive generations of ethnic and national members and for the regulation of their interests through myths of ethnic descent and symbols of territory and community. (See A. D. Smith 1998, ch. 8)

This emphasis on culture, in the broadest sense, introduces some flexibility into ethnic membership, which in normal circumstances allows for a degree of demographic replenishment and cultural borrowing, and hence social and cultural adaptation. This suggests that, contrary to approaches that sharply distinguish between an open and flexible *civic* nation and a rigid and closed *ethnic* nation, the *ethnic* components constitute only one, albeit ever-present, set of (often contested) elements within the totality of modern nations, and they can also encourage openness and receptiveness to outside influences. The history of modern Catalan nationalism is a case in point. (See Miller 1995; A. D. Smith 1995, ch. 4)[18]

There are, however, circumstances, internal and external, that bring to power nationalist intelligentsias who, in their quest for authenticity and cultural purity, increasingly seek to purge their cultures of foreign elements and ultimately of outsiders. Despite the very different emphases on *genealogy* or *ideology* in myths of descent, the drive for cultural homogeneity and purity is more common in the case of *ethnic* nationalisms, that is, those whose criterion of national membership is genealogical rather than territorial. This point is the focus of Chapter Seven, on *Ethnic Nationalism and the Plight of Minorities*, which analyses the dire effect of cultural homogenization and purificatory ethnic nationalisms on ethnic minorities and the consequent flow of refugees, and hence on the stability of regional inter-state orders.

5. Ethnic myths and symbols

Of particular importance among the cultural components of ethnicity are myths of ethnic origin and election, and symbols of territory and community.

Myths of origin and descent constitute the primary definers of the separate existence and character of particular *ethnies*. As Chapter Two on *National Identity and Myths of Ethnic Descent* illustrates, they include accounts of the time and place of the community's origins, and trace the lines of descent from presumed common ancestors; thus Turks trace their ancestry to Central Asia in the first millennium, and to their founding father, Oghuz Khan, and Jews do likewise to Abraham and Canaan (or even to Ur or Haran). Equally important for the survival of *ethnies* has been the development of myths of ethnic election. These may be missionary or covenantal in character. Missionary election myths exalt their *ethnies* by assigning them god-given tasks or missions of warfare or conversion or overlordship; so the Franks or the medieval French monarchs interpreted their role as latter-day king Davids defending the new Israel (France and/or the Church), and the Russian Tsars came to see in Orthodox Russia a third Rome, the only truly Christian kingdom after the fall of Constantinople. Covenantal election myths tend to set the chosen people apart from their profane surroundings, through a covenant between the deity and the elect, namely, a conditional promise of continued divine favour in return for constant observance of divine commands and ceaseless performance of a singular moral and ritual code, such as the Israelites were enjoined to practise in the Old Testament. These variations and their consequences are explored in Chapter Four on *Chosen Peoples*, and more briefly in Chapter Ten on *The Resurgence of Nationalism?*. (See Armstrong 1982, chs. 6–7; Akenson 1992)

Symbols of territory and community take a variety of forms. They include emblems of difference (flags, totems, coins, ritual objects), hymns and anthems, special foods and costume, as well as representations of ethnic deities, monarchs and heroes—like Pharoah's double crown, the Jewish Menorah or the fleur-de-lys. Particular interest and significance attaches to the symbolism of ancestral or sacred territory and the development of *ethnoscapes*—landscapes endowed with poetic ethnic meaning through the historicization of nature and the territorialization of ethnic memories. These poetic landscapes often come to be associated with crucial events and personages in the history of the ethnic community and may be invested with sacred significance, a powerful motif of ethnic nationalism, explored in Chapter Five, *Nation and Ethnoscape*.

6. 'Ethno-history'

A further major theme concerns the multiple, changing and uneven nature of *ethno-history*. By *ethno-history* is meant the ethnic members' memories and understanding of their communal past or pasts, rather than any more *objective* and dispassionate analysis by professional historians. Such a mode of historical discourse has three facets: it is multi-stranded and contested; it is always subject to change; and it is globally uneven.

Given the multiplicity of interests, needs and outlooks of members of any community, the likelihood of a single, unified version of the communal past emerging in any relatively free society must be minimal. In fact, the past is as much a zone of conflict as the present, and we can therefore expect to find, at any given point in time, two or more versions of the ethnic past, often in competition or conflict. This was the case in Greece throughout the nineteenth century, when a classical *Athenian* version of Hellenism held by westernised intelligentsia and merchants was pitted against a Greek Orthodox popular ethno-history which harked back to the medieval glories of the Byzantine empire, a point underlined in Chapter Eight, on *Zionism and Diaspora Nationalism*. A similar conflict erupted in France in the nineteenth and early twentieth centuries, and particularly during the Dreyfus Affair, when a medievalizing monarchist and Catholic vision of French ethno-history was challenged by a secular, revolutionary and classicizing interpretation of the French past. (See Campbell and Sherrard 1968, ch. 1; and Gildea 1994, chs. 3, 7)

If *ethno-history* is always multi-stranded and contested, this implies a continuous process of reinterpretation of national identities. Homi Bhabha's dualism of traditional *pedagogical* and everyday practical *performative* narratives of *the people* fails to capture the complexity of a situation in which every generation fashions its own interpretations of national identity in the light of its reading of the ethnic past or pasts. The fund of ethnic elements, the ethno-historical heritage handed down through the generations, is always being reinterpreted and revised by various social groups in response to internal differences and external stimuli. Hence, British, Japanese or Egyptian *national identity* is never fixed or static: it is always being reconstructed in response to new needs, interests and perceptions, though always within certain limits. (Bhabha 1990, ch. 16)

From a comparative standpoint, the incidence of ethno-history is markedly uneven. Some communities can boast a *rich* or well-documented, and eventful, ethnic past; others can only summon up the barest memories and sketchiest traditions. (For example, Russian or Arab ethno-histories are eventful and abundantly documented, while Slovak and Estonian ethno-histories are more sketchy and poorly recorded). This *unevenness* of ethno-historical cultural resources is itself a source of national competition and conflict, as the less well endowed communities seek to attain cultural parity with the better endowed. Hence, the appeal for Finns of the national epic of the *Kalevala*, edited in 1835 by Elias Lonnrot, as they strove to free themselves from Russian political and Swedish cultural domination—a theme taken up in Chapter Eight, on *Zionism and Diaspora Nationalism*, in the context of richly documented ethno-histories with vivid memories of *golden ages*, as well as in the concluding chapter. (See Branch 1985, Introduction)

7. Routes to Nationhood

Another central ethno-symbolic concern is the manner in which nations in the modern world have come to be formed. Armstrong, indeed, presents a complex schema on the emergence of nations, showing how a variety of factors operating at broader or narrower levels, combine to create the terrain and impetus for particular nations. These factors include differences in nomadic and sedentary lifestyles with associated nostalgias; the influence of great religious civilizations like Islam and Christianity; the impact of imperial administrations and *mythomoteurs* (constitutive political myths); the differences in ecclesiastical organization; and, at the lowest and most dependant level, the role of language *faults* and of particular languages. (Armstrong 1982, ch. 9)

As Chapter Four on *Chosen Peoples* illustrates, I have sought to identify *patterns* of nation-formation, depending on the initial ethnic starting-point. The important distinction here is between *lateral* and *vertical ethnies*. The former are aristocratic and extensive, their boundaries are ragged, and they rarely (seek to) penetrate culturally or socially the middle or lower classes. The latter are demotic and intensive, their boundaries are compact, barriers to entry are relatively high, and their culture spreads across all classes, if unevenly at times. There are also immigrant *ethnies*, or rather, part-*ethnies*, which have hived off from the main body to set up colonies and gradually form a separate new *ethnie*. We can then trace the routes by which modern nations have been formed from these three ethnic *bases*: a route of *bureaucratic incorporation* by which aristocratic *ethnies* may forge strong states and incorporate outlying regions and lower classes into their upper-class ethnic culture and symbolism; a route of *vernacular mobilization* whereby an indigenous intelligentsia uses folk culture to mobilize middle and lower strata and create ethnic nations; and finally, an *immigrant-colonist* route in which the founding immigrant part-*ethnie* is supplemented by waves of pioneering colonizers who together create a *plural* or polyethnic immigrant nation and culture. (See A. D. Smith 1989)

8. *The longevity of nationalism*

The final theme of ethno-symbolism concerns the power and durability of nations and nationalism. Nationalism is a modern ideological movement, but also the expression of aspirations by various social groups to create, defend or maintain *nations*—their autonomy, unity and identity—by drawing on the cultural resources of pre-existing ethnic communities and categories. Nationalism, defined as *an ideological movement for attaining and maintaining identity, unity and autonomy of a social group some of whose members deem it to constitute an actual or potential nation*, has proved a powerful instrument for forging a world of nations based on pre-existing ethnic ties and sentiments; and it is one that has by no means run its course.[19]

These aspirations for nationhood can be found in pre-modern epochs, but they are particularly widespread and powerful in the modern era. This suggests that nationalisms, as well as nations, are likely to be recurrent phenomena in future, as they were in past epochs (Billig 1995). However, the underlying ground of their persistence is not simply their frequency and intensity in the modern epoch. Both frequency and intensity are products of deeper causes, namely the ability of modern nationalisms to draw sustenance from the pre-existing memories, myths, symbols, and traditions of each ethnic community and region. Where such memories, myths, symbols, and traditions are either lacking or negative—conflictual, ambiguous, and disintegrative—the attempt to create new communities and cultural identities is likely to prove painfully slow and arduous, especially where the new identities lack clear boundaries and must compete with well established and deep-rooted identities and communities. This is the theme explored in Chapter Nine, on *National Identity and the Idea of European Unity*, in the context of attempts to create a European cultural identity that could underpin the drive for European economic and political union. These attempts raise serious doubts about the possibility of transcending nations and superseding nationalism, since the very idea of 'Europe', insofar as it can be pinned down and given systematic coherence, appears as a pale reflection of the much more rooted, vivid and tangible national identities. Here, again, I have employed an ethno-symbolic approach to uncover some of the deeper, unspoken cultural myths, memories and assumptions about the 'new Europe'. (See Delanty 1995; Benda-Beckman and Verkuyten 1995)

The ambiguities and nebulous character of European cultural identity contrast strongly with the dramatic and powerful diaspora nationalisms of the Greeks, Jews, and Armenians with their rich memories of golden ages of saints and heroes, their stark symbols of trauma and suffering, and their potent popular myths of glorious restoration in their age-old homelands, discussed in Chapter Eight on *Zionism and Diaspora Nationalism*. The implication, spelt out in the concluding chapter, is that the continuing power of myths, symbols, and memories of ethnic chosenness, golden ages and historic homelands has been largely responsible for the mass appeal of ethnic nationalism in the aftermath of the Cold War and the demise of the Soviet empire; and that we are therefore unlikely to witness the early transcendence of ethnicity or the supersession of nationalism.

PLAN OF THE BOOK

These are the major themes and considerations that account for the plan of the book, which is divided into two parts.

Part One is more theoretical and historical in focus.

Chapter One considers the relationship between nationalism and those historians who have sought to describe its course and explain its appeal. In particular, it explores the assumptions and myths in the work of historians who have investigated the phenomena of nations and nationalism, from Michelet, Acton, and Renan to Seton-Watson, Hobsbawm, and Breuilly.

Chapter Two is an early statement of some ethno-symbolic concerns. It reveals the importance of an ethno-symbolic approach in uncovering the crucial role of myths of ethnic descent in the formation of modern nations and national identities. It explores the nature and consequences of such myths in their different versions, in England, France, Greece, Turkey, and Israel, and emphasizes the differences between 'genealogical' and more 'ideological' myths of descent.

Chapter Three applies these arguments to the question of 'national identity' in ancient and medieval epochs, both on the theoretical and the historical levels. Setting aside the sweeping claims of perennialists and modernists, it enquires how far it is possible to speak of nations before the modern epoch, notably in antiquity, and whether the term 'nation' can have a single, clear and unambiguous meaning in both pre-modern as well as modern epochs.

Chapter Four looks at the role of myths of ethnic election and the beliefs in chosen peoples as critical factors in the survival of ethnic groups, from the covenantal model of the ancient Israelites to the looser missionary models of many peoples in Europe and outside. It also explores the implications of these beliefs, and their subsequent transformation in the rise of modern nations.

Chapter Five, the final chapter in Part One, considers the nature and role of the territorial dimensions of ethnic communities and nations. It explores the central role of the territorialization of memory and of 'ethnoscapes' in the formation of nations, laying particular emphasis on the sacralization of historic territories in aggravating and prolonging conflicts between nations.

Part Two is more empirical and contemporary in focus.

Chapter Six provides a general account of the role of nationalist ideologies and movements in the formation of modern nations. Comparing the ethno-symbolic approach with other perspectives, such as perennialism and modernism, it shows how nationalism can best be understood as a form of 'political archaeology', particularly on the part of intelligentsias intent on the reconstruction of modern nations.

Chapter Seven applies this ethno-symbolic approach to the ways in which demotic ethnic nationalisms politicize cultures and seek to purify their communities of alien elements. This 'darker side of nationalism' has particularly serious consequences for ethnic minorities within the boundaries of these demotic communities, and it helps to explain the incidence and flow of ethnic refugees all over the world.

Chapter Eight is a comparative study of diaspora nationalisms and, in particular, of Zionism. It emphasizes the role of myths, memories and symbols of ethnic chosenness, trauma, and the 'golden age' of saints, sages, and heroes in the rise of modern nationalism among the Jews, Armenians, and Greeks—the archetypal diaspora peoples.

Chapter Nine considers the current debates about European unity and national identity. It emphasizes the significance of myths, memories, symbols and traditions, or their absence, in recent attempts to forge European unity and create a European cultural identity. It also explores the potential of a European 'family of cultures' for greater cultural unity, while pointing to the difficulties of a nebulous analogy of the nation competing with well entrenched and vivid national identities.

Chapter Ten, the final chapter, provides a concise overall statement of the ethno-symbolic approach, and applies its insights to the current resurgence of nationalism since the collapse of the Soviet Union. It emphasizes the deeper roots of the persistence and variety of ethnic nationalisms in the uneven distribution of ethno-history and 'golden ages', the impact of religious ideals, notably of myths of ethnic election, and the differential nature of ancestral 'homelands'.

Notes

1. Another fashionable approach, or rather set of approaches, which we can term 'post-modernist', views the nation as a composite or hybrid construct of various cultural, social, and ethnic groupings. But such approaches hardly amount to a separate explanatory paradigm (or aim to provide one). As Chapter Five, on *Gastronomy or Geology?*, attempts to show, they really accept the modernist paradigm and apply it to contemporary Western polyethnic states. (See A. D. Smith 1998, ch. 9)

2. For these nationalist metaphors, see Pearson (1993). Some nationalists adopt a voluntarist view, according to which people must belong to a nation, but can choose to which nation they wish to belong, a tradition epitomized in Ernest Renan's lecture, *Qu'est-ce que la nation?* (1882), a reply to Heinrich Treitschke's ethnic German justification for the annexation of Alsace-Lorraine. See Guibernau (1996, ch. 1).

3. For all his 'primordialism', Clifford Geertz (1963) considers kinship groups too small and hence politically irrelevant. As for endogamy, it is again the belief, rather than any documented fact, that is significant.

4. For Eller and Coughlan (1993), cultural primordialism is non-rational and asociological insofar as it places primordial attachments outside the domain of social interaction and construction in an unexplained realm of 'emotion'. But, as Grosby (1994) demonstrated in his response, this is to narrow our understanding of the 'sociological' and to miss out other important kinds of human relationship that are neither constructed nor part of a means–end causal chain.

5. This is a view put forward by John Armstrong (1982; 1995), though on occasion he combines it with a more specific 'continuous perennialism' in respect of the French and Russians, for example. For a clear-cut example of this 'continuous perennialism' in respect of the British Isles, see Hastings (1997, chs. 2–3).

6. I have recently explored this question again in A. D. Smith (1998, chs. 7–8). Even Hastings (1997) concedes that most nations are modern, and post-date the French Revolution.

7. I have conflated the earlier (1964) and later (1983) formulations of Gellner's theory. Both Nairn and Hechter use Gellner's earlier version; Nairn acknowledges his debt to Gellner's specific concept of uneven development.

8. Gellner (1983, ch. 3) is clearly concerned with this issue, and accepts the advantages of cultural legacies from the past for nation-creation. Yet, in his last work (1997, ch. 15), Gellner takes a stronger line, arguing that most nations do not have 'navels'; they are invented for them. For this debate and my reply, see A. D. Smith (1996).

9. For similar analyses that stress the centrality of the 'modern state' in the genesis and diffusion of nationalism, see Giddens (1985, chs. 4, 8) and Mann

(1993, ch. 7; 1995). I have discussed their contributions, along with Breuilly's, more fully in A. D. Smith (1998, ch. 4).

10. Kedourie's analysis also suffers from a degree of idealism, in that nationalism is seen as the intellectual product of a fusion of ideas of self-determination derived from Kant with ideas of cultural diversity derived from Herder. This heady brew spreads like an epidemic and, like an opiate, it destroys those who administer the drug, as well all those on whom it is inflicted. Kedourie's one-sided and hostile portrait of nationalism overlooks its constructive aspects, and its vital role in creating, as well as controlling, social and political change.

11. Anderson's 'imagined community' is generically related to Hobsbawm's 'invented tradition', so important in the latter's eyes for the creation of nations. But Anderson reveals a more profound and positive appreciation of the persisting role of nations and nationalism, and a greater sensitivity to the underlying cultural changes that made national imaginings possible. See A. D. Smith (1998, ch. 6).

12. Hobsbawm (1990, ch. 2) elaborated his earlier analysis of 'invented traditions' (Hobsbawm and Ranger 1983) by distinguishing an earlier nineteenth century mass civic-political nationalism from a late-nineteenth century divisive ethno-linguistic variety of nationalism. But, despite his acknowledgement of 'proto-national' regional, linguistic and religious communities, he refused to allow them any influence on the rise of a state-creating modern nationalism which he suggested was largely a product of the need of capitalist élites to control the recently mobilized and enfranchised masses through the use of national 'invented traditions'.

13. There are important differences between Armstrong, Hutchinson and myself. Hutchinson (1987; 1994) argues for the importance of cultural nationalism, but also suggests a role for pre-modern ethnicity in, for example, Irish nationalism. Armstrong (1982) adopts a mainly phenomenological approach, but couples it with a social 'boundary' approach derived from Fredrik Barth; yet he also assigns a major role to myths and symbols in the preservation of ethnic identities over *la longue durée*.

14. For this definition of the nation, see A. D. Smith (1991, ch. 1). For a general discussion of the problems of defining the concept of the nation, see Connor (1994, ch. 4). Though the distinction between *ethnies* and nations is crucial, it does not correspond to the chronological or the sociological divide between pre-modernity and modernity. Not only do many *ethnies* persist (or are crystallized) in late modernity and also become 'modernized'; a few nations antedate modernity (chronologically and sociologically) and owe little or nothing to the processes of 'modernization'.

15. This is very much the view put forward by the editors and most of the contributors to Tonkin *et al.* (1989); reacting against the idea that the 'past determines the present', they have opted for an equally unilateral understanding in which, for the most part, 'the present shapes the past'—or, at any rate,

our understanding of it. One could equally well claim that our 'understanding' of the past is inevitably shaped by the frameworks of meaning handed down from previous generations, even when we dissent from their particular views of the past. (See also Eriksen 1993) The question of continuities of nations is also bedevilled by definitional problems. For Walker Connor (1994, ch. 9) we can only speak of mass nations; nations only exist when a majority of the designated population participates (indeed votes) in public life; whereas for Adrian Hastings (1997, ch. 1) nations can be said to exist when a significant minority of the population outside the ruling élite reveal a national consciousness, in which case we can speak of medieval nations.

But are these 'nations' in the full sense of the term (a modern, and modernist, sense?), or only potential or 'pre-national' peoples? Perhaps we should avoid trying to draw too hard-and-fast lines between *ethnies* and nations in each case, but rather identify processes (of territorialization, homogenization, legal standardization, etc.) by which nations are formed, often discontinuously, out of pre-existing *ethnies*.

16. That is why cultural nationalism, as Hutchinson (1987, ch. 1) highlights, is so important for the creation of nations. This was also probably the case with pre-modern *ethnies*. A religious culture provided the foundation for the crystallisation and persistence of fluid ethnic categories. From this standpoint, nationalist 'political archaeology', for all its rhetoric, is not as fictive and fantastic as modernists are apt to portray.

17. This suggests that the fashionable distinction between 'ethnic' and 'civic' nations and nationalisms is not as clear-cut as is often assumed. (See Breton 1988) Western 'civic' nations assume a fundamental ethnic core which has allowed them to tolerate a measure of cultural hybridity through immigration and intermarriage. This is because the more cultural elements of language, territory, and history can be separated to some extent from their ethnic moorings, so allowing outsiders to join the nation and assimilate its culture.

18. The open, assimilatory character of Catalan linguistic nationalism can be contrasted with the relatively closed and more exclusive character of Basque religious and 'racial' nationalism. For a rich and illuminating study of these ethnic nationalisms, see Conversi (1997).

19. For this definition of nationalism, see A. D. Smith (1991, ch. 4). On globalization and nationalism, see Billig (1995, esp. ch. 6) and Guibernau (1996, ch. 7).

References

AKENSON, DONALD 1992 *God's Peoples: Covenant and Land in South Africa, Israel and Ulste*, Ithaca: Cornell University Press.

ANDERSON, BENEDICT 1991 *Imagined Communities: Reflections on the Origins and Spread of Nationalism*, Second Edn, London: Verso.

ARMSTRONG, JOHN 1982 *Nations before Nationalism*, Chapel Hill: University of North Carolina Press.

ARMSTRONG, JOHN 1995 'Towards a theory of nationalism: consensus and dissensus', in Sukumar Periwal (ed.): *Notions of Nationalism*, Budapest: Central European University Press, 34–43.

BENDA-BECKMANN, KEEBET VON, and VERKUYTEN, MAYKAL (eds.) 1995 *Nationalism, Ethnicity and Cultural Identity in Europe*, Utrecht University: ERCOMER.

BERGHE, PIERRE VAN DEN 1978 'Race and ethnicity: a sociobiological perspective', *Ethnic and Racial Studies*, 1, 4, 401–11.

BERGHE, PIERRE VAN DEN 1995 'Does race matter?', *Nations and Nationalism*, I, 3, 357–68.

BHABHA, HOMI (ed.) 1990 *Nation and Narration*, London and New York: Routledge.

BILLIG, MICHAEL 1995 *Banal Nationalism*, London: Sage.

BRANCH, MICHAEL (ed.) 1985 *Kalevala, The Land of Heroes*, trans. W. Kirby, London: The Athlone Press and New Hampshire: Dover.

BRASS, PAUL 1991 *Ethnicity and Nationalism*, London: Sage.

BRETON, RAYMOND 1988 'From ethnic to civic nationalism: English Canada and Quebec', *Ethnic and Racial Studies* 11, 1, 85–102.

BREUILLY, JOHN 1993 *Nationalism and the State*, Second Edn, Manchester: Manchester University Press.

—— 1996 'Approaches to nationalism', in Gopal Balakrishnan (ed.) *Mapping the Nation*, London and New York: Verso, 146–74.

CAMPBELL, JOHN and SHERRARD, PHILIP 1968 *Modern Greece*, London: Ernest Benn.

CONNOR, WALKER 1994 *Ethno-Nationalism: The Quest for Understanding*, Princeton: Princeton University Press.

CONVERSI, DANIELE 1997 *The Basques, the Catalans and Spain: Alternative Routes to Nationalist Mobilisation*, London: C. Hurst & Co.

DELANTY, GERARD 1995 *Inventing Europe: Idea, Identity, Reality*, Basingstoke: Macmillan.

ELLER, JACK and COUGHLAN, REED 1993 'The poverty of primordialism: the demystification of ethnic attachments', *Ethnic and Racial Studies* 16, 2, 183–202.

ERIKSEN, THOMAS HYLLAND 1993 *Ethnicity and Nationalism*, London and Boulder, Col.: Pluto Press.

GEERTZ, CLIFFORD 1963 'The integrative revolution', in Clifford Geertz (ed.) *Old Societies and New States*, New York: Free Press.

GELLNER, ERNEST 1964 *Thought and Change*, London: Weidenfeld and Nicolson.

—— 1983 *Nations and Nationalism*, Oxford: Blackwell.

—— 1997 *Nationalism*, London: Weidenfeld and Nicolson.

GIDDENS, ANTHONY 1985 *The Nation-State and Violence*, Cambridge: Polity Press.

GILDEA, ROBERT 1994 *The Past in French History*, New Haven and London: Yale University Press.

GROSBY, STEVEN 1994 'The verdict of history: the inexpungeable tie of primordiality—a reply to Eller and Coughlan', *Ethnic and Racial Studies* 17, 1, 164–71.

GUIBERNAU, MONTSERRAT 1996 *Nationalisms: The Nation-State and Nationalism in the Twentieth Century*, Cambridge: Polity Press.

HASTINGS, ADRIAN 1997 *The Construction of Nationhood: Ethnicity, Religion and Nationalism*, Cambridge: Cambridge University Press.

HECHTER, MICHAEL 1975 *Internal Colonialism: The Celtic Fringe in British National Development, 1536–1966*, London: Routledge and Kegan Paul.

HOBSBAWM, ERIC 1990 *Nations and Nationalism since 1780*, Cambridge: Cambridge University Press.

HOBSBAWM, ERIC and RANGER, TERENCE (eds.) 1983 *The Invention of Tradition*, Cambridge: Cambridge University Press.

HOROWITZ, DONALD 1985 *Ethnic Groups in Conflict*, Berkeley and Los Angeles: University of California Press.

HUTCHINSON, JOHN 1987 *The Dynamics of Cultural Nationalism: The Gaelic revival and the Creation of the Irish Nation State*, London: Allen and Unwin.

HUTCHINSON, JOHN 1994 *Modern Nationalism*, London: Fontana.

JOHNSON, LESLEY 1995 'Imagining communities: medieval and modern', in Simon Forde, Lesley Johnson and Alan Murray (eds.) *Concepts of National Identity in the Middle Ages*, Leeds: School of English, University of Leeds, 1–19.

KEDOURIE, ELIE 1960 *Nationalism*, London: Hutchinson.

—— (ed.) 1971 *Nationalism in Asia and Africa*, London: Weidenfeld and Nicolson.

KOHN, HANS 1967 *The Idea of Nationalism*, Second Edn, New York: Collier-Macmillan.

LEVI, MARIO ATTILIO 1965 *Political Power in the Ancient World*, trans. J. Costello, London: Weidenfeld and Nicolson.

LLOBERA, JOSEP 1994 *The God of Modernity*, Oxford: Berg.

MANN, MICHAEL 1993 *The Sources of Social Power*, Vol. II Cambridge: Cambridge University Press.

—— 1995 'A political theory of nationalism and its excesses', in Sukumar Periwal (ed.) *Notions of Nationalism*, Budapest: Central European University Press, 44–64.

MILLER, DAVID 1995 *On Nationality*, Oxford: Oxford University Press.

NAIRN, TOM 1977 *The Break-up of Britain: Crisis and Neo-Nationalism*, London: New Left Books.

PEEL, JOHN 1989 'The cultural work of Yoruba ethno-genesis', in Tonkin *et al.* (1989), 198–215.

PINARD, MAURICE and HAMILTON, RICHARD 1984 'The class bases of the Quebec independence movement: conjectures and evidence', *Ethnic and Racial Studies* 7, 1, 19–54.

REYNOLDS, SUSAN 1983 'Medieval *origines gentium* and the community of the realm', *History* 68, 375–90.

—— 1984 *Kingdoms and Communities in Western Europe, 900–1300*, Oxford: Clarendon Press.

SETON-WATSON, HUGH 1977 *Nations and States*, London: Methuen.

SMITH, ANTHONY D. 1981 *The Ethnic Revival in the Modern World*, Cambridge: Cambridge University Press.

—— 1986 *The Ethnic Origins of Nations*, Oxford: Blackwell.

—— 1989 'The origins of nations', *Ethnic and Racial Studies* 12, 3, 340–67.

—— 1991 *National Identity*, Harmondsworth: Penguin.

—— 1993 'Ethnic election and cultural identity', *Ethnic Studies* 9, 9–25.

—— 1995 *Nations and Nationalism in a Global Era*, Cambridge: Polity Press.

—— 1996 'Memory and modernity: some reflections on Ernest Gellner's theory of nationalism', *Nations and Nationalism* 2, 3, 358–88.

—— 1998 *Nationalism and Modernism: A Critical Survey of Recent Theories of Nations and Nationalism*, London and New York: Routledge.

TILLY, CHARLES (ed.) 1975 *The Formation of National States in Western Europe*, Princeton: Princeton University Press.

TIPTON, LEON (ed.) 1972 *Nationalism in the Middle Ages*, New York: Holt, Rinehart and Winston.

TONKIN, ELISABETH, McDONALD, MARYON and CHAPMAN, MALCOLM (eds.) 1989 *History and Ethnicity*, London and New York: Routledge.

WALEK-CZERNECKI, M. T. 1929 'Le role de la nationalité dans l'histoire de l'anti-quité', *Bulletin of the International Committee of the Historical Sciences* 2, 2, 305–20.

1

Nationalism and the Historians*

The history of nationalism is as much a history of its interlocutors as of the ideology and movement itself. Exactly because it appears so protean and seems so elusive, nationalism reveals itself only in its various forms, or rather the forms given to us by its proponents and critics. That is why nationalism is so often considered an 'historical movement' *par excellence*. Not only did it emerge in a given epoch of European history, and not only does it manifest itself in specific historical situations. Nationalism is also profoundly 'historicist' in character: it sees the world as a product of the interplay of various communities, each possessing a unique character and history, and each the result of specific origins and developments.

But, beyond this, there is a more specific sense in which we may term nationalism a profoundly 'historical' movement. Historians figure prominently among its creators and devotees; but they have also led the way in seeking to assess and understand the phenomenon of nationalism. That historians should contribute in such large measure to so 'historicist' a movement, is not surprising, given the common elements in early European nationalism and the historiography of the romantic epoch. Michelet, Burke, Muller, Karamzin, Palacky and many others, provided the moral and intellectual foundation for an emerging nationalism in their respective communities. Along with the philologists, the historians have in many ways furnished the rationale and charter of their aspirant nations.[1]

Historians have also been among nationalism's sharpest critics and opponents, especially since the Second World War. Indeed, most of them have been sceptical of its ideological claims, if not downright hostile. They have attributed to nationalism a variety of harmful consequences, ranging from absurd social and cultural policies to totalitarian terror and global destabilization. This attitude has been conditioned by a number of widely held assumptions about the nature of the phenomenon. Historians have generally seen nationalism as a doctrine or principle or argument; it has

* *International Journal of Comparative Sociology* XXXIII, 1–2 (1992) pp. 58–80.

been nationalism rather than the nation that has exercised their imagination, with a few exceptions. This doctrine or principle has often been regarded as an idée fixe, a motive force that remains constant beneath its many disguises. Alternatively, nationalism is equated with 'national sentiment', a feeling of belonging to, and identification with, the nation. The nation is then seen as serving individual and collective needs for warmth, strength and stability which assume much greater importance once the ties of family and neighbourhood are loosened. In that sense, nationalism may be functional for society in the modern era.[2]

But the costs are high. There is no reason, for the critical historian, why a group of human beings should not prefer to live, work, and be governed together, perhaps on the basis of some cultural tie or shared historical experiences; and they may be better governed by representatives of their own community than by others. But this liberal doctrine must not be confused with the Continental and Romantic varieties of nationalism, which treat individuals as members of immutable communities which can only be free if they are self-governing.[3] Such a doctrine spells disaster for all, particularly in ethnically mixed areas, where it can only exacerbate existing differences and historic antagonism.

Speaking generally then, the historical understanding of the complex phenomenon of nationalism is grounded on a rather narrow definition of the field and a similarly specific mode of explanation. The latter is largely contextual, psychological, and diffusionist. It insists, rightly in my view, in locating nationalism and the concepts characteristic of this movement in the context of European thought and history, at least as far as the origins of nationalism are concerned; these concepts and ideas can only be understood within that historical framework. Because modern Europe witnessed a breakdown in its modes of community, economy and political order, the psychic advantages and aspects of nationalism are emphasized; and the functions it performs for disoriented individuals and dislocated communities receive special attention. Finally, the favoured mechanism for explaining the spread of nationalism to Asia, Africa, and Latin America is a mixture of imitation and reaction: élites, especially intellectuals, adopt and adapt Western ideas of the nation and national regeneration. Nationalism flourishes in the specific circumstances of European imperialism and colonialism; but its diffusion is largely self-propelled and self-reproducing, once a tiny stratum of intellectuals has made its appearance in the recipient country[4] (Perham 1963; Hodgkin 1964).

Latterly, two other aspects of the historians' understanding of nationalism have become more visible, aspects which are shared by scholars from neighbouring disciplines. The first is the constructed nature of the nation. Not only is nationalism regarded as purely contingent and logically untenable: the nation itself, the object of every nationalism's endeavours, is artificial, a concept and model of social and cultural organization which is the product of the labours of self-styled nationalists bent on attaining power and reaping the rewards of political struggle. The nation is an invented category; it has roots in neither nature nor history. This leads into the second recent feature: the modernity of nations and nationalism. The past to which nationalists aspire is mythical: it exists only in the minds of nationalists and their followers, even when it is not cynically fabricated for present political purposes. The nation dates from the moment of nationalist success: it is a purely modern concept and the product of quite modern processes like bureaucracy, secularization, revolution and capitalism. Here the historians' understanding converges with the political scientist's, the sociologist's and the anthropologist's; except that for the historian, the initial emergence of the ideology and movement of nationalism is fairly securely dated to the last quarter of the eighteenth century and the first decade of the nineteenth, the period from the Polish Partitions and American War of Independence to the Prussian and German reaction to the French Revolution and Napoleonic conquests.[5]

THREE HISTORICAL RESPONSES TO NATIONALISM

Given the historical nature of their subject-matter and their own professional outlook, it would be surprising if historians did not conform to the general academic pattern, which discloses a close relationship between the ways in which scholars characterize and explain nationalism and their own *Sitz im Leben*, and that of their community; with ensuing differences in the basic meanings attached by each generation and group of historians to the concepts of nation and nationalism. This can be immediately seen in the typical early responses of historians and others to nineteenth-century nationalisms.

Early historians of the national idea tended to see the nation as a bulwark of individual liberty. This is of course the stance of Michelet in his *Historical View of the French Revolution*; writing in the mid-nineteenth century, Michelet reaffirmed a Rousseauan vision of the return to nature and human sociability. The 'spontaneous organization of France', born in 1789, had ushered in the era of fraternity, of 'Man fraternizing in the presence of God', as Michelet put it. In the fraternity, 'there are no longer either rich or poor, nobles or plebeians; there is but one general table, and provisions are in common; social dissensions and quarrels have disappeared; enemies become reconciled; and opposite sects, believers and philosophers, Protestants and Catholics, fraternize together.'[6]

This religion of patriotism is also the worship of man, and the motive force of modern French and European history. For the 'child upon the altar (of the festival of the confederation) is France, with all the world surrounding her. In her, the common child of nations, they feel themselves united . . .', and Michelet singles out Italy, Poland and Ireland, countries with nationalist movements belonging to the Young Europe movement of Mazzini, as fraternal sympathizers of France, even during the Revolution, revealing the power of an idea in modern history.

By the 1880s, nationalist principles were firmly entrenched in French politics, following the loss of Alsace-Lorraine in 1871. Renan, in opposing the principle of voluntary historical solidarity to that of an organic ethno-linguistic unity as the basis of the nation, remained true to the liberal spirit. 'Nations', he wrote, 'are nothing eternal. They had a beginning, they will have an end. The European confederation will probably replace them. But this is not the law of the century in which we live. At present, the existence of nations is good and even necessary. Their existence is a guarantee of liberty which would be lost if the world had only one law and one master . . .'. For Renan, the spirit of liberty was best embodied in a definition of the nation that was social psychological, one that refused any kind of reduction, whether biological, linguistic, economic, or geographical. 'Let us not abandon the fundamental principle that man is a rational and moral being before he is penned up in this or that language, before he is a member of this or that race, before he adheres to this or that culture.' So, 'A nation is a soul, a spiritual principle. . . . A nation is a great solidarity, created by the sentiment of the sacrifices which have been made and of those which one is disposed to make in the future. It presupposes a past; but it resumes itself in the present by a tangible fact: the consent, the clearly expressed desire to continue life in common. The existence of a nation is a plebiscite of every day, as the existence of the individual is a perpetual affirmation of life.' (Renan 1882; Kohn 1955: 135–40)

In trying to remain true to liberal principles in opposition to von Treitschke's militarism and racial nationalism, Renan may have overstated the voluntaristic aspects of the nation. What he really wants to affirm is the primacy of politics and shared history in the genesis and character of nations. Unlike the East, Western Europe saw the rise, after the demise of the Carolingian empire, of various nations which were fusions of populations. 'Even by the tenth century', he claims, 'all the inhabitants of France are French. The idea of a difference of races in the population of France has completely disappeared with the French writers and poets after Hugues Capet. The distinction between the noble and the serf is highly emphasised, but this distinction is in no way an ethnic distinction . . .'. The important point for Renan is social and psychological: shared experiences and common memories (and forgotten things). He does not explain why the West evolved the kind of nation, which he thinks is new in history, based on shared experience and selective memory, while the East failed to do so and retained its pattern of ethnic distinctiveness.

A more conservative response to the proliferation of nationalism can be found in Lord Acton's essay criticizing Mazzini's ideal of political nationality, which he characterized as an expression of political idealism. While the English concept of libertarian nationality looks back to 1688 and tends 'to diversity and not to uniformity, to harmony and not to unity', the French ideal of racial collective nationality partakes of the character of 1789 and 'overrules the rights and wishes of the inhabitants, absorbing their divergent interests in a fictitious unity; sacrifices their several inclinations and duties to the higher claim of nationality, and crushes all natural rights and all established liberties for the purpose of vindicating itself'. For Acton, the theory of national unity makes the nation a source of despotism and revolution; but the theory of liberty regards it as the bulwark of self-government, and the foremost limit to the excessive power of the State. (Acton 1948: 166–95)

It follows that, for Acton, multi-national empires are superior to nations, the Austrian empire to France. A State which is incompetent to satisfy different races condemns itself; a State which labours to neutralize, to absorb, or to expel them, destroys its own vitality; a State which does not include them is destitute of the chief basis of self-government. The theory of nationality, therefore, is a retrograde step in history. He concludes that 'nationality does not aim either at liberty or prosperity, both of which it sacrifices to the imperative necessity of making the nation the mould and measure of the State. Its course will be marked with material as well as moral ruin, in order that a new invention may prevail over the works of God and the interests of mankind'.

In fact, Acton has here slightly shifted his target, from the French theory of nationality to the nation itself. But what concerns us is Acton's sense of the constructed nature of the nation. Not only are its claims less important than those of traditional authority and individual liberty; it is really an outgrowth, a product of the denial of corporate rights by state absolutism. Acton is reacting against the movement for Italian unification; hence, his focus on nationalism and a theory of unity rather than secession. Both his arguments and his historical analysis are tied to mid-nineteenth century developments on the Continent; except for his conviction of the artificiality and modernity of the nation, they would evoke few chords in African or Asian states in the contemporary era. Yet his underlying assumptions continue to inspire academic analyses even today.

Not all conservative reactions were so hostile to nationalism. Max Weber, sociological historian and German nationalist, regarded nations as conflict groups and bearers of unique cultural values. Echoing Renan, Weber declares that 'A nation is a community of sentiment which would adequately manifest itself in a state of its own; hence, a nation is a community which normally tends to produce a state of its own'. (Gerth & Mills 1947: 176) The nation is also the focus of the cultural values that define its individuality: 'The significance of the 'nation' is usually anchored in the superiority, or at least irreplaceability, of the cultural values that can only be preserved and developed through the cultivation of the individuality (Eigenart) of the community'. (Weber 1968, III, Ch. 3: 926)

Like the other historians considered so far, Weber has left us with no historical account of the rise of nationalism, though he seems to have intended to do so. All we have are sections on ethnicity, the nation, and nationalism in *Economy and Society*, in which his basic 'political' approach to the subject is evident. For, not only did Weber consider the State and the nation required each other in the modern world, as do the bureaucrats and intellectuals, the bearers of the respective concepts; it was political action, more than anything, which could transform ethnic communities into nations, as the case of Alsace with its French political memories so clearly demonstrated for Weber. As he put it, 'This can be understood by any visitor who walks through the museum of Colmar, which is rich in relics such as tricolors, *pompier* and military helmets, edicts by Louis Phillippe and especially memorabilia from the French Revolution; these may appear trivial to the outsider, but they have sentimental value for the Alsatians. This sense of community came into being by virtue of common political and, indirectly, social experiences which are highly valued by the masses as symbols of the destruction of feudalism, and the story of these events takes the place of the heroic legends of primitive peoples'.[7] (Weber 1968, I/II, ch. 5: 396)

We cannot be sure how far Weber regarded nations as modern, let alone inventions or artificial. In his work, for perhaps the first time, we meet the problem of the relationship between ethnicity and nationalism which has exercised some latter-day scholars. This concern, however, was far from a third typical response to nineteenth-century nationalism, the socialist and Marxist historical evaluation. Not that Marx or Engels devoted any systematic attention to the phenomenon; their attitudes must be gleaned from passing references in articles on foreign policy or in revolutionary pamphlets or essays. (Davis 1967, chs. 1–3; Cummins 1980). But their legacy to Marxist historians is clear in its main outlines: nations are communities of language and natural sympathies, as Engels put it; the great or 'leading' nations, furthest advanced on the road of capitalism, must be supported against reactionary absolutist states like Tsarist Russia or small, backward nations like Serbia or the Czechs; the working-class 'has no stake in the fatherland', though its struggle must first of all be with its own national bourgeoisie; and nationalism may only be supported by socialists where it hastens the overthrow of feudalism or, as in Ireland, bourgeois domination. To which Engels added, à propos Poland, that national independence is the pre-condition of social development, and that (as Hegel had claimed) only those nations which in the past had built their own states, would be able to do so in the future, and so deserved the support of socialists.[8]

It was left to subsequent Marxist historians to take up these purely 'instrumental' positions and attempt to understand the phenomena of nations and nationalism in historical terms. Kautsky, Lenin, and Luxembourg, despite their disagreements, extended the basically 'instrumentalist' analysis of Eastern European nationalisms as tools of the feudal or bourgeois classes and diversions from proletarian revolution, though Lenin was prepared to concede the popular reality of the Eastern nationalism with which he had to contend. (Davis 1967; Talmon 1980, Pt. II, ch. 8 and Part III and Part VI/2: 111). But it was left to Karl Renner and Otto Bauer to provide a more rounded Marxist account of nationalism.

Of course, theirs was also a programmatic statement. It was designed to meet the immediate needs of the Austrian Social Democrats, confronted with the problems of multi-nationalism within the empire and the party. To support their extra-territorial solutions and their concept of personal and cultural nationality, Renner and Bauer adopted definitions of the nation that led them away from the political and territorial conceptions of Marx and Engels. For Bauer, in particular, the nation was a 'community of fate', with its own character and culture. It was shaped by material factors, but close proximity and communication in a shared history and culture made the national bond even more powerful than class ties. Bauer, nevertheless, insisted on the individual's right to choose his cultural nationality, as the latter gradually evolved. In the case of the Germans, Bauer traced their national community back to the tribal horde living in isolation and sharing everything. With agricultural settlement, some parts of the horde broke away or fused with other groups; but the central stem was split in the Middle Ages on class lines, with the barons and clergy constituting the real nation. Later, with the rise of towns and a money economy, they were gradually enlarged by the addition of the bourgeoisie and educated middle class; and now socialism was broadening the national base still further through the inclusion of the working-class. It was in this spirit that the 1899 Brunn Congress of the Austrian Social-Democratic Workers' party called for a democratic federal state of nationalities, viewed as cultural-historical communities without territorial rights. (Bauer 1924; Talmon 1980, Part III, ch. 7)

TYPOLOGIES AND EVALUATIONS

Bauer's is perhaps the first full-length study of nationalism, from an historical standpoint, albeit a political one dictated by very specific political circumstances. It reflects the growing importance of nationalism as a political ideology and movement, and as a subject of academic investigation in its own right. It was in the 1920s that Carlton Hayes and Hans Kohn began their close dissections of nationalist ideologies and attempted to order its varieties into definite, recurring types. Hayes' work is perhaps the first to adopt a more neutral stance, one that seeks to distinguish the various strands of nationalist ideology. If his distinctions between Humanitarian, Traditional, Jacobin, Liberal, and later Economic and Integral nationalisms describe pure types rather than concrete trends or instances, which in practice mingle the different strands, they do sensitize us to the complexities of nationalist ideology. They also reveal, beneath the analytical discourse, the moralistic periodization of the first full-length histories of nationalism. (Hayes 1931; A. D. Smith 1971, ch. 8)

A more influential typology, Hans Kohn's dichotomy of 'Western' voluntaristic and 'Eastern' organic nationalism, also discloses an underlying moral purpose. For Kohn, nationalism in England, France, and America is rationalist, optimistic, and pluralist. Couched in terms of the social contract, it answered to the aspirations for political community of the rising middle classes with their ideal of social progress. Across the Rhine, however, and eastwards into Russia and Asia, social backwardness and the weakness of the middle classes produced a much more emotional and authoritarian nationalism, based on the lower aristocracy and intelligentsia, and appealing to the folk instincts of the masses. Later, Kohn subdivided his Western type into 'individualist' and 'collectivist' sub-categories, found respectively in the Anglo-Saxon countries and in France. (Kohn 1967a, esp. chs. 5, 7; Kohn 1955)

As this last distinction suggests, it is the ideology of nationalism rather than the movement or community, that forms the object of Kohn's interest. This accords with our characterization of most historians' picture of nationalism, and the moralistic concerns which have often animated their research, concerns that were understandably pressing during the Second World War, when Kohn wrote his major study. Kohn does, however, attempt to link his ideological types with their social settings, albeit somewhat crudely; and to show some of the pre-modern group sentiments among Greeks, Jews and others, that went into the formulations of modern nationalism. In other words, Kohn's 'modernism' (the belief in the complete modernity of nations and nationalism) is tempered by his inclusion of pre-modern ethnic motifs; and this in turn implies a separate role for 'national sentiment', a role not attributable solely to nationalist ideologues. Indeed, even a cursory inspection reveals that Kohn's many books include not only detailed analyses of specific nationalist ideologies like Pan-Slavism, but studies of the social and political setting of a wider 'national consciousness' in Jacobin France, nineteenth-century Germany or early modern Switzerland. (Kohn 1957; 1960; 1965 and 1967b)

This wider consciousness seems also to form the object of the brief study, *Nationalism and After* (1945) by Edward Hallett Carr. Carr's attitude to nationalism is not wholly negative: he speaks of the development of that community of national thought and feeling, of political and cultural tradition, which is the constructive side of nationalism. Generally, however, Carr, like Acton whom he quotes at the outset, sees nationalism as a denial of individualism and democracy, of liberty and equality; though the nation, as an historical group, has a 'place and function in a wider society', it must not be allowed to impede its own supersession in an interdependent regional or world order. (Carr 1945, II, 39; Shafer 1955)

In his historical account, Carr distinguishes three periods of nationalism: an early modern epoch in which the new national unit was identified with the person of the monarch, international relations being simply the rules governing the intercourse of dynastic states, with 'mercantilism' as the characteristic economic policy; the era from the French Revolution till 1914, in which a popular and democratic political nationalism fathered by Rousseau was diffused throughout Europe under the aegis of an international economic order grounded on free trade, expansion and the financial dominance of London; and finally the period from the late nineteenth century to the Second World War, which saw the incorporation of the masses into the fully socialized nation, its growing economic nationalism, and the sheer proliferation of European nations, leading to totalitarian regimes and total warfare. Carr considers the prospects for a reversal of nationalism's appeal encouraging; his failure to allow for the possibility of a wave of anti-colonial nationalisms, or renewed European and Third World secession nationalisms, suggests again the moral and teleological basis of his penetrating analysis, as well as its Eurocentrism. Again, given the enormity of the issues at stake in the 1939–45 War, and his own social location, this is unsurprising. (Carr 1945, I)

As long as fascism continued to be regarded as the logical denouement of nationalism, a European focus and a periodization in terms of moral progression seemed to make sense. But, the moment a more global and less moralistic standpoint, which differentiated fascism from various kinds of nationalism, began to be adopted, chronological typologies were seen to be inadequate. Thus, in his earlier work, Louis Snyder had opted for a common four-stage periodization, as follows:

1815–1871 —'integrative' nationalism
1871–1900 —'disruptive' nationalism
1900–1945 —'aggressive' nationalism
1945–?   —'contemporary' nationalism

In his later work, Snyder opts for a geographical typology, including a 'fissiparous' European nationalism, a racial Black nationalism in Africa, a politico-religious nationalism in the Middle East, a messianic one in Russia, a 'melting-pot' one in the United States, and anti-colonial nationalisms in Asia, and populist ones in Latin America. (Snyder 1954; 1968: 64–7). It is not clear that such general, and necessarily overlapping, regional types, do more than point up the global diffusion of nationalism, but they serve at least to correct the Eurocentrism of earlier typologies.

This shift in geopolitical focus is apparent in a number of typologies proposed by historians and others, contrasting the European experience with that of the Third World, or parts of it. Here we may mention Kenneth Minogue's typology of European 'ethnic', Pan and diaspora, and 'underdeveloped' Third World nationalisms (Minogue 1967; ch. 1); John Plamenatz' distinction between the nationalisms of those with a high level of cultural resources and education, like the nineteenth-century Germans and Italians, and those with poor cultural resources like the Slavs and Africans, whose nationalism is therefore imitative and competitive (Plamenatz 1976); and E. K. Francis' contrast, taken from Meinecke, between 'ethnic' nations and nationalisms, based on a belief in common descent and identity, and 'demotic' nations which share administrative and military institutions and common territory and mobility.[9]

Perhaps the most influential of these recent typologies is Hugh Seton-Watson's distinction between, first, the 'old, continuous nations' like the English, French, Castilians, Dutch, Scots, Danes, Swedes, Poles, Hungarians and Russians, and the 'new' nations of the Serbs, Croats, Rumanians, Arabs, Africans and Indians, whose national consciousness succeeded the spread of nationalism and were largely its products; and then within this last category, three kinds of nationalist movement, secession, irredentism, and 'nation-building' nationalisms. In his *Nations and States* (1977), Seton-Watson elaborates these distinctions (which Tilly had also used in relation to state-building) with a wealth of historical examples. They serve to organize his account, which shifts the object of interest away from nationalism as an ideology to the processes which encourage the formation of national consciousness, processes like geography, the state, religion and language. (Seton-Watson 1965; 1977, chs. 1–2)

NATIONS AS NATIONALIST CONSTRUCTS

I said that historians generally aim to arrive at a contextual understanding of nationalism, that is, an understanding of the meanings which the participants attributed to the concept of the nation according to the concrete circumstances in which they were placed. For this reason, the problem of explanation is often seen as an attempt to grasp, first, the various traditions of nationalist thought and experience, and second, the manner in which such traditions are diffused to other peoples. An example of the first kind of attempt is Salo Baron's excellent analysis of the varieties of nationalist experience, at least in Europe, viewed in relation to different religious traditions such as Protestantism, Catholicism, Orthodox Caesaro-Papism and Judaism. If nations are modern and largely the product of the labours and ideas of nationalists, the latter can only be grasped in the context of definite traditions in which religion played the dominant role. However secular the nationalist doctrine, it cannot be understood in all its empirical variety outside this religious matrix, as many case studies were to demonstrate.[10] An example of the second type of attempt is Trevor-Roper's explanation of the diffusion of ideas from the 'historic'

nationalisms of Germany, Italy, and Hungary to the 'secondary' nationalisms of Czechs, Poles, and Jews. Quite apart from the validity of the
distinction itself, the imitative role of the East European intelligentsias who
react against the West, but take up its nationalist ideas, requires further
elucidation. Why should these particular ideas prove so attractive, and what
accounts for the prominence of the intellectuals? (Trevor-Roper 1961;
A. D. Smith 1971, ch. 2)

An answer to both questions, and one which accords to religious
traditions a determining role, is provided by the work of Elie Kedourie.
In his initial study, Kedourie aimed at a contextual understanding of
European nationalism from its invention in early nineteenth century
Germany to its later diffusion by native intellectuals in Eastern Europe and
the Middle East. Concentrating more on the varieties of nationalism than
the growth of nations, Kedourie traces the evolution of notions of diversity, autonomy of the will, and linguistic purity, to the peculiar concerns
of the European philosophical tradition from Descartes to Kant and Fichte,
and the alienation of German-speaking intellectuals. The context, then,
in which the example of the French Revolution and the ideals of the German
Romantics captured the imaginations of the frustrated youth, was specifically modern and European, and it involved a radical breakdown of
traditional communities like the family and church, and their accom-
panying political habits. Here the social psychological base is apparent:
nationalist movements, he argues, are seen to satisfy a need, to fulfil a want.
Put at its simplest, the need is to belong together in a coherent and
stable community. So that nationalism here is treated as the outcome of
the spirit of an age in which old communities and traditions had fallen
to the onslaught of Enlightenment doctrines and in which disoriented youth
craved the satisfaction of their need to belong.[11]

In a later work, *Nationalism in Asia and Africa* (1971), Kedourie
extended this strictly 'modernist' analysis in two directions. The first was
spatial and sociological. In attempting to explain why native élites in Africa
and Asia adopted the western ideals of nationalism Kedourie developed a
diffusionist model in which both Western institutions and ideas were spread
to other continents by the regimenting effects of modernizing colonialisms
and the Western education of indigenous intellectuals, who then suffer
discrimination at the hands of colonial administrations in their native lands;
Kedourie cites in particular the examples of Surendranath Banerjea,
Edward Atiyah, and George Antonius. Imitation is here combined with
psychological resentment at social rejection by the West. On the other side,
the original analysis is extended back in time. In returning to the 'cult of

the dark gods', African and Asian intelligentsias were nevertheless imitating, not only the historicism of European intellectuals, but also their revolutionary chiliasm, their belief in the perfectibility of this world, which had its roots in the visions of Christian millennialism. Tracing European nationalist ideals to their origins in the heterodox doctrines of Joachim of Fiore, the Franciscan Spirituals and the Anabaptists of Munster, whose activities Norman Cohn had so vividly recorded, Kedourie is able to affirm that:

We may say in short that the mainspring of nationalism in Asia and Africa is the same secular millennialism which had its rise and development in Europe and in which society is subjected to the will of a handful of visionaries who, to achieve their vision, must destroy all barriers between private and public.[12] (Kedourie 1971, Introduction)

In tracing this particular lineage of nationalism, Kedourie does not mean to imply that nations and nationalism are not peculiarly modern phenomena; or that they have historical roots beyond the imaginings and activities of nationalist intellectuals. Despite his respect for different historical traditions, the emphasis falls on the power of nationalism as a doctrine to conjure the nation in place of decayed traditional communities, and on the activities of modern, rationalist intellectuals in serving as creators and revolutionary agents of modern nations and nationalisms.[13]

This sense of the modernity and 'constructed' nature of the nation is widely shared by contemporary historians of all persuasions, as well as by scholars in other disciplines. Not all of them would, however, ascribe the predominant role in the process of construction to the ideologues of nationalism. John Breuilly, for example, restricts the definition of nationalism to political arguments designed to mobilize, co-ordinate and legitimize support for the capture of state power. These arguments presuppose the existence of the nation with its own peculiar character, seeking independence and possessing priority over every other interest or value. Such a doctrine emerges in opposition to state power, and becomes the basis for mobilizing and co-ordinating civil society during the early modern period in Europe, when the split between state and society became apparent. On this basis, Breuilly distinguishes three kinds of nationalist opposition, secession, unification, and reform movements, each of which may emerge in nation-states and in states which do not define themselves as nations, for example, empires or colonies. This six-fold classification can then be used to compare the nationalist politics of both Europe and the Third World, in ways that illuminate the uses of nationalist arguments for élites and others in the struggle for state power. For Breuilly, the role of culture and intellectuals is supportive; nationalism is not primarily a matter of identity or communication, but simply a cultural mode of opposition (and more rarely governmental) politics, which equates the historicist notion of the unique nation with the political concept of the universal 'nation-state'. By this means, nationalists are able to tap all sorts of non-political resources in a society for the purpose of mobilizing political opposition. The nationalist solution to the problem of alienation which was the inevitable product of the growing division between state and society, was to regard each unique society or 'nation' as the natural (and only) basis of a territorial state, lest alien societies do violence to the unique national spirit. Breuilly regards this fusion of a cultural and political concept of community as spurious, but acknowledges its wide appeal in all continents (Breuilly 1982; Introduction and Conclusion).

This analysis is typical of the dominant 'modernist' and 'instrumentalist' school of historical, and sociological, thought about nations and nationalism. Not only are nations recent constructs of partisan ideologues. Nationalism is also an instrument of legitimation and mobilization, through which leaders and élites stir up mass support for their competitive power struggle. Not only nationalists, but non-nationalists like Bismarck, can tap atavistic emotions and manipulate the fears and resentments of the masses by appealing to their chauvinism and heightening their sense of cultural difference. If Breuilly's political realism concedes rather less to intellectuals and their ideals among the upper and middle classes, he still reserves for them a place in igniting mass sentiment, which can be channelled for élite political ends.[14] (Breuilly 1982, ch. 16).

A similar 'instrumentalism' pervades the essays in the volume edited by Eric Hobsbawm and Terence Ranger, entitled *The Invention of Tradition* (1983). It must be said that not all the essays support the book's *leitmotif*, the novelty and even fabrication of traditions which masquerade as immemorial. It is, for example, clear from Prys Morgan's careful account of the revived *eisteddfodau* in the mid-eighteenth century that new practices were meshed with much older customs and traditions; on the other hand, the incorporation of the neo-Druidic Gorsedd into the *eisteddfod* of 1819 was a stroke of pure invention on the part of Iolo Morganwg.[15] Hobsbawm, however, regards 'that comparatively recent historical innovation, the 'nation', with its associated phenomena: nationalism, the nation-state, national symbols, histories and the rest as closely bound up with 'invented traditions', and as resting on exercises in social engineering which are often deliberate and always innovative'. Nations are neither ancient nor natural: on the contrary, much of what subjectively makes up the modern 'nation' consists of such constructs and is associated with appropriate and, in general, fairly recent symbols or suitably tailored discourse (such as 'national history'). In his concluding essay, Hobsbawm analyses the spate of invented traditions in late nineteenth-century France, Germany, and the United States—education manuals, public ceremonies, public monuments and buildings, the use of collective personifications like Marianne or the 'Deutsche Michel', commemorative anniversaries, the use of flags and anthems—and links them causally to the increasing rapidity of social change and in particular to the rise of mass political democracy. It was then that rulers and states discovered the uses of mass irrationality, though this does not mean that invented national traditions are themselves irrational responses to the breakdown in social structure and political hierarchies, for they clearly fulfil widespread social and psychological needs in the modern era.[16]

His conclusions are of a piece with Hugh Trevor-Roper's account of the invention of the Highlands tradition from the late eighteenth century, after the Jacobite defeat at Culloden. From Rawlinson's 'invention' of the small kilt in the 1730s, through MacPherson's 'rediscovery' of Ossian in the early 1760s and Walter Scott's creation of Scottish literary tourism to the 'clan' tartans published by Colonel David Stewart in 1822 and the *Vestiarium Scotium* (1842) and *The Costume of the Clans* (1844) of the 'Sobieske Stuart' brothers, who sought to revive an almost vanished medieval Scottish Highlands civilization, the threads of fabricated traditions were woven into the created new nation of Scotland, aided by Victoria's devotion to Balmoral and English bourgeois concern for the healthy pleasures of Highlands life.[17] The point, of course, is that any connection with life in the medieval Highlands, which till the seventeenth century under the MacDonald Lords of the Isles constituted a Hebridean variant of an overflow Irish culture, is purely fictitious: the traditions of the nations are as recent as the nation itself.

That is also the burden of Benedict Anderson's recent reflections on the origins and spread of nationalism, in his *Imagined Communities* (1983). The nation is an abstraction, a construct of the imagination; it is a community which is imagined as both sovereign and limited. It emerges when the realm of church and dynasty recede, and no longer seem to answer to mankind's craving for immortality. The nation, with its promise of identification with posterity, can help us to overcome the finality of death and oblivion; but that only becomes possible when a new conception of homogenous, empty chronological time replaces medieval concepts of simultaneous time. Nations are created in the historical and sociological imagination, through identification with generalised communal heroes set in equally generalized but vividly detailed locations and times; though we can never meet them, we can 'know' our fellow-citizens, the members of our cultural nations, through these identifications and descriptions in newspapers, journals, novels, plays, and operas. This has become a reality through what Anderson calls 'the technology of print capitalism', which spawned the first real commodity, the mass-produced printed book. Together with the possibilities of travel and the 'administrative pilgrimages' of colonial élites, the rise of printed literature and the press has made it possible to 'narrate' the nation and imaginatively to 'construct' it. In different parts of the world and successive epochs, this process of construction took different forms, from the 'vernacular' literary and philological nationalisms of Europe to the 'official' nationalism of the authoritarian empires and the Marxist nationalism of communist states like Vietnam and China. But the underlying cultural and economic processes were broadly similar, and their result was everywhere the same basic model of imagined community we call the 'nation'.[18] (Anderson 1983)

IDENTITY AND CONTINUITY

This brief discussion of the work of some historians, and a few others, who concerned themselves with the nature and history of nations and nationalism, has been necessarily selective and partial. I have been concerned to bring out the main lines of their treatment, rather than the historiographical detail. This has allowed us to grasp the stages of historical treatment, which correspond roughly, as I intimated at the outset, to the historians' own situation and epoch. The first of these periods or stages lasts, roughly, from the mid-nineteenth century to the 1920s; with the exception of the full-length treatment of Bauer, who is not a historian in the strict sense, the treatments are in essay or section form, and addressed to particular nationalist situations in Europe. It is only in the second period that we encounter serious attempts by historians to concentrate on the field of nationalist phenomena, and to look closely at the varieties of ideology and the periodization of nationalism. On the whole, it is national*ism*, in the sense of an ideology rather than a sentiment, at the expense of nations, that preoccupies historians like Hayes, Snyder, Kohn, and Shafer; and the emphasis is less on systematic explanation of the rise and appeal of nationalism, than on narration and classification of its sub-types. It is really only in the third period, since the 1950s, that historians have devoted greater attention to a rigorous search for situational or general factors that serve to explain the genesis and course of particular movements or of nationalism-in-general. In this period, too, there is a growing interest in national sentiment and the nation as explananda. Although some historians continue to devote their attention to the ideology, several others combine this with consideration of its role in creating nations or augmenting or fostering national consciousness. Equally, there is a growing interest in what might be termed sociological factors as possible causes of the origins and appeal of nationalism, and in cross-fertilization with other disciplines in approach and method.[19]

In the light of these different concerns and this variety of approaches, can we speak of an historical perspective on nationalism *tout court*? That would be going too far. What we can do is to list the main characteristics common to most historians' picture of nations and nationalism, and to ask how far the resulting image corresponds to, and helps to explain, the many facets of this complex phenomenon.

Of these characteristics, three stand out, especially in recent accounts by historians. The first is the scepticism, and even hostility, to nationalism which was mentioned at the outset. It takes the form of emphasizing the inherently absurd and destructive tendencies of nationalism. This is a motif that runs right through the three periods of historical investigation in the field. It is, of course, not peculiar to historians: scholars in political science and international relations also fasten on the destabilizing effects of nationalism for states and for inter-state order. Nevertheless, historians by and large appear to display greater scepticism and hostility than others, perhaps because they are keenly aware of the disturbing psychological aspects of national sentiment and nationalism. At times, this awareness makes them liable to the charge of psychologism, or reducing a phenomenon that manifests itself at several levels to just one, the social psychological. But perhaps the more serious charge is that, by taking the ideology as their prime explanandum, they overlook or bypass the importance of processes of nation-formation which are to some extent independent of the activities of nationalist ideologues. If some sociologists have been guilty of missing out those activities, some historians have perhaps given them too much attention and explanatory weight.

One effect of this tendency among historians is to underplay some of the functional, even 'constructive' aspects, of nationalist endeavours. Once those activities are placed within the context of a process of 'nation-formation' (not the same as 'nation-building'), which for various reasons may be under way, they may assume a greater validity and practical utility than is often conceded. It is not uncommon for this process to throw up a cultural renascence and a range of new communal ventures; if some of these border on the absurd or pernicious, others are clearly salutary and regenerative, notably in the fields of music, art and literature, and various fields of scholarship.[20]

Allied to the historians' general assumptions about the poverty of nationalism is their conviction that nations are artificial communities with largely fabricated ties. Hence, the common enterprise of 'deconstructing the nation', shared with many anthropologists; and the need to uncover the ideological aims of nationalist manipulators who tap the atavistic emotions of the masses for their partisan ends. This is the subject of a lively debate between Paul Brass and Francis Robinson on the formation of Pakistan and the role of nationalist élites in forging, or reacting to, the Muslim sentiments of the masses in North India. (Taylor and Yapp 1979; Sathyamurthy 1983)

But, as Hobsbawm concedes, only some traditions have mass resonance, and only some of them prove durable. The nation, as he points out, is the most important of the lasting 'invented traditions'.[21] If so, in what sense shall we regard it as 'invented' or 'constructed'? Why does this 'invention' so often and in such different cultural and social settings appear to strike such a deep chord and for so long? No artifice, however well-constructed, could survive so many different kinds of vicissitude or fit so many different conditions. Clearly there is more to the formations of nations than nationalist fabrication, and 'invention' must be understood in its other sense of a novel recombination of existing elements.[22]

The so-called 'artificiality' of nations and nationalism is closely allied to the third characteristic of the historians' general image: the modernity of nations and nationalism. Now, the historians are surely correct in maintaining that nationalism, as an ideology and a movement, seeking to attain and maintain autonomy, unity and identity for a social group deemed by some of its members to constitute an actual or potential 'nation', is a product of the late eighteenth century. It was then that a specifically nationalist doctrine arose, claiming that the world is divided into distinct nations, each with its peculiar character, that nations are the source of all political power, that human beings are free only insofar as they belong to an autonomous nation, and that international peace and security depend on all nations being autonomous, preferably in states of their own. It was only in the eighteenth century that such ideas gained currency, in the specific context of the European inter-state system.[23]

Not all historians accepted, however, the correlate of this view, namely the modernity of the nation. An older generation of historian, particularly on the Continent, looked for and found nations even in antiquity, among Greeks, Jews, Persians, and Egyptians.[24] Others were equally convinced of their presence among French and English, Scots and Swiss, in the Middle Ages. (Coulton 1935; Handelsman 1929; Koht 1947). There are partisans of these views to this day, though their number is small.[25]

Today, however, most historians accept the modernity of the 'nation', and they differ only as to more detailed dating for the emergence of particular nations, and about the factors which facilitated their emergence. The nation is seen as an exclusively modern concept and type of social organization, requiring specifically 'modern' conditions of state bureaucracy, capitalism, secularism, and democracy to bring it into being.

Three points can be made about this conception. The first is that it too contains a 'mythical' element, in the sense of a dramatic interpretation which is widely believed and which while referring to past events, serves present purposes or future goals. The 'myth of the modern nation' refers back to a premodern era which is 'nationless', and dramatizes the narrative of modernization giving birth to nations; and the nations in this picture represents a more or less regrettable stage in human history, part of the radical break between traditional, agrarian and modern, industrial societies, to be superseded once full modernity is attained. Such a 'counter-myth' seeks to relativize nationalism and to dismiss and explain the claims and assumptions of the nationalist myth itself. (Tudor 1972; A. D. Smith 1988)

The second point is that, even on the assumptions made by the 'modernist' conception of nationalism, there are important differences between groups of nations, both in type and in periodization. Of course, much depends on the definition of the 'nation' espoused. But let us suppose that by the term 'nation' we mean a large, territorially bounded group sharing a common culture and division of labour, and a common code of legal rights and duties, the kind of attributes which would be uncommon in antiquity and the early medieval era.[26] Even with such a 'modernist' definition, the kind of distinction that Hugh Seton-Watson, and in another context, Charles Tilly have drawn, between slowly emerging, continuous nations (and states) in Western and Northern Europe, and the later 'nations of design', created by and in the era of nationalism, must be observed. It is clear that in the West the process of 'nation-formation' was unforeseen and unintended, with states being forged around dominant ethnic communities, and in turn gradually becoming national states. Elsewhere such processes required external stimuli and planned activism. (Seton-Watson 1977, chs. 2–3; Tilly 1975, Introduction and Conclusion)

Of course, this must not be taken to imply that something like the 'nation' had already emerged in the fifteenth century in England, France, and Spain; this was decidedly not Seton-Watson's claim. Rather, he was pointing to two quite different routes in the formation of nations, and to the need to trace the origins of one of these trajectories back into the Middle Ages, a trajectory that was not really completed (if it is ever complete) until the nineteenth century, as Eugen Weber has so well reminded us in the case of France and its regions.[27]

This leads to my last point. If it is conceded that some of the processes which enter into the formation of nations go back to the medieval era, and perhaps even earlier, then perhaps it becomes legitimate and necessary to enquire how pre-modern communities relate to what we call 'modern nations', in order to understand better why such nations have so wide an appeal in the modern world. The real trouble with the modernist picture of nationalism, assumed by so many historians and other scholars, is a certain historical shallowness. By locating the nation and nationalism exclusively in the transition to a modern era and treating them as products of 'modernity', one makes the task of explaining the return to the past and the felt continuities with an ethnic past, more difficult. The balance between continuity and discontinuity has been upset, and this makes the modern quest for collective identity so baffling—unless of course one invokes a catch-all 'need to belong'. But as we said, that need is variable, and in any case it does not explain why it so often attaches itself to the 'nation' rather than other communities.

This is why it is so necessary and important to look at the cultural models of pre-modern community which may help to explain why so many people are drawn to the nation as their primary focus of loyalty and solidarity in the modern world. Not only may we point to specific continuities of the kind noted by John Armstrong in his study of medieval Christian and Islamic ethnic identities, notably in the realm of myth, symbol and historical memory which Renan singled out.[28] The fact that many parts of the world had been socially and culturally structured in terms of different kinds of ethnic community (or *ethnie*) in antiquity and the medieval era, as they continue to be to this day, and that *ethnies* share some elements with modern nations (myths of ancestry, memories, some cultural elements, perhaps a territory and a name), may afford a better point of departure for the study of the transformations and revivals involved in the formation of modern nations and the role played by nationalism in those processes. Even if elements of ethnicity are 'constructed' and 'reconstructed' and sometimes plainly 'invented', the fact that such activities have been operating for centuries, even millennia, and that several *ethnies* while changing their cultural character have nevertheless persisted as identifiable communities over long periods, suggests that we ignore the presence and influence exerted by such communities on the formation of modern nations at our peril.[29]

My purpose here has not been to fit every historian of nationalism into a preconceived framework, but only to draw out what I took to be the main points of an underlying argument to be found in many of their writings on this subject. Clearly, there are historians who do not subscribe to the currently dominant trends, and for whom the nation is more than a modern construct and nationalism not only the genie of disruption which is often portrayed. Nevertheless, it is interesting that a wide spectrum of historians have and do subscribe to the general 'modernist' portrait which I have delineated, and share in the general scepticism and suspicion of nationalism, to which they attribute many of the world's ills.

Whether this verdict on so protean a phenomenon as nationalism is justified is an open question. But the underlying analysis from which it springs, while engendering many fascinating insights, poses as many problems as it resolves.

Notes

1. The role of nationalist historians in promoting nationalism has not, as far as I know, been the subject of a full-length study; but Hans Kohn's work has several chapters on the contributions of particular historians to specific movements, for example, Muller and von Treitschke in Kohn (1965); see also Kohn (1961) on Michelet, and Kohn (1960) on Palacky.

2. As for example in the Royal Institute of International Affairs' *Report on Nationalism* (1939) or the study by Michelat and Thomas (1966). For a case study using such a definition, see Klausner (1960).

3. For the Whig doctrine, see Mill (1872) and the comments on Lord Acton's critique, below.

4. For a social psychological theory of European 'neo-nationalism', see Mayo (1974); for an evaluation of such approaches, A. D. Smith (1978).

5. A few historians, like Marcu (1976), place the origins of national*ism* as an ideology in the sixteenth century; but most place it in the era of the 'democratic

revolution', with Palmer (1940) and Godechot (1965); see Kohn (1967b) and Kamenka (1976).

6. J. Michelet, *Historical View of the French Revolution*, tr. C. Cocks, London, S. Bell & Sons 1890, III, chs. X–XII, pp. 382–403, cited in Kohn (1955, 97–102).

7. All history, Weber concludes, shows how easily political action can give rise to the belief in blood relationship, unless gross differences of anthropological type impede it. Weber (1968, 393).

8. On Hegel's theory of the 'history-less peoples' and Engels' use of it, see Rosdolsky (1964); more generally, see Fisera and Minnerup (1978) and Connor (1984).

9. Francis (1968); also the distinction between 'ethnic' and 'political' nations in Krejci and Velimsky (1981); cf. Symmons-Symonolewicz (1970).

10. Baron (1947), with an analysis of the founding fathers' views of the relationship between religion and nationalism.

11. Kedourie (1960, especially 101); the burden of his book, however, is to castigate nationalism as a doctrine of the Will, and one which is beyond the control even of its devotees.

12. See also Cohn (1957) on millennial movements in medieval Christendom. For some comments on the links between nationalism and millennialism, see A. D. Smith (1979, ch. 2).

13. Hence the anthology of nationalist writings collected in Kedourie (1971). On the role of intellectuals in nationalism, see Gella (1976) and Seton-Watson (1960, ch. 6). For class and nationalism, see Shafer (1938).

14. In this Breuilly is close to the position adopted by Nairn (1977, chs. 2, 9) on the intelligentsia.

15. P. Morgan, *From a Death to a View: The Hunt for the Welsh Past in the Romantic Period*, in Hobsbawm & Ranger (1983). (Edward Williams was the real name of Iolo Morganwg).

16. E. Hobsbawm, Introduction: *Inventing Traditions* (esp. 13–14) and ch. 7 (esp. 270–83) in Hobsbawm & Ranger (1983). It is interesting how attractive this idea of the nation fulfilling needs is to historians of all persuasions; it encourages the cautionary note.

17. H. Trevor-Roper, *The Invention of Tradition: The Highland Tradition of Scotland*, in Hobsbawm & Ranger (1983).

18. I have included Anderson, though his account is as much sociological as historical, because of its attention to historical contexts and sequences of events; and his emphasis on the nation as a construct of the imagination accords well with the understanding of many historians today.

19. There is, of course, no hard and fast distinction between these three periods; and some elements, notably the sense of artifice in the phenomenon of the nation, echo throughout. Similarly, it is possible to find sociological elements in earlier periods, in Bauer, Kohn, Carr and of course Max Weber. For parallel sociological paradigms or approaches, see A. D. Smith (1983).

20. The term 'nation-building' really refers to a nationalist programme of building the institutions and roles of the 'nation-state'. In practice, it is more

concerned with 'state-building' than 'nation-creation'. Whereas the term 'nation-formation' refers to all those processes, intended or not, that contribute to the emergence of the nation and national consciousness. These will normally include social and cultural activities of nationalists; but they may also cover the military and political activities of kings and ministers, the rates of population increase and urbanization, and the decline of churches and empires. All these may enter into a process of 'nation-formation', but not of 'nation-building'. On the role of the visual arts in late-eighteenth century Western Europe in the formation of conceptions of the nation, see Rosenblum (1967), Herbert (1972) and A. D. Smith (1987).

21. Hobsbawm & Ranger (1983, esp. 6–7, 10–11, 13–14, and 303–5); also the essay by G. Mosse, *Mass Politics and the Political Liturgy of Nationalism*, in Kamenka (1976).

22. For this meaning of 'invention', see Banks (1972).

23. For this statement of nationalist doctrine, and definition of nationalism as a movement, see A. D. Smith (1973, section 2). 'National sentiment' and consciousness of 'national' difference arose rather earlier, however, encouraged perhaps by the emerging European state system sanctioned by the treaty of Westphalia; see on this Kemilainen (1964) and Tilly (1975); also Howard (1976).

24. For example, Walek-Czernecki (1929) and, more critically, Hadas (1950).

25. For example, Levi (1965); Huizinga (1970); and, more critically, Reynolds (1983), for whom the medieval kingdoms, though not nations in the modem sense, were based on communities of custom and descent and resembled 'ethnic states'; this is elaborated in Reynolds (1984, ch. 8).

26. For definitions of the 'nation', see Rustow (1967, ch. 1) and A. D. Smith (1973, section 2); for the 'modernist' and 'perennialist' images of the nation, see A. D. Smith (1984).

27. On processes of nation-formation in England and France, see Strayer (1963); and more generally, Orridge (1982). For France between 1870 and 1914, see E. Weber (1979).

28. Armstrong (1982); and for the Irish case, see Hutchinson (1987).

29. As argued in A. D. Smith (1986). But this does not preclude an important role for a 'returning intelligentsia', especially in the many, smaller, 'demotic' *ethnies*, which lack state power to help them 'reconstruct' the nation.

References

ACTON, L. 1948 *Essays on Freedom and Power*. Glencoe, Illinois: Free Press.

ANDERSON, B. 1983 *Imagined Communities: Reflections on the origin and spread of nationalism*. London: Verso Editions and New Left Books.

ARMSTRONG, J. 1982 *Nations before Nationalism*. Chapel Hill: University of North Carolina Press.

BANKS, J. 1972 *The Sociology of Social Movements*. London: Macmillan.

BARON, W. 1960 *Modern Nationalism and Religion*. New York: Meridian Books.

BREUILLY, J. 1982 *Nationalism and the State*. Manchester: Manchester University Press.

BAUER, Otto 1924 *Die Nationalitätenfrage und die Sozialdemokratie*. (1908), 2nd edn., Vienna: Volksbuchhandlung.

CARR, E. H. 1945 *Nationalism and After*. London: Macmillan.

COHN, Norman 1957 *The Pursuit of the Millennium*. London: Secker & Warburg.

CONNOR, W. 1984 *The National Question in Marxist-Leninist Theory and Strategy*. Princeton: Princeton University Press.

COULTON, G. C. 1935 Nationalism in the Middle Ages, *Cambridge Historical Journal*, 5, 15–40.

CUMMINS, I. 1980 *Marx, Engels and National Movements*. London: Croom Helm.

DAVIS, H. B. 1967 *Nationalism and Socialism: Marxist and Labor Theories of Nationalism*. London and New York: Monthly Review Press.

FISERA, V. C. and G. MINNERUP 1978 Marx, Engels and the National Question, in E. Cahm and V. C. Fisera (eds.): *Socialism and Nationalism*. Vol. 1, Nottingham: Spokesman.

FRANCIS, E. 1968 The ethnic factor in nation-building, *Social Forces*. 68, 338–46.

GELLA, A. (ed.) 1976 *The Intelligentsia and the Intellectuals*. Beverley Hills: Sage Publications.

GERTH, Hans and MILLS, C. Wright (eds.) 1947 *From Max Weber, Essays in Sociology*. London: Routledge and Kegan Paul.

GODECHOT, J. 1965 *France and the Atlantic Revolution of the Eighteenth Century*. 1770–1799, New York: Collier-Macmillan.

HADAS, M. 1950 National Survival Under Hellenistic and Roman Imperialism, *Journal of the History of Ideas* 11, 131–9.

HANDELSMAN, M. 1929 Le role de la nationalite dans l'histoire du Moyen Age, *Bulletin of the International Committee of the Historical Sciences* 2/2, 235–46.

HAYES, C. 1931 *The Historical Evolution of Modern Nationalism*. New York: Smith.

HERBERT, R. 1972 *David, Voltaire, Brutus and the French Revolution*. London: Allen Lane.

HOBSBAWM, E. and RANGER, T. (eds.) 1983 *The Invention of Tradition*. Cambridge: Cambridge University Press.

HODGKIN, T. 1964 'The relevance of "Western" ideas in the derivation of African nationalism', in J. R. Pennock (ed.): *Self-government in modernising societies*. Englewood Cliffs: Prentice-Hall.

HOWARD, M. 1976 *War in European History*. London: Oxford University Press.

HUIZINGA, J. 1970 Patriotism and nationalism in European history, in *Men and Ideas: Essays on History, the Middle Ages and the Renaissance*. (trans. J. S. Holmes and H. van Marle), New York: Harper and Row.

HUTCHINSON, J. 1987 *The Dynamics of Cultural Nationalism; The Gaelic Revival and the Creation of the Irish Nation State*. London: Allen and Unwin.

KAMENKA, E. (ed.) 1976 *Nationalism, the nature and evolution of an Idea.* London: Edward Arnold.

KEDOURIE, E. 1960 *Nationalism.* London: Hutchinson.

KEDOURIE, E. (ed.) 1971 *Nationalism in Asia and Africa.* London: Weidenfeld & Nicolson.

KEMILAINEN, A. 1964 *Nationalism, problems concerning the Word, the Concept and Classification.* Yvaskyla: Kustantajat Publishers.

KLAUSNER, S. 1960 Why they chose Israel, *Archives de Sociologie des Religions* 9, 129–44.

KOHN, H. 1955 *Nationalism: its meaning and history.* Princeton: Van Nostrand.

—— 1957 *Nationalism and Liberty: The Swiss Example.* New York: Macmillan.

—— 1960 *Pan-Slavism.* 2nd ed., New York: Vintage Books.

—— 1961 *Prophets and Peoples.* New York: Collier Books.

—— 1965 *The Mind of Germany.* London: Macmillan.

—— 1967a *The Idea of Nationalism.* 2nd ed., New York: Collier-Macmillan.

—— 1967b *Prelude to Nation-States: the French and German Experience. 1789–1815,* New York: Van Nostrand.

KOHT, H. 1947 The Dawn of Nationalism in Europe, *American Historical Review.* 52, 265–80.

KREJCI, Y. and VELIMSKY, V. 1981 *Ethnic and Political Nations in Europe.* London: Croom Helm.

LEVI, M. A. 1965 *Political Power in the Ancient World.* (trans. 3. Costello), London: Weidenfeld & Nicolson.

MARCU, E. D. 1976 *Sixteenth-century Nationalism.* New York: Abaris Books.

MAYO, P. 1974 *The Roots of Identity: Three National Movements in Contemporary European Politics.* London: Allen Lane.

MICHELAT, G. and J-P. H. THOMAS 1966 *Dimensions du nationalisme.* Paris: Librairie Armand Colin.

MILL, J. S. 1872 *Considerations on Representative Government.* London.

MINOGUE, K. 1967 *Nationalism.* London: Batsford.

NAIRN, T. 1977 *The Break-up of Britain.* London: New Left Books.

ORRIDGE, A. 1982 Separatist and autonomist nationalisms: the structure of regional loyalties in the modern state, in C. Williams (ed.): *National Separatism.* Cardiff: University of Wales Press.

PALMER, R. 1940 The national idea in France before the Revolution, *Journal of the History of Ideas* I, 95–111.

PERHAM, M. 1963 *The Colonial Reckoning.* London: Fontana.

PLAMENATZ, J. 1976 *Two types of Nationalism,* in Kamenka (1976).

RENAN, E. 1882 *Qu'est-ce qu'une Nation?,* Paris: Calmann-Levy.

REYNOLDS, S. 1988 Medieval *origines Gentium* and the community of the realm, *History* 68, 375–90.

—— 1984 *Kingdoms and Communities in Western Europe. 900–1300,* Oxford: Clarendon.

Rosdolsky, R. 1964 Friedrich Engels und das Problem der 'Geschichtslosen Volker', *Archiv für Sozialgeschichte* 4, 87–282, Hanover.

Rosenblum, R. 1967 *Transformations in late Eighteenth-century Art*. Princeton: Princeton University Press.

Royal Institute of International Affairs 1939 *Nationalism: A Report*, ed. Edward H. Carr, London: Oxford University Press.

Rustow, D. 1967 *A World of Nations*. Washington, D.C.: The Brookings Institution.

Sathyamurthy, T. 1983 *Nationalism in the Contemporary World*. London: Frances Pinter.

Seton-Watson, H. 1960 *Neither War, Nor Peace*. London: Methuen.

—— 1965 *Nationalism, Old and New*. Sydney: Sydney University Press.

—— 1977 *Nations and States*. London: Methuen.

Shafer, B. C. 1938 Bourgeois nationalism in the pamphlets on the eve of the French Revolution, *Journal of Modern History* 10, 19–38.

Shafer, B. C. 1955 *Nationalism, Myth and Reality*. New York: Harcourt Brace.

Smith, A. D. 1971 *Theories of Nationalism*. London: Duckworth, and New York: Harper & Row.

—— 1973 *Nationalism*, A Trend Report and Annotated Bibliography, *Current Sociology*, 21/3, Mouton, The Hague.

—— 1978 The Diffusion of Nationalism, *British Journal of Sociology* 29, 234–48.

—— 1979 *Nationalism in the Twentieth Century*. Oxford: Martin Robertson.

—— 1983 Nationalism and classical social theory, *British Journal of Sociology* 34, 19–38.

—— 1984 Ethnic Myths and Ethnic Revivals, *European Journal of Sociology* 25, 283–305.

—— 1986 *The Ethnic Origins of Nations*. Oxford: Blackwell.

—— 1987 *Patriotism and Neo-Classicism: The 'Historical Revival' in French and English Painting and Sculpture*, 1746–1800, unpublished Ph.D. thesis in the University of London.

—— 1988 The myth of the 'Modern Nation' and the myths of nations, *Ethnic and Racial Studies* 11, no. 1, 1–26.

Snyder, L. 1954 *The Meaning of Nationalism*. New Brunswick: Rutgers University Press.

—— 1968 *The New Nationalism*. Ithaca: Cornell University Press.

—— 1976 *The Varieties of Nationalism, A Comparative View*, Hinsdale, Illinois: The Dryden Press.

Strayer, J. 1963 The historical experience of nation-building in Europe, in K. W. Deutsch & W. Foltz (eds.): *Nation-building*. New York: Atherton.

Symmons-Symonolewicz, K. 1965 Nationalist movements: an attempt at a comparative typology, *Comparative Studies in Society and History* 7, 221–30.

—— 1970 *Nationalist Movements: A Comparative View*. Meadville, PA.: Maplewood Press.

TALMON, J. L. 1980 *The Myth of the Nation and the Vision of Revolution*. London: Secker & Warburg.

TAYLOR, D. and M. YAPP (eds.) 1979 *Political Identity in South Asia*. London and Dublin, SOAS, Curzon Press.

TILLY, C. (ed.) 1975 *The Formation of National States in Western Europe*. Princeton: Princeton University Press.

TREVOR-ROPER, H. 1961 *Jewish and Other Nationalisms*. London: Weidenfeld & Nicolson.

TUDOR, H. 1972 *Political Myth*. London: Pall Mall Press/Macmillan.

WALEK-CZERNECKI, M. T. 1929 'Le role de la nationalite dans l'histoire de l'antiquite', *Bulletin of the International Committee of Historical Science* 2/2, 305–20.

WEBER, E. 1979 *Peasants into Frenchmen*. London: Chatto and Windus.

WEBER, M. 1968 *Economy and Society*. Eds. G. Roth and C. Wittich, New York: Bedminster Press.

2

National Identity and Myths
of Ethnic Descent*

While the study of ethnic identity and national movements has flourished
in the last decade, little attention has been devoted to the meanings and
visions underlying them in the social consciousness. These meanings and
visions are encapsulated in distinctive ethnic myths which, like all myth,
bring together in a single potent vision elements of historical fact and
legendary elaboration to create an overriding commitment and bond for
the community. Of course, such myths often change their symbolic forms
and content over time in relation to different perceptions of significant
others outside the community and varying degrees of conflict or competition with those outsiders (Kriesberg 1982). Yet no national movement
and no persisting ethnic identity can emerge without a bedrock of shared
meanings and ideals, which guide action and determine the direction
of social change. Even an 'instrumentalist' view of ethnicity, which sees
ethnic ties as largely situational, must come to terms with the basic myths
and symbols which endow popular perceptions of ethnic boundaries and
identities with meaning and sentiments, and which mediate changes in
those identities set in motion by external forces (Brass 1979; Armstrong
1982). It is the structure and content of these neglected myths, and their
role in social movements, that provide the main focus of this chapter.

Naturally, such myths and symbols possess many features—formal,
aesthetic, psychological, social, and political—which merit attention; but
in a chapter of this kind, it is only possible to focus on certain aspects. Here
I am interested in their potentialities for group identity and collective action;
and that is why I accord considerable importance to the distinction
between different modes of ethnic myth-making. Broadly speaking, it is
possible and useful to distinguish myths that cite _genealogical_ ancestry
from those which trace a more _ideological descent_, between 'biological' and

* _Research in Social Movements, Conflict and Change_, vol. 7, pp. 95–130.

'cultural-ideological' myths. In the former, filiation is the basic principle of myth-construction: the chroniclers and poets trace generational lineages, and rest their claims for high status and power on a presumed biological link with a hero, a founder, or even a deity. The community, according to this mode of myth-making, is descended from a noble and heroic ancestor, and for that reason is entitled to privilege and prestige in its own and other peoples' estimations. The biological link also ensures a high degree of communal solidarity, since the community is viewed as a network of interrelated kin groups claiming a common ancestor, and thereby marking them off from those unable to make such a claim. Thus alleged ties of 'blood' form the basis for a strictly 'primordialist' sense of belonging and identity (Fishman 1980).

Against such biological modes of tracing descent, we find another equally important set of generational linkages: those that rest on a cultural affinity and ideological 'fit' with the presumed ancestors. What counts here are not blood ties, real or alleged, but a spiritual kinship, proclaimed in ideals that are allegedly derived from some ancient exemplars in remote eras. The aim is to recreate the heroic spirit (and the heroes) that animated 'our ancestors' in some past golden age; and descent is traced, not through family pedigrees, but through the persistence of certain kinds of 'virtue' or other distinctive cultural qualities, be it of language, customs, religion, institutions, or more general personal attributes.

What I shall argue is that within given ethnic communities since the French Revolution (or slightly earlier), both kinds of national myth-making emerge and persist in an often contrapuntal relationship. They thus both divide, and unite, the communities whose identity and consciousness they underpin. They divide them, because, as the case-studies make clear, different modes of myth-making are embraced by opposing strata; and they unite them because, out of this tension of opposites, there emerges a greater sense of dynamic activism, and an enhanced communal self-consciousness. Beyond that, myths of ethnic descent are vital both for territorial claims and for national solidarity; a section of the essay is devoted to showing how, in England, France, Turkey, Greece, and Israel, these myths have not merely underwritten, but have actually inspired such claims and solidarities, acting as 'title-deeds' and as ideals guiding action. There are several other issues arising out of a consideration of the structure and content of myths of descent; but it is not possible, within the space allowed, to analyse all or even most of them. The last section, however, is devoted to a brief examination of the conditions of emergence, and the adherents or 'bearers', of the myths; as well as to a restatement, with some elaborations, of the principal themes and arguments, in the hope of stimulating further studies of these and other aspects of the role of ethnic myths of descent.

COLLECTIVE IDENTITY AND MEANING

The passion for tracing pedigrees is not a peculiarly modern pastime nor a passing fashion. Both individually and collectively, it has a venerable history. From the Alcmaeonids to Alex Haley, families and individuals have traced and publicized their ancestry; the desire to 'know whence we came' is not confined to particular civilizations or epochs. Reasons for the quest vary. Noble families like the Alcmaeonids, the Farnese, or the Tudors used their pedigrees to justify their 'right' to wield political or ecclesiastical power; the author of Luke traced back Jesus' ancestry to the house of King David to vindicate his claim to messianic kingship in Judea. Claims to illustrious lineage may help to legitimate newfound wealth, or bolster the shaky prestige of families entering novel and unrecognized occupations. More recently, we find an affirmation of lowly origins as a legitimation of status; in an ostensibly egalitarian milieu with a puritanical ideology it may be wiser to trace one's ancestry to the peasantry, the working-class or kidnapped slaves.

But, behind the ever-changing needs and purposes of individuals, a more obstinate question obtrudes. It is well summed up by King Oedipus in the moment that precedes the shattering revelation of his true origins; into his mouth Sophocles has put these words:

Let all come out, However vile! However base it be, I must unlock the secret of my birth. The woman, with more than woman's pride, is shamed by my low origin. I am the child of Fortune, The giver of good, and I shall not be shamed. She is my mother; my sisters are the Seasons; My rising and my falling march with theirs. Born thus, I ask to be no other man Than that I am, and will know who I am. (Sophocles 1947: 55)

It is the question of individual identity, which is always a matter of social and spiritual location. For in that location lies a sense of security, so indispensable to the much-desired individuality and uniqueness of persons and families alike; it is through such claims to uniqueness that dignity and power are conferred in society. And when we speak of the 'crisis of identity' felt by so many marginal and powerless intellectuals, especially in the Third World, it is just this loss of security and location within a traditional milieu and its stable value-system that we have in mind (Shils 1960).

As with families, so with ethnic communities and nations. Here, too, we witness the same passion for tracing origins and pedigrees, the same quest to discover a true identity, to 'know who I am'. Nor is the quest confined to the modern era. Hesiod's *Theogony* charts the origins of the Greek people in antiquity, along with lineages of the gods; the Bible similarly presents detailed genealogies of Abraham's ancestors and descendants to locate the children of Israel among the 'families' of the earth.[1] Ancestry and foundation myths were widespread in Africa and Asia from early times; we meet them again among the Romans and Franks, who both claimed Trojan descent, and later among several medieval kingdoms which thereby legitimated their claims to rule a cohesive community.[2]

It is well to bear this widespread practice and its antiquity in mind, when we turn to the modern era, which is the focus of my concern. Not only does it attest the importance of ethnic myths of descent in themselves, a dimension often neglected by historians and social scientists alike; it also suggests links between premodern and modern eras, which must modify to some extent, at least, the generally held view that national sentiment and nationalism are exclusively modern phenomena (Kohn 1967; Kedourie 1960; Hayes 1931; Carr 1945; Emerson 1960; Kamenka 1976; Gellner 1964, ch. 7).

Nevertheless, when due allowance has been made, there are some novel elements in the modern era of myth-making and pedigree-tracing. To begin with, these activities are far more widely diffused; no aspirant ethnic group can be without its myth of descent, if it is to secure any recognition from competitors. Since the late eighteenth century, spokesmen for every ethnic community have made frequent appeals to their alleged ancestry and histories, in the struggle for recognition, rights, and independence. In the course of these struggles, ethnic spokesmen have drawn on, or in some cases invented, a 'myth of origins and descent' which then inspired writers and artists to recreate for their publics the events, atmosphere, and heroic examples of remote, archaic eras found in the epics and sagas of Homer and Aeschylus, Dante, Ossian, and the *Edda*. By 1800 most of Western Europe was caught in the romantic quest for origins; by 1850 it had spread to Eastern Europe, and during the next century was diffused to Asia and Africa (Honour 1968; Vaughan 1978; Irwin 1966).

Second, the new era of myth-making was united by a common ideology, nationalism, which embodied a global vision of the 'true' relations between social and political units and of the relations between members or 'citizens' and their collectivities. Ethnic myths of descent figure prominently in the nationalist *Weltanschauung*. As a community of culture and a distinctive unity, the nation not only has a past; the roots of its unique identity *must* reside in its origins and genealogy. In order to claim the new status of 'nation', a community's spokesmen had therefore to advance a case which rested, at least in part, on the conviction of ethnic ancestry and common history. And third, a revolutionary element was injected into the new era of ethnic myth-making. Nationalism became a vehicle for rapid social change, for mobilizing people, for claiming a 'homeland' by redrawing the map, and for destroying local, and regional ties in the interests of the centre and the whole community. So the ethnic myth became a charter for revolution, for turning established arrangements upside down, and creating new political communities on the basis of a sense of community derived from historic memories and a myth of common descent. Where previously, these myths were utilized to uphold cultures and kingdoms, today they can just as easily be made to serve the interests of forgotten and submerged communities aspiring to national status and territorial recognition (Deutsch & Foltz 1963; Mayo 1974; Esman 1977).

Insofar as these myths are accorded separate treatment, they are usually assumed to serve and legitimate the needs and special interests of ethnic groups or particular strata within them. Much of what I have claimed so far, can be read as support for this view. But the 'instrumental' approach leaves a good deal unexplained. Why is it really necessary to return to the past in order to legitimate present actions? How does unearthing archaic epochs satisfy the desire for a blueprint for the future? Why is such myth-making so universal and intensely felt? In a secular age of rationalism, capitalism, and bureaucracy, why should so many feel the need to trace out their collective roots and genealogies? Why, in short, root society and politics in culture and biology?

If, on the other hand, we posit with Weber a universal drive for meaning and inner consistency, we may be in a better position to illuminate those areas left unexplained by instrumental approaches.[3] Nationalism, after all, has emerged as an ideological movement in an era of widespread religious doubt and secularism, in which many traditional myths, and beliefs are under challenge. Given the processes of widespread mobility, uprooting and emigration, many of the old values and beliefs are unable to satisfy this drive for meaning and consistency or guide significant sections of the population. The old cognitive homeland is no longer habitable; and exile, which in earlier times had been successfully incorporated into traditional belief-systems, has become too fluctuating and unstable a state to endure without benefit of a compass. In this respect, some communities are more fortunate than others. Their ethnic ties have been preserved into the modern era, along with their sense of common ancestry. Others have felt the need to reforge, or even invent, those ties and myths which had dissolved or become forgotten. In all cases, however, the descent myths themselves, once unearthed and disseminated, have come to exercise a powerful fascination, and not just for intellectuals, because they provide a framework, albeit a malleable one, for social solidarity and a resolution of the crisis of insecurity through the provision of collective identities. It is only in terms of a myth of ethnic descent that both groups and individuals can 'make sense' of their relocation, and the challenge posed by the bureaucratic state to the old cosmic images. By placing the present in the context of the past and of the community, the myth of descent interprets present social changes and collective endeavours in a manner that satisfies the drive for meaning by providing new identities that seem to be also very old, and restoring locations, social and territorial, that allegedly were the crucibles of those identities.[4]

But the provision of myths of descent to counter insecurity and meaninglessness, is apt to prove a difficult and controversial undertaking. For one thing, the historical record is often scanty or biased. For another, alternative narratives and interpretations may have been handed down the generations. The myths themselves, as we shall see, are made up of several components, with differing sources, and they may well come to possess alternative meanings, and uses, for the various classes and status groups that comprise the ethnic community or nation. This is often a source of persistent conflict, so much so that the national tradition may be marked by a deep-seated cleavage based on rival concepts of identity, as occurred in England, France, and nineteenth century Greece. In these cases, two modes of interpreting 'descent' come into conflict, the one cultural and ideological, the other more strictly genealogical and biological. Yet, even this conflict fails to break the overall mould of ethnic myth-making, or the sense of meaning and security engendered by it.

COMPONENTS OF ETHNIC MYTHS

Every nationalist movement will possess myths of descent that are, in some respects, unique. Nevertheless, they possess a common form that can be usefully broken down into its component myths. I shall consider each, briefly.

A Myth of Temporal Origins, *or When We Were Begotten*

One of the main tasks of nationalist historians is to date the community's origins, and so locate it in time and in relation to other relevant communities. Fixed points in time act as barriers to the flood of meaninglessness; they are essential gauges of collective development; and they place the 'generations of our ancestors' in a definite linear succession stretching back to the sacred moment of birth (Debray 1977). It is no wonder that dramatists and artists eagerly turned back to the legends of primeval origins recounted in the biblical story of Creation, in Hesiod's *Theogony*, and in the creation myths of the *Edda* and the *Veda*. Nor is the popularity of such foundation-myths as the Oath of Brutus, which led to the expulsion of the Tarquins and the founding of the Roman republic, or the Oath of the Rütli, by which the three Swiss forest cantons around Lake Lucerne swore to drive out the Habsburgs from their valleys in 1307, surprising; Zurich town hall commissioned Fussli to paint the confederates in 1778, while the Oath of Brutus became immensely popular in late eighteenth-century England and France, as the tide of republicanism began to run high.[5]

Of course, even here there may be deep divisions over the antiquity of the community. The date of 'foundation' may vary between classes and epochs; for some, Hengist and Horsa were the true founders of Saxon liberties and English rights, for others the Norman Conquest marked the foundation of the state and monarchy, not to mention the claims for ancient Britons (Kohn 1940; Hill 1958: ch. 3). Given the paucity and unreliability of the evidence, particularly in the seventeenth century, the conflict over the 'Norman Yoke' was ideological rather than genealogical. A similar conflict was to develop in France a century later. Yet in these and other cases, nobody questioned the need to establish the antiquity and ancestry of the community; the demonstration was vital, both for self-esteem and security, and for external recognition.

A Myth of Location and Migration, *or Where We Came from and How We Got Here*

Not all ethnic communities possess a fully elaborated myth of spatial origins, but all have some notions. Space is, after all, the other dimension necessary for a framework of self-identification, and assumes special importance where claims to 'territory' are being pressed. Here, historicism furnishes the nationalist with 'evidence' in his struggle for autonomy and independence. A large part of the cultural history of the Arab-Israel dispute, for example, can be written in terms of historicist claims to the strip of territory between the Jordan and the Mediterranean from Dan to Beersheba or Eilat; especially as regards the original habitat of the contending parties, with 'evidence' from archaeology, linguistics, history, and anthropology often selectively interpreted (Haim 1962; Hertzberg 1960). Indeed, where the community has been divorced from what it regards as its original habitat, as with Jews, Armenians, and Greeks, or where an original territory has been renounced for another, as with the Ottoman Turks, the question of spatial origins looms especially large.

Spatial origins, of course, legitimate control over land and scarce resources, even where mass migration memories are lacking (Weber 1968). Equally important, however, is their role in controlling change by locating it firmly in a distinctive area and niche. In this way, uprooted individuals are 'restored', if not physically, at least symbolically, to 'their' homeland; they become true citizens of a nation with an acknowledged and distinctive territory, which fixes the place of the community in the 'family of nations'. To counter the 'homelessness' characteristic of modern life, the nationalist constructs out of the sense of spatial origins and a given territory a 'homeland'; this homeland will help to define the nation, by marking its boundaries and providing its 'home'. So another barrier is created against flux, in this case the flux of aimless movement and ceaseless wanderings (Debray 1977; Johnson 1968).

A Myth of Ancestry, *or Who Begot Us and How We Developed*

It does not really matter whether the common ancestor or founding father is *mythical* or quasi-historical; Hellen served for the ancient Greeks as well as Abraham for the Jews, Arminius for the Germans as much as Oguz Khan for the Turks. What is important about the ancestor myth is the symbolic kinship link between all members of the present generation of the community, and between this generation and all its forebears, down to the common ancestor. The power of this myth can be felt in writers as far apart as Blyden and Edmond Fleg, with their reverence for Ethiopian and Israelite ancestors; neither claimed a real kinship relationship. On the contrary, the quest for genealogical roots in family or clan is transposed to the communal level, and thereby becomes symbolic. What these men, and so many others, appear to be affirming is the principle of filiation as the key to historical development from a common source, the transmission of certain spiritual values within the lines of descent, and thereby the solution to the problems of relationships and cohesion in modern, complex societies (Wilson 1968; Hertzberg 1960; Fleg 1943).

Once again, the search for roots and ancestry is not without its problems. The metaphor of the tree, with its organic intimations, may prove problematic, especially for communities marked by temporal or spatial discontinuities; it is not easy to accommodate revolution and dispersion within this schema, let alone immigration and intermarriage. There is, again, the problem of evidence, so much of it conflicting or simply lacking. Alternatively, there is the possibility of constructing rival genealogies, used for opposite purposes by different strata.

Yet, all these problems are more than outweighed by the sense of location and security conferred by a myth of ancestry with its comforting metaphor of family ties recreated among dispersed city migrants and transposed to the communal level. Such myths afford a means of rooting and classifying the uprooted and declassified in what can so easily appear a chaotic social world, and thereby of identifying one's friends as 'kinsmen' in opposition to unfriendly outsiders, who are excluded from belonging by the absence of roots and kinship ties. In fact, the satisfaction of the drive for meaning and security afforded by these myths is even more important than their short-run uses as instruments of immediate mobilization and integration. A sense of common ancestry confers sentiments of prestige and dignity through an 'ethnic' fraternity, one based upon alleged kinship ties; and herein lie the seeds of that transformation, through a biological or genetic interpretation, by which the 'ethnic community' becomes the 'race' (van den Berghe 1967; Cohen 1976).

A Myth of the Heroic Age, *or How We Were Freed and Became Glorious*

While definitions of grandeur and glory vary, every nationalism requires a touchstone of virtue and heroism, to guide and give meaning to the tasks of regeneration. The future of the ethnic community can only derive meaning and achieve its form from the pristine 'golden age' when men were 'heroes'. Heroes provide models of virtuous conduct, their deeds of valour inspire faith and courage in their oppressed and decadent descendants. The epoch in which they flourished is the great age of liberation from the foreign yoke, which released the energies of the people for cultural innovation and original political experiment. The most influential examples reach back into Near Eastern antiquity: the Mosaic liberation of the Israelites from Egypt and the subsequent glories of the Davidic kingdom; the liberation of Athens and Greece from the tyrants and Persian invasions, culminating in the Periclean age; the expulsion of the Tarquins from Rome, and the founding of the Republic with its selfless heroes, Brutus the consul, Scaevola and Cincinnatus; and the Hegira of Muhammad and the Age of the Companions, which witnessed the great Islamic conquests.

In the wake of these exemplars, many nationalist historians tried to reconstruct equivalent 'golden ages' for their communities, using sagas like the *Edda* and *Kalevala* and the lays of 'Ossian' and the Nibelunglied.[6] Very often, no great distinction was made between myth and history, since for the sophisticated 'myth' signified a poetic form of history, an archetypal set of motifs thought to embody the real 'essence' of the people and the true character and individuality of the community. Archaeology, too, was treated in this same 'reconstructive' and 'regenerative' mode; Frankish, Saxon, Etruscan, Mycenaean, Hittite, Assyrian, and Egyptian artefacts and sites were quickly assimilated into the romanticizing mainstream of ethnic myth-making, to buttress a particular vision of history and destiny (Daniel 1971).

Similar selectivity was employed for that key concept of nineteenth-century Europe, the hero. Thus early Greek nationalists might liken certain *klephtic* leaders during the War of Independence to Achilles; what mattered was not any actual similarity, let alone the historicity of Achilles, only the qualities attributed to the hero and his ability to inspire emulation and guide action. It would be wrong to say that antique heroes were manipulated or distorted, let alone invented, to serve present ends, as some maintain.[7] Rather, the heroes of old brought into the open, at least for the literate classes, those qualities of courage, wisdom, self-sacrifice, zeal, and stoicism, which they felt to be so conspicuously lacking in the present generation, and which seemed to act as an antidote to oppression and a spur to liberation. In these alleged qualities of the hero were mirrored the best of the community's traditions, its authentic voice in the moment of its first flowering, so sadly silent today, so badly needed to halt exile and decline.

The golden age served yet another purpose. As a vehicle of historical and archaeological reconstructions, it could be used to dramatize the 'atmosphere' and picturesque uniqueness of the people's past, and of the events and personages which composed it. That way historicists underlined a theme dear to their hearts: the diversity of history and the potential for active intervention in a world of cultural pluralism. For, if ethnic uniqueness is the stuff of history, change and growth proceed at different rates and ways in the different communities, and these may also influence each others' progress; this leaves more room for elements of subjective choice, active liberation, and conscious mastery than in a determinate scheme of universal growth, such as the evolutionists posited (Nisbet 1969; A. D. Smith 1976, chs. 3–4).

\A Myth of Decline, *or How We Fell into a State of Decay*

Unlike unilinear evolutionism, nationalism stresses the reality of retrogressions and the role of human volition. The tree never grows straight, the river always meanders, even turns back in erratic loops. But, if seized with ethnic consciousness, men can unbend the tree and set the river back on course. Then, of course, the golden age will be renewed and the heroes will return.

But how did that glorious age pass away, why have the heroes become the generations of the oppressed? Because, the old virtues were forgotten, moral decay set in, pleasure and vice overcame discipline and self-sacrifice, the old certainties and hierarchies dissolved, the barbarians burst through. . . . The myth of decline tells us how the community lost its anchor in a living tradition, how the old values became ossified and meaningless, and how, as a result, common sentiments and beliefs faded to give way to rampant individualism and the triumph of partisan interests over collective ideals and communal solidarity. The form of the explanation may be Durkheimian, but the reasons for the decline and the solutions proffered by the nationalists are quite different. To the nationalist myth-maker, present alienation is simply an inner exile or homelessness, literal or figurative, and mirrors external oppression or lack of self-rule. We are strangers to ourselves because we have no clear idea of the real, the historic, self, the collective identity formed many generations back, from which each and every individual identity takes its life and meaning. Hence, self-exile and communal aimlessness. It is the leitmotif of so many intellectuals who bewailed the sad plight of their community, from Korais and Afghani to Banerjea and Blyden. In each case, their point of departure was the degenerate state of their country, in comparison not only with a technologically and educationally superior Western civilization, but with the underlying genius of the community, revealed in its purest form during the golden age of authentic heroism (Kedourie 1971).

A Myth of Regeneration, *or How to Restore the Golden Age and Renew Our Community as 'in the Days of Old'*

Here we move from the sphere of explanatory myth to that of prescriptive ideology: from an idealized, epic history to an account of 'required actions', or rationale of collective mobilization. But, even here, myth is not absent: it informs the central concept of nationalism, that of regeneration, together with the associated notions of authenticity and autonomy. But these notions can only represent ideal states, unattainable in an imperfect world; given the nature of social and geopolitical relations, they must always remain unfulfilled. Psychologically compelling if logically incoherent, they present the 'drama' of nationalism and its quasi-messianic promises alongside other quite realistic and concrete goals, such as attaining independence, creating the conditions for self-sustaining growth, building up national institutions, pursuing cultural homogenization and social integration, demarcating the 'homeland', and creating a world of cultural diversity and pluralism.

Of especial interest, from the standpoint of ethnic myths of descent, are the notions of authenticity and regeneration. The first is illuminated by myths of origins and descent, since they furnish the criteria for judging what is inauthentic or impure; that was the function that Fichte and his followers conferred on philology, a discipline which traced out linguistic descent and origins to reveal what was instrinsic to the pure, authentic language group, and what was foreign and extraneous (Kohn 1965; Reiss 1955). The second, regeneration, with its metaphors of 'rebirth' and 'reawakening', continues this drama of self-purification, so necessary to collective salvation, by placing the act of liberation in an ideal world of heroic imagery and naturalistic metaphor. A fundamentally historical event is thereby endowed with a deeper symbolic significance, derived from the re-enacting of the early drama of liberation and the subsequent golden age. By returning to one's origins, the links in the long chain of the generations are reforged.[8]

Having rehearsed and analysed the components that typically make up the substratum of ethnic 'myths of origins and descent', on which nationalisms base their ideals and programmes, we are now in a better position to grasp the consequences of collective action entailed by nationalism's belief-system. These are:

Special Identity

The claim to a *special identity*, in virtue of the principle of cultural diversity and the uniqueness of the community's golden age and heroism. The nationalist spokesmen claim the right to a particular freedom, that of developing a specific culture through an ethnically responsive press, judiciary, church and educational system, and an ethnically aware literature and art. This is the typical demand of cultural nationalism and its intellectual representatives, which in turn requires the cultivation of an individual style of creation and action—in food, dress, customs, leisure activities, work, morals, and politics. Herder's influence is especially apparent in this sphere, since he, above all, argued the need for cultural individualism and populism, for the creation of a living style of doing things, born of popular experience and activity (Berlin 1976).

Obviously the quest for a special identity serves the 'need' for communal solidarity and fraternity; for it sharpens boundaries between communities and points up similarities between members and differences with non-members. Moreover, the myth of descent suggests a rationale for these differences. Equally, however, quests for identity require certain types of action and behaviour—in education, recreation, worship, habits, politics and so on—which in turn heighten solidarity and exclusiveness. To identify oneself with particular others entails a range of actions, associations, and sacrifices that bind one to the chosen and sever one from those outside the circle (Barth 1969, Introduction; Armstrong 1982).

Special Dignity

The claim to a *special dignity*, in virtue of antiquity and pedigree. What is often sought is a status confirmation—for dominant communities—or status reversal—for suppressed minorities. Dating and periodizing the history of the community become essential tools for these ends; so does the pursuit of genealogies. But these activities and their results also *define* a status; once you concede the validity of this sort of reasoning and activity, once it becomes widely practised, it automatically entails a special status, the conferring of a definite prestige on those for whom it is utilized. The chosen community becomes a 'victim' of the claims made on its behalf, its members come to 'feel' they are entitled to a certain respect.

Specific Territories

The claim to *specific territories*, in virtue of spatial origins, migrations or history. Ethnic myths are vital 'evidence' for territorial 'title-deeds'; association of the people with historic events and persons resident within a particular terrain is a *sine qua non* of the quest for a recognized 'homeland' (Smith 1981a; also Breuilly 1982: ch. 3). But, equally, the title-deeds which derive their meaning from ethnic myths are charters for collective aspirations and actions; they validate, even direct, the struggle for land and recognition.

Any title-deed refers to an historically defined terrain, for which validation is by 'historic right' rather than actual possession; hence the Liberian ('back-to-Africa'), Armenian, and Zionist restorative movements, whose title-deeds were based on ancient 'right' and which required mass migrations of community members (Wilson 1968: Pt. I; Hovannisian 1967; Halpern 1961). Title-deeds are also used to validate population transfers and direct their course, as with the Greco-Turkish population exchange of 1922 (Campbell & Sherrard 1968: ch. 5); alternatively, they may influence the course of action in multiethnic states towards territorial division or partition, as in Ulster and Cyprus, or at least promote intractable territorial disputes, as have occurred in Alsace, Tyrol, Transylvania, the Jura, and the Ogaden. In each case historic title-deeds derived from a special reading of history based upon ethnic myths of descent, have given content to other needs and grievances; the solidarity that they have inspired has given the ensuing conflict its peculiar form and intensity of commitment.

Specific Autonomy

The claim to a *specific autonomy*, in virtue of a previous, distant era of liberty, the heroic, golden age, now lost through oppression and neglect. Independence and autarchy are important channels for communal autonomy, but they do not exhaust it; such freedom, once attained, has its own imperatives for action. But it is not any freedom; it is a collective liberty in which the self's laws are those of the nation-to-be, and a specific liberty for that community in those conditions. The demands of that freedom are peculiar to an historic era and community and they vary according to the aspects that appear to be deficient. Such quests for autonomy are often felt to represent merely a 'restoration' of ancient, lost rights and freedoms; thus the Basques today seek a return of their *fueros*, their statutes of autonomy which men of noble blood once enjoyed (Greenwood 1977). The struggle for autonomy is always specific; and it is always conditioned, and given its meaning, by a lingering sense of the heroic era before the community's decline, and by the desire to recover the liberties and rights enjoyed in that golden age.

IDEOLOGICAL AND GENEALOGICAL MYTHS

Identity; dignity; territory; autonomy: these are the basic aspirations and dimensions of the drama of regeneration which the ethnic myth of descent explains and inspires in the participants. Not only does it legitimize these aspirations and unite these dimensions; it energizes and feeds them like an explosive charge, whose roots *seem* indeed quite 'primordial'

to members of ethnic communities and immune to the process of ration-
alization (Shils 1957; Geertz 1963).

Yet, deep within what appears to the outside as a unifying myth, are
hidden many tensions and contradictions, which parallel and illuminate
the social contradictions within most communities. Just as national solidarities are often flawed by class conflicts, religious cleavages, or regional
divisions, so the ethnic myth itself reveals divergent traditions from which
different strata and groups within the ethnic community may draw
strength, identity, and meaning. Of particular importance is the distinction between *ideological* and *genealogical* myths, between ethnic myths that
trace descent through cultural and ideological affinity with presumed
ancestors and epochs, and those that draw on a more strictly genealogical
pedigree and links of alleged kinship. These differences become important,
both for claims to territory or 'title-deeds', and for conceptions of national
solidarity through regeneration. They may, indeed, lead to quite distinct,
even opposed courses of action, with serious repercussions for the community.
In the examples that follows, I shall concentrate particularly upon this
twofold aspect, the territorial and the regenerative, and upon how these
aspirations were influenced by competing types of ethnic myth.

England

It is sometimes contended that a specifically English nationalism succumbed
during the eighteenth century to a grander British nationalism, founded
on the Union with Scotland and the British empire; and that today a peculiarly English nationalism is hardly visible (Seton-Watson 1979; cf. Seton-
Watson 1977: ch. 2). It is true that since 1707, English nationalism has
added new dimensions of vast scope, yet these have always been harnessed
to the English core. Even that core has several layers, and these are
reflected, and given their meaning, by rival ethnic myths of origin current at different periods and within different strata.

Thus, in 1658 Sir Thomas Browne, discussing the Walsingham urns, could
speak about 'our British, Saxon and Danish forefathers'; a century earlier,
Englishmen had claimed Brutus as their ancestor (cf. Dixon 1976: 25). In
the seventeenth century, Levellers and others opposed their Saxon birthrights to the oppressive 'Norman Yoke' of the monarchy; in the eighteenth,
Sir William Stukeley argued the case for British ancestry (Dixon 1976: 26;
Kohn 1940).

Towards the end of the eighteenth century, the American and French
wars stimulated a powerful revival of national sentiment, particularly

under the leadership of the younger Pitt; it was heralded and accompanied by the rise of such new national institutions as the British Museum
and Royal Academy, and the neo-classical school of patriotic art, especially
'history painting', led by Benjamin West, Füssli, Hamilton, Blake, and
Flaxman; the Roman and medieval motifs chosen by these artists ante-
dated the analogous movement in France (Plumb 1965: Pt. III, ch. 6; Irwin
1966; Smith 1979a).

But it was in the nineteenth century that full-scale interpretations of
English development based upon myths of ancestry and descent gained
wide currency; following Burke's emphasis upon tradition and freedom
embodied in parliamentary institutions, the Whigs and the Loyal Associations, founded by Arthur Young in 1792, looked back with nostalgia to
the image of peaceful evolution and liberty represented by the Glorious
Revolution of 1688, the gradual growth of representative government, and
the origins of Parliament in the 'free' institutions of Germanic tribes. This
image of ancient origins was opposed to the medievalism of Tory views.
Disraeli, for example, looked to the medieval paternalism of the noble classes
to solve the problem of the 'two nations'; this was also the function of his
concept of race. It was in this context that Galton's views became popular, as Mosse puts it:

Since the idea of inherited genius could be ascribed to a whole people who had
proved so adept at governing themselves, it was a mere step to ascribing this to
the hereditary genius of a race. (Mosse 1963: 60)

But, although racism had a considerable following in the later nineteenth
century in Britain, the liberal ideal of self-government, so integral a part
of English national consciousness, tended to preclude the kind of extreme
biological racialism found in France, Germany or Austria at this time (Banton
1967; Weiss 1977). At the same time, debates in archaeology, particularly
with regard to the Saxon origins traced by men like Kemble and Wright
in England and Germany/Denmark, lent support for a strong *English*
ethnic identity operating within the wider imperial circle.[9]

This sense of Englishness, moreover, is by no means dead. Enoch
Powell, at least, has been quite explicit about the need to sustain an
English consciousness, which, he believes, has survived within the bosom
of empire. Tom Nairn cites his speech to the appropriately-named Royal
Society of St. George, founded in 1894, a society that has consistently
championed the 'indefeasible birthright' of the Englishman, and his
'ever-present, far down and deeply-rooted; too dormant, too unassertive,
unaggressive yet uneradicable' racial instinct.[10] Powell argued that, unlike

other empires, the British empire left the 'nationhood of the mother country' unaltered and continuous; so the present generation discovers affinities with earlier generations of English; they find themselves 'once more akin to the old English'. Nairn, indeed, links this latterday romantic English nationalism with that of the intelligentsia in the early part of this century, with Housman and Vaughan-Williams and the Georgians, and with the pageantry of empire (Nairn 1977: 262–5). But he also claims that Powellite romantic nationalism, with its easy descent into racism, serves to compensate for a lack, not of national traditions and institutions, but of a popular myth of the mobilized people. English history since 1688 can boast no such myth; its course has been predominantly patrician, and constitutional. Hence, a romantic conservative nationalism, without a trace of populism.[11] Whether, of course, a Bennite populism might excite the kind of nationalism that Nairn feels to be absent in England and present almost everywhere else, is open to doubt. So is its necessity. There are signs, after all, that such a popular nationalism does exist, albeit without overt political voice. In the love of rural England; in such pageants as the State opening of Parliament, Trooping the Colour, the Cenotaph Service for the World Wars' Dead or the last night of the Promenade concerts; in the widespread adulation of monarchy and royalty; in the powerful hold exerted by memories of two World Wars, especially the Dunkirk spirit; in the recurrent lamentations over national economic performance and praise of parliamentary liberties; in the national union traditions of the English working class; we find here fragmented, but powerful, elements of a popular English national consciousness. Perhaps the lack of a 'significant other' to serve as a traditional enemy, coupled with an island location, and the continuing prevalence of alternative class images of Englishness, has muted this consciousness (Birch 1977: ch. 3 and 136–8; Marwick 1974: 153–99). Yet, in time of danger, even the deep-seated opposition between a more genealogical myth of descent found among Tories and the upper classes, and based upon monarchical and aristocratic tradition, and the ideological myth which, stemming from Puritan radicalism, looks back to Saxon liberties and birthrights and forward to working class socialism, can coalesce to present to the outside world a clear image of English identity, if not yet of regeneration.

France

English ethnic myths since the eighteenth century have been potent sources in the shaping of a national sense of solidarity which surfaces in times of crisis; but, on the whole, they have not helped to foster or guide radical social change. It has been otherwise in France. Since the mid-eighteenth century French history has witnessed a competitive interplay between the genealogical myths of the monarchy and upper classes, and the more ideological myths of the third and fourth estates. Together, these myths inspired drives towards territorial expansion, and communal regeneration. Thus, the Crown, long engaged in a process of territorial consolidation from the times of Philip Augustus, acquired in 1733 the territory of Lorraine; during the Revolution, the patriot governments of the third estate acquired Avignon and Venaissin through plebiscite, and advanced French borders through war to what Danton preached were France's 'natural frontiers' (Kohn 1967: Pt. I). Similar motives of the territorial expansion of French civilization and ethnic culture under-pinned the acquisition of colonies in America, Africa and southern Asia under both monarchical and republican regimes, and was fed by Anglo-French rivalries and periodic threats to the integrity and safety of the *patrie*.

Whereas ethnic history tended towards the territorial unity and expansion of France, whatever the regime or class in power, its impact upon communal regeneration was more complex. During the mid-eighteenth century both Crown and *parlements* vied for legal supremacy and looked to historical precedent to bolster their claims (Palmer 1940; Palmer 1959: Pt. I, 89, 449–51). It was, in fact, in the propaganda of the *parlements* that the concept of the 'nation' and its ancient liberties (now being allegedly undermined by centralizing royal governments) became prominent. Partly to counteract this propaganda, and link the monarchy more closely with the concept of a French nation, the Crown and its ministers of the arts and public works from de Tournehem onwards (in 1746) initiated a series of educational and artistic reforms designed to produce a generation of patriotic propagandists for the regime (Loquin 1912; Leith 1965). In addition, Marigny and especially his successor, d'Angiviller, commissioned some important series of paintings on national themes from medieval French history, notably the 1773 series on St. Louis, and the 1776–7 series on the Anglo-French Wars and the virtues of Du Guesclin and Bayard (Cummings 1975). French heroic motifs like the *Entry of the French into Paris* in 1436 or the *Burghers of Calais* entered the artistic repertoire alongside depictions of episodes from the reign of Henri IV.[12] These 'medieval' national themes found favour again under the Restoration; even after Napoleon's Concordat, troubadour medieval-ism became increasingly popular, linked as it was with ideas of sacred kingship and the Catholic revival (Detroit 1975; also Markham 1975: 67–70, 108–110, 177–8).

At the same time, the ancient idea that Frenchmen were descended from the Trojans and Romans, took root and presaged a deep-seated rift in French national consciousness. In the early part of the eighteenth century, the Comte de Boulainvilliers had lamented the decline of the Frankish aristocracy; at the end of the century Siéyès inverted the idea, holding that the Frankish aristocracy were little better than foreign usurpers of a Gallic realm linked to the great Roman empire (Barzun 1932; Poliakov 1967). The 'real' nation, the Third Estate, were true descendants of those republican heroes of ancient Rome who had in their day sworn to abolish tyranny, just as their latterday successors were preparing to do. Like Rousseau and David, Siéyès and the Jacobins after him saw in Cato, Brutus, and the Horatii exemplars of a republican virtue and martial heroism that was also quintessentially French; and in the period preceding the outbreak of Revolution, writers and artists like David and Lemierre looked to the historians of classical antiquity, above all to Charles Rollin, for patriotic inspiration and the sources of a new ethnic myth of primordial simplicity and civic solidarity that would release and mobilize the energies necessary for social change (Crow 1978; Rosenblum 1967: ch. 2).

Both the 'Roman' and the 'medieval' ethnic myths served to promote the claims to special identities, dignity and autonomy. At the same time, their rivalry, repeated throughout the nineteenth century and especially during the prolonged Dreyfus Affair, and mirroring class cleavages, weakened national social cohesion, while reinforcing the sense of French identity in the long run and helping to stimulate a radicalism of both Left and Right. Both myths were 'regenerative' in impulse, if for different strata; in their rites and celebrations, especially during the moments of revolution, the French rehearsed their sense of identity and destiny in periodic acts of self-renewal (Durkheim 1915: 346, 427, esp. 214). Moreover, the genealogical and ideological myths overlapped, in intent if not content. Both aimed to inculcate 'virtue', albeit through different models; both aimed to inspire self-sacrifice, if for differently conceived communities. The noble deaths of a Bayard or Du Guesclin are, after all, only the medieval counterparts of those of a Cato, Germanicus or Seneca. Of course, the 'medieval' genealogical myth promoted the ideals of hierarchy, organic social order and the sacred, the whole tradition of counter-revolution from Bonald to Maurras (Weiss 1977; Nolte 1969); but even that was a radical, mobilizing myth, compared to the conservative myth of Norman England.

As for the 'Roman' myth, which proclaimed the spiritual affinity of patriot Frenchmen with republican Romans, the enthusiasm and sense of solidarity it inspired stemmed directly from its belief in a common ideological ancestor and a golden age of virtue, which we Frenchmen, as true patriots and brothers of the *patrie,* will restore. Together, these myths have created an ideal of France which, even today, is capable of radical self-renewal and of generating new movements for social change and national self-assertion, whether in the radical elements in Gaullism or in student revolts.

Turkey

Myths of origin have played a particularly important role in shaping Turkish national identity, since until the end of the nineteenth century, the very word 'Turk' had pejorative connotations (Lewis 1968: 343). Its rehabilitation was due, in the first place, to the 'outside Turks', mainly Tatars and Azeris in Tsarist Russia, and was then adopted by Turks within the Ottoman empire. Its restoration parallels exactly the growing sense of identity and dignity of the submerged Turkic-speaking communities (Karal 1965).

Under the impact of Russia's southward thrust and its pan-Slavic, Christian ideology, Ottoman statesmen and intellectuals began to reform the edifice of empire and search for new modes of solidarity (Davison 1963). At the same time, Western scholars and orientalists began to take an interest in Ottoman studies, and in the Turkish and Mongol ancestry of the Ottomans. Important in this respect were the theories of men like Joseph de Guignes, whose *General History of Huns, Turks, Mongols and other Western Tatars* appeared in 1756–58; Arthur Lumley Davids, whose *Grammar of the Turkish Language* was published in 1832; Celaleddin Pasa, a converted Polish exile, whose *Ancient and Modern Turks* was published in 1869; and especially the Hungarian scholar, Arminius Vambery (1832–1913), whose account of his *Journey to Central Asia* was published in 1879, and the important French Orientalist, Leon Cahun (1841–1900), who summed up his 'Turanian' theories in his *Introduction to the History of Asia,* published in 1896 (Kushner 1977: 9–10). All these works lavished praise upon the Turkic-speaking peoples, and located their original 'home' in Central Asia; several of them linked the Turkish language with the Hungarian, Finnish, Mongol, Estonian, and other 'Finno-Ugric' languages. The Ottomans themselves were traditionally traced (by Ottoman writers) to the tribe of Khayi Khan, a branch of the Oguz Turks, who had been forced by the Mongols to migrate westwards to the domains of the Seljuk Turks, at the time of Ertugrul. Towards the end of the century, these traditional Ottoman themes were coupled with European research to produce a consciousness in Ottoman intellectuals that Turkish history was their own history; this was evident in Suleyman Pasa's *Universal History* (1877), Ahmed Midhat's *History of Modern Times* (1887) and especially Necib Asim's *History of the Turks* (1900) (Kushner 1977: 28–33; Lewis 1968: 345–8).

This historicism was both genealogical and ideological in character. On the one hand, men like Midhat and Tevfik were keen to trace the pedigree of the Ottomans among the Turkish tribes of Central Asia; on the other, they were intent on tracing a cultural and ideological affinity with the qualities and virtues of their alleged Turkish ancestors, whose antiquity vied with the Greeks, Jews and Persians in the ancient Near East, according to the circle of writers around Ahmed Cevdet's paper, *Ikdam* (founded in 1894) (Kushner 1977: 18–19, 31, 37–40). There were also clear territorial implications. Even if pan-Turanianism was rejected, pan-Turkism implied a strong concern for, if not actual union between, the Ottoman Turks and those of Russia and Central Asia; and it led inevitably to attempts to join the 'new' Anatolian homeland of the Turks with their 'original' Central Asian one, with disastrous consequences for Young Turk policies during the First World War (Landau 1981: ch. 2; Lewis 1968: ch. 7). Here the influence of Mehmed Tevfik, who had extolled Oguz Khan already in 1889, and of Murad, who later became a leading Young Turk, was all too evident; genealogy and ideology alike promoted that racial myth of descent which enabled grandiose title-deeds to be drawn up on behalf of a soon-to-be-revived Turkish people, whose Ottoman state bastion was no longer tenable. (Landau 1981: 32; Kushner 1977: 29). In all this, one aim of these Turkist historians was clear: to free their people of self-contempt and self-ignorance through historicist education. The temporary bifurcation between a wider racial and linguistic pan-Turanianism and a more strictly ethnic pan-Turkism was soon settled in favour of the latter, but both served to raise the pride in self of Turkish intelligentsia and restore the credibility of the Turkish community. In the end, a more limited westernizing Anatolian Turkism won out; Ataturk turned his back on foreign adventures and the Central Asian homeland, yet his followers remained profoundly influenced by their pan-Turkist background, including the Hittite myth and the belief in a 'Turkification' of Anatolia and its peasant stock (Kushner 1977: ch. 5; Lewis 1968: 357–61; cf. also Berkes, 1964). Nor is the pan-Turkist social myth dead today; it lives on in the extreme Right parties in Turkey, and in organizations like the *Association of Pan-Turkists* (founded in 1962), even if its territorial implications have given way to its regenerative potential (Landau 1981: chs. 4–6).

Greece

Whereas Turkish myths of descent tended to blur the lines between genealogical and ideological impulses and promote an ethnic myth with strong racial and territorial implications, Greek myths were counterposed to each other in often open rivalry. On the one hand, there was the 'Hellenic' myth which can be traced back to the neo-Platonist Pletho in the early fifteenth century, developed by Theophyllus Corydaleus in the early seventeenth century, and finally elaborated by Adamantios Korais in the late eighteenth century; according to it, present-day inhabitants of Greece were descended from the ancient Hellenes, since they shared their language and culture, and only the values of classical Athenian antiquity could therefore serve as the basis for Greek self-renewal today (Campbell and Sherrard 1968: 22–43). Language played an important role in this ideological myth; unfortunately, the intellectuals disagreed on the appropriate version of Greek, some like Katartzis and Rhigas favouring the more 'demotic' forms spoken in the Morea, and others like Korais throwing their weight behind a 'purified' form which was a mixture of classical Greek and the modern Greek spoken by the educated middle classes (Koumarianou 1973). This difference mirrored a split between intelligentsia and peasantry, and became intertwined with the claims of the alternative 'Byzantine' imperial myth, which the Orthodox clergy and their congregations (most of whom were peasants and shepherds) espoused. In this more traditional image, the restoration of Christ's kingdom on earth was coeval with the wresting of power from infidels, Turks or Franks, and the restoration of the Byzantine hierocratic *imperium* (Frazee 1969: 20–25; Sherrard 1959). Within this empire, Greek was the natural language of religious communion and the Greeks would once again become its spiritual and temporal rulers, as, in fact, with the advance of the Phanariots in the administration of the Porte, they already appeared to be doing. Here, too, genealogical elements became intertwined with religio-ideological myths; for, despite the fact that the leading 'princely' Phanariot families can be shown to have originated in the provinces during the sixteenth and seventeenth centuries, claims of aristocratic Byzantine ancestry were made by and for them, and their self-image and vision of the world was saturated by Byzantinism. Like the Orthodox Patriarchate, they dreamed not of the regeneration of Greece, (with a few exceptions like Rhigas Velestinlis, whose 'Balkan federation' of 1796–7 was little more than a semi-secular Byzantine democracy), but of the impending restoration of the Byzantine empire and its religious culture (Mango 1973; Stavrianos 1961: ch. 9; Dakin 1972: chs. 1–2).

But, as Rhigas' example shows, Hellenism and Byzantinism were not mutually exclusive, even though their inspiration and spirit was mutually opposed. In a sense, both were 'revolutionary', since even the restoration of Byzantium demanded popular mobilization (and foreign intervention). Both, too, had dramatic territorial consequences, though here they led in opposite directions. The Hellenic ideal, centered on Athens, was western in orientation and based upon mainland Greece; the Byzantine myth, centred on Constantinople, looked to the east and spanned the area from Moscow to Alexandria (Henderson 1971; Demos 1958). In the event, however, Western intervention, by confining the new Greek state to the Morea and southern central Greece and thereby excluding so many Greek-speaking communities, helped to promote the '*Megale Idea*' (Great Idea), the quest for a much larger, inclusive Greek state stretching into Thrace and Asia Minor, which had been the dream of the Byzantine restoration, with disastrous consequences, both military and economic, for Greek regeneration (Dakin 1972; Campbell and Sherrard 1968: chs. 4–5; also Jelavich 1977: chs. 5, 12, 18).

Even the Hellenic ideal has been sharply criticized for holding back economic and educational development in Greece, despite the romantic claims of Korais and his followers; both Hellenism and Byzantinism appear to be backward-looking ideologies, characteristic of the Greek intelligentsia and clergy (Pepelassis 1958). In their time, however, both myths provided vital foci of identity; even if they collided at times, they helped to rally purely sectional interests—clerical, bourgeois, intellectual, *klephtic*—into a single struggle for national regeneration. In terms of enhanced dignity, territorial expansion and autonomy, both ethnic myths initiated and guided subsequent policies, even when they later promoted internal divisions. Of course, the content of the myths differed greatly; their golden ages, the heroes they revered, the reasons for decline they propounded, were entirely divergent. Even the location of origins, in the one case Asia Minor, in the other the Peloponnese, differed, as did their mythic genealogies of descent. In the end, too, an ideological Hellenism, geared to western thought and rational institutions, won out, mainly through force of external circumstances. Yet, in the origins and development of the Greek nation-state during the nineteenth century, both myths played a vital formative role in identifying the nature of 'Greek' character and guiding its regeneration in the light of their theories of origins.

Israel

As with the Greeks, a myth of descent was preserved among the Jews, enshrined in their sacred traditions. It traced Jewish origins to the land of Canaan, whither Abram of Ur had wandered at God's command; it preserved the memory of collective slavery and deliverance from Egypt, a return to Canaan under Moses, the promulgation of a divine Law, and the flowering of a golden age under David and Solomon. Thereafter, despite the efforts of Temple priests, the land was divided, Israel carried into Assyrian captivity and oblivion, and Judah ultimately also deported for its sins to Babylon. The myth suggested a second renaissance after the return to Jerusalem, another war of liberation under the Maccabees and a final decline and captivity under the Romans in A.D. 70 (Baron 1960: ch. 7; Noth 1960).

Thereafter, a bifurcation appears. The traditional interpretation, advanced by most rabbis, traced the line of descent through Talmudic Judaism to the medieval and Polish (*Ashkenazi*) rabbis; likewise, they traced the descent of their East European communities in the Diaspora through the fleeing German medieval communities back to those late Roman exiles in Gaul and Germany. On the other hand, during the early nineteenth century, the Jewish enlightenment intellectuals (*Maskilim*) tended to omit the medieval genealogical links and extol the cultural renaissance of Iberian Jewry, in which it saw a later reflection of that of ancient Israel and Judah in its own land (cf. Greenberg 1944: vol. I, chs. 2–3; Eisenstein-Barzilay 1959). Thus, the nineteenth-century conflict between rabbis and enlighteners, between a 'western' and 'eastern' outlook in Jewry, was guided and given meaning by two contrasting myths of descent, one more genealogical in character, the other more cultural and ideological in intent.

Again, as in the case of Greece, it was the secular and more ideological of these images that provided the main stimulus to territorial innovation and social regeneration. During the epoch of the Berlin and Galician enlightenment in the early nineteenth century, the Davidic kingdom and the Mosaic liberation assumed the status of the golden age for thinkers and novelists alike; it was re-education in that (more secular) image that was to be the key to national regeneration (Meyer 1967; Eisenstein-Barzilay 1959a). Again, the parallel with Korais is illuminating; both in matters of education and language reform, the Jewish and Greek intelligentsia pursued similar courses, sustained by their interpretations of history, especially the myth of origins and descent. In this development, they received unexpected support from the wealthier sections of Western Jewry, whose Reform

Judaism likewise sought to return to 'purer' forms and dispense with rabbinic accretions (Plaut 1963; Meyer 1967); in this they followed the 'revolutionary' thrust of philosophers and historians like Zunz, Graetz, Krochmal and Samuel Luzzatto, who began to forge the notion of a 'Jewish community' divorced from 'Judaism', that is, of an ethnic community one of whose creative expressions is the Jewish religion (Katz 1958; Dinur 1969). Such a separation was an essential precondition of any political movement of the Jewish people, including the Zionism of Moses Hess and, later, Leo Pinsker; in this context, Hess' revolutionary concern with the liberation of the Exodus and with the 'Sabbath of History' to be achieved by a mass return to Jerusalem, becomes a natural extension of the 'ideological' myth propounded by the Jewish intelligentsia which he had temporarily forsaken for world socialism (Hess 1958).

Since that time, two currents have been at work within Zionism: a strictly secular myth, at once territorial and liberal, such as Herzl and Nordau embraced; and a more socio-cultural myth, based upon a return to the Zion of traditional hopes, of which Achad Ha'am and Russian Jewry were the exponents (Vital 1975: chs. 6–7, 9–10). These two currents reflected differing concerns and the demographic split in European Jewry: on the one hand, a 'Western' outlook (based upon western European Jewry) whose object was to save individual Jews in a 'homeland' of their own, be it in Uganda, Argentina, or any politically convenient territory, as Zangwill argued; on the other, an 'Eastern' concern with 'Jewishness' as well as Jews, and therefore, a commitment to Palestine as the only 'homeland' capable of regenerating a 'distorted' Jewish diaspora into a true nation (Halpern 1961: 4–5; Herzberg 1960, Introduction). If the Western vision was attuned to the needs of wealthy, educated élites in process of assimilation (albeit chequered), the Eastern ideal spoke to and for the Jewish masses of Russia and Poland.

Within the latter ideal, however, two historicist myths were at work. The one was a traditional, religious myth of Jewish descent which we have traced; it was represented by a variety of Orthodox Zionists from Mohilever and Kalischer to Rabbi Avraham Kook. (Hertzberg 1960: Pt. VII) Its focus is the continuity of Israel. It refuses to reject the millennial diaspora, or the divinely-ordained two thousand year exile that links ancient Israel with its modern rebirth. It even seeks to remould the modern state into a quasi-theocracy, using the medieval diaspora canons of Orthodox Judaism; under the Begin government, and especially through the vanguard Gush Emunim movement, this myth has succeeded in moving and guiding both territorial policy in the West Bank and social and cultural programmes of religious regeneration (Gutman 1979; Segre 1980). The other great myth, which linked up with the secular, ideological concerns of the nineteenth-century enlighteners, was espoused by the various labour and socialist movements of the second and third immigrations (*Aliyot*). They all sought to 'overleap' the two thousand years of diaspora 'servitude' and oppression, so as to link up ideologically with an idealised Palestinian commonwealth of ancient Israelite peasants, shepherds and warriors, whose agrarian egalitarianism furnished a truly Rousseauan basis for that Davidic cultural and political renaissance, now being so memorably sung by the Hebrew revival poetry of a Bialik or Tchernikowski (Elon 1971: chs. 4–5; Halkin 1970). By returning to Palestine and working on and 'with' the land, as recommended by that mystic socialist A.D. Gordon, modern and alienated Jews might come to feel a deep kinship and affinity with their ancestors, whose material culture was now being unearthed in a romantic fervour of archaeological rediscovery; and would thereby come to experience a personal and collective regeneration (Hertzberg 1960: Pt. VI, 368–87). A few of these messianic pioneers even went so far as to proclaim themselves 'Canaanites'; most, however, aimed to slough off their petit-bourgeois 'pariah' status in an increasingly oppressive diaspora, to rediscover their ancestral roots in the land of their forefathers, and thereby create a new Israeli secular nation, free of the burden of the diaspora they had evacuated. But it was not to be. The terrible realization of the meaning of Hitler's Holocaust forced these socialist heirs of the enlightenment spiritually back towards the diaspora; and they embarked on an often painful quest to reassess the diaspora and reintegrate the 'lost' two thousand years into their Zion-centred ideological myth (Elon 1971: ch. 8; Hertzberg 1960, Introduction).

SOCIAL CLEAVAGE AND ETHNIC REGENERATION

From this brief survey, some recurrent features of ethnic myths of descent become apparent. They may be summarized as follows:

1. They designate the basic cultural entities of social relations;
2. They link past to future states of the unit, and act as models;
3. They possess external referents of comparison, even implicitly;
4. They designate a space and time for action, a territorial programme;
5. They contain impulses for collective action, mobilizing people;
6. They are developmental, assuming the possibility of change;

7. They are partly voluntaristic, in that successive generations may add to the heritage and even regenerate themselves;
8. They tend to be multiple, even competing, for any one entity.

Obviously, it would be possible to analyse each of these dimensions in some detail. I shall confine my attention to the last four, and especially the role of conflicting myths in creating frameworks of meaning and impulses for national regeneration; in other words the achievement of an ever developing identity, even solidarity, through social tensions and conflicts.

The Location of Ethnic Myths

In order to grasp the functions of ethnic myths, we need to have some idea of their characteristic location. Historically and sociologically, these myths emerge into the political daylight at certain junctures; these are usually periods of profound culture clash, and accelerated economic and social change. Very often, too, there is a definite threat, political or military, from outside to the viability of the community. That occurred, for example, during the prophetic and the Hellenistic periods in ancient Judea, and no doubt brought into the open the priestly myths of descent among the Jews of antiquity (Weber 1952; Tcherikover 1970). A similar conjunction of culture clash, economic change and military conflict (this time between Ptolemies and Seleucids) stirred a Pharaonic myth of descent, particularly in the writings of Manetho the priest, as the core of a strong Egyptian national sentiment under the Ptolemies (Grimal 1968: 210–41). A similar myth surfaced in the Egypt of Zaghlul and Taha Husain some two millennia later, again under the impact of rapid westernization, economic development and political turbulence in the Middle East after the First World War (Safran 1961). More generally, the vast increase in the political emergence of ethnic myths all over Europe from 1800 onwards, can be attributed to the same complex of factors, culture clash, commercialization and the Napoleonic and Russo-Turkish wars (Kohn 1967: ch. 8).

We may also observe the tendency for such myths to emerge during periods of incipient secularization, or the threat thereof. Even in the ancient examples I have cited, it was Hellenic rationalism that appeared to pose an insidious threat to traditional Jewish and Egyptian religion (or Phoenician-inspired paganism before 600 B.C.) (Tcherikover 1970; Hengel 1980). This is hardly surprising. As indicated earlier, ethnic myths of descent, often contained within their religious chrysalis, become autonomous and prevalent at the moment when tradition is under attack, and men seek alternative antidotes to their sense of estrangement and insecurity. In that sense, the myths represent a means of adapting to rapid change, of mediating between an untenable but much-regretted religious tradition and an ardently-sought but often fearful social change and modernization. That these myths also reflect the hopes and possibilities of social development mirrors the involvement of the community in new economic networks of commerce, and, in the modern era, of capitalist industrialism, and the breakdown of traditional economic isolation and subsistence structures (Geertz 1963).

Hence, we may say that typical conditions for the emergence and social location of ethnic myths are:

1. prolonged periods of warfare, involving the community directly or as an affected 'third party' and threatening it;
2. incipient secularization or its threat, as the nub of a wider clash of cultures, usually between a technologically superior, more 'rationalistic' civilization and a more traditional backward one, a clash that divides the community over the value of its tradition today;
3. incipient commercialization, breaking down the community's isolation and involving it in an external economic network based upon a superior material culture and technology.

The Appeal of Ethnic Myths

Cui bono? Whom do the myths serve? Broadly speaking, in the first place, the intellectuals, the humanistic ones at the outset, the more technically oriented ones later; and secondly, the professional intelligentsia, both humanistic and technical.

Historicism is the special preserve of intellectuals, whose status and social role is thereby greatly enhanced. No wonder Weber held them to be the missionaries of the national ideal; for everywhere the intellectuals have special access to 'culture values' and hence they 'usurp the leadership of a "culture community"' (Weber 1947: 176). The intellectual is the interpreter, *par excellence*, of historical memories and ethnic myths. By tracing a distinguished pedigree for his nation, he also enhances the position of his circle and activity; he is no longer an ambiguous 'marginal' on the fringes of society, but a leader of the advancing column of the reawakened nation, the leaven in the movement of national regeneration. And since myths and memories are capable of infinite interpretation and multiform dissemination, the educator-intellectuals, especially historians and linguists, help to 'recreate' a sense of ethnicity out of the chronicles, traditions, memories and artefacts at their disposal. In this way, the intellectual leaves his study to enter upon a new social role as national pedagogue and artist (Smith 1981: ch. 5; Feuer 1975: 202).

Whom does he teach and enchant? In the first place, the ever-growing stratum of the intelligentsia, whose new professional skills require an arena, openings and recognition (Gella 1976; Gouldner 1979). But these are exactly the needs to which the historicist myth of descent can minister. To begin with, it provides a territorial arena, the 'homeland', free of interference from church, aristocracy or bureaucracy, one in which the professionals can find employment and use their diplomas and talents. Second, the regenerated community which the myth inspires furnishes openings for their skills in its schools, hospitals, laboratories, press, and legal practices, and latterly in its corporations and mass party machines. And finally, by legitimating social change and demanding social regeneration, the ethnic myth creates a new climate in which the skills and talents of the intelligentsia are eagerly sought and rewarded. This is not to deny the role of other factors in this process of restratification; it is only to underline the part played by such historicist myths in providing new frameworks in which the intelligentsia can gain recognition. There are, therefore, quite practical reasons why the ethnic myth should have such resonance among professionals and why it becomes an almost unquestioned assumption, once the national ideal has been achieved (Smith 1981: ch. 6).

The intelligentsia are not the only constituency of the ethnic message of the intellectuals. The bourgeoisie may be attracted by such myths; not so much for historical features and artistic resonance, as for the culture and education they inspire in literature and the arts, which satisfy the bourgeoisie's need for cultivation to counteract their (and their children's) *nouveau-riche* status. Besides, the myths are important in legitimating territorial claims and national integration; hence in the formation of adequate markets for their products. And, on a more general level, the myths help to define the national 'public' which forms the audience for intellectuals and intelligentsia; they foster a sense of ethnic community and citizenship among the 'middle classes'.

And finally, such is the malleability of an historical myth, we may find it being adapted by populist intellectuals to the alleged needs of peasants and workers; the peasants, especially, become quasi-sacred objects of nationalist concern, since they carry many memories and myths (ballads, dances, crafts, customs, social organisations, tales, and dramas) which the nationalist intellectuals draw upon for the construction of their ethnic myth of descent, and its programme of regeneration (Smith 1979: ch. 5; Nairn 1977: ch. 2).

Social Cleavage and Competing Myths

As we saw, each nationalism usually contains more than one myth of descent. This split in their images of past and future tells us much about the divisions in the social and cultural life of a community experiencing rapid change, and the difficulties it faces in trying to achieve social integration. On one level, competing myths of ethnic regeneration constitute an index of the failure to achieve social cohesion, of the persistence of old divisions and the emergence of new ones. The calls to unity in England, France, Turkey, Greece, and Israel are sounded at exactly the point at which this unity is gravely imperilled by external forces of change. Different strata seize on rival myths and competing modes of myth-making to serve their 'ideal interests'; and in their hands, the myths themselves gradually become modified to suit their interests. Identities and descent-patterns come to serve the outlooks and interests of competing classes and status-groups within the community in the struggle for leadership of the emergent nation (cf. Weber 1947, Introduction).

Of special importance is the distinction between ideological modes of myth-making and genealogical pedigrees. Generally speaking, conservatively-oriented groups tend to stress the union of generations of descent and the patterns of family lineage, to shore up their power and prestige; such groups include the upper clergy, aristocracy, upper bourgeoisie intent on intermarriage with the upper classes, and sometimes the higher bureaucrats. On the other side, radical aspirant strata will trace their lineage through some ideological affinity with a model of antique nobility, from which they claim spiritual descent; that was the case with the Third Estate in 1789 who looked back to the Romanized Gauls against the Frankish usurpers and identified with Roman mores and ideals, seeing in Cato, Regulus, and Brutus their heroic ancestors. Similarly, radical strata among Greeks and Jews identified, not with their immediately traceable ancestors whom they tended to reject with all they stood for, but with a remote, idealized classical era of heroes and virtue, with Periclean Athens or Davidic Israel.[13] Indeed, the more revolutionary the stratum, the more does ideological affinity appear to outweigh genealogical pedigree.

In support of this contention, we may cite the case studies analysed and other examples. Of the former, the prototype is the Third Estate in 1789, mentioned above: their cult of *Brutus* encapsulated the drive for liberty from tyrants, for a republican solidarity and for the heroic nobility of stoic Romans (Herbert 1972; Antal 1939). The radical Greek intelligentsia, similarly, identified with the liberal ideals of classical Athens against the claims of a Byzantine clerical Orthodoxy; the more revolutionary among them, like Rhigas Pheraios and Korais, traced the ideals of the French Revolution and the Enlightenment to what they regarded as their common spiritual ancestor, the philosophical and artistic heritage of ancient Greece (Koumarianou 1973; Mouzelis 1978). In England, the radical tradition of the Levellers, taken up by the circle around Godwin and Blake over a century later, looked to the ancient Saxon liberties as their bulwark against foreign, i.e. Norman, usurpation (Hill 1958; Bindman 1977). And the radical socialist Zionist pioneers who went out to work the land in Palestine in the early years of this century, were equally inspired by a vision of egalitarian independence in ancient agrarian Davidic Israel or post-Exilic Judea under Ezra and Nehemiah (Elon 1971, ch. 8; Vital 1975). Other examples are furnished by India, where the radicalism of Tilak's appeal to the lower middle and incipient working classes in Bombay and Calcutta around 1900, took its inspiration from the cults of Shivaji and Kali, and a special reading of the *Bhagavad-Gita*, in which a spiritual descent to modern India from the ancient heroes served to inspire the Hindu masses to activist fervour (Adenwalla 1961; Crane 1961; Heimsath 1964); and by Ireland, where the Gaelic revival, fostered by radical and mainly Catholic strata in the 1890s, sought to recreate an organic vision of a 'lost' island civilization which has been a spiritual beacon to Europe in the early Middle Ages (Lyons 1979: chs. 2, 4; Sheehy 1980: ch. 6). And in early twentieth-century Egypt, the radical-liberal Coptic and Muslim middle classes led by Zaghlul, looked back to the myth of the Pharaonic past and its splendours as an impulse towards freedom and dignity, and a heroic inspiration in the struggle for a liberated modern Egyptian community (Ahmed 1960; Safran 1961; Vatikiotis 1968).

The Regenerative Potential of Ethnic Myths

In the short term, then, competing myths mirror and accentuate social cleavages. But in the longer term, their tension and interplay serves to mobilize popular action and regenerate the community. Rival myths may push policy in different directions; but they also limit the options and present a circle of assumptions and dynamic impulses which help to raise the self-consciousness of ethnic members. Hence, at another level, ethnic myths of descent provide frameworks of developmental meaning which underpin the sense of community among all strata, and answer to the problems of insecurity shared by members. In the longer term, the rival definitions of national identity tend to merge; by provoking encounters

with other national communities, by seeking title-deeds to disputed territories, they coalesce to form a community which, while still riven by social
conflicts, has become more unified at the level of history and culture, and
more sharply differentiated from other cultural communities.

Seen in this light, competing myths of descent and the social cleavages
they highlight, are analogous to family feuds in which each branch or
individual aims to achieve its due within the overall nexus of kin security
and status. By reaching back into an ideal antiquity, myths of descent
confer grandeur and glamour upon the often banal strivings for sectional
interests characteristic of most national communities today. Even more,
images of a distant past, and the ethnic myths that form their heart, achieve
a hold over the perceptions of various strata and an almost sacred and
magical status in the minds of their members. But, since in the final
analysis, the myths, for all their differences, refer to the selfsame community
and its history, different sections of the community find themselves enclosed
within one national circle, a single orbit of common security and destiny,
a clearly bounded social and territorial identity. From this orbit and
identity it becomes progressively more difficult to opt out. The myths not
only inspire, and even require, certain kinds of regenerative collective action;
they answer the all-important questions of identity and purpose which
religious tradition no longer seems able to resolve. In the shape of the ancient
heroes, they give us our standards of collective morality; in the promise
of new modes of solidarity and fraternity, they provide cures for our homelessness and alienation; in the return to primordial origins of kinship, they
seem to minister to our need for security. By telling us who we are and
whence we came, ethnic myths of descent direct our interests like Weber's
'switchmen' and order our actions towards circumscribed but exalted
goals. By 'replacing' us as links in an unbroken chain of generations, the
myths of descent disclose our national destinies.

Notes

1. Hesiod: *Theogony* 211–32, and *Works and Days* 109–201, for the Creation myth
   and the Five Ages of Man; the flood of Deucalion and Pyrrha, and the story
   of their son, Hellen, and his offspring, Dorus, Aeolus, Ion and Achaeus, is
   told by Apollodorus and Pausanias; for Abraham's ancestry back to Shem,
   cf. *Genesis* 11: 10–27.

2. For the Trojan ancestry myth of the Romans, cf. the *Aeneid*. I am indebted to Susan Reynolds for pointing to the existence of such a myth among the Franks in the early medieval era. (S. Reynolds: 'The political theory of nationalism: a medieval variant?', unpub. mss. 1981).

3. Weber himself links this drive for meaning with the growth of intellectualism: it is the intellectual who transforms the concept of the world into the problem of meaning. As intellectualism suppresses belief in magic, the world's processes become disenchanted, lose their magical significance, and henceforth simply 'are' and 'happen' but no longer signify anything. As a consequence, there is a growing demand that the world and the total pattern of life be subject to an order that is 'significant and meaningful' (Weber 1966: ch. 8, p. 125).

4. This survival of elements of what Durkheim called the 'conscience collective' and even of 'mechanical solidarity' into modern, industrial society, forms the essential background to his study of the functions of myth and ritual in all societies; Durkheim (1964, esp. Bk. 11/2, and Conclusion); and *idem* (1915, esp. Conclusion).

5. For the Brutus tale, cf. Livy II, 5, and Valerius Maximus V, viii, 1. For an analysis of its portrayals in late eighteenth century art, cf. Rosenblum (1961, 8–16). On the Oath of the Rütli, cf. Thürer (1970, 25); its so-called 'judges' clause' contains the typical nationalist sentiment that 'we will accept no judge in our valleys who shall have obtained his office for a price, or who is not a native and resident among us'; cf. also Steinberg (1976, 13–15). On Füssli's painting in the Zürich Rathaus, Antal (1956, pp. 71–4).

6. On these myths, Guirand 1968; 232–4, 245–80, 299–308; the 'Ossianic' lays of Macpherson (1760–63) were very popular in late eighteenth-century Europe (cf. Okun 1967).

7. This incident, in which the *klephtic* leader, Nicotsaras is said to have replied to a Greek scholar who likened his prowess to that of Achilles: 'What nonsense is this and who is Achilles? Did the musket of Achilles kill many?', is cited by Stavrianos (1961, ch. 9); for the debate about 'manipulation' of the past and of mass emotions, cf. the essays by Brass and Robinson in Taylor & Yapp (eds.) (1979); Kedourie (ed.) (1971, Introduction).

8. The metaphor of 'links in the chain' of generations comes from Dubnow (1958, 326). Examples of 'regenerationist' nationalism can he found in Thaden (1964); Binder (1964); and Heimsath (1964).

9. Saxon themes had also figured in the English national revival in the arts of the 1780's, in the work of Füssli, Kauffmann, Mortimer, Blake and Flaxman, based on Hume's popular *History of England* (1763), and Bishop Percy's *Reliques of Ancient English Poetry* (1762); cf. Irwin (1979, 14–17); Bindman (1977, 22–26).

10. Nairn (1977, 258–9), discusses this Society and its journal, *The English Race*; for other champions of the Right before and after 1914, including

Chamberlain, Milner, Belloc, Chesterton, Beaverbrook and Mosley, cf. J. R. Jones: 'England', in Rogger and Weber (eds.) (1966).

11. From another political standpoint, the same charge of English national pride, nostalgia and complacency is made by Birch (1977, 135–8).
12. Both themes were painted by Berthelemey in 1787 and 1782, respectively; Brenet painted the death of Du Guesclin in 1777, and Beaufort depicted Bayard's death in 1781; Danloux, Suvée and later Ingres treated incidents from the reign of Henri IV. On these and other paintings, cf. Rosenblum (1967, chs. 1–2) and Cummings (1975).
13. It may, of course, be a 'Right revolutionary' myth, as with Mussolini's return to antique Roman models (cf. Nolte 1969).

References

ADENWALLA, M. 1961 'Hindu Concepts and the Gita in early Indian thought'. pp. 16–23 in R. Sakai (ed.), *Studies on Asia*. Lincoln: University of Nebraska Press.

AHMED, J. 1960 *The Intellectual Origins of Egyptian Nationalism*. London: Oxford University Press.

ANTAL, F. 1956 *Fuseli Studies*. London: Routledge and Kegan Paul.

ANTAL, F. 1966 *Neoclassicism and Romanticism, and Other Studies*. London: Routledge and Kegan Paul.

APTER, D. (ed.) 1963 *Ideology and Discontent*. New York: Free Press.

ARMSTRONG, J. 1982 *Nations before Nationalism*. Chapel Hill: University of North Carolina Press.

BANTON, M. 1967 *Race Relations*. London: Tavistock Publications Ltd.

BARON, S. 1960 *Modern Nationalism and Religion*. New York: Meridian Books.

BARTH, F. (ed.) 1969 *Ethnic Groups and Boundaries*. Boston: Little, Brown and Company.

BARZUN, J. 1932 *The French Race*. New York: Columbia University Press.

BERKES, N. 1964 *The Development of Secularism in Turkey*. Montreal: McGill University Press.

BERLIN, I. 1976 *Vico and Herder*. London: Hogarth Press.

BINDER, L. 1964 *The Ideological Revolution in the Middle East*. New York: John Wiley.

BINDMAN, D. 1977 *Blake as an Artist*. Oxford: Phaidon.

BIRCH, A. 1977 *Political Integration and Disintegration in the British Isles*. London: Allen and Unwin.

BOWKER, G. and J. CARRIER (eds.) 1976 *Race and Ethnic Relations*. London: Hutchinson.

BRASS, P. 1979 'Elite groups, symbol manipulation and ethnic identity among the Muslims of South Asia.' pp. 35–77 in Taylor and Yapp (eds.), *Political Identity in South Asia*, SOAS. London: Curzon.

BREUILLY, J. 1982 *Nationalism and the State*. Manchester: Manchester University Press.

CAMPBELL, J. and P. SHERRARD 1968 *Modern Greece*. New York: Praeger.

CARR, E. 1945 *Nationalism and After*. New York: Macmillan.

COHEN, P. 1976 'Race relations as a sociological issue'. In Bowker and Carrier.

CRANE, R. I. 1961 'Problems of divergent developments within Indian national-ism, 1895–1905', pp. 1–15, in R. Sakai (ed.), *Studies in Asia*. Lincoln: University of Nebraska Press.

CROW, T. 1978 'The Oath of the Horatii in 1785: Painting and Pre-Revolutionary Radicalism in France', *Art History* I: 424–71.

CUMMINGS, F. 1975 'Painting under Louis XVI, 1774–89'. pp. 31–43 In Detroit Institute of Arts, *French Painting, 1774–1830: The Age of Revolution*. Detroit: Wayne State University Press.

DAKIN, D. 1972 *The Unification of Greece, 1770–1923*. London: Ernest Benn.

DANIEL, G. 1971 *The First Civilisations*. Harmondsworth: Penguin.

DAVISON, R. 1963 *Reform in the Ottoman Empire, 1856–76*. Princeton: University Press.

DEBRAY, R. 1977 'Marxism and the national question', *New Left Review* 105: 29–41.

DEMOS, R. 1958 'The Neo-Hellemc Enlightenment, 1750–1820', *Journal of the History of Ideas* 19: 523–41.

DETROIT INSTITUTE OF ARTS 1975 *French Painting, 1774–1830: The Age of Revolution*. Detroit: Wayne State University Press.

DEUTSCH, K. and W. FOLTZ (eds.) 1963 *Nation-Building*. New York: Atherton.

DINUR, BEN-ZION 1969 *Israel and the Diaspora*. Philadelphia: Jewish Publication Society.

DIXON, P. 1976 *Barbarian Europe*. Oxford: Elsevier-Phaidon.

DUBNOW, S. 1958 *Nationalism and History* (ed.). K. Pinso. Philadelphia: Jewish Publication Society of America.

DURKHEIM, E. 1915 *The Elementary Forms of the Religious Life*. Trans. J. Swain. London: Allen and Unwin.

—— 1964 *The Division of Labour in Society*. Trans. E. Simpson. New York: Macmillan.

EIENSTEIN-BARZILAY, I. 1959 'National and anti-national trends in the Berlin Haskalah'. *Jewish Social Studies* 21: 165–92.

—— 1959a 'The background of the Berlin Haskalah'. pp. 183–97 in J. Blau (ed.), *Essays in Jewish Life and Thought*. New York: Columbia University Press.

ELON, A. 1971 *The Israelis, Founders and Sons*. London: Weidenfeld and Nicolson.

EMERSON, R. 1960 *From Empire to Nation*. Cambridge: Harvard University Press.

ESMAN, M. ed. 1977 *Ethnic Conflict in the Western World*. Ithaca: Cornell University Press.

FEUER, L. 1975 *Ideology and the Ideologists*. Oxford: Basil Blackwell.

FISHMAN, J. 1980 'Social theory and ethnography'. pp. 69–99 in P. Sugar (ed.), *Ethnic Conflict and Diversity in Eastern Europe*. Santa Barbara: ABC-Clio.

FLEG, E. 1943 *Why I am a Jew*. London: Victor Gollancz.

FRAZEE, C. 1969 *The Orthodox Church and Greek Independence, 1821–52*. London: Cambridge University Press.

GEERTZ, C. 1963 'The integrative revolution'. *Old Societies and New States*. New York: Free Press.

—— 1963a 'Ideology as a Cultural System'. In Apter.

GELLA, A. (ed.) 1976 *The Intelligentsia and the Intellectuals*. Beverley Hills: Sage Publications.

GELINER, E. 1964 *Thought and Change*. London: Weidenfeld and Nicolson.

GOULDNER, A. 1979 *The Rise of the Intellectuals and the Future of the New Class*. London: Macmillan.

GREENBERG, L. 1944 *The Jews of Russia*. New Haven: Yale University Press.

GREENWOOD, D. J. 1977 'Continuity in change: Spanish Basque ethnicity as a historical process'. pp. 81–102 in M. Esman (ed.), *Ethnic Conflict in the Western World*. Ithaca: Cornell University Press.

GRIMAL, P. 1968 *Hellenism and the Rise of Rome*. London: Weidenfeld and Nicolson.

GUIRAND, F. (ed.) 1968 *New Larousse Encyclopedia of Mythology*. London: Hamlyn.

GUTMAN, E. 1979 'Religion and its role in national integration in Israel'. *Middle East Review* XII:3 1–36.

HAIM, S., (ed.) 1962 *Arab Nationalism, An Anthology*. Berkeley & Los Angeles: University of California Press.

HALKIN, S. 1970 *Modern Hebrew Literature*. New York: Schocken Books.

HALPERN, B. 1961 *The Idea of the Jewish State*. Cambridge: Harvard University Press.

HAYES, C. 1931 *The Historical Evolution of Modern Nationalism*. New York: Smith.

HEIMSATH, C. 1964 *Indian Nationalism and Hindu Social Reform*. Princeton: Princeton University Press.

HENDERSON, G. P. (ed.) 1971 *The Revival of Greek Thought*. Edinburgh: Scottish Academic Press.

HENGEL, M. 1980 *Jews, Greeks and Barbarians*. London: SCM Press Ltd.

HERBERT, R. 1972 *David, Voltaire, Brutus and the French Revolution*. London: Allen Lane.

HERTZBERG, A. (ed.) 1960 *The Zionist Idea, A Reader*. New York: Meridian Books.

HESS, M. 1958 *Rome and Jerusalem*. Trans. M. Bloom. New York: Philosophical Library.

HILL, C. 1958 *Puritanism and Revolution*. London: Martin, Secker and Warburg.

HONOUR, H. 1968 *Neo-Classicism*. Harmondsworth: Penguin.

HOVANNISIAN, R. 1967 *Armenia, the Road to Independence*. Berkeley: University of California Press.

IRWIN, D. 1966 *English Neo-Classical Art*. London: Faber and Faber.

—— 1979 *John Flaxman, 1755–1826*. London: Studio Vista.

JELAVICH, B. & C. 1977 *The Establishment of the Balkan National States, 1804–1920*. Seattle: University of Washington Press.

JOHNSON, H. G. (ed.) 1968 *Economic Nationalism in Old and New States*. London: Allen and Unwin.

JONES, J. R. 1966 'England'. pp. 29–70 in H. Rogger and E. Weber (eds.) *The European Right*. Berkeley: University of California Press.

KAMENKA, E. (ed.) 1976 *Nationalism*. London: Edward Arnold.

KARAL, Z. 1965 'Turkey: From Oriental Empire to modern national state'. pp. 59–81 in G. Metraux and F. Crouzet (eds.), *The New Asia*. New York: Mentor.

KATZ, J. 1958 'Jewry and Judaism in the 19th century'. *Journal of World History* 4: 881–900.

KEDOURIE, E. 1960 *Nationalism*. London: Hutchinson.

—— (ed.) 1971 *Nationalism in Asia and Africa*. London: Weidenfeld and Nicolson.

KOHN, H. 1965 *The Mind of Germany*. New York: Macmillan.

—— 1967 *The Idea of Nationalism*, 2nd ed. New York: Macmillan.

—— 1967a *Prelude to Nation-States: the French and German Experience, 1789–1815*. New York: van Nostrand.

—— 1940 'The origins of English Nationalism'. *Journal of the History of Ideas 1: 69–94*.

KOUMARIANOU, C. 1973 'The contribution of the Greek Intelligentsia towards the Greek independence movement, 1798–1821'. pp. 67–86 in R. Clogg (ed.), *The Struggle for Greek Independence*. London: Macmillan.

KRIESBERG, L. 1982 *Social Conflicts*. 2nd ed. Greenwich, Conn: Prentice-Hall.

KUSHNER, D. 1977 *The Rise of Turkish Nationalism*. London: Frank Cass.

LANDAU, J. 1981 *Pan-Turkism in Turkey*. London: C. Hurst and Co.

LEITH, J. A. 1965 *The Idea of Art as Propaganda in France, 1750–99*. Toronto: University of Toronto Press.

LEWIS, B. 1968 *The Emergence of Modern Turkey*. London: Oxford University Press.

LOQUIN, J. 1912 *La Peinture d'Histoire en France de 1747 a 1785*. Paris: Henri Laurens.

LYONS, F. S. 1979 *Culture and Anarchy in Ireland, 1890–1939*. London: Oxford University Press.

MANGO, C. 1973 'The Phanariots and the Byzantine tradition'. pp. 41–66 in R. Clogg (ed.), *The Struggle for Greek Independence*. London: Macmillan.

MARWICK, A. 1974 *War and Social Change in the Twentieth Century*. London: Methuen.

MARKHAM, F. 1975 *Napoleon and the Awakening of Europe*. Harmondsworth: Penguin.

MAYO, P. 1974 *The Roots of Identity*. London: Allen Lane.

MEYER, M. A. 1967 *The Origins of the Modern Jew: Jewish Identity and European Culture in Germany, 1749–1821*. Detroit: Wayne State University Press.

MOSSE, G. 1963 *The Culture of Western Europe*. London: John Murray.

MOUZELIS, N. 1978 *Modern Greece, Facets of Underdevelopment*. London: Macmillan.

NAIRN, T. 1977 *The Break-up of Britain*. London: New Left Books.

NISBET, R. 1969 *Social Change and History*. London: Oxford University Press.

NOLTE, R. 1969 *Three Faces of Fascism*. Trans. L. Vennewitz. New York: Mentor Books.

NOTH, M. 1960 *A History of Israel*. London: Adam and Charles Black.

OKUN, H. 1967 'Ossian in painting'. *Journal of the Warburg and Courtauld Institutes* XXX: 327–56.

PALMER, R. 1959 *The Age of the Democratic Revolution*. Princeton: Princeton University Press.

PALMER, R. 1940 'The National Idea in France before the Revolution'. *Journal of the History of Ideas* 1: 95–111.

PEPELASSIS, A. 1958 'The image of the past and economic backwardness'. *Human Organisation* 17: 19–27.

PLAUT, W. 1963 *The Rise of Reform Judaism*, New York.

PLUMB, J. 1965 *England in the Eighteenth Century*. Harmondsworth: Penguin.

POLIAKOV, L. 1967 'Racism in Europe'. pp. 223–25, in Reuck and Knight (ed.): *Caste and Race*. London: Ciba.

REISS, H. S. (ed.) 1955 *The Political Thought of the German Romantics, 1793–1815*. Oxford: Blackwell.

REUCK, A. DE and J. KNIGHT (eds.) 1967 *Caste and Race*. London: Ciba.

REYNOLDS, S. 1981 'The political theory of nationalism: a medieval variant'. Unpub. MSS.

ROSENBLUM, R. 1967 *Transformations in Late Eighteenth Century Art*. Princeton: Princeton University Press.

ROSENBLUM, R. 1961 'Gavin Hamilton's "Brutus" and its aftermath', *Burlington Magazine* 103: 8–16.

SAFRAN, N. 1961 *Egypt in Search of Political Community*. Cambridge: Harvard University Press.

SAKAI, R. 1961 *Studies on Asia*. Lincoln: University of Nebraska Press.

SEGRE, D. 1980 *A Crisis of Identity: Israel and Zionism*. Oxford University Press.

SETON-WATSON, H. 1977 *Nations and States*. London: Methuen.

—— 1979 'Nationalism, Nations and Western Policies', *Washington Quarterly* 211: 91–103.

SHERRARD, P. 1959 *The Greek East and the Latin West*. London.

SHEEHY, J. 1980 *The Rediscovery of Ireland's Past*. London: Thames and Hudson.

SHILS, E. 1957 'Primordial, personal, sacred and civil ties'. *British Journal of Sociology* 7: 113–45.

SHILS, E. 1960 'Intellectuals in the political development of new states.' *World Politics* 12: 329–68.

SMITH, A. D. 1976 *Social Change*. London and New York: Longman.

SMITH, A. D. 1979 *Nationalism in the Twentieth Century*. Oxford: Martin Robertson.

—— 1981 *The Ethnic Revival*. London: Cambridge University Press.

—— 1979a 'The "historical revival" in late eighteenth century England and France'. *Art History* 2: 156–78.

—— 1981a 'States and homelands: the social and geopolitical implications of National Territory'. *Millennium* 10: 187–202.

SOPHOCLES 1947 *King Oedipus*. Trans. E. F. Watling. Harmondsworth: Penguin.

STRAVRIANOS, L. S. 1961 *The Balkans since 1453*. New York: Holt.

STEINBERG, J. 1976 *Why Switzerland?* London: Cambridge University Press.

TCHERIKOVER, V. 1970 *Hellenistic Civilisation and the Jews*. New York: Athenaeum.

THADEN, E. C. 1964 *Conservative Nationalism in Nineteenth Century Russia*. Seattle: University of Washington Press.

THÜRER, G. 1970 *Free and Swiss*. London: Oswald Wolff.

VAN DEN BERGHE, P. 1967 *Race and Racism*. New York: John Wiley.

VATIKIOTIS 1968 *Modern History of Egypt*. London: Weidenfeld and Nicolson.

VAUGHAN, W. 1978 *Romantic Art*. London: Thames and Hudson.

VITAL, D. 1975 *The Origins of Zionism*. Oxford University Press.

WEBER, M. 1947 *From Max Weber, Essays in Sociology*. (eds.) H. Gerth and C. Mills, (eds.). London: Routledge and Kegan Paul.

—— 1952 *Ancient Judaism*. New York: Free Press.

—— 1965 *The Sociology of Religion*. Trans. E. Pischoff. London: Methuen.

—— 1968 *Economy and Society*. New York: Bedminster Press.

WEISS, J. 1977 *Conservatism in Europe, 1770–1945*. London: Thames and Hudson.

WILSON, H. S. (ed.) 1968 *The Origins of West African Nationalism*. London: Macmillan.

3

The Problem of National Identity:
Ancient, Medieval and Modern?*

ABSTRACT

To grasp the similarities and differences between modern and pre-modern collective cultural identities, we need to move beyond the dominant paradigms of perennialism and modernism and their conflicting passions and, aided by clear working definitions of key terms in the field, construct ideal types of ethnicity and nationality. This procedure allows us to assess evidence from a number of examples of collective identities in both the ancient and medieval worlds, independently of the dominant assumptions. The resulting picture reveals that, while national identity is mainly a modern phenomenon, pre-modern ethnic communities and identities are widespread and processes of national formation and representation are found in all epochs. Though the 'empirical' approach has its problems, it is more sensitive to historical context and nuance, and conveys a fuller picture, than the dominant perspectives in the field today.

'*A passionate man cannot teach*'. Partisans cannot be scholars. We expect political ideologies like nationalism to instil a spirit of absolute commitment and self-sacrifice, but political dogmatism of this kind sits ill with the spirit of detachment that scholarship seeks. In an era when, for all the studied disdain of Western scholars and statesmen, nationalism has reasserted itself, when national aspirations, conflicts and tragedies fill the air, is it too much to ask that scholarship free itself from these enveloping passions? Would this imply that a nationalist—and an anti-nationalist—cannot study nationalism and understand the problem of national identity? (For Hillel's maxim in *The Mishnah*, Aboth 2.6, see Danby 1933, 448; cf. Hobsbawm 1990: 12–13.)

* *Ethnic and Racial Studies*, Volume 17, Number 3, July 1994.

Such a ruling would be rather harsh. It would certainly make us question a number of recent theories of national identity and nationalism. For despite the scholarly air of unconcerned objectivity, few subjects continue to engage the passions so vividly. But we must also recognize the protean nature of nationalism which, like the river god Achelous, can change its shape at will. The evil that nationalism has wrought certainly lives on, but the good is not necessarily interred with its bones. It may blossom later and bear fruit. Recognition of the many-sided nature of nations and nationalisms may help to calm the passions, both the scepticism and hostility of so many of the 'modernist' school of Western scholars who associate nationalism with Nazism, and the sympathy of the old school for the 'primordial' nation (Emerson 1960; Connor 1978; Breuilly 1982).

THE THEORETICAL DEBATE

As things stand today, however, these passions continue to inform, not just the content of national identity, but also recent theoretical debates about these issues. Broadly speaking, we can distinguish two antagonistic schools of thought about nations and nationalism: the 'perennialists' and the 'modernists'. In addition, there is a more fundamental divide over the nature of ethnic ties between the 'primordialists' and the 'instrumentalists', that is, between those who regard the ethnic community as in some sense 'primordial' and those who regard it as a malleable 'instrument' (see Geertz 1963; A. D. Smith 1984).

I shall be mainly concerned with the debate between the perennialists and modernists over the antiquity of nations and nationalism. But it is necessary first to say something briefly about the other debate on the nature of ethnic ties, and more particularly about the concept of 'primordialism'. As recent debates have revealed, there are different positions included under the wide rubric of primordialism. One is the position adopted by many (but not all) nationalists, namely, that ethnic communities and nations are 'natural', that they are part of the natural order, just like speech or physiognomy. Another is the recent attempt by sociobiologists to explain ethnic ties in terms of genetic reproductive success and inclusive fitness, the ethnic community representing an extended family in time and space (Van den Berghe 1979).

A third position, often confused with these, is that put forward initially by Edward Shils and Clifford Geertz. Here, the primordial sentiment was *attributed* to the participants. It was and is the members of ethnic communities and nations who feel their communities are primordial, existing almost 'out of time' and having an 'ineffable' binding and almost overpowering quality. It is no part of this approach to suggest that such communities *are* primordial, only that the members *feel* they are. In this sense—what one might term a 'participant's primordialism'—the concept of the primordial plays an important part in our understanding of phenomena like national identity (Shils 1957; Geertz 1963; Stack 1986; Grosby 1991; Eller and Coughlan 1993).

This last position, not to mention the other two, is at present distinctly out of fashion among scholars of ethnicity and nationality. Most of them are of the 'instrumentalist' persuasion. They regard ethnic ties as a social and political resource, a socially constructed repertoire of cultural elements that afford a site for political mobilization, especially where the ties of social class are in decay. At the same time, some of these scholars are profoundly aware of the durable nature of ethnic boundaries and border mechanisms, which are actually intensified by transactions across the border. I am not sure, however, whether they would thereby concede to a primordial element in ethnic ties, with the exception of John Armstrong. (See Barth 1969; Glazer and Moynihan 1975; Brass 1979; but also Armstrong 1982.)

Turning to the second debate over the antiquity of the nation, the perennialist perspective is regarded as a rather unsophisticated misreading of the history of collective cultural identities. The feeling that members of a nation may have that their nation is ancient, even immemorial, may be widespread; but to go on from this to see ancient Greeks or Egyptians, for example, as nations in the same sense as their modern counterparts is to commit the sin of 'retrospective nationalism' (See Levi 1965; Brandon 1967; cf. also Tipton 1972).

According to this modernist perspective, nations and nationalism are not only logically contingent; they are sociologically necessary only in the modern world. There was no room for nations or nationalism in agrarian society, for there was no need to unify the tiny élite strata and the vast mass of peasant food-producers and tribesmen subdivided into their many local cultures. Nor was there any chance of generating a sense or ideology of the nation from an aristocratic or clerical culture that stressed its élite status. Only in the era of modernization, argue modernists like Deutsch, Kautsky, Gellner and Nairn, was there any need, or possibility, of unifying a disparate and mobile population. Hence, the pivotal role played by the intelligentsia and mass public education in the genesis of nations, in providing both the ideology and the leadership of modern, industrial societies (Kautsky 1962; Gellner 1964, 1983; Deutsch 1966; Nairn 1977, chs. 2, 9; cf. A. D. Smith 1988).

The modernist standpoint clearly regards nations as well as nationalism as products of the modern era subsequent to the French and Industrial revolutions, the outgrowth of specifically modern phenomena like capitalism, industrialism, the bureaucratic state, urbanization, and secularism. In this way, nations and nationalism are functional for an industrial society, providing its essential cement, the necessary solidarity without which it could disintegrate. Nationalism has become the 'religion surrogate' of modernity.

Some scholars would go further. They argue that nations are recent cultural artefacts, emerging from an era of 'print-capitalism', reading publics, and political mobilization. They are creations of nationalist intelligentsia or other classes who re-present and picture them to others through books, newspapers and works of art. Much of the nation's symbolism, mythology, and history is deliberately produced and invented. In short, nations are best seen as *imagined political communities*, imagined as both sovereign and spatially finite (Anderson 1983; cf. Hobsbawm and Ranger 1983).

This kind of 'social constructionism', for all its insights and influence today, does not in my view take us very far, for several reasons. We may readily concede the role of invention and imagination in the formation of particular nations, without regarding either nations or nationalisms as largely constructs of the imagination. To read the nation as a printed text to be decoded may reveal much of the recurrent imagery and language of nationalism, but it tells us little about the genesis and course of either particular nations and nationalisms or of nationalism in general. Nor does it help us to understand why only certain political and/or ethnic communities became nations, and which these are. Secondly, while nationalist intelligentsias obviously played important roles in the creation of particular nations, they required antecedent cultural ties and sentiments in a given population if they were, and are, to strike a deep popular chord and forge durable nations. Finally, the idea that thousands, even millions, of men and women have let themselves be slaughtered for a construct of their own or others' imaginations, is implausible, to say the least. It illustrates the yawning gulf between a cognitive approach to the nation and an understanding of it as a focus for moral and political mobilization (see A. D. Smith 1991b).

In fact, the modernist view is as much a myth as perennialism, where myth is understood as a dramatization and exaggeration of elements of truth in the tale it tells of a heroic past which serves the present. The modernists' 'myth of the modern nation' exaggerates the gulf between tradition and modernity, the impossibility of nations in traditional agrarian societies and their necessity in modern, industrial ones. It thereby assumes what we need to explore and demonstrate empirically, that is, the modernity of national identity and nationalism (see Tudor 1972; A. D. Smith

THE PROBLEM OF DEFINITION

If we are to move beyond the sweeping certitudes of these reductions, we shall need to proceed more cautiously, using the maximum empirical evidence at every step. We also need to try and unravel the tangled terms like nation, nation-state, national identity, and nationalism, that bedevils progress in this field. Only then can we begin to move forward and deal with the question of the nature of collective cultural identities in the pre-modern and modern epochs, and how far and in what ways they differ or resemble one another.

Let me start with the term 'nationalism'. It is used in different ways, according to context. We can distinguish four main usages:

1. the whole process of growth of nations and national states;
2. sentiments of attachment to and pride in the nation;
3. an ideology and language (discourse) extolling the nation;
4. a movement with national aspirations and goals.

We can put aside the first usage; it is a broad, umbrella concept for a whole series of processes that we shall want to delineate separately.

The second usage is more germane. 'National sentiment', though often confused with nationalism, should be distinguished from both the ideology/language and the movement of 'nationalism'. One can have nationalist movements and ideologies in a given unit of population, without any real diffusion of national sentiment in that population. Nationalist ideologies and movements frequently start out as ideologies and movements of small minorities of intellectuals, as has occurred in several states in Africa and Asia this century. The reverse can also be found, though rarely; the English (arguably) had a widely diffused national sentiment at certain stages in their history, but little in the way of a nationalist ideology or movement.[1]

It is therefore, useful to distinguish between nationalism, the ideology and movement, and national sentiment, the feelings of collective belonging to a nation. The ideology and movement, on the other hand, usually go together. One could, of course, have the ideology without the movement, in the sense that one might identify a few writers who held nationalist beliefs but who were too few to form a movement with political demands; but the reverse is inconceivable, by definition. In practice, there is a relatively swift transition from the early nationalist intellectuals to the birth of a nationalist movement, so I shall treat the third and fourth usages together as a single phenomenon, the 'ideological movement' of nationalism, while recognizing the possibility that they might be separable (see Hroch 1985).

What is the ideology and what are the goals of this ideological movement? The ideology can be briefly summarized:

1. the world is divided into nations, each with its own character and destiny;
2. the nation is the sole source of political power, and loyalty to it overrides all other loyalties;
3. everyone must belong to a nation, if everyone is to be truly free;
4. to realize themselves, nations must be autonomous;
5. nations must be free and secure if there is to be peace and justice in the world (A. D. Smith 1973, section 2; 1983, ch. 7; Breuilly 1982, Introduction).

These propositions form the 'core doctrine' of nationalism everywhere, at all times. They are the central tenets preached by the founders of nationalism: Rousseau, Burke, Herder, Jefferson, Fichte, Mazzini, Korais, and others. It follows that the modernists are right when they underline the modernity of nationalism, the ideological movement, dating as it does from the late-eighteenth century in Western Europe. Any other nationalist ideas and motifs are specific to particular nationalist movements and national communities; but they are secondary to the central tenets of the core doctrine. Nationalism also differs from what is sometimes meant by 'patriotism', which strictly speaking is a sense of attachment to a country or state. Nationalism is an ideological movement on behalf of a nation, a cultural-historical community which may or may not at that moment have its own homeland or state. (Whereas patriotism is commonly thought to be positive, nationalism may be positive or negative, depending on the viewpoint of the participant or analyst. In fact, it is often both at the same time, in the sense that it has both constructive and destructive effects).

What, then, are the goals of nationalist movements? There are three main recurrent goals: national identity, national unity, and national autonomy. For nationalists, the nation must possess a particular character or identity and what Max Weber called 'irreplaceable culture values'. It must also be united, both as a compact territorial unit and as a fraternity of citizens, as preached by the *patriots* of the French revolution. Finally, the nation must be free. It must be master of its destiny, a subject of history, and not liable to external interference. It must obey only its own 'inner laws' (see Hobsbawm 1990, ch. 1; A. D. Smith 1991a, ch. 4). Hence, we can define nationalism as an ideological movement for attaining and maintaining identity, unity, and autonomy on behalf of a population deemed by some of its members to constitute an actual or potential 'nation'.

What then of the 'nation'? Can we describe it simply as an imagined political community, limited but sovereign? That would lead us to include Iceland and the former Soviet Union, as well as the Roman and Chinese empires behind their *limes* or walls, as well as ancient and medieval city-states like Tyre, Corinth and Pisa. Since any community above the level of the face-to-face is imagined, this kind of definition is more suggestive than helpful.[2]

The defect of such subjectivist and voluntarist definitions, even Renan's, is that any self-selecting group, provided its aspirations are spatially limited, can claim to be a nation. That would rule in all kinds of grouping—churches, sects, professions, and voluntary associations—which have nothing to do with our understanding of what is meant by the term, nation. On the other hand, objectivist, cultural definitions of the nation come up against the vast numbers of cultural categories that could claim the status of nation, the particularity of each national experience and the many per-mutations of the objective elements of culture (language, religion, customs), something especially true of language which the German romantics regarded as the touchstone of the nation (Akzin 1964; Haugen 1966; Gellner 1983; Edwards 1985, ch. 2).

The only way to break out of the resulting impasse, I believe, is to for-mulate an ostensive definition derived from the images and ideas of the nation held by most or all nationalists. The question is: do all or most nationalists possess common images and ideas of the nation? Can these be merged into some ideal type? Does not such a procedure come per-ilously close to the modernist tenet which holds, in Gellner's words, that

Nationalism is not the awakening of nations to self-consciousness: it invents nations where they do not exist—but it does need some pre-existing differentiating marks to work on, even if, as indicated, they are purely negative . . .

with all the social constructionist implications that have been criticized (Gellner 1964: 168)?

I think not. A procedure for *defining* the nation needs to be sharply separated from one for generating explanations of nations, nationalism, and national identity. Appealing to the common images and ideas of the nation held by nationalists for the purpose of defining the nation is not to be confused with a procedure for explaining the rise of nations and nationalisms. In other words, our definitional procedure should not prejudge the relationship between nations and nationalism.

In fact, we can, I think, extract some common ideas and motifs of the nation common to most, if not all, nationalists, and thereby establish an ideal type of the nation for purposes of comparison. Such an ideal type, derived from the three goals of national identity, unity and autonomy, would include:

1. the growth of myths and memories of common ancestry and history of the cultural unit of population;
2. the formation of a shared public culture based on an indigenous resource (language, religion, etc.);
3. the delimitation of a compact historic territory, or homeland;
4. the unification of local economic units into a single socio-economic unit based on the single culture and homeland;
5. the growth of common codes and institutions of a single legal order, with common rights and duties for all members.

These motifs, commonly found in the writings and speeches of nationalists everywhere, help us to define the nation as a named cultural unit of population with a separate homeland, shared ancestry myths and memories, a public culture, common economy, and common legal rights and duties for all members (see Connor 1978; Gellner 1983, ch. 5; A. D. Smith 1991a, chs. 1, 4).

There are several points about this definition. It is inevitably a modernist definition, in the sense that its very concepts such as public culture, common economy, and common legal rights derive their meaning from developments in and of the modern epoch. Our understanding of these terms is infused with 'modern' connotations. It may be that there were parallels for each of these concepts in pre-modern epochs, and we shall explore this. It must be admitted, however, that the *definition* of the nation is framed in modern, and one must add, modernist terms, while nevertheless recalling our earlier refusal thereby to sanction automatically a modernist *explanation*.

Secondly, it treats subjective elements like myths and memories as objective realities. In one sense, everything in the definition is subjective, conceived by nationalists and others. In another sense, each element has an empirical referent, a piece of territory, a chronicle or epic poem, a law-code, a material and institutional embodiment, summing up recurrent activities, such as national markets, courts, and rituals.

Thirdly, there is no mention in the definition of the state. While I accept Weber's dictum that 'A nation is a common bond of sentiment whose adequate expression would be a state of its own, and which therefore normally tends to give birth to such a state', the qualification 'normally' suggests that the nation is first and foremost a social and cultural community independent of the state, and that like Poland after the Partitions it can exist without 'a state of its own'. State and nation are often linked in practice, but they should be kept conceptually distinct, even in that misnomer, the 'nation-state' (Connor 1972; Tivey 1980, Introduction).

Finally, the definition makes no mention of ethnic identity. Nevertheless, the nation is closely related to ethnic phenomena. It is, in my view, a sub-category of, and development out of, the far more common phenomenon of the ethnic community, which is itself a development out of the global phenomenon of the ethnic category. We start from a world divided into ethnic categories, that is, cultural units of population with some sense of kinship or ancestry, some common dialects and deities, but little collective self-awareness, few shared memories, and no common name or territory or solidarity. Only travellers, missionaries and scholars may note their close affinity, and perhaps by their activities help to weld them together, as did the missionary pastors of Bremen who reduced the Ewe dialects to a common Anlo script, or the native missionaries among the Yoruba tribes whose cultural work helped to unify them in the mid-nineteenth century (Welch 1966; Peel 1989).

From these categories certain processes of ethno-genesis give rise to fully-formed ethnic communities, or what the French term *ethnies*, which we may define as named human populations with shared ancestry myths, historical memories and common cultural traits, associated with a homeland and having a sense of solidarity, at least among the élites. In this definition, the sense of shared birth and ancestry, common to the Greek *ethnos* and the Latin *natio*, is pivotal. It gives rise to all the real and metaphorical kinship connotations of nationality, to be found in the Israelite ethnic genealogies of the Patriarchs but equally powerfully, though more metaphorically, in the *fraternité* of the revolutionary *patriots* of 1789 (Noth 1960; Kohn 1967; Hertz 1944; cf. for the term *natio*, Zernatto 1944; Kemilainen 1964; and for *ethnos*, Tonkin, McDonald and Chapman 1989, Introduction).

Ethnies, then, are named groups with shared ancestry myths and memories or 'ethno-history', with a strong association, though not necessarily possession of, a historic territory or homeland. The élites often have a vivid sense of solidarity, a sense of distinctive 'people-hood'; these are the aristocratic 'lateral' *ethnies*. Where this ethnic sentiment is widely diffused to other strata of the community, we may speak of demotic 'vertical' *ethnies* (see Connor 1978; A. D. Smith 1986, chs. 2–4).

COLLECTIVE CULTURAL IDENTITIES IN ANTIQUITY

This long excursus into definitions was necessary, if we are to advance any substantive arguments about the nature of collective cultural identities in the pre-modern and modern epochs. It also encourages us to move beyond the sweeping generalizations of the competing perspectives of perennialism and modernism, whose dogmas blind us to the nuances and complexities of historical realities in various periods in different parts of the world. In what follows, I can only concentrate on a few examples from the many that could be studied, testing the working definitions sketched above against the collective cultural identities presented in the historical record, first in the ancient world and then in the medieval era, and comparing them implicitly with the national identities of the modern era.

   In the ancient world, I would argue, human beings were for the most part divided into fairly fluid ethnic categories and some more durable ethnic communities, or *ethnies*. A few of the latter—Persians, Egyptians, Israelites—possessed states of their own, that is, states run by and for members of the dominant *ethnie*, even when members of other ethnic categories resided on their territory, as the Israelites lived before the Exodus in the north-east Egyptian province of Goshen. The question that might be asked is whether such 'ethnic states' can be termed nations, according to our criteria, as scholars of an earlier generation were wont to do (Walek-Czernecki 1929; Koht 1947).

   Ancient Egypt, for example, a community named after the god (HaKa-Ptah, in Greek, Ai-guptos), regarded itself as separate, chosen and central, the community of inhabitants of 'the land', with everyone else as outsiders to that provident territory. The community had its native Pharaohs who mediated for Amon-Re, the representative of the Egyptian pantheon, its Memphite Theology of creation and ancestry myths, its shared memories of Menes' union of Upper and Lower Egypt, and its king-lists and chronicles. Moreover, the Egyptians, of all ancient communities, had the most clear-cut attachment to their land, a function perhaps of their radical separation from other communities by the eastern and western deserts, and of the unity provided by the life-giving Nile. On the other hand, the boundaries of ancient Egypt were neither as clear-cut nor as well-policed as those of its modern counterpart; nor was its economic life as unified, given the divisive power of the regions and nomarchies, and the chronic differences between Upper and Lower Egypt, represented in the Pharaoh's two crowns. These factors militated against a single division of labour throughout the country, and supported the localism of Egyptian economic life (Frankfort *et al.* 1947; Frankfort 1954, ch. 4; Atiyah 1968, ch. 1; Trigger *et al.* 1983).

It is not only in the economic sector, but also in the sphere of culture and education, that the designation of ancient Egypt as a 'nation' can be questioned. For one thing, the sons of nobles and priests had a much more privileged education than that afforded to commoners' sons. For another, different classes had diverse funerary practices, as well as different rights and duties; there were also rival priesthoods and competing temple centres. On the other hand, the Pharaoh sought to enact ordinances for the whole population, and to represent the community as a whole in its relations with the divine pantheon, and in the many common temple rituals, thereby helping to forge over time a sense of collective Egyptian history and destiny (see Beyer 1959; David 1982).

Following our criteria and working definitions, then, ancient Egypt resembles more an 'ethnic state' than a nation. In contrast, many Old Testament scholars have regarded ancient Israel as a nation from the time of David and Solomon, if not earlier. The evidence adduced includes a collective name (or names), vivid creation and ancestry myths, and shared memories of the Exodus, conquest and wars with the Philistines, recorded in the books of Judges and Samuel. There is also the well-known description of the sacred territory of Israel, stretching from 'Dan to Beersheba', in Numbers 34 and Joshua 22[3] (Noth 1960; Grosby 1991).

Ancient Israel was also distinctive and relatively unified in terms of public culture. Admittedly, this was a religious culture, centred on Temple worship, the cult of the Sabbath, the three pilgrim festivals, and the New Year and Day of Atonement; but then several modern nations have a predominantly religious culture, including Ireland, Morocco and Iran. It is, of course, difficult to say from the surviving evidence how many ordinary Israelites of the First Temple period participated in this public religious culture. Certainly, popular participation was much greater in post-Exilic times, especially after the Ezraic reforms, and in the area round Jerusalem. Much later, after the Hasmonean reforms, a public culture of the synagogue established itself in town and countryside and gained a following in the Roman period. By the Mishnaic period, after the destruction of the Temple, the idea of a religious culture embracing 'all Israel' was well-established under the sages, a culture dominated by law (Torah and Halakha, or Oral Law). This, in turn, suggests that in a period when the distinctions between Priests, Levites and People had all but lost their meaning, a uniform code of law with common rights and duties embraced all Jewish males[4] (see Neusner, 1961; *Cambridge History of Judaism* 1984, vol. 1, pp. 14–17).

There was less unity in the economic sphere. In terms of produce and modes of existence, Galilee and the coastal area round Caesarea were separate from the Judean centre round Jerusalem. Moreover, production in the villages was predominantly local. Hence, the compact territorial and economic unity often found in modern nations was lacking, though a clear sense of the Lord's land and its indigenous resources inspired much Zealot thinking of the period. Clearly, ancient Israel in the later Second Temple era was well on the way to becoming a nation, and it seems that significant sections of the population saw themselves as members of a distinctive nation, in a sense of the term not unlike the one that is prevalent today. Of course, it is easy to fall into the trap of a retrospective nationalism, such as arguably informs Brandon's well-known thesis about Zealot guerrilla nationalism; yet, as other scholars have shown, ancient Israel in this period possessed those attributes of distinctive Hellenistic political communities—a capital, temple, territory, leadership and army as well as a unifying ideology—that testify to a national consciousness and existence (Brandon 1967, ch. 2; Alon 1980, vol. I, chs. 7–8; cf. Zeitlin 1988: 130–48; Mendels 1992).

The discussion of ancient Israel clearly reveals the fluid historical processes whereby an ethnic category (Israelite slaves in Egypt) becomes a clearcut *ethnie* through the Mosaic reforms, and then part of the community comes to approximate, after many vicissitudes, to a nation. This is not to suggest some kind of necessary evolutionary development, but rather a typological series from the broader, encompassing category to the narrower. Undoubtedly, the narrowest category, the nation, is found predominantly in the modern epoch, something that requires separate explanation; but that does not preclude its presence in earlier epochs, and ancient Israel in this period, according to our criteria, may well be designated a nation.

The other well-known case of ethnic consciousness in antiquity, the ancient Hellenes, presents a more complex picture. They are often portrayed as a *Kulturnation*, but we are in fact dealing with at least three levels of collective identification: with the territorial city-state and its shared myths, memories and public culture, its clearly demarcated borders and in some cases legal uniformity; with the linguistic subculture—Dorian, Ionian, Aeolian, Boeotian—and its separate genealogies, tribal organizations, calendars, dialects and architectural styles; and with the Hellenic community and its common worship of the Olympian pantheon, its Greek language and script, its Homeric epics, its games, festivals and colonies, and later, its pan-Hellenic rhetoric. All these circles of allegiance overlapped one another; the public cultures of the city-states were mostly variants of a wider Hellenic culture; the genealogies, styles and dialects of the linguistic subgroups were again variants of the Hellenic culture and also used by political factions of rival city-states; while the Hellenic community was being continually defined and pressed into the service both of individual city-states and of linguistic groups of city-states, such as Pericles' bid for pan-Hellenic supremacy for Athens or the Spartan (Dorian) League (Fondation Hardt 1962; Alty 1982).

Only the widest Hellenic circle could constitute a national identification. Given the lack of any economic unity, however, the differences in laws and public culture throughout Hellas and the ragged nature of Greek boundaries stretching from the Black Sea to Sicily and Magna Graecia, ancient Hellas is closer to a loose ethnic community than to a nation. No wonder that the *philosophes* and Rousseau looked back to the city-republics of Sparta, Athens and Rome, rather than to Greece! (Rosenblum 1967; Cohler 1970).

The other well-known example of a cohesive *ethnie* from the ancient world is the Persian. That the Persian rulers of the far-flung Achaemenid empire were conscious of the separate identity of Medes and Persians, in contrast to other ethnic communities, is evident not only from Persian records, like Darius's Behistun inscription, but also from the sculptural representations of ethnic groups bearing gifts for the New Year ceremony, in the reliefs of the Apadana staircase at Persepolis. How far this Persian *ethnie* then, or later, in the Sassanid empire, could be said to constitute a nation with a common public culture, clear-cut territory, legal membership and economic unity, rather than simply an ethnic state, is unclear, not least because of problems in interpreting often textually defective or ambiguous documents. The same is true of other *ethnies* in the ancient world—Sumerians, Elamites, Babylonians, Assyrians, Hittites, Hurrians, Arameans, Philistines and Phoenicians; in some cases, we may speak of ethnic kingdoms (Elamites, Hittites, Assyrians), in others (Arameans, Arabs) of a series of culturally cognate but separate political units, and in yet others (Sumerians, Philistines and Phoenicians) of a network of culturally homogenous city-states which are often in civil conflict (see Moscati 1962; Frye 1966; Wiseman 1973).

ETHNIES AND NATIONS IN MEDIEVAL EUROPE

For these reasons we should not allow ourselves to be seduced by either the modernist or the perennialist paradigms of nationality. How far we may speak of a widespread conception and presence of national identities in the ancient world, and what these signify, is a question that requires detailed empirical investigation of particular cases and their processes of nation-formation. My argument is simply that use of the criteria of ethnicity and nationality proposed here does not prejudge the presence or absence of nations and national identities for any particular period or continent.

The same kind of reasoning applies *mutatis mutandis* to later epochs and other areas. In principle, the same kind of open-ended investigation could help us to analyse processes of ethnic and national formation for areas like the Far East—Japan, Korea, China and Tibet in the late first millennium AD—or Latin America—notably Mexico and Peru—from the first to the mid-second millennium AD, or for part of the Middle East and Horn of Africa (Arab Caliphates, Persia, Seljuq Turks, Mamluk Egypt, Monophysite Ethiopa) in the same period (see Katz 1972, chs. 9–10, 13; Ullendorff 1973, ch. 4; Armstrong 1982, ch. 3).

It is for medieval Europe, however, that this kind of comparative investigation is most relevant and necessary. For it has been a long and powerful tradition here, informed by a romantic genealogical nationalism, that traces the roots, the 'true' origins, of several modern European nations to an early medieval seedbed. Museum and gallery exhibitions to this day insinuate in their guides and catalogues similar presuppositions, overtly or subtly impregnated with a philological and archaeological nationalism that tells us much about the continuing hold of this kind of ethno-history, even in a rational, 'post-modern' era (see Hobsbawm and Ranger 1983, chs. 3, 7; Horne 1984; Johnson 1992).

We need to separate out these issues of affiliation from those of comparative analysis. The question, for example, whether Kievan 'Rus was in any sense the 'true ancestor' of modern Russia or whether the medieval Muscovite state bore much resemblance to later Tsarist or Soviet Russia, should not be confused with attempts to evaluate the nature of collective cultural ties in these polities *in their own right*, and not as the prelude to, or seedbed of, something else. The same arguments apply in the parallel Greek case, where it is customary to trace national affiliation to the classical or Byzantine heritage and communities (see Portal 1969; cf. Campbell and Sherrard 1968, ch. 1; and Carras 1983).

The Russian case is peculiarly complex. Kievan 'Rus, at least, was undoubtedly highly heterogeneous ethnically, with Varangians, Slavs, Chazars and others intermingling along the Dnieper route to Constantinople. There was greater ethnic homogeneity among the later north-east Slav settlements, especially after the Orthodox Church had consolidated their culture in the fourteenth century, in opposition to both the Mongols and the Latin West. Certainly, by the sixteenth century, a distinctive ethno-political identity had evolved among ruling and clerical circles, buttressed by the political myth of the Third Rome and Byzantine succession. By 1500, indeed, Muscovite Russia approximated to an ethnic state, but thereafter, the incorporation of vast tracts of land with culturally alien *ethnies* (Tartars, Ukrainian Cossacks, Mari and others) undermined any cultural or economic unity that may have existed, while the reimposition of serfdom under the new class of boyar landowners ruled out any possibility of common legal rights and duties for all members of the community (see Cherniavsky 1975; Pipes 1977, especially ch. 9).

There is an instructive comparison here with the formation of national identity in France. In both, the guiding *mythomoteur* was dynastic; the land, people and dynasty were closely related. Both communities, too, had a vivid myth of ethnic election, memorably resonated by St. Joan in France, but circulating well beforehand among the clergy. In this myth, the French, like their Russian counterparts, were seen as a 'chosen people' with a God-given mission to unbelievers, schismatics and aliens. In both the Church, centred in France on the archbishopric of Rheims, played a leading part in defining the nature of ethno-political identity; and in both cases, the medieval state and community have often been seen as the true ancestors of the modern nation (Armstrong 1982: 152–59; Reynolds 1983; and for the modern French myth, Citron 1988).

But the French case diverged from the Russian as a result of vastly different geopolitical circumstances: a growing dynastic public culture in France expanded during the later medieval era to cover a limited and *compact* territory, hemmed in by other European powers. Even the later annexations (Brittany, Lorraine, Avignon, Venaissin, Nice) did not alter the fact and sense of a compact territory with 'natural' frontiers based on the original hexagon, a shape that goes back to the Carolingian era, to the *regnum* of Charles the Bald (with the exception of Lorraine, of course). By the later stages of the Anglo-French wars there was a clear identification of the French state, community and sacred realm, within definite boundaries that excluded, for example, England. On the other hand, economic unity had to wait for centuries, until the late-nineteenth century, according to Eugene Weber, and the same was true for common legal rights for all Frenchmen, let alone French women. But, then, the same has been true of most Western states. To deny the title of 'nation' to communities that lacked economic unity or full legal rights for all members would be unduly restrictive and posit a rather static view of the nation as a target to be attained once and for all, rather than a set of processes and a growth of consciousness, as I am suggesting. If we reject the idea that nations can only be 'mass nations', then our task is to trace the growth of the French nation from the time of the Anglo-French wars, if not earlier, and relate it to a pre-existing *ethnie* originating with the Frankish *regnum*[5] (Weber 1979; Connor 1990).

Similar cautions apply in tracing the growth of an English (not British) community in the Anglo-Saxon and Anglo-Norman periods. From Bede and others it would appear that educated Englishmen of the eighth century saw themselves as a named community of common descent with myths of common ancestry and shared historical memories of migration across the seas from northern Europe, followed by battles with the native Briton inhabitants. By this period, too, there was a growing public culture based on the organization of the Church and subsequently on the court of the kingdom of Wessex in its struggles with the Danes. Given the rivalries between the Anglo-Saxon kingdoms, territorial borders were only stabilized in the tenth century, with a body of common laws and a measure of common trade emerging in the eleventh century, despite the predominance of local economies. Can we speak here of the nucleus of an English nation? (Reynolds 1984, ch. 8; Howe 1989; cf. L. Smith 1984).

In the subsequent Anglo-Norman period, we can also discern a growing unity in a number of spheres: language and culture, laws and institutions, stronger trading links despite the predominance of feudal tenures, and new myths of common descent, formulated by Geoffrey of Monmouth in his compilation of the pedigrees of the British kings. It was not, however, until the thirteenth and fourteenth centuries that we find an increased sense of common English identity and destiny, and some would place this development after the long-drawn-out wars with Scotland and France. Here, too, the political effects were felt later. Only with the Tudors does centralization of the state gain real momentum and help to determine the shape and course of an English (later British) national identity. The overall picture of the course of English medieval histories represents therefore a series of movements into and out of sociopolitical structures approximating to the pure types of *ethnie*, ethnic state and nation, rather than any simple linear progression from ethnic category to ethnic community to nation.

Indeed, it is only from the late-fifteenth century that we can begin to speak confidently of a growing sense, among the élites at least, of an English national identity (Geoffrey of Monmouth 1966, Introduction; MacDougall 1982; Corrigan and Sayer 1985; Mason 1985).

One more example may help to clarify these distinctions. The Swiss Confederacy is often cited as a counter-example to the importance of language for nationality, the need for cultural homogeneity and the central role of the state. From the modernist perspective, Switzerland represents an anomaly. This holds also for the perennialist perspective, which treats Switzerland as an immemorial nation, at least from the Oath of the Rütli in 1291. It is extremely doubtful whether the Alemannic tribes around the newly opened St. Gotthard Pass possessed much sense of a common ethnicity, divided as they were by grandiose mountain ranges and speaking cognate dialects in their valleys. By this time, they had evolved a cantonal jurisdiction, their rights subject to confirmation by the region's overlord, in this case Rudolf of Habsburg. Only when such confirmation failed to materialize and the first oaths of the *Eidgenossenschaft* were sworn between representatives of the forest cantons, did a process of ethnic formation commence, binding together a string of local communities who had constituted no more than a very loose ethnic (Alemannic) category. In the course of prolonged struggles with the Habsburgs and Burgundians, the various Swiss cantons and city-republics produced a fund of sagas, songs, rituals and laws embodying and chronicling their memories, myths, symbols and traditions, including the legend of William Tell (originally recounted in the *White Book of Sarnen* of the 1470s and unconnected with Stauffacher's revolt and the founding Oath of the Rütli) whose exploits recalled an earlier, less mercenary, heroic ethos at variance with the one later espoused by the victorious Confederacy under the leadership of the burghers of Berne, Lucerne and Zürich (Thurer 1970: 236; Steinberg 1976, ch. 2; Kreis 1991, ch. 4).

There followed a long period of consolidation of the Old Confederacy and of divisions produced by Zwingli's Reformation. The sixteenth century also marked the moment of transition from a purely Alemannic to a wider community incorporating Protestant as well as French-speaking cantons like Fribourg and Geneva. Here was the seedbed of a possible Swiss political community, though, given the repressive and exclusive nature of the patrician urban oligarchies that held power, its realization was postponed for two centuries. Not till the late-eighteenth century, after the Enlightenment had produced a movement of national renewal among the intelligentsia of Berne, Zürich and Geneva, did it prove possible to dissolve the Old Confederacy and inaugurate a modern national community, first in the form of the Helvetic Republic under French auspices, and then in 1848 with a modern federal constitution (Kohn 1957; Warburton 1976; and especially Im Hof 1991).

Thus, from about the late-fifteenth century, it seems reasonable to speak of a Swiss *ethnie* with common name, ancestry myths, historical memories, replicated social and cultural institutions and a growing sense of historic territory. This was reflected in a clear sense of common Swiss identity and destiny. Economic unity and common rights and duties were certainly lacking, as was a shared public culture for all Swiss men (let alone women) at this period; while the changing shape of the Confederacy's territories, and the differing statuses of new and some older cantons, meant that before 1798 any Swiss 'nation' resembled a patchwork of partly contiguous local territories rather than the compact fraternal unity espoused by nationalists in the nineteenth century and really only achieved after 1848. So, despite some early processes of nation-formation, it is difficult to describe the Swiss Confederacy as a nation, rather than as an ethnic community, before 1798.[6]

CONCLUSION

Inevitably, in any discussion of the problems of defining the concept of national identity and dating the emergence of nations, there is an arbitrary element. In this case, it involves my starting-point, the appearance in the later eighteenth century in Western Europe and America of the ideological movement called nationalism. This seems to be the one fixed point in a field otherwise marked by flux and paradox, and it has important social and political consequences. This was recognized by a number of scholars, as the title of John Armstrong's book, *Nations before Nationalism*, indicates. The emergence of nationalism marks a critical divide in the history of ethnicity and nationality. For only after 1800 has it been possible for every self-aware *ethnie* and political community to claim the title of nation and strive to become as like the nationalists' pure type of the nation as possible. Before the eighteenth century, no such doctrine or movement was available to confirm nations in their status, or guide would-be nations to their goal; and so it was not possible before that time to create 'nations by design' (Armstrong 1982; cf. Tilly 1975, and Seton-Watson 1977, chs. 2–3).

From this fixed point, we can go on to construct the ideal or pure type of the nationalists' ideal of the nation everywhere. Yet, it is important also to realize that the pure type itself is not a fixed standard, since its features are actually social and political *processes*. The formation of nations includes collective myth-making and ethno-historical selection, ethnic territorialization, cultural assimilation and mass public education, economic unification and legal standardization. It also includes processes of collective representation, of the growth of collective consciousness among ever wider strata of the designated population. These processes are not inevitable; they can often be reversed. That is why nationalisms arise to 'awaken the people' and stir them from their slumber. This means that nationalism, the ideological movement, is part of reversible nation-forming processes, which it influences and shapes and hastens but does not produce or construct.

A key question arises here: can these processes of nation-formation exist independently of nationalism? Were there nations before nationalism? Clearly, unless we arbitrarily restrict the notion of the nation to mass nations, the origins of such nations as the French, English and Dutch can be traced back well before the nationalist era. What about nations in yet earlier epochs? Can we discover there, too, the nation of the nationalists' vision? It is important to treat this question on its own merits, independently of the rival perennialist and modernist perspectives, and irrespective of what occurred in the same geographical area in subsequent periods of history. Whether the English or French constituted nations in the seventh or fourteenth century is not to be confused with the issue of their relationship to the modern English or French nations. It must be determined by independent criteria drawn from the processes selected for inclusion in the ideal type of the nation. Adoption of such a procedure reveals the complexity of the empirical issues and rules out the possibility of uncovering law-like regularities or sweeping generalizations in this field.

There are several objections to the ideal-type procedure. The first is that the argument is circular. It sets out from a nationalist vision of what constitutes the concept of the nation, one which is infused with the modern European context of its initial formulation, and it then examines how far pre-modern collective formations approximate to the ideal type of the nation drawn from the nationalist vision, that is, how far collective formations far removed in epochs and continents from eighteenth- and nineteenth-century Europe conform to this nationalist ideal. Is this not to adopt a retrospectively nationalist criterion? Should we not recognize that the very meaning of the concept of the nation is contextual, that is, it is specific to the time and place of its appearance?

To accept such a relativist criticism would, of course, rule out the possibility of comparison and general explanation, and lead to a *reductio ad absurdum*: every nation and nationalism would be incommensurable, even conceptually, because, by definition, its historical appearance is specific. That would underwrite the irreducible particularism which nationalism extols. However, the terms and concepts of the discourse of nationalism are also general and comparative; though each nation and nationalism has its specific features, it is also related to a wider conceptual framework of 'nationalism in general' of which it forms an instance.[7]

There is the additional problem with this procedure of how 'we moderns' are to grasp the inner meaning of the terminology of collective identity of each distinct era in its own terms and without any modern presuppositions. How can we know whether the terms and concepts of ethnicity and nationality of pre-modern epochs correspond in any way to our own modern ones? (Does 'modern' here bear the original meaning of 'recent', 'just now' (*modo*), or a more sociological one of a new stage of history marked by machine-power technology, industrialism, the bureaucratic state and the like?)

In one sense, the problem is insuperable. Either one accepts that modern society is radically different from pre-modern society, so that every term of analysis is also different in the two kinds of society, and pre-modern ethnicity and nationality simply cannot be compared with modern ethnicity and nationality; or one does not, and then these terms and concepts can be related to each other across the modernization divide, because the similarities are more important than the differences. Clearly, this is something that cannot be settled by a purely 'empirical' method that must treat the terms of definitions as valid for all eras to allow useful comparisons, irrespective of their historical context.

In another sense, I am not sure that the dilemma is insuperable. It is possible to recognize the radically different nature of (sociologically) modern societies, while treating collective cultural identities through the ages and across continents on a single continuum and as part of a single discourse that spans the epochs and zones. This does not mean ignoring differences in historical context—or for that matter, of geographical context. (Do ethnicity and nationality, common legal rights and public culture bear quite different meanings in China, Ethiopia and Mexico, even in the modern epoch, let alone in antiquity or the medieval era? Does the 'context' only change with modernization?) Nor does it ignore the changes that terms and concepts may undergo with modernity (as with *natio* to nation). At the same time, this procedure allows us to frame general concepts and language that can accommodate comparisons across epochs and continents, as part of the social scientific enterprise, while being sensitive to changes in many of the key terms of that language.

A third objection to the ideal-type procedure adopted here is that the data found in pre-modern epochs will not permit definitive answers to the questions under consideration here. We rarely possess the records of the vast majority of pre-modern cultural units of population, of the peasants, tribesmen and artisans, or of most women. We have to rely on the testimonies and relics of a tiny fraction of the population, usually the clergy, but also a few nobles, bureaucrats, and merchants. Other relics include buildings and artefacts—sculptures and paintings, craft objects, inscriptions and the like—which often have recognizable regional or ethnic styles, though inferences from such artefacts are by their nature limited.

To this we may reply that it would be foolish to imagine that we can arrive at full answers to such questions even in the modern world. The best we can hope for is an approximation to the realities of a given epoch or area. Besides, the historical record, even in pre-modern epochs, often contains sufficient accounts of political, religious, military and economic activities to allow us to make reasonable inferences about ethnic or national motivations, as has been demonstrated in a study of the Ionian and Dorian sentiments of many of the participants in the Peloponnesian war, based on a close reading of the accounts of Herodotus and Thucydides (Alty 1982).

A last objection is the classical sociological one: so what? Where can such an exercise in nuanced analysis lead? For historians, perhaps, this is not an important objection, but for social scientists trained to search for large-scale regularities there is a question of theoretical yield. Unfortunately, the nationalists have a point. The field of nations and nationalisms is one of particularities, variations and nuances. It is a field of cultural plurals. No wonder that Max Weber, with his historical training, hesitated to give us the book on the formation of national states that he promised us. Hence, too, his recommendation, which I have followed here, to use the ideal-type method, in order to allow some means of comparison and contrast.

But there are other uses of this method. By creating a framework for examining the nature of collective cultural identities, the ideal type is useful for the identification of key processes in the formation of *ethnies* and nations, something that is critical if we are ever to formulate a more general model or theory. Secondly, in by-passing the all-or-nothing formulations of perennialists and modernists, the ideal-type method can help us to search for the varieties of collective identities, and the similarities and differences between ethnic and national identities. Thirdly, this method can provide a touchstone for discovering whether there may be substantial relationships between ethnic and national communities in the same area in successive historical periods and this, in turn, may help us to determine which nations emerged and why.

Finally, the ideal-type approach emphasizes the need for caution in predicting the demise of ethnic and national identities. Nations may not be immemorial, nor is nationalism perennial. At the same time, the long history of ethnic identification suggests the rootedness and functionality of ethnic and national ties and identities in so many periods and areas of the world. We are all too aware of how politically controversial is the problem of the nature and antiquity of ethnic or national identity of French and English, Germans and Poles, Arabs and Jews, Tamils and Sinhalese, and how easily these questions generate rivalries, hatreds and wars even today. In seeking more balanced and many-sided answers to such complex and controversial questions, social scientists and historians may help us to gain a deeper understanding of a rich and fascinating sphere of human existence, and also make a modest contribution to a saner and more tolerant approach to human diversity.

Notes

1. This is true only of some periods. There were strong cultural and political nationalist movements in puritan England, and again at the end of both the eighteenth and nineteenth centuries; see Kohn (1940); Colls and Dodd (1986); Newman (1987); and more generally, Samuel (1989). One could also argue that where national sentiment is widely diffused and territorial claims have been satisfied, as in Norway, Switzerland and Holland, there is little need for an explicit nationalist movement.

2. Why cannot city-states become nations? Presumably because their public cultures and myths were variants of wider ethno-linguistic and religious cultures, and their descent myths harked back to a common ancestor of cognate city-states, as in Sumer, Phoenicia and ancient Greece. Does this apply to a city-state like Venice, which was formed after the breakdown of a common Roman-Italian culture? What of republican Rome itself, with its *populus Romanus* in contradistinction to the barbarian *nationes*? Do not Rome's dual foundation myths (Romulus, Aeneas), its later exclusiveness to foreigners, its very public culture and uniform legal codes, make the later Roman republic appear like a dominant 'nation' at the head of a growing empire, in the same way as the English (through Britain) came to rule a large empire? (For Roman myths and attitudes, see Ogilvie 1976; Balsdon 1979.)

3. See also Deuteronomy 11, 12. The settlement of the Israelite tribes on the sacred land is discussed by Grosby (1991, especially p. 240) where the conjoining of a distinctive 'people' with a specific sacred 'land' is a 'characteristic referent in the shared beliefs constitutive of nationality, ancient and modern: a people has its land and a land has its people'.

4. It can also be argued that the early Mosaic code enjoins such equality of rights and duties on all Israelite males at a very early period; see Zeitlin (1984, ch. 3).

5. This is the recent position of Connor (1990). The rise of nations, he argues, can only be dated from the emancipation of the masses and the spread of national sentiment and rights to the majority of the population, including women. The indicator here is the enfranchisement of the majority of the population, which would place the emergence of nations in the West in the early-twentieth century. This raises a number of questions. Is this not a rather arbitrary criterion of the presence of the nation? Where is the 'cut-off' point in such a quantitative account? Does this not suggest that the nation is a target that must be attained, or perhaps a moving target that always eludes our grasp? (See Nettl and Robertson 1968, Part I.)

6. With the proviso that there is nothing inevitable about this process, we may agree with Im Hof (1991, Introduction) that elements of a later Swiss national identity can be traced back as far as the later fifteenth century.

7. Gellner (1983) distinguishes explanations of the rise of particular nationalisms and explanations of nationalism in general. We seek both kinds of explanation, of course, but there remains a tension, not least between historians and social scientists, over the importance accorded and the methodology adopted, to one or the other.

References

AKZIN, B. 1964 *State and Nation*. London: Hutchinson.

ALON, G. 1980 *The Jews in their Land in the Talmudic Age*. vol. 1, Jerusalem: Magnes Press, Hebrew University.

ALTY, J. H. M. 1982 'Dorians and Ionians', *Journal of Hellenic Studies*. vol. 102, no. 1, pp. 1–14.

ANDERSON, B. 1983 *Imagined Communities: Reflections on the Origins and Spread of Nationalism*. London: Verso.

ARMSTRONG, J. 1982 *Nations before Nationalism*. Chapel Hill, NC: University of North Carolina Press.

ATIYAH, A. S. 1968 *A History of Eastern Christianity*. London: Methuen.

BALSDON, J. V. P. 1979 *Romans and Aliens*. London: Duckworth.

BARTH, F. (ed.) 1969 *Ethnic Groups and Boundaries*. Boston, MA: Little, Brown and Co.

BEYER, W. C. 1959 'The civil service in the ancient world', *Public Administration Review*. vol. 19, pp. 243–49.

BRANDON, S. G. F. 1967 *Jesus and the Zealots*. Manchester: Manchester University Press.

BRASS, P. 1979 'Elite groups, symbol manipulation and ethnic identity among the Muslims of South Asia', in David Taylor and Malcolm Yapp (eds.): *Political Identity in South Asia*. London and Dublin: School of Oriental and African Studies, Curzon Press Ltd., pp. 35–77.

BREUILLY, J. 1982 *Nationalism and the State*. Manchester: Manchester University Press.

Cambridge History of Judaism 1984 *Vol. 1, Introduction: The Persian Period*, W. D. Davies and L. Finkelstein (eds.), Cambridge: Cambridge University Press.

CAMPBELL, J. and SHERRARD, P. 1968 *Modern Greece*. London: Ernest Benn.

CARRAS, C. 1983 *3,000 Years of Greek Identity—Myth or Reality?* Athens: Domus Books.

CHERNIAVSKY, M. 1975 'Russia', in Orest Ranum (ed.), *National Consciousness, History and Political Culture in Early-Modern Europe*. Baltimore and London: The Johns Hopkins University Press, pp. 118–43.

CITRON, S. 1988 *Le Mythe National*. Paris: Presses Ouvriers.

COHLER, A. 1970 *Rousseau and Nationalism*. New York: Basic Books.

COLLS, R. and DODD, P. (eds.) 1986 *Englishness, Politics and Culture*. London, Sydney, Dover, New Hampshire: Croom Helm.

CONNOR, W. 1972 'Nation-building or nation-destroying?' *World Politics*. vol. 24, pp. 319–55.

—— 1978 'A nation is a nation, is a state, is an ethnic group, is a . . .', *Ethnic and Racial Studies*. vol. 1, no. 4, pp. 378–400.

—— 1990 'When is a Nation?', *Ethnic and Racial Studies*. vol. 13, no. 1, pp. 92–103.

CORRIGAN, P. and SAYER, D. 1985 *The Great Arch: English State Formation as Cultural Revolution*. Oxford: Blackwell.

DANBY, H. (ed.) 1933/67 *The Mishnah*. Oxford: Oxford University Press.

DAVID, A. R. 1982 *The Ancient Egyptians: Beliefs and Practices*. London and Boston: Routledge and Kegan Paul.

DEUTSCH, K. 1966 *Nationalism and Social Communication*. 2nd ed., New York: MIT Press.

EDWARDS, J. 1985 *Language, Society and Identity*. Oxford: Blackwell.

ELLER, J. D. and COUGHLAN, REED M. 1993 'The poverty of primordialism: the demystification of ethnic attachments', *Ethnic and Racial Studies*, vol. 16, no. 2, pp. 18–202.

EMERSON, R. 1960 *From Empire to Nation*, Cambridge, MA: Harvard University Press.

FONDATION, H. 1962 *Grecs et Barbares, Entretiens sur l'Antiquité classique*, VIII, Geneva.

FRANKFORT, H. 1954 *The Birth of Civilisation in the Near East*. New York: Anchor Books.

FRANKFORT, H. *et al.* 1947 *Before Philosophy.* Harmondsworth: Penguin.

FRYE, R. 1966 *The Heritage of Persia.* New York: Mentor.

GEERTZ, C. 1963 'The integrative revolution', in C. Geertz (ed.): *Old Societies and New States.* New York: Free Press.

GELLNER, E. 1964 *Thought and Change,* Weidenfeld and Nicolson.

—— 1983 *Nations and Nationalism.* Oxford: Blackwell.

GEOFFREY OF MONMOUTH 1966 *The History of the Kings of Britain.* (trans. L. Thorpe), Harmondsworth: Penguin.

GLAZER, N. and MOYNIHAN, D. (eds.) 1975 *Ethnicity: Theory and Experience.* Cambridge, MA: Harvard University Press.

GROSBY, S. 1991 'Religion and nationality in antiquity', *European Journal of Sociology,* vol. XXXII, pp. 229–65.

HAUGEN, E. 1966 'Dialect, language, nation', *American Anthropologist.* vol. 68, no. 4, pp. 922–35.

HERTZ, F. 1944 *Nationality, in History and Politics.* London: Routledge & Kegan Paul.

HOBSBAWM, E. 1990 *Nations and Nationalism since 1780.* Cambridge: Cambridge University Press.

HOBSBAWM, E. and RANGER, T. (eds.) 1983 *The Invention of Tradition.* Cambridge: Cambridge University Press.

HORNE, D. 1984 *The Great Museum.* London and Sydney: Pluto Press.

HOWE, N. 1989 *Migration and Mythmaking in Anglo-Saxon England.* New Haven and London: Yale University Press.

HROCH, M. 1985 *The Social Preconditions of National Revival in Europe.* Cambridge: Cambridge University Press.

IM HOF, ULRICH 1991 *Mythos Schweiz: Identität—Nation—Geschichte, 1291–1991,* Zürich: Neue Zürcher Verlag.

JOHNSON, L. 1992 'Imagining communities', paper given to Conference on *Imagining Communities: Medieval and Modern.* Centre for Medieval Studies, University of Leeds, 23 May 1992.

KATZ, F. 1972 *The Ancient American Civilisations.* London: Weidenfeld and Nicolson.

KAUTSKY, J. H. (ed.) 1962 *Political Change in Underdeveloped Countries.* New York: John Wiley.

KEMILAINEN, A. 1964 *Nationalism, Problems Concerning the Word, Concept and Classification.* Yvaskyla: Kustantajat Publishers.

KOHN, H. 1940 'The origins of English nationalism', *Journal of the History of Ideas.* vol. 1, pp. 69–94.

—— 1957 *Nationalism and Liberty: The Swiss Example.* New York: Macmillan.

—— 1967 *Prelude to Nation-States: The French and German Experience, 1789–1815.* New York: Van Nostrand.

KOHT, H. 1947 'The dawn of nationalism in Europe', *American Historical Review.* vol. 52, pp. 265–80.

KREIS, G. 1991 *Der Mythos von 1291: Zur Entstehung des schweizerischen Nationalfeiertags.* Basel: Friedrich Reinhardt Verlag.

Levi, M. A. 1965 *Political Power in the Ancient World*. (trans. J. Costello), London: Weidenfeld and Nicolson.

MacDougall, H. A. 1982 *Racial Myth in English History: Trojans, Teutons and Anglo-Saxons*. Montreal: Harvest House, and Hanover, NH: University Press of New England.

Mason, R. A. 1985 'Scotching the Brut: the early history of Britain', *History Today*. vol. 35, (January), pp. 26–31.

Mendels, D. 1992 *The Rise and Fall of Jewish Nationalism*. New York: Doubleday.

Moscati, S. 1962 *The Face of the Ancient Orient*. New York: Anchor Books.

Nairn, T. 1977 *The Break-up of Britain*. London: New Left Books.

Nettl, P. and Robertson, Roland 1968 *International Systems and the Modernisation of Societies*. London: Faber.

Neusner, J. 1961 *Max Weber Revisited: Religion and Society in Ancient Judaism*. Oxford: Oxford Centre for Postgraduate Hebrew Studies.

Newman, G. 1987 *The Rise of English Nationalism: A Cultural History 1740–1830*. London: Weidenfeld and Nicolson.

Noth, M. 1960 *The History of Israel*. London: Adam and Charles Black.

Ogilvie, R. M. 1976 *Early Rome and the Etruscans*. London: Fontana Paperbacks.

Peel, J. 1989 'The cultural work of Yoruba ethnogenesis', in Elizabeth Tonkin, Maryon McDonald and Malcolm Chapman (eds.), pp. 198–215.

Pipes, R. 1977 *Russia under the Old Regime*. London: Peregrine Books.

Portal, R. 1969 *The Slavs: A Cultural Historical Survey of the Slavonic Peoples*. (trans. Patrick Evans), London: Weidenfeld and Nicolson.

Reynolds, S. 1983 'Medieval *Origines Gentium* and the community of the realm', *History*. vol. 68, pp. 375–90.

—— 1984 *Kingdoms and Communities in Western Europe, 900–1300*. Oxford: Clarendon.

Rosenblum, R. 1967 *Transformations in late Eighteenth Century Art*. Princeton, NJ: Princeton University Press.

Samuel, R. (ed.) 1989 *Patriotism, The Making and Unmaking of British National Identity*. London and New York: Routledge.

Seton-Watson, H. 1977 *Nations and States*. London: Methuen.

Shils, E. 1957 'Primordial, personal, sacred and civil ties', *British Journal of Sociology*. vol. 7, pp. 111–45.

Smith, A. D. 1973 'Nationalism, a trend report and annotated bibliography', *Current Sociology*. vol. 21, no. 3, The Hague: Mouton (ed.)

—— 1976 *Nationalist Movements*. London: Macmillan.

—— 1983 *Theories of Nationalism*. 2nd ed., London: Duckworth, and New York: Holmes and Meier.

—— 1984 'Ethnic myths and ethnic revivals', *European Journal of Sociology*. vol. 25, pp. 283–305.

—— 1986 *The Ethnic Origins of Nations*. Oxford: Blackwell.

—— 1988 'The myth of the "Modern Nation" and the myths of nations', *Ethnic and Racial Studies*. vol. 11, no. 1, pp. 1–26.

SMITH, A. D. 1991*a* *National Identity*. Harmondsworth: Penguin.

—— 1991*b* 'The nation: invented, imagined, reconstructed?', *Millennium, Journal of International Affairs*. vol. 20, no. 3, pp. 353–68.

SMITH, L. M. (ed.) 1984 *The Making of Britain: The Dark Ages*. London: Macmillan.

STACK, J. F. (ed.) 1986 *The Primordial Challenge: Ethnicity in the Contemporary World*. New York: Greenwood Press.

STEINBERG, J. 1976 *Why Switzerland?*. Cambridge: Cambridge University Press.

THÜRER, G. 1970 *Free and Swiss*. London: Oswald Wolff.

TILLY, C. (ed.) 1975 *The Formation of National States in Western Europe*. Princeton, NJ: Princeton University Press.

TIPTON, L. (ed.) 1972 *Nationalism in the Middle Ages*. New York: Holt, Rinehart and Winston.

TIVEY, L. (ed.) 1980 *The Nation-State*. Oxford: Martin Robertson.

TONKIN, E., McDONALD, M. and CHAPMAN, M. (eds.) 1989 *History and Ethnicity*. ASA Monographs 27, London and New York: Routledge.

TRIGGER, B. G., KEMP, B. J., O'CONNOR, D. and LLOYD, A. B. 1983 *Ancient Egypt, A Social History*. Cambridge: Cambridge University Press.

ULLENDORFF, E. 1973 *The Ethiopians, An Introduction to Country and People*. 3rd ed., London: Oxford University Press.

VAN DEN BERGHE, P. 1979 *The Ethnic Phenomenon*. New York: Elsevier.

WALEK-CZERNECKI, M. T. 1929 'Le role de la nationalité dans l'histoire de l'antiquité', *Bulletin of the International Committee of Historical Sciences*. vol. 11, no. 2, pp. 305–20.

WARBURTON, T. RENNIE 1976 'Nationalism and language in Switzerland and Canada', in A. D. Smith (ed.), *Nationalist Movements*. pp. 88–109.

WEBER, E. 1979 *Peasants into Frenchmen: The Modernisation of Rural France, 1870–1914*. London: Chatto and Windus.

WELCH, C. 1966 *Dreams of Unity: Pan-Africanism and Political Unification in West Africa*. Ithaca, NY: Cornell University Press.

WISEMAN, D. J. (ed.) 1973 *Peoples of the Old Testament*. Oxford: Clarendon Press.

ZERLIN, I. 1984 *Ancient Judaism*. Cambridge: Polity Press.

—— 1988 *Jesus and the Judaism of His Time*. Cambridge: Polity Press.

ZERNATTO, G. 1944 'Nation: the history of a word', *Review of Politics*. vol. 6, pp. 351–66.

l

4

Chosen Peoples: Why Ethnic Groups Survive*

ABSTRACT

The persistence of ethnic communities is a neglected area of research. The study of *ethnies* over long time-spans requires comparison of different patterns of ethnic survival, in terms of symbols and myths of ethnic election. Such myths can be found in the ancient Near East, in Judea, Greece, Armenia, Persia, as well as Byzantium, Russia and Western Europe, mobilizing and inspiring ethnic survival. Four main patterns of ethnic survival are outlined: imperial-dynastic, communal-demotic, emigrant-colonist and diaspora-restoration. In each case, modern nationalism reinforces and politicizes the old myths of ethnic election and its forms and intensity can be explained in terms of these patterns of ethnic survival.

Why do some ethnic groups survive, and others perish? What are the factors that help to sustain ethnic communities? How far do the many national conflicts that we witness today across the globe stem from the conditions of ethnic persistence?

I need hardly say how important such questions have become in the contemporary world. The last two decades have seen a surge of ethnic sentiments and movements, first in the West and latterly in Eastern Europe and the former Soviet Union. Several states in Africa—Chad, Sudan, Ethiopia, Angola, and South Africa—are wracked by ethnic dissension. In the Middle East and Asia, the frequency and intensity of ethnic conflicts have, if anything, increased in recent years: Druse, Kurds, Azeris, Armenians, Sikhs, Tamils, Tibetans, Uigurs, Achinese, and Moro are demanding autonomy, if not outright independence; while the larger conflicts of Indo-China, India and Pakistan, and Arabs and Israelis, show little sign of abating.

* Inaugural Lecture delivered at the London School of Economics and Political science on Thursday 25 April 1991. *Ethnic and Racial Studies* Volume 15, Number 3, July 1992.

Thus it is a matter of some urgency to seek a broader understanding of the roots of ethnic conflicts and nationalist movements that threaten the peace of the world. It would be easier, and more comforting, to view these conflicts as so many symptoms of modernization, secularization, the globalization of capitalism, or the birth-pangs of a general democratization of society. In these perspectives, ethnic movements and nationalism, like neo-traditionalism, feminism and the green movements, are seen as populist and non-rational reactions to the exponential advances of technology and communications, the great shifts in population and economic power, and the general bureaucratization of social life in the modern world: so many diversions and obstacles to the great march of history.[1]

Evolutionary perspectives like these, for all their lingering popularity, tend to be profoundly misleading, even dangerous. Many of the movements I have mentioned attract growing support, often from the educated classes in democratic states. All of them answer to deep-seated aspirations and needs in modern society. Above all, they draw their power from fundamental ethnic, gender, religious, and regional cleavages that modern economic and political processes often reinforce.

Here I shall concentrate on some of the underlying conditions of modern ethnic conflicts, which can, I believe, be traced to the different patterns of long-term ethnic survival across the globe. The study of ethnic survival is a subject that could absorb the labours of many scholars, singularly and together, over many years. Here I can only touch on some key issues in this vast field, with examples drawn mainly from Europe and the Middle East.

THE STUDY OF ETHNIC SURVIVAL

The terms 'ethnic' and 'ethnicity' have attracted wide-ranging debates and are used in a variety of ways. For my purposes, the study of ethnic survival, two levels of ethnicity and ethnic identity, individual and collective, must be distinguished. For the investigation of *long-term ethnic persistence*, individual sentiments and attitudes, though important, are secondary. The focus here is rather on the social and cultural properties of ethnic communities, that is, collective cultural units claiming common ancestry, shared memories and symbols, whether they constitute majorities or minorities in a given state.

For the same reason, we cannot confine our attention to rates of ethnic attrition at the level of the individual, or to processes of ethnic assimilation or resistance in modern *immigrant* societies, as much of the literature would suggest. We need to consider persistence and change in *all* ethnic communities, or *ethnies, over long time-spans*—what the Annales school termed the *longue durée*—and in many kinds of society, pre-modern as well as modern. At any rate, that is how I propose here to approach the phenomenon of ethnic survival.[2]

Such a study requires an initial working definition of the object of explanation. The term 'ethnic' is generally taken to refer to *cultural* rather than biological attributes, despite the recent revival of interest in kin selection and genetic inheritance as explanations of ethnic solidarity (Van den Berghe 1978; 1979). Be that as it may, it is with cultural units wider than the family that individuals identify when they belong to, and feel solidarity with, ethnic communities. Yet the family metaphor retains its importance. When people identify with *ethnies,* they feel a sense of wider kinship with a fictive 'super-family', one that extends outwards in space and down the generations in time (Horowitz 1985, ch. 2).

Ethnies also possess common codes and shared symbols and myths of common descent from a putative ancestor. These codes, symbols and myths and the associated historical memories of common past experiences, albeit selectively remembered, are the main features of collective cultural identities in most societies; and they serve to differentiate *ethnic* from other types of human group and social bond. Belonging to an ethnic community endows members with the sense of sharing in a vastly extended 'family' which claims descent from a single, usually heroic and glorious, ancestor.[3]

An *ethnie* is defined, however, not only by historical memories, codes and ancestry myths, but also by its possession, or loss, of an historic territory or 'homeland'. Over the generations, the community has become identified with a particular, historic space, and the territory with a particular cultural community. The homeland need not be the cradle of the community, but it must provide the terrain, the 'soil', for its 'creative genius' at some (suitably distant) epoch in its history. The Jews traced their origins to Ur and Harran in Mesopotamia, but realized themselves in the land of Canaan. The Turks traced their forebears to Oguz Khan in the steppes of Central Asia, but their cultures flourished in Anatolia and northwest Iran, after the conquest of the Seljuqs from the eleventh century A. D. (B. Lewis 1968, ch. 10; Kushner 1976).

We can now define an ethnic community, or *ethnie,* as a *named human group claiming a homeland and sharing myths of common ancestry, historical memories and a distinct culture.* In addition, we should normally expect an ethnic community, or segments thereof, to express sentiments of solidarity, even if only the urban classes share in the ethnic culture.[4]

'Ethnic survival', in turn, would entail the persistence over several generations of each of the attributes of ethnic communities: a collective name, a homeland, myths of common ancestry and the like. This is a fairly stringent definition of ethnic survival. It means that we cannot speak of communities like the Greeks, Chinese and Japanese surviving, simply because they may have retained their names and homelands for over two millennia. They would also have had to retain their memories, symbols, traditions and culture—everything, in fact, that made them distinctive. Given the massive changes undergone by most societies, and the vast time-spans involved, this criterion would effectively rule out most *ethnies,* quite apart from the practical problems of furnishing adequate evidence of survival in periods where records are meagre (see Armstrong 1982; Smith 1984*b*).

For these reasons I shall adopt a less severe test of ethnic survival. Ethnic communities can reasonably be said to have survived in something like their earlier forms, if *successive generations continue to identify with some persisting memories, symbols, myths and traditions.* In other words, ethnic survival does not require the retention of one's culture, intact; nor of one's homeland, as the Armenian and Jewish examples demonstrate; nor even of one's former religion, as the introduction of Buddhism in Japan or the Islamization of Iran suggests, *provided that* the new religion enshrines the ancient symbols, memories and myths, or at least some of them—which is what happened in Iran during the New Persian literary renaissance of the tenth and eleventh centuries A.D. (Frye 1966, ch. 6; Cambridge History of Iran 1975, IV, chs. 1, 19).

If the problem of conceptualizing 'ethnic survival' is complex, that of explaining how and why some *ethnies* survived while others were absorbed or dissolved is still more baffling. In theory, we should be able to attempt some kind of multivariate analysis of the conditions and rates of ethnic survival or dissolution, assuming always that we had clear measures of such survival. However, in practice the historical evidence is often too scanty, and the number of possible factors involved is too great, to make this a feasible project. Ethnic survival depends on a whole range of conditions from the demographic and economic to the cultural and political; while on the other side, well-documented cases of long-term ethnic survival are few. This means that we can expect only limited and uncertain results from a large outlay of time and effort. Perhaps we may be able to isolate a few very general conditions of ethnic persistence, such as the effects of organized warfare or religion. However, for such insights we hardly require statistical techniques (see Armstrong 1982, ch. 9; Smith 1988).

Perhaps this is why the historical and anthropological case-study approach has proved so attractive. Detailed studies like Braudel's of some of the conditions of French identity, Richard Frye's analyses of ancient and medieval Persia, and Salo Baron's social and religious history of the Jews, make us vividly aware of the many special circumstances that ensure or disrupt ethnic continuity. They also reveal the diverse elements that go into the making of French, Persian, Jewish, or whatever, ethnic identity over the *longue durée* (Baron 1952–76; Frye 1975; Braudel 1989).

Few of these case studies, however, directly address issues of ethnic survival. These have to be inferred from the narrative of events or from discussions of quite different issues. Nor does the analysis of a single case, however illuminating, allow one to control for particular factors or isolate those elements crucial to ethnic survival from surrounding circumstances. Only *comparisons* of different patterns of ethnic survival, on the basis of some hypotheses, can enable us to grasp some of the necessary conditions that facilitate long-term ethnic survival. It is to comparisons on the basis of one such hypothesis that I now turn.[5]

MYTHS OF ETHNIC ELECTION

It is worth recalling first the very different factors and hypotheses from which a comparative analysis of the patterns of ethnic survival can depart. The ones usually highlighted are political in nature: the degree of a community's autonomy, its political will to survive; and its leadership qualities. Sometimes analysis will focus on economic and ecological variables; the possession of specific homelands, their location, extent and population, and the presence of various material resources, facilities and skills for the support of a community. Yet another set of hypotheses treats *ethnies* as networks of communication, and seeks to ascertain how customs, language and other symbolic codes bind the members of communities together over generations (see Deutsch 1966; Krejci and Velimsky 1981).

Each of these approaches, and the hypotheses that derive from them, can make valuable contributions to the study of ethnic survival, and they merit further intensive comparative investigations. It is worth remembering, however, that ethnic communities can, and have, survived over long periods without political autonomy, without a homeland of their own, even without a common language—as the linguistic divisions in Switzerland remind us—though this is rare. In such cases, other social and psychological factors appear to compensate for these absences.

This suggests that we need to pay more attention to the subjective elements in ethnic survival, such as ethnic memories, values, symbols, myths, and traditions. The reason is that long-term ethnic survival depends, in the first place, on the active cultivation by specialists and others of a heightened sense of collective distinctiveness and mission. The members of an ethnic community must be made to feel, not only that they form a single 'super-family', but that their historic community is unique, that they possess what Max Weber called 'irreplaceable culture values', that their heritage must be preserved against inner corruption and external control, and that the community has a sacred duty to extend its culture values to outsiders. Persians, Armenians, Poles, Russians, Chinese, Koreans, Japanese, Americans, Irish, English, and French, to name but a few, have all cultivated this sense of uniqueness and mission by nurturing ethnic values and traditions, through myths of distant origins and symbols and memories of a golden age of former glory.[6]

We can go further. Myths of common ancestry and memories of a golden age may unite and inspire the members of an ethnic community over several generations. Yet what is even more important for ethnic survival is to cultivate a *myth of ethnic election*. Those communities that managed to formulate and cultivate such a belief have succeeded in prolonging the specific collective life of their members over many generations. The creation and dissemination by specialists of the belief that 'we are a "chosen people"' has been crucial for ensuring long-term ethnic survival.

A myth of ethnic election should not be equated with plain ethnocentrism. Ethnic communities have quite commonly regarded themselves as the moral centre of the universe and as far as possible affected to ignore or despise those around them. A myth of ethnic election is more demanding. To be chosen is to be placed under moral obligations. One is chosen on condition that one observes certain moral, ritual, and legal codes, and only for as long as one continues to do so. The privilege of election is accorded only to those who are sanctified, whose life-style is an expression of sacred values. The benefits of election are reserved for those who fulfil the required observances. The classical expression of such beliefs among the ancient Israelites is to be found in the book of Exodus (ch. 19):

Now therefore if ye will obey my voice indeed and keep my covenant, then shall ye be a peculiar treasure unto me from all peoples; for all the earth is mine; and ye shall be unto me a kingdom of priests and an holy nation (Exodus 19: 5–6; cf. Deuteronomy 7: 13 and 10: 12–22).

The covenant here refers to a code of morality, law, and ritual, set out in detail in the book of Deuteronomy, which the Israelites must observe if they are to remain chosen and redeemed by God. Only by keeping these laws and ceremonies can the community and its members be saved.[7]

ELECTION MYTHS IN THE MIDDLE EAST AND EUROPE

Even in antiquity, the Jews were by no means the only people to have believed that they were 'chosen'. Intimations of such ideas can be found over a millennium earlier in ancient Egypt and Mesopotamia. In the lands of Sumer and Akkad, (now southern Iraq), the scattered city-states, while prizing their independence, acknowledged their ethnic kinship, particularly in times of crisis. The kings of one or other of the city-states united the Sumerians periodically, while worship of Enlil, chief god of the Sumerian pantheon, at his shrine in Nippur, acted as a religious focus for the Sumerian city-states. During the Sumerian revival under the Third Dynasty of Ur in the late third millennium BC, a greater sense of common ethnicity found expression in nostalgia for an earlier Sumerian golden age. Yet the sense of ethnic election was muted and indirect. It was vested in the king, as Enlil's representative on earth, and it was through kingship that any covenant between the gods and the community was mediated (Kramer 1963, ch. 7; Roux 1964, ch. 10).

Ethnocentrism was more marked in ancient Egypt. The land of Ptah was compact, united and more homogeneous than the lands of Sumer and Akkad. There was greater emphasis on divine election of the 'god-king', notably in the political propaganda of New Kingdom Pharaohs like Tuthmosis III, Hatshepsut and Horemhab.[8] There was correspondingly less stress on the community's election, with or without moral conditions. At the same time, the characteristic Egyptian sense of cultural superiority to aliens, those who lived outside 'the land' (of Egypt), was accentuated after the Theban Pharaohs had driven out the Asiatic Hyksos dynasty in the sixteenth century B.C. Once again, however, the sense of election rose and fell with the monarchy and the state, though it lingered on into Hellenistic and Roman epochs.[9]

We cannot be sure, but a clear-cut theology of communal election in the ancient world seems to have originated in ancient Israel, though the forms of that relationship owed much to Near Eastern, especially Hittite, models. The central Israelite belief was that the sole God, the Lord of the universe, is working out His purpose for all His creatures, and has chosen a particular people to bring salvation to humanity. God's favour, however, is conditional on the fulfilment by the chosen of detailed moral and ritual codes. 'You only have I known of all the families of the earth; therefore

I will punish you for all your iniquities'. Amos's prophetic judgement is unequivocal.[10] Later prophets, responding to the social and geopolitical position of Israel, hemmed in between Egypt and Asyria, elaborated on the moral dimensions of divine election. God's promise to Abraham that 'in thee shall all the families of the earth be blessed' is transformed by the Second Isaiah into the belief that Israel, the suffering servant, is chastised in order to bring salvation to all peoples. God uses Israel's enemies, the Assyrians and Babylonians, to redeem a purified Israel and thereby the world; while the Exodus from Egypt and the Covenant at Sinai are part of God's redemptive plan for humanity as a whole.[11]

Such a conception imposes a heavy burden on the chosen. They are continually required to live up to strict moral standards. Backslidings are liable to severe punishment. This affords great scope for prophets, judges, sages and other moral crusaders to warn their kinsmen and thereby periodically to reaffirm the distinctive qualities and unique destiny of the community. Later, this close relationship with God, with its inescapable moral demands on the community, became the social and psychological mainspring of Jewish survival in their long diaspora.[12]

Ideas of ethnic election, dynastic and communal, can be found among several other peoples of the ancient Near East. Here I can only mention a few. Among the Persians, the belief in ethnic chosenness has surfaced in various guises during their long history. The great Achaemenid kings, Cyrus and Darius, inherited the idea of the monarch's divine election from earlier empires and reserved for themselves the characteristic virtues of the Medes and Persians: truth, order and justice. Cyrus records how he 'constantly sought after order and equity for the black-headed people [of Babylon]' whom Marduk made him conquer; while Darius's rock inscriptions at Behistun emphasize the wisdom of living according to the precepts of the great Persian god, Ahura-Mazda, and dwell on the special mission of a Persian king to his many subjects (Dentan 1983: 86, 89–94).

Such themes were taken up much later by the Sassanid Persian rulers of Iran. The Zoroastrian temple religion was encouraged, and in the sixth century A.D. Chosroes I instigated a revival of old Persian symbols, myths and rituals. To this period, too, we can trace the origins of the *Book of Lords*, which recorded the exploits of the great Persian aristocratic families, chosen warriors defending Iran against the land of Tur'an. Though the Zoroastrian state religion ultimately failed to mould the Persians into a moral community, it did help to instil a sense of unique identity and destiny, which laid the basis for the New Persian cultural renaissance (Frye 1966: 239–61; Cambridge History of Iran 1983, 111/1, ch. 3B).

Much later, under the Safavid dynasty in the sixteenth century, the adoption of Islamic Shi'ite beliefs gave a new moral dimension to Persian identity. The present century has seen a fervent renewal of Shi'ite national-religious community and missionary destiny—in contrast to the abortive attempts of the Pahlavis to recreate ancient Aryan imperial traditions (Avery 1965; Keddie 1981, chs. 1–3).

Further west, a powerful myth of election emerged in the mountain kingdom of Armenia after its conversion to Orthodox Christianity by St. Gregory in A.D. 301. The Romans and Byzantines contended for several centuries with the Persian Sassanid monarchs for control of Armenia, which finally lost its chance of independence after the disastrous battle of Avarayr in A.D. 451, despite a brief revival under the Bagratids in the ninth century. In this respect, Armenia resembled the Judean kingdoms, from which its rulers and nobles claimed descent. Both stood at the strategic crossroads of warring empires, and both peoples were spurred by political adversity to form a moral community and reinterpret their historical destinies in spiritual terms. The growing theological rift with Byzantine Orthodoxy, especially after the Council of Dvin (A.D. 554), and Armenian pride in being the 'first Christian nation', cemented their belief in ethnic election and divine mission, a belief that the Armenian clergy nurtured throughout the Armenian diaspora.[13]

Yet another Christian realm whose legitimacy rested on a dynastic myth of election was the Ethiopian kingdom of Aksum and its successors. The Aksumite kings may have adopted their Monophysite form of Christianity in the fourth century from Coptic sources, but it retained many Judaic features, brought perhaps from the southern Arab kingdoms. Successive Ethiopian kingdoms on the Abyssinian plateau derived their legitimacy from the symbolism of the Lion of Judah and the claim to royal descent from Solomon and the Queen of Sheba through Menelik. In the so-called 'Solomonic' dynasty from the thirteenth century, the ruling Christian Amhara nobles began to participate in this royal myth of election, which inspired a cultural revival and mobilized the community for resistance to Muslim invaders and the Falashas.[14]

We need not dwell at length on the powerful myths of election that have surfaced periodically among the Arabs and their kingdoms, notably during the Islamic conquests and in the period of the Crusades. The fact that Islam, like Christianity, is a world-religion, has not prevented the emergence of narrower ethnic myths within its domain. In some ways, Islamic allegiance has added a crusading fervour. Particularly among the Arabs, it has stimulated a pride in their language, culture and achievements and a sense of election and collective destiny that continue to exert a power-ful influence on Middle Eastern politics to this day.[15]

Myths of election also helped to sustain ethnic communities in Europe. The ancient Greek encounter with the Persian empire had produced a height-ened ethnocentrism, a sense of moral and cultural superiority to the sur-rounding 'barbarians', even a pan-Hellenic ideology—though, unlike the foundation myths of the Romans, it never succeeded in uniting the Greek city-states into a moral or political community. Only after the adoption of Orthodox Christianity in the Roman East, did Hellenism gradually acquire a moral dimension. The Byzantine Christian ideal was essentially dynas-tic and universal; yet it slowly became centred on the Greek-speaking inhab-itants of an empire which by the ninth century had lost its western and eastern provinces, and which came to adopt Greek as its language of state in place of Latin and foster a classical Greek revival (Baynes and Moss 1969, ch. 1.). Much later, especially after the Crusader sack of Constantinople in A.D. 1204, a defensive Byzantine Hellenic population became even more convinced of its elective status and imperial mission—as if the destiny of the world hung on the correct liturgical observance of the only true Christian doctrine in the only genuine Christian empire (Sherrard 1959; Armstrong 1982: 178–81).

When that empire was at last extinguished in A.D. 1453, the same dream found a home further north and fed the burgeoning imperial ambitions of the Muscovite Russian state. The realm of the Russian Tsars became the sole bastion of Orthodoxy in an heretical world, the Third Rome, proclaimed by the Orthodox Russian clergy in the early sixteenth century. In the words of one of their leaders, Joseph of Volokolamsk monastery: 'In piety, the Russian land now surpasses all others'. From Ivan the Terrible on, the Tsar was elevated into a redeemer-figure, a 'father' to his chosen people in holy 'mother Russia'. By the nineteenth century, Slavophiles came to regard the Russian peasant community as the repository of truth, purity and wisdom—a religious conception that fed Tolstoyan and populist ideals and one that persists to this day in the writings of some neo-Russian nationalists.[16]

Similar myths can be found further west. They emerged, for example, in the Frankish kingdom in the eighth century, which the reigning Pope Paul likened to a 'new kingdom of David', occupying a place like that of the people of Israel. Similar language was used much later by Pope Boniface at the end of the thirteenth century, when he stated that '. . . the kingdom of France is a peculiar people chosen by the Lord to carry out the orders of heaven'—a status and mission that Joan of Arc, and many French leaders after her, have fought to retain and execute.[17]

Similar beliefs could be found in contemporary Scotland, in the language of the Declaration of Arbroath of 1320, in the growing sense of Swiss Confederation from 1291, among the defeated Welsh and Irish, in Hussite Bohemia, in Elizabethan England, in Calvinist Holland and, across the ocean, in the American colonies and Catholic Mexico.[18]

In all these instances, myths of ethnic election have helped to mobilize communities and ensure their survival over long periods. Because the ethnic myth is a dramatic tale that links the present with a communal past, and one that is widely believed, it helps to draw the members into a distinctive community, conferring on them a special aura, that of 'the elect'. Through its symbolism, it strives to unify different classes and regions, spreading ethnic culture outwards from the urban centres and the specialist strata, who guard the traditions, thereby creating a more participant society (Kirk 1973; cf. Tudor 1972 and Thompson 1985).

Myths of ethnic election may also strengthen a community's attachment to its historic territory. By regarding the homeland as God-given, it ties the elect to a particular terrain. Only the sacred land and the sanctified soil are fit for the elect, and they can only be redeemed in the land where their fathers and mothers lived, their heroes fought and their saints prayed. To be worthy of forefathers who laid down their lives in these holy mountains and by the banks of these sacred rivers, must we not return to the ancient virtues and forsaken ways? The Swiss, who recall the heroism of Sempach and Morgarten, who extol the shining purity of the Jungfrau, who to this day re-enact the drama of William Tell, have they not converted an egalitarian myth of chosenness into the basis of their state and society, the condition of their continued freedom and prosperity? (Kohn 1957; Thürer 1970).

Finally, myths of ethnic election can incite a community to expansion and war. The conviction of possessing the only true faith, and a higher morality and civilization, has inspired and justified many a missionary movement and imperialist drive to those who 'live in darkness'—be it medieval Armenians seeking converts in the Caucasus, Arabs engaged in righteous *jihad*, or Western nations imposing white 'civilization' on Asians and Africans.[19]

PATTERNS OF ETHNIC SURVIVAL

In pre-modern eras, myths of ethnic chosenness spread to most areas of the world: to the Americas, Southern Asia, the Far East and Africa, as well as to Europe and the Middle East. Yet the belief in ethnic election has operated in different ways. Here I shall briefly distinguish four patterns of ethnic persistence and four ways in which myths of election help to sustain ethnic communities.

1. I call the first pattern *imperial-dynastic.* The myth of election is attached to the ruling house and dynasty, from which the community tends to take its main symbols and culture, and with which it is always associated. Thus, the Norman myths, within Normandy, were elaborated by clerics and chroniclers around the exploits of the ruling dukes from Rollo in A.D. 913 onwards. The chroniclers assumed that the Norman community shared in the special status and glory of its ruling house as a *regnum*, a kingdom of common customs and descent (Davis 1976; cf. Reynolds 1984, ch. 8).

This conjunction of dynasty, land and people was repeated on a grander scale in the later Western kingdoms of France, England and Spain. In all three, myths of election centred on the ruling house, with coronation and anointing ceremonies underlining the semi-divine status of the monarch. Over the centuries the kingdom and its people came to share in this elective status, as John of Gaunt's eulogy of England, 'This other Eden, demi-paradise', reminds us; until the point where the people themselves become the elect as citizens of a modern nation.[20] Poland illustrates clearly this process of transfer. In the medieval and Renaissance periods, the Polish myth of election was attached to the kingdom and its Catholic rulers. With the decline of the dynasty and the dissolution of the state in the late-eighteenth century, the people gradually became the focus of collective redemption. Sections of the nineteenth-century Polish intelligentsia, notably the great poet Adam Mickiewicz, interpreted Poland's role as that of a 'suffering Christ' among the nations, soon to rise again— while the Polish Catholic Church remained sufficiently close to the people to furnish an ethnic resource into this century. So, Poland avoided the fate of those aristocratic *ethnies*, where royal defeat and destruction of the state entailed the demise of the community itself, as occurred in Burgundy or ancient Assyria; instead, Poland was transformed after 1918 into a citizen-nation (Halecki 1955; Davies 1982).

2. A second pattern of ethnic survival, the *communal-demotic*, attaches the myth directly to the people in their sacred land. In these cases the community has usually been conquered and is struggling to preserve its former rights and way of life, claiming that its members are the original inhabitants and their culture is the vernacular. That was the claim of Celtic communities in Wales and Ireland. The Welsh myth of election pictured the community as the lost tribes of Israel, a latterday chosen people, whose

original form of Christianity had been transplanted to ancient Britain by Joseph of Aramathea. Together with the Welsh language, folk poetry and the medieval bardic contests, these beliefs helped to nurture a sense of unique Welsh identity, especially after the English conquest and the incorporation of Wales.[21]

Ireland exhibited a similar mixture of pagan and Christian motifs in its election myths. The Irish 'golden age' was variously located in the pagan Celtic era of the High Kings of Tara, and the heroes of the Ulster cycle of ancient sagas; or in the great epoch of Irish monastic learning, art and missionary activity after St. Patrick's conversion of Ireland in the fifth century. The latter period, especially, furnished rich materials for later Irish myths of election, as literary scholars, archaeologists and poets in the eighteenth and nineteenth centuries envisaged the national restoration of an original Irish community in its *insula sacra*, its sacred island home (Sheehy 1980; Hutchinson 1987).

3. The third pattern is that of the *emigrant-colonist*. Again the myth is attached to the people; but this time to a people on the move. They have left or fled their old homelands and are bent on building new communities in new homelands, often with little regard for the indigenous inhabitants. The elect are the immigrants and their descendants. Theirs is a settler community and mission. They carry with them their values, memories and traditions, regarding themselves as chosen by God for a providential destiny that will abolish the old order and inaugurate a new society.

The prototype here is the biblical exodus of the children of Israel from Egypt across the Red Sea. It has served as a model of their destiny for Anglo-Saxon tribes crossing the Channel into Britain, after the Roman legions had been withdrawn, the land of milk and honey being replaced by England's green and pleasant land (Howe 1989). Many centuries later another crossing, this time of an ocean by the Pilgrim Fathers fleeing religious oppression, became part of the foundation charter of the new American homeland, with its promise of freedom in a new Jerusalem.[22]

4. A final pattern, that of *diaspora-restoration*, also attached the myth of election to a community on the move; only this time it was to one moving in a reverse direction, back to the old homeland. The return of the community to its ancestral home from which it had been exiled became the precondition of collective redemption. Zionism is the classic instance, with its secular fulfilment of ancient Jewish religious aspirations. Yet we meet the same pattern among Armenians yearning to return to Mount Ararat, among eighteenth-century diaspora Greeks longing for a

restoration of Hellas, among Liberians, and other Black Americans intent on returning to Africa, and latterly among some communities deported by Stalin to distant parts of the Soviet Union. In each of these cases, as the great Greek educator, Adamantios Korais, so clearly realized, the restoration of a diaspora to its ancestral home involved not merely the physical return of a people, but also its spiritual regeneration through education and political mobilization.[23]

These four patterns of ethnic persistence and renewal do not pretend to be exhaustive. However, they reveal the importance of beliefs in chosenness for ethnic survival. They also show the different ways in which such beliefs operate. Sometimes they fuel expansion, sometimes popular revolt, at still other times mass migration and movements of restoration. They also expose the community to different risks: the ossification of the ethnic community through overdependence on the state, popular instability and extremism, dissipation of communal energy through schism or assimilation. These dangers are familiar to ethnic leaders. In each generation priests, scribes, prophets, bards, mandarins, even nobles, have warned the people of these dangers, and by prescribing remedies for communal ills have actively cultivated the sense of ethnic identity and destiny.

Each of these patterns also reveals certain key factors in ethnic survival. *Warfare* and a warrior ethos are generally prominent in the dynastic-imperial pattern. The elect consist of righteous warriors under their redeemer-princes and faithful caliphs, and ethnic chosenness is borne on the spears and shields of missionary knights such as the Hungarian or Catalan nobility. As with the battles of the ancient Israelites against the Philistines, memories of victory and defeat became incorporated into the sacred history of a chosen people and its warrior-deity.[24]

Popular revolt stands at the heart of the communal-demotic pattern. Theirs is no simple fate of passive endurance, but rather the ideal of a purified people, mobilized in defence of its heritage. Vernacular mobilization is the *leitmotif* of survival among Irish and Basques, Czechs and Georgians, Kurds and Sikhs, and many more communities that have drawn on their native languages, traditions, symbols and memories for comfort and inspiration (Anderson 1983, ch. 5; cf. Pech 1976; Smith 1989).

Wandering has become the dominant theme of both emigrant and diaspora patterns. For the first, it is a migration to the promised land, with a providential destiny that excludes indigenous peoples and slaves. For the diaspora type, long exile evokes a fervent nostalgia, an ardent desire to recover an original home exclusive to the chosen community.[25]

FROM ETHNIC SURVIVAL TO NATIONAL LIBERATION

Even such a brief survey as this reveals how widespread has been the sense
of ethnic identity as a source of social and political solidarity throughout
recorded history. Particular ethnic communities may have formed and
dissolved over the centuries, but ethnicity has been a recurrent feature of
culture and social organization in every continent in pre-modern epochs.
So, how have ethnic communities fared in the modern world, and what
role do myths of ethnic election play today?

It is tempting to think that, in a secular era of rationality and materi-
alism, such myths, like ethnicity itself, are outmoded and irrelevant. Such
a view would be misleading and singularly myopic. Not only does traditional religion continue to play a major part in the lives of many people
in the contemporary world; ethnic attachments remain as potent today as
at any period in the past, and are, if anything, becoming more widespread
and intense.

Yet what of the earlier myths of chosenness? Are they not now at best
instruments of mobilization, cynical political devices by which a Nasser
or Nkrumah, a Gandhi or de Gaulle, can manipulate mass emotions for
partisan political ends? There lies the rub. It is no accident that the names
of these charismatic figures conjure up images of nationalism in their respective countries. For in the language and symbolism of modern nationalism we find the contemporary equivalent of the old beliefs in ethnic election.

Nationalism may be defined as a *doctrine of autonomy, unity and identity for a group whose members conceive it to be an actual or potential nation*.
Through its symbols and ceremonies, it legitimates the unique cultures
and diverse experiences of each ethnic community and makes them the
measure of political life. For nationalists, the nation is a *body of citizens
bound by shared memories and a common culture, occupying a compact territory with a unified economy and identical rights and duties*. In nationalist mythology, each nation has a distinctive past and unique destiny,
answering to its 'true nature'. The patriot's sacred duty is to recover the
nation's authentic past and repossess its homeland. That is the only way
to rediscover 'our' inner freedoms and realize our 'true selves' (Smith
1971/83, ch. 7; 1973; Connor 1978).

The twofold influence of Rousseau and Herder, the return to untram-
melled nature and the rediscovery of authentic history, is evident here. So
too is the continuity with pre-modern myths of ethnic election. Nationalism has secularized and universalized the old religious beliefs in chosen
peoples. Thus, in olden times, the Hellenic community was chosen by God

as the vessel and vehicle of true Christian Orthodoxy under its priest-king in Constantinople. Today the Greeks can see themselves as a beacon of liberty and reason, the *fons et origo* of Western civilization, and the original home of democracy. That is why their unique culture values have to be preserved, and why the language and culture of Sophocles and Plato must be cultivated in the hearts and minds of successive generations of Greeks.[26]

Myths of ethnic chosenness not only underpin peoples and cultures; they also provide charters and title-deeds of sacred homelands. So, where there is more than one title-deed to the same territory, the probability of ethnic conflicts and nationalist wars is greatly increased. The closer the association between unique people and historic homeland, the more exclusive becomes the nationalism of embattled communities, whether in the Balkans or the Middle East, India or the Caucasus. Economic grievances and state interference may exacerbate such antagonisms, but the roots of conflict must be sought in the underlying patterns of long-term ethnic survival in particular areas and in their sustaining myths of election. If all are chosen, what chance compromise, what price peace? Even a cursory glance at the modern world reveals the continuing power of these ethnic beliefs. Imperial national states were fortified in their sense of invincible superiority by modern nationalism, and we were soon treated to the unedifying spectacle of national imperialisms claiming the right to civilize so-called 'primitive peoples'. For the many subordinated popular *ethnies*, nationalism has offered a political panacea. From the Bretons and Finns to the Kurds and Somalis, it has sought to revitalize their myths, politicize their vernacular cultures, mobilize their peoples and turn them into political actors. Even in immigrant and diaspora societies, nationalism has reinforced old myths of chosenness and given them new political meanings (Smith 1991, ch. 6).

CONCLUSION

In this way nationalism, though a modern and initially secular ideology, has breathed new life into ancient myths and old beliefs. It has strengthened existing myths of ethnic chosenness and kindled new ones wherever ethnic groups have begun to crystallize and demand recognition. We do not have to look to the consequences of industrialization, the inequalities of capitalism or the cold oppression of bureaucracy, nor even to the hopes of democracy, important though these may often be, to explain why ethnic antagonisms are so intense and nationalist conflicts so frequent.

Whether in Spain or Sri Lanka, the Horn of Africa or the Caucasus, the Baltic states or Kurdistan, the forms and intensity of these struggles derive in large part from the history of ethnic relations in each of these areas, and from the underlying patterns of ethnic survival and belief that I have attempted to trace.

To grasp the forms and intensity of these conflicts, we need knowledge and understanding of each community's *ethno-history*, the shared memories and beliefs of the members of particular *ethnies*, and of the cultural activity of the community's intelligentsia. Most of all, we need to explore the continuing impact of ethnic myths, symbols and traditions in popular consciousness, and the way they continue to condition attitudes and behaviour to immigrants, minorities and outsiders, even in the most apparently rationalist and pragmatic societies.

The study of ethnic survival and its beliefs is a vast and relatively virgin terrain for research. I have only touched on one corner of this terrain, and have explored briefly only one of several necessary conditions of ethnic survival. Research in this field is essential if we are to begin to understand, and so perhaps to ameliorate, the many social and political problems in this area. For to imagine that we can address such deep-rooted problems by often *ad hoc* economic or political means is to ignore at our peril the underlying conditions of such conflicts.

By the same token, to imagine that nationalism's day is drawing to its end is to close our eyes to the continuing impact of older ethnic structures and beliefs, which modern nationalism has revitalized and which contemporary global forces are actually spreading and recycling (Hobsbawm 1990, ch. 6; cf. Smith 1990).

Since the roots of modern nations and nationalism lie so deep in the history of chosen peoples, it is premature to invoke the owl of Minerva, even in the West. When the prospect of European unification is invoked to suggest the imminent supersession of nationalism, we should recall the tale of Samson, whose strength ebbed when his hair was shorn, only to return in greater force when it grew again. Let us hope that we shall show more understanding and greater foresight than the Philistines.

Notes

1. For an attempt to locate several of these movements in an action and meaning frame of reference in the Western world, see Melucci (1989).

2. For an original analysis of the large literature on the chances of ethnic survival of immigrant white ethnics in the United States, see Gans (1979).
3. For the importance of ancestry myths, see Schermerhorn (1970). For the difficulties of delimiting *ethnies* from other collective identities such as religion and class, see Armstrong (1982), to whose pioneering work in this field I am much indebted.
4. For a fuller discussion of the features of *ethnies,* see Smith (1986, ch. 2); for the term *ethnies,* see Heraud (1963).
5. I know of no attempt to address this issue in *comparative* terms, except Armstrong (1982). For some comparative analyses of 'nation-formation', see Bendix (1964), Deutsch (1966), and Seton-Watson (1977).
6. For Weber's phrase, see Weber (1978, III, ch. 3, p. 926). For the Swiss case, see Steinberg (1976). For a discussion of myths of the 'golden age', see Smith (1984a).
7. This is the burden of the priestly book of Deuteronomy, especially chapter 30; see Seltzer (1980, I, ch. 2).
8. On this royal propaganda, see Van Seters (1983, ch. 5, esp. pp. 172–81), who quotes Hatshepsut's cliff temple inscription in Middle Egypt: 'I have raised up that which had gone to pieces formerly, since the Asiatics were in the midst of Avaris in the Northland. They ruled without Re . . .' (p. 174).
9. For the expulsion of the Hyksos from Egypt c. 1580 B.C., see Trigger *et al.* (1983, pp. 149–60; 173–4). For a comparison with Mesopotamian conceptions of divine kingship, see Frankfort (1948, pp. 5–12; 299–312).
10. Amos 3:2; but cf. the more 'universalistic' outlook at Amos 9:7, which likens Israel to the Ethiopians, Philistines and Syrians in God's eyes; cf. also Hosea 11:1, for the idea of Israel as God's child.
11. See, for example, Isaiah 41:8–10; 43:1–21; 49:14–18; also Jeremiah 2:1–3; 4:1–4; and 31 *passim;* Hosea 11:13–14. See on this Zeitlin (1984, chs. 7–8).
12. See the classic study of Jewish messianism by Klausner (1956); cf. R. J. Werblowski: 'Messianism in Jewish history', in Ben-Sasson and Ettinger (1971, pp. 30–45), and Yerushalmi (1983).
13. For the early history of Christian Armenia, see Lang (1980, chs. 7–8); for the Jewish links, see Armstrong (1982, ch. 7). For the evolution of Armenian Christianity, see Atiya (1968, pp. 315–28).
14. On the Solomonic tradition in the *Kebra Nagast* ('Glory of the Kings'), the Ethiopian national epic, see Edward Ullendorff: 'The Queen of Sheba in Ethiopian tradition', in James B. Pritchard (1974; pp. 104–14); and cf. Ullendorff (1968) for more details, and Kessler (1985) for the Falashas and Jewish elements in Ethiopian Christianity.
15. On these Arab dimensions of Islam, see Carmichael (1967) and B. Lewis (1970). For the modern period, see Sharabi (1970); for medieval Islamic identities, see Armstrong (1982, ch. 3).
16. For the medieval Russian beliefs, see M. Cherniavsky: 'Russia', in Ranum (1975; pp. 18–43), and Pipes (1977, ch. 9). For nineteenth-century Slavophile ideals, see Thaden (1964); for recent neo-Russian expressions among the Orthodox

and the nationalists, including *Pamyat* and *Veche,* see Dimitry Pospielovsky: 'The "Russian Orientation" and the Orthodox Church: from the early Slavophiles to the "Neo-Slavophiles" in the USSR', in Ramet (1989, pp. 81–108).

17. See Armstrong (1982, pp. 152–9) and Bloch (1961, II, pp. 431–7). For St. Joan, see Warner (1983). For a recent critical analysis of French myths of election, in Third Republic (and later) history texts, see Citron (1988).

18. For the text and background of the Declaration of Arbroath, see Duncan (1970); for the Swiss beliefs, see Kohn (1957). For a more general discussion, see Smith (1984a).

19. For a clear example of western cultural imperialism, that of the French in West Africa, see Lewis (1965). For a similar, if more aloof, imperialism in China, see Dikötter (1990).

20. For French myths of dynastic election, see Kantorowicz (1951) and Armstrong (1982, pp. 152–9). For English-British myths, see Kohn (1940), MacDougall (1982) and Mason (1985).

21. For Welsh myths, see Williams (1985) and P. Morgan: 'From a death to a view: the hunt for the Welsh past in the romantic period', in Hobsbawm and Ranger (1983).

22. See Tuveson (1968) and O'Brien (1988) for American puritan providentialism. We meet the same sentiments in early settlement Australia, which 'is truly a land flowing with milk and honey', according to Barron Field's *Geographical Memoirs* of 1825 (cited in Smith 1960, p. 185).

23. See the analysis of Korais in Kedourie (1971, Introduction). For the birth of Zionism, see Vital (1975); for Armenian diaspora nationalism, see Nalbandian (1963) and Walker (1980); for back-to-Africa movements, including Garveyism, among American Blacks, see Draper (1970).

24. For Christian and Muslim warrior myths, see Armstrong (1982, ch. 3); for Israelite beliefs, see M. Weinfeld, 'Divine intervention in war in ancient Israel and in the ancient Near East', in Tadmor and Weinfeld (1986; pp. 121–7); more generally, see Smith (1981).

25. For such immigrant nationalisms, see Seton-Watson (1977, ch. 5); and compare the contemporary protests of Aborigines, American Indians and Mohawks.

26. For Rousseau's influence, see Cohler (1970); and for that of Herder, Berlin (1976). For modern Greek myths, see Kitromilides (1979) and Carras (1983).

References

ANDERSON, B. 1983 *Imagined Communities: Reflections on the Origin and Spread of Nationalism.* London: Verso Books.

ARMSTRONG, J. 1982 *Nations before Nationalism*. Chapel Hill, NC: University of North Carolina Press.

ATIYA, A. S. 1968 *A History of Eastern Christianity*. London: Methuen.

AVERY, P. 1965 *Modern Iran*. London: Ernest Benn.

BARON, S. W. 1952–76 *A Social and Religious History of the Jews*. New York: Columbia University Press.

BAYNES, N. H. and MOSS, H. St. L. B. (eds.) 1969 *Byzantium: An Introduction to East Roman Civilisation*. Oxford, London and New York: Oxford University Press.

BENDIX, R. 1964 *Nation-building and Citizenship*. New York: John Wiley.

BEN-SASSON, H. and ETTINGER, S. (eds.) 1971 *Jewish Society Through the Ages*. London: Valentine, Mitchell & Co.

BERLIN, I. 1976 *Vico and Herder*. London: Hogarth Press.

BLOCH, M. 1961 *Feudal Society*, 2 vols., London: Routledge and Kegan Paul.

BRAUDEL, F. 1989 *The Identity of France*, vol. I, London: Fontana Press.

CAMBRIDGE HISTORY OF IRAN (1983, vol. III, parts 1 and 2: *The Seleucid, Parthian and Sassanian Periods*); (1975, vol. IV, *The Period from the Arab Invasion to the Saljuqs*). Cambridge: Cambridge University Press.

CARMICHAEL, J. 1967 *The Shaping of the Arabs*. New York: Macmillan.

CARRAS, C. 1983 *3,000 Years of Greek Identity—Myth or Reality?*. Athens: Domus Books.

CITRON, S. 1988 *Le Mythe National*. Paris: Presses Ouvriers.

COHLER, A. 1970 *Rousseau and Nationalism*. New York: Basic Books.

CONNOR, W. 1978 'A nation is a nation, is a state, is an ethnic group, is a . . .', *Ethnic and Racial Studies*, vol. 1, no. 4, pp. 377–400.

DAVIES, N. 1982 *God's Playground: A History of Poland*, 2 vols., Oxford: Clarendon Press.

DAVIS, R. H. 1976 *The Normans and Their Myth*. London: Thames and Hudson.

DENTAN, R. C. (ed.) 1983 *The Idea of History in the Ancient Near East*. New Haven, CT: American Oriental Society.

DEUTSCH, K. 1966 *Nationalism and Social Communication*, 2nd ed., Boston, MA: MIT Press.

DIKÖTTER, F. 1990 'Group definition and the idea of "race" in modern China (1793–1949)', *Ethnic and Racial Studies*, vol. 13, no. 3, pp. 430–32.

DRAPER, T. 1970 *The Rediscovery of Black Nationalism*. London: Secker and Warburg.

DUNCAN, A. A. M. 1970 *The Nation of Scots and the Declaration of Arbroath*. (1320) London: The Historical Association.

FRANKFORT, H. 1948 *Kingship and the Gods*. Chicago, IL: University of Chicago Press.

FRYE, R. 1966 *The Heritage of Persia*. New York: Mentor.

—— 1975 *The Golden Age of Persia*. London: Weidenfeld & Nicolson.

GANS, H. 1979 'Symbolic ethnicity', *Ethnic and Racial Studies*, vol. 2, no. 1, pp. 1–20.

HALECKI, O. 1955 *A History of Poland*. London: J.M. Dent & Sons.

HERAUD, G. 1963 *L'Europe des Ethnies*. Paris: Presses d'Europe.

HOBSBAWM, E. and RANGER, T. (eds.) 1983 *The Invention of Tradition*. Cambridge: Cambridge University Press.

HOBSBAWM, E. 1990 *Nations and Nationalism since 1780*. Cambridge: Cambridge University Press.

HOROWITZ, D. 1985 *Ethnic Groups in Conflict*. Los Angeles and London: University of California Press.

HOWE, N. 1989 *Migration and Mythmaking in Anglo-Saxon England*. New Haven, CT, and London: Yale University Press.

HUTCHINSON, J. 1987 *The Dynamics of Cultural Nationalism: The Gaelic Revival and the Creation of the Irish Nation State*. London: Allen and Unwin.

KANTOROWICZ, E. H. 1951 'Pro patria mori in medieval political thought', *American Historical Review*, vol. 56, pp. 472–92.

KEDDIE, N. 1981 *Roots of Revolution: An Interpretive History of Modern Iran*. New Haven, CT, and London: Yale University Press.

KEDOURIE, E. (ed.) 1971 *Nationalism in Asia and Africa*. London: Weidenfeld & Nicolson.

KESSLER, D. 1985 *The Falashas, the Forgotten Jews of Ethiopia*. New York: Schocken Books.

KIRK, G. S. 1973 *Myth, its Meanings and Functions in Ancient and Other Cultures*. Cambridge: Cambridge University Press.

KITROMILIDES, P. 1979 'The dialectic of intolerance: ideological dimensions of ethnic conflict', *Journal of the Hellenic Diaspora*, vol. 6, no. 4, pp. 5–30.

KLAUSNER, J. 1956 *The Messianic Idea in Israel*. London: Allen and Unwin.

KOHN, H. 1940 'The origins of English nationalism', *Journal of the History of Ideas*, vol. 1, pp. 69–94.

—— 1957 *Nationalism and Liberty: The Swiss Example*. New York: Macmillan.

KRAMER, S. N. 1963 *The Sumerians*. Chicago: University of Chicago Press.

KREJCI, J. and VELIMSKY, V. 1981 *Ethnic and Political Nations in Europe*. London: Croom Helm.

KUSHNER, D. 1976 *The Rise of Turkish Nationalism*. London: Frank Cass.

LANG, D. M. 1980 *Armenia, Cradle of Civilisation*. London: Allen and Unwin.

LEWIS, B. 1968 *The Arabs in History*. 5th ed., London: Hutchinson & Co.

—— 1970 *The Emergence of Modern Turkey*. London: Oxford University Press.

LEWIS, W. H. (ed.) 1965 *French-Speaking Africa: The Search for Identity*. New York: Walker.

MACDOUGALL, H. A. 1982 *Racial Myth in English History: Trojans, Teutons and Anglo-Saxons*. Montreal: Harvest House and Hanover, New Hampshire: University Press of New England.

MASON, R. A. 1985 'Scotching the Brut: the early history of Britain', *History Today*, vol. 35, (January), pp. 26–31.

MELUCCI, A. 1989 *Nomads of the Present: Social Movements and Individual Needs in Contemporary Society*. London: Hutchinson Radius.

NALBANDIAN, L. 1963 *The Armenian Revolutionary Movement: the Development of Armenian Political Parties Through the Nineteenth Century*. Berkeley: University of California Press.

O'BRIEN, C. C. 1988 *God-land: Reflections on religion and nationalism*. Cambridge, MA: Harvard University Press.

PECH, S. 1976 'The nationalist movements of the Austrian Slavs in 1848', *Social History*, vol. 9, 336–56.

PIPES, R. 1977 *Russia under the Old Regime*. London: Peregrine Books.

PRITCHARD, J. B. (ed.) 1974 *Solomon and Sheba*. London: Phaidon Press Limited.

RAMET, P. (ed.) 1989 *Religion and Nationalism in Soviet and East European Politics*. Durham and London: Duke University Press.

RANUM, O. (ed.) 1975 *National Consciousness, History and Political Culture in Early-Modern Europe*. Baltimore and London: Johns Hopkins University Press.

REYNOLDS, S. 1984 *Kingdoms and Communities in Western Europe. 900–1300*, Oxford: Clarendon.

ROUX, G. 1964 *Ancient Iraq*. Harmondsworth: Penguin.

SCHERMERHORN, R. 1970 *Comparative Ethnic Relations*. New York: Random House.

SELTZER, R. M. 1980 *Jewish People, Jewish Thought*. New York: Macmillan.

SETON-WATSON, H. 1977 *Nations and States*. London: Methuen.

SHARABI, H. 1970 *The Arab Intellectuals and the West: The Formative Years. 1875–1914*, Baltimore and London: Johns Hopkins University Press.

SHEEHY, J. 1980 *The Rediscovery of Ireland's Past*. London: Thames & Hudson.

SHERRARD, P. 1959 *The Greek East and the Latin West, A Study in the Christian Tradition*. London: Oxford University Press.

SMITH, A. D. 1971/83 *Theories of Nationalism*. 2nd. ed., London: Duckworth and New York: Holmes and Meier.

—— 1973 'Nationalism, A Trend Report and Annotated Bibliography', *Current Sociology*, vol. 21, no. 3.

—— 1981 'War and ethnicity: the role of warfare in the formation, self-images and cohesion of ethnic communities', *Ethnic and Racial Studies*, vol. 4, no. 4, 375–97.

—— 1984*a* 'National identity and myths of ethnic descent', in *Research in Social Movements, Conflict and Change*, vol. 7, pp. 95–130.

—— 1984*b* 'Ethnic myths and ethnic revivals', *European Journal of Sociology*, vol. 25, pp. 283–305.

—— 1986 *The Ethnic Origins of Nations*. Oxford: Blackwell.

—— 1988 'Social and cultural conditions of ethnic survival', *Journal of Ethnic Studies, Treatises and Documents*, vol. 21, pp. 15–26, Ljubljana.

—— 1989 'The origins of nations', *Ethnic and Racial Studies*, vol. 12, no. 3, pp. 340–67.

—— 1990 'Towards a global culture?', *Theory, Culture and Society*, vol. 7, pp. 171–91.

—— 1991 *National Identity*. Harmondsworth: Penguin.

SMITH, B. 1960 *European Vision and the South Pacific*. London: Oxford University Press.

STEINBERG, J. 1976 *Why Switzerland?* Cambridge: Cambridge University Press.

TADMOR, H. and WEINFELD, M. (eds.) 1986 *History, Historiography and Interpretation*. Jerusalem: Magnes Press, Hebrew University.

THADEN, E. 1964 *Conservative Nationalism in Nineteenth Century Russia*. Seattle, WA: University of Washington Press.

THOMPSON, L. 1985 *The Political Mythology of Apartheid*. New Haven, CT, and London: Yale University Press.

THÜRER, G. 1970 *Free and Swiss*. London: Oswald Wolff.

TRIGGER, B. G., KEMP, B. J., O'CONNOR, D. and LLOYD, A. B. 1983 *Ancient Egypt, a Social History*, Cambridge: Cambridge University Press.

TUDOR, H. 1972 *Political Myth*. London: Pall Mall Press Ltd, Macmillan.

TUVESON, E. L. 1968 *Redeemer Nation: the Idea of America's Millenial Role*. Chicago and London: Chicago University Press.

ULLENDORFF, E. 1968 *Ethiopia and the Bible*. Oxford University Press.

VAN DEN BERGHE, P. 1978 'Race and ethnicity: a sociobiological perspective', *Ethnic and Racial Studies*, vol. 4, no. 4, pp. 401–11.

—— 1979 *The Ethnic Phenomenon*. New York: Elsevier.

VAN SETERS, J. 1983 *In Search of History: Historiography in the Ancient World and the Origins of Biblical History*. New Haven, CT, and London: Yale University Press.

VITAL, D. 1975 *The Origins of Zionism*. Oxford: Clarendon Press.

WALKER, C. 1980 *Armenia, the Survival of a Nation*. London: Routledge.

WARNER, M. 1983 *Joan of Arc*. Harmondsworth: Penguin.

WEBER, M. 1968 *Economy and Society*, vol. 1, G. Roth and C. Wittich (eds.), New York: Bedminster Press.

WILLIAMS, G. 1985 *When Was Wales?*, Harmondsworth: Penguin.

YERUSHALMI, J. H. 1983 *Jewish History and Jewish Memory*. Seattle, WA, and London: University of Washington Press.

ZEITLIN, I. 1984 *Ancient Judaism*. Cambridge: Polity Press.

5

Nation and Ethnoscape*

Current views of the rise of nations and nationalism emphasize the role of the modern state in constructing nations and engendering national loyalties and conflicts. In the work of Eric Hobsbawm, Benedict Anderson, and Anthony Giddens, to name some of the most original scholars in the field, nations owe their existence and borders to the growth of modern, centralized states, their reflexive bureaucratic penetration and their ethnographic controls.[1] To this perspective, Michael Mann and Charles Tilly have added a military dimension: prolonged inter-state warfare, fed by capitalism, determines the reach of states and the mobilization of their citizen populations as nations.[2] Clearly, there is much to commend in this view, particularly its insistence on the central role of the political domain in creating nations and engendering national conflicts. But it tends to privilege a western pattern of state-to-nation formation, without giving sufficient weight to the alternative route of ethnic nationalism forging the state which we witness in Eastern Europe and parts of Asia. It also tends to neglect the role of popular mobilization, and the consequent return by the intelligentsia to ethno-history and vernacular culture. Perhaps most critically, this state-centred modernism attaches no weight to the properties of territory and the role of ancestral homelands. It is this last aspect that I wish to develop here.[3]

Whatever else it may be, nationalism always involves an assertion of, or struggle for, control of land. A landless nation is a contradiction in terms. Ethnic communities (or *ethnies*) may be severed from their historic territories, as has been the case with such diaspora communities as the Armenians, Jews and Greeks. But the creation of nations requires a special place for the nation to inhabit, a land 'of their own'. Not any land; an historic land, a homeland, an ancestral land. Only an ancestral homeland can provide the emotional as well as physical security required by the citizens of a nation.[4]

* *Oxford International Review* 8, 1997, 8–16.

THE GROWTH OF 'ETHNOSCAPES'

Now what we so frequently observe is the often fervent attachment of populations to particular stretches of territory, and their readiness, in certain circumstances, to defend them to the last inch.

Everyday strategic and political calculations by élites claiming title deeds to particular lands become, under these circumstances, invested with powerful emotional connotations and cultural meanings. In particular, we find many groups of people endowing with a particular collective emotion a specific terrain which they occupy, whether it be a local district, a region or a wider ethnic territory. What is at stake is the idea of an historic and poetic landscape, one imbued with the culture and history of a group, and vice versa, a group part of whose character is felt by themselves and outsiders to derive from the particular landscape they inhabit, and commemorated as such in verse and song.

Of course, these poetic and historic landscapes vary in extent. Some are historic 'mini-scapes', relatively small localities which support groups of villages such as we might find in valleys or along the shores of lakes. Over time, the inhabitants develop networks and local cultures which are clearly recognizable, as with the various groups in the Carpathian valleys or in the outlying regions of Mexico. The limits of the valley or district circumscribe the outlook and culture of the group, and become a subject of myth and tradition. Other terrains we might term historic 'ethnoscapes' cover a wider extent of land, present a tradition of continuity and are held to constitute an ethnic unity, because the terrain invested with collective significance is felt to be integral to a particular historical culture community or *ethnie*, and the ethnic community is seen as an intrinsic part of that poetic landscape.

How does this association between the group and the terrain come about? More particularly, how do ethnoscapes emerge? At its simplest, the terrain in question is felt over time to provide the unique and indispensable setting for the events that shaped the community. The wanderings, battles and exploits in which 'our people' and their leaders participated took place in a particular landscape, and the features of that landscape are part of those experiences and the collective memories to which they give rise. Often the landscape is given a more active, positive role; no longer merely a natural setting, it is felt to influence events and contribute to the experiences and memories that moulded the community. This is especially true of ethnoscapes, where the landscape is invested with ethnic kin significance, and becomes an intrinsic element in the community's myth of origins and shared memories. In this way, the Alps were thought to influence the nature and early development of the Swiss *Eidgenossenschaft*, and the dykes the character and rise of the Dutch states.

But there is a further way in which historic miniscapes and particularly ethnoscapes emerge: as witnesses to the group's survival as a cultural community, for the land forms the last resting place of 'our ancestors' and of our forefathers and foremothers. The graves of the forebears testify to the uniqueness and antiquity of particular landscapes; this piece of land has a special place in the hearts and minds of the members of this community, just as this community has a special affinity with a particular historical landscape, commemorated in monuments and chronicles and celebrated in epic and ballad.[5] The land as a historically unique and poetic landscape, as a decisive influence over historical events and as the witness to ethnic survival and commemoration over the *longue durée*: these are all components of a general process of 'territorialization of memory'. They help to bring about a close association between a given landscape and a particular community, such that a people is felt to belong to a specific territory and a territory to a particular people. On this basis, larger ethnoscapes emerge in which a sense of kin relatedness and emotional continuity is developed through a chain of generations living, working, dying and being buried in the same historic terrain.

The sense of continuity and genealogy induces a particular veneration; the poetic landscape is revered as an 'ancestral homeland' and the ethnoscape becomes an intrinsic part of the character, history and destiny of the culture community, to be commemorated regularly and defended at all costs lest the 'personality' of the ethnic or regional community be impugned. That is why many new states pay so much attention to inculcating a love and veneration for particular ethnoscapes and lavish so much praise on the natural features of the territory they control. It is another example of the process by which nature becomes historicized and its features celebrated; at the same time the community and its history becomes naturalized, and its development comes to be seen as part of the natural order.[6]

How is this close identification between the community and its landscape achieved in practice? By attaching specific memories of 'our ancestors' and forebears, particularly if they are saintly or heroic, to particular stretches of territory. For example, leaders and educators of the community may locate the deeds of heroes and great men at specific sites, 'poetic spaces' eulogized in the chronicles and ballads recited down the generations, thereby binding their descendants to a distinct landscape endowed with ethno-historical significance. Across the landscape lie the 'sites of memory'; the fields of battle, the monuments to the fallen, the places of peace treaties, the temples of priests, the last resting places of saints and heroes, the sacred groves of spirits and gods who guard the land.

For the ancient Israelites who settled the promised land, the sites of battle, the resting places of the Ark of the Covenant, the place of the Temple, the sites of miracles and the tombs of prophets and rabbis, became invested with awe and sacred meaning, they helped to define the extent and character of an ethnoscape, a land uniquely theirs even as they belonged to the land. Similarly, for the Swiss, the lakes and mountains, valleys and fields, defined their history while simultaneously being invested with historic meanings as the sites of battles and treaties, oaths and heroic exploits. The Swiss Confederation may have developed through the contingencies of battle, dynastic alliances and trade networks; but equally important for that development were the territorialized memories and symbols, myths and traditions which invested events with collective meaning and purpose for the people.[7]

SACRED TERRITORIES

The territorialization of memory is an important part of the explanation of ethnic and national identities, but it fails to account for the passions and conflicts, and the associated mass mobilization, involved in some claims to territorial title deeds. How can we account for some of the most vehement assertions of national identity and the most bitter and intractable ethnic conflicts? Of course, many factors are at work in a complex and protracted antagonism of the kind that we saw over Alsace and Sudetenland, and which we witness today in Ulster, Bosnia, Palestine and the Caucasus.

But, if we concentrate on the popular level of analysis, we can grasp the special significance which certain stretches of territory hold for a large proportion of the members of particular ethnic communities. In these cases, certain areas of land come to possess a special symbolic and mythic meaning, and some ethnoscapes are endowed with a sacred and extraordinary quality, generating powerful feelings of reverence and belonging. Here again the Swiss case is instructive. The heartland of the Swiss Confederation, the *Innenschweiz*, with its mountains encircling the lake of Lucerne, witnessed the Oath of the Rütli and the legends surrounding the heroic figure of William Tell.

More generally, success in battle on the mountain slopes and passes engendered in the Swiss peasants and herdsmen a simple faith in divine providence, exemplified by the ability of faithful and virtuous shepherds to triumph over far more powerful enemies. In this way, an association between a pure and virtuous people and an unspoilt and unmolested land became a corner-stone of later Swiss national consciousness; and it continues to influence contemporary Swiss self-images and attitudes to the outside world.[8]

Ethnoscapes become sacred in a variety of ways. One is the result of the nature of the inhabiting community. Where an *ethnie* is also a community of believers and a 'holy people' adhering to a single sacred lifestyle, repeated performance of sacred acts in fulfilment of the mission with which the community is entrusted sanctifies the land and turns it into a reward for faithful observance of a 'covenant'. That is how the ancient Israelites eventually came to see their ethnoscape; the promised land became a holy land fit for a nation of priests. Similarly the ideal of France as a sacred kingdom like ancient Israel emerged only through the mission of the Carolingian and Capetian monarchs who took it upon themselves to defend the holy Catholic faith, like so many latterday King Davids.[9]

The holy deeds of 'our ancestors' may also confer a sacred quality on an ethnoscape. These legendary or historical figures are venerated by the people for the benefits, material and spiritual, that they bestow on the community, and for the divine blessings they bring on the people. So the places where holy men and heroes walked and taught, fought and judged, prayed and died, are felt to be holy themselves; their tombs and monuments became places of veneration and pilgrimage, testifying to the glorious and sacred past of the ethnic community. Holy towns and temples like Mecca, Qom, Amritsar and Jerusalem and miraculous sites such as Lourdes, Yasna Gora and Guadeloupe, bear witness to the holy men and women of past ages of faith, and sacred fields of battle such as Avarayr, Kossovo and Blood River testify to the Armenian, Serb and Afrikaner martyrs whose virtue and self-sacrifice sanctified the land of 'our ancestors'.

A territory can also become sacred through a quest for liberation and utopia. The promised land becomes a land free from oppression, a land where a liberated community can build a New Jerusalem. This is very much what the American and Afrikaner settlers sought to do on prairie and veldt, modelling themselves on the biblical Exodus and seeking to drive out the indigenous inhabitants of the land in their purificatory zeal to uphold a moral and ritual ideal. Confidently seeing themselves as an elect, these fervent believer-pioneers came to idealize the 'virgin' land and the frontier as sacred elements of their self-images, and to see them as instruments and rewards of a providential national destiny.[10]

IRREDENTISM AND MARTYRDOM

In the modern era, nationalism has sought to harness these pre-existing ethnic, religious and regional sentiments and meanings for its own ends. Broadly speaking, this involved two processes: the national re-education of the young; and the inculcation of a spirit of self-sacrifice. As far as re-education was concerned, this meant a mass standardization of outlook, values, knowledge and skills in a national framework around the trinity of literature, history and geography. As the German Romantics realized, these were the pre-eminent disciplines for imbuing the young with a national outlook and feeling, for they revealed, more than most, the inner rhythms of the nation and its profound roots in the past. Nationalism, as the right education of the collective will, had to inculcate a profound knowledge and keen identification with the father- or motherland as a sacred and inviolable ancestral homeland, the only guarantor of its history and destiny. The knowledge and love of the homeland became therefore an integral part of a national programme of mass education, and it drew on the prior attachments of the people to their ethnoscapes.[11]

But such re-education was not an end in itself. It served to prepare the spirit of the young for a life of service to the nation, and if necessary of heroic martyrdom. For the true nationalist hero was a martyr, sacrificing his or her life for nation and ancestral homeland, and in death hallowing both. Love of the sacred homeland inspired the martyr's death, a love and devotion that fed on tales of analogous exploits long ago. Following this logic, modern Greek nationalists held up the example of such classical 'martyrs' as Achilles before Troy or Leonidas and the Spartan three hundred at Thermopylae, and French revolutionary nationalists looked back to the self-sacrifice of ancient Roman republican heroes like the Horatii or Brutus the consul.[12]

Of course, we must not forget that individuals and communities had always fought and died for strips of territory, whether in the Swiss Alps, the Spanish plateaux or the Russian steppe. The power of the modern ideal of defending a homeland regarded as sacred derives as much from ancient traditions of sacred sites and historic ethnoscapes as from the ideology of nationalism with its demand for its own authentic ethnoscape for each unique nation. The amalgamation of these two sources of mass martyrdom is the work of modern intellectuals, but it also takes place more inchoately at the popular level, as 'the people' and their ideas influence the élites 'from below'. One result has been the readiness, as Anderson noted, of large numbers of people to lay down their lives willingly for the nation and its homeland, as the great monuments and huge cemeteries of two World Wars so tragically testify.[13]

The ideas of 'ethnoscape' and 'sacred territory' are especially prominent in cases of irredentism or where two communities compete for possession of the selfsame homeland territories. The very term, irredenta, has religious connotations: the people and territory in question are spiritually as well as physically lost, and their 'redemption' requires reincorporation in the motherland and restoration to the fatherland. This is how French nationalists saw the lost territories and peoples of Alsace and Lorraine, the Italians those of Trieste, Fiume and the south Tyrol, and the Greeks 'unredeemed' Epirus, Thrace and Crete. For French, Italian and Greek nationalists, the recovery of these lands was a sacred duty, because the territories as well as their ethnic kin were integral parts of the ancestral homeland and had to realize their true destiny by being liberated from their unnatural state of alien oppression.[14] Similar ideals motivate Irish and Serb nationalists in respect of Ulster and Kossovo. For the former, it is a question of recovering the lost six counties severed from the Republic by the Treaty of 1921, the more so as Ulster constituted one of the four ancient provinces of Ireland and was the sacred home of the heroes of the epic Ulster Cycle, rediscovered at the end of the nineteenth century by Standish O'Grady and Lady Gregory. But the selfsame province is equally sacred as the home of an elect Protestant community, the province freed by the Battle of the Boyne from Catholic control. In the marches of the Orange Order, the sanctity of this ethnic territorial dispensation is annually confirmed, as the ancestral homeland of a covenanted Ulster-Scots Protestant community.[15]

In similar vein, Serbs look on the province of Kossovo as the original heartland of the Serb people, which can on no account be surrendered to its Albanian majority. In part, Milosevic's nationalist policies which began with the reassertion of Serb claims over Kossovo derive from strong historic attachments to this venerated area which saw the demise of the medieval Serbian empire at the hands of the Ottomans in the Serbian defeat in 1389 on the field of Kossovo Polje. This is still a place of pilgrimage for Serbs, just as the epic ballads of Kossovo and their hero, Marko, continue to hold a special place in Serb hearts. But, even where the sacred land in question cannot be described as a heartland, its symbolism may still evoke powerful attachments. We witness a vivid contemporary example of this, in the fervour of the Greek rejection of the attempt by the newly independent Macedonians of former Yugoslavia to appropriate, as the Greeks see it, the name and symbols of the ancient Macedonian kingdom of Philip and Alexander the Great, which the Greeks have come to regard as part of their sacred lands and heritage.[16]

But perhaps the most dramatic example of a contested land which forms the object of an irredentist movement is that of the West Bank of the river Jordan. While for Palestinians these lands form the heartland of their people, with Jerusalem a city sacred to Muslims, for Israeli Jews, and especially the Orthodox, Judea and Samaria represent the cradle of their people and integral parts of the land that God promised His elect. The *Gush Emunim* (Bloc of the Faithful), in particular, have insisted on settling these lands in the teeth of fierce Palestinian opposition on both religious and ethnic grounds, citing a literal interpretation of the biblical boundaries 'from Dan to Beersheba'. Although this reading is either not shared or treated as a minor issue by most Israelis, the *raison d'etre* for a separate Israeli national state in Palestine is bound up with an ethnic understanding of Jewish history and community, and involves respect for Jewish sacred traditions. Hence, not even the most secular Jew can afford to dismiss entirely the biblical rationale for an Israeli state in Palestine. The fact that Judea and Samaria are marked by many sacred and historic sites and ancient memories, notably in Jerusalem, infuses what would otherwise be a difficult security and political issue with powerful ethno-religious attachments which make it impossible for governments to ignore popular opinion in the search for peace.[17]

In all these cases, large numbers of people can and have been mobilized and martyred in the defence or annexation of lands deemed to be 'ours by right', intrinsic elements of the ancestral homeland, whose loss would seriously impair, and whose recovery would restore, the integrity of the nation and its ethnoscape. Where these lands are by tradition sanctified, the site of sacred acts and memories, even greater fervour and attachments can be evoked, and even larger numbers of people can be mobilized for battle and death. The fraternity of the nation is then lived in and through the sacrifice of its citizens in defence of the fatherland or motherland, seen as the permanent and unchanging bedrock of the nation, and the sacred soil which nourishes its historic culture.

CONCLUSION

In a brief review like this, it is impossible to do justice to the many cases of sacred ethnoscapes at the centre of national reassertions and ethnic conflicts. The influence exerted by these ethnic attachments has been largely neglected. However, in arguing for the importance of sacred homelands in understanding the roots of national identity and ethnic conflict, I do not mean to imply that all ethnic or national conflicts revolve around territories deemed to be sacred, much less that most conflicts in the world involve territorial disputes. This is clearly not the case. One can think of many conflicts (class, regional, religious, ideological) that do not involve national or ethnic territory, just as one can think of many nationalisms (in, say, Africa) whose main preoccupations are economic, cultural and political.

On the other hand, insofar as any nation must have recognized territory and clear-cut borders and any nationalism that wants to build a community must do so on a stretch of land which is acknowledged as belonging by right to that community, they must both appeal to historical geography as a vital ingredient of their *raison d'etre*. The territory they come to occupy by chance must be turned into a historic necessity. Land must become an ancestral homeland and landscape an ethnoscape. Only in this way can land and landscape inspire popular devotion and mass sacrifice, both of which are necessary if an often heterogenous population is to be moulded into a 'nation'. That is why, where there are no pre-existing traditions of sacred lands, nationalism itself seeks to sanctify the nation's homeland, making it part of a national salvation drama of collective history and destiny. Where such sacred traditions do exist, nationalists seek to turn the perceptions and attachments of the populace to the ethnoscape—its fertility, its beauty, its sustenance and its solace—to their own political ends.

But, by the same token, the invocation of these deep and potent sentiments can prove destructive; the popular base, once mobilized, can outrun élite political strategies. This is particularly true in cases like India and Sri Lanka where contested lands are felt to be sacred land, where rival ethno-religious traditions provide the basis for territorial political dispensations. For if nationalism has territorialized religion and ethnicity, older religious beliefs and sentiments about sacred homelands can feed and overflow the political goals of élites. This is why it is so important to explore the sacred meanings of ethnoscapes and ancestral homelands, if we are to understand the foundations of so many modem national identities and the roots of some of the most bitter and protracted ethnic conflicts.

Notes

1. See Giddens (1985), pp. 116–21; 212–21; Hobsbawm (1990); and especially Anderson (1991), pp. 121, 170–80, for this state-centred modernism.
2. See Tilly (1975), Introduction; and Mann (1993), esp. pp. 221 ff., who nevertheless concedes a place for earlier discursive literacy networks.
3. In the second edition of his book, Breuilly (1993) gives more weight to ideological factors; cf. the populist appeal to 'mass sentiments' analysed in Nairn (1977), Chapter 2.

4. For diaspora communities, see Sheffer (1986). For the concept of *ethnie*, see Anthony D. Smith (1991), Chapter 2.
5. See Im Hof (1991); and Schama (1987), Chapter 1.
6. For the concept of poetic landscapes, see Anthony D. Smith (1986), Chapter 8.
7. See the volumes edited by Pierre Nora (1984 and 1986). For the ancient Israelites and their promised land, see Zeitlin (1984); for the medieval Swiss, see Im Hof (1991).
8. For the 'invention' of the Oath of the Rütli, see Kreis (1991).
9. On the mission of the French kings, see Armstrong (1982).
10. For the sense of providential destiny among the American settlers, see Tuveson (1968): for the Afrikaner sense of ethnic mission, see Akenson (1992) Chapter 3; on myths of ethnic election, see Anthony D. Smith (1992).
11. The nationalist assumptions of the German Romantics are dissected by Kedourie (1960) and Anthony D. Smith (1983), Chapter 1.
12. For the classical models of modern Greek nationalism, see Campbell and Sherrard (1968); for those of the French *patriots*, see Rosenblum (1967).
13. See Anderson (1991) Chapters 1 and 5; cf. Mosse (1994).
14. On irredentism generally, see Horowitz (1985) Chapter 6.
15. On the sense of a covenanted community among the Ulster-Scots, see Akenson (1992).
16. For Serb historical myths, see Singleton (1985) Chapter 3; Greek attitudes to Macedonia, see Poulton (1995) Chapters 8–9.
17. For the ideology of *Gush Emunim* see Weissbrod (1996); for Jewish beliefs in ethnic election, see Akenson (1992).

References

AKENSON, D. 1992 *God's Peoples* Ithaca: Cornell University Press.
ANDERSON, B. 1991 *Imagined Comniunities: Reflections on the Origin and Spread of Nationalism* London: Verso.
ARMSTRONG, J. 1982 *Nations before Nationalism* Chapel Hill: University of North Carolina Press.
BREUILLY, J. 1993 *Nationalism and the State.* Second Edition Manchester: Manchester University Press.
CAMPBELL, J. and SHERRARD, P. 1968 *Modern Greece* London: Ernest Benn.
GIDDENS, A. 1985 *The Nation-State and Violence* Cambridge: Polity Press.
HOBSBAWM, E. 1990 *Nations and Nationalism since 1780* Cambridge: Cambridge University Press.
HOROWITZ, D. 1985 *Ethnic Groups in Conflict* Berkeley and Los Angeles: University of California Press.

IM HOF, U. 1991 *Mythos Schweiz: Identität—Nation—Geschichte, 1291–1991* Zürich: Neue Zurcher Verlag.

KEDOURIE, E. 1960 *Nationalism* London: Hutchinson.

KREIS, G. 1991 *Der Mythos von 1291: Zur Enstehung des Schweizerischen Nationalfeiertags* Basel: Friedrich Reinhardt Verlag.

MANN, M. 1993 *The Sources of Social Power.* Vol. 11 Cambridge: Cambridge University Press.

NAIRN, T. 1979 *The Break-up of Britain: Crisis and Neo-Nationalism* London: New Left Books.

NORA, P. (ed.) 1984/86 *Les Lieux de Memoire*, Vol. 1: *La Republique* Vol. II: *La Nation* Paris: Gallimard.

ROSENBLUM, R. 1967 *Transformations in late Eighteenth Century Art* Princeton: Princeton University Press.

SCHAMA, S. 1987 *The Embarrassment of Riches* London: Fontana Press.

SHEFFER, G. (ed.) 1986 *Modern Diasporas in International Politics* London, Madrid, Sydney: Croom Helm.

SINGLETON, F. 1985 *A Short History of the Yugoslav Peoples* Cambridge: Cambridge University Press.

SMITH, A. D. 1983 *Theories of Nationalism.* Second Edition London: Duckworth and New York: Holmes and Meier.

—— 1986 *The Ethnic Origins of Nations* Oxford: Basil Blackwell.

—— 1991 *National Identity* Harmondsworth: Penguin.

—— 1992 'Chosen peoples: why ethnic groups survive', *Ethnic and Racial Studies*, Vol. 15, No. 3, pp. 436–56.

TILLY, C. (ed.) 1975 *The Formation of National States in Western Europe* Princeton: Princeton University Press.

TUVESON, E. L. 1968 *Redeemer Nation: The Idea of America's Millennial Role* Chicago and London: University of Chicago Press.

WEISSBROD, L. 1996 '*Gush Emunim* and the Peace Process: Modern Religious Fundamentalism in Crisis, *Israel Affairs*, Vol. 3, No. 1 (1996), pp. 86–103.

ZEITLIN, I. 1984 *Ancient Judaism* Cambridge: Polity Press.

PART II

Myths and Memories of Modern Nations

6

Gastronomy or Geology?
The Role of Nationalism in the
Reconstruction of Nations*

ABSTRACT

This article considers the debate that has recently developed in studies of nationalism between those scholars who see the nation as a modern and constantly changing construction *ex nihilo* and those who see it as an immemorial, unchanging communal essence. It outlines the so-called 'gastronomical' and 'geological' metaphors of nation formation and suggests a synthetic model which balances the influence of the ethnic past and the impact of nationalist activity. It shows that the central question which has divided theorists of nationalism is the place of the past in the life of modern nations. The author recognizes the role of nationalists in national mobilization but stresses that nationalists are not social engineers or mere image makers as modernist and post-modernist accounts would have it, but rather social and political archaeologists whose activities consist in the rediscovery and reinterpretation of the ethnic past and through it the regeneration of their national community.

Is the nation a seamless whole or an à la carte menu? Is it an immemorial deposit that archaeology has recovered and history explained, or a recent artefact that artists have created and media chefs purveyed to a bemused public? Are nationalists to be compared with intrepid explorers of an often distant past, or with social engineers and imaginative artists of the present? Does nationalism create nations, or do nations form the matrix and seedbed of nationalisms?

The debate that has developed around these themes represents a radical attempt to rethink the problem of nations and nationalism in the modern

* *Nations and Nationalism* 1 (1), 1995, 31–23.

world. But it also has far wider and deeper ramifications for our understanding of history and ethnicity. Here I want to explore some of these themes and recommend a position that places nations and nationalisms within a much longer historical trajectory, one which does justice both to the created and the received elements of national identity, and attempts to grasp the explosive energy of nationalisms.

THE NATION AS CULTURAL ARTEFACT

Let me start with the nation, and specifically with the gastronomic theory of the nation. According to this view, nations are composed of discrete elements and their cultures possess a variety of ingredients with different flavours and provenances. For example, English national identity was shaped by various influences in the past—Celtic, Roman, Saxon, Danish, Norman—and English culture today is composed of a number of ingredients from the Caribbean, Cyprus, Eastern Europe, and India. In this century, with so much immigration and intermarriage, there is no such thing as a pure English (I do not mean British) nation or culture. Today's symbol of Englishness is the 'ploughman's lunch'. Its ingredients (bread, cheese, pickles) may be venerable, but they are not peculiar to the English, and their juxtaposition was a commercial fabrication of the 1960s. Similarly, the choice of Constable's painting of *The Hay Wain* as the quintessential symbol of an 'English' landscape was a Victorian and Edwardian invention; just as the kilt and tartans as the symbol of the Scottish Highlands was an invention of the age of Walter Scott.[1]

In one sense, there is nothing particularly new here. The idea that nations are in some sense 'invented' goes back to Renan. The notion of the English nation as a cocktail of cultural ingredients is found in Daniel Defoe and it was generalized by a number of scholars including Kedourie, who stressed the recent and invented quality of nations and nationalism. What we have in the 'gastronomic' theory is no more than the logical conclusion of this line of argument.

But, if we look a little closer, we will see a major difference. The older theorists—Deutsch, Kedourie, Gellner, J. H. Kautsky, Hugh Seton-Watson, Tom Nairn, Charles Tilly—all assumed that nations, once formed, were real communities of culture and power: circumscribed, but potent, unifying, energizing, constraining. They were, if you like, what Durkheim would have called 'social facts', with the qualities that he attributed to social facts: generality, exteriority, constraint. They were also social actors, indeed the largest and most powerful social actors on the political stage, and as such, they could not be fragmented and shattered into a thousand pieces like the mechanical nightingale of the Hans Andersen fairy-tale. They were real, singing nightingales, even if they could not, or would not, cure sick emperors or put obsolete empires back together again.

For the 'gastronomic' theory, however, the nation is like the artificial nightingale. It is a piece of social engineering. Speaking of the 'nation' and its associated phenomena: nationalism, the nation-state, national symbols, etc., Eric Hobsbawm tells us: 'All these rest on exercises in social engineering which are often deliberate and always innovative, if only because historical novelty implies innovation'.[2] In other words, nationalists and their followers have put together the various ingredients of the nation—history, symbols, myths, languages—in much the same way as pub owners put together the ploughman's lunch. In doing so, they often select elements with diverse origins, particularly if, as so often happens in moden societies, the state's boundaries include various ethnic communities. So, the modern nation is a composite artefact, cobbled together from a rich variety of cultural sources.

But there is a further element in the recent radical rethinking of the concepts of nations and nationalism: its insistence on the imagined quality of the national community and the fictive nature of unifying myths. There is a polemical, satirical intent here: to unmask the nation and reveal the power games of nationalism. Specifically nationalist instruments of élite manipulation are symbolic: they involve the creation of a culture-ideology of community, through a series of emotive symbols and myths, communicated by print and the media. But in fact it is ultimately a specious community, one that parades as a collective cure for the modern disease of alienation between state and society, and operates through historical fictions and literary tropes, of the kind that Benedict Anderson and his followers have described.[3]

France during the Third Republic provides a classic example of the way in which the imagined community of the modern nation has been constructed, indeed invented. Between 1870 and 1914, the high period of 'ethno-linguistic' nationalism, according to Eric Hobsbawm, republican nationalist French leaders sought to 'create France' and 'Frenchmen' throughout the area of the French state by institutional and cultural means. Military service for all, a regimented mass, public education system, inculcation of the spirit of glory and *revanche* against Prussia, colonial conquests and assimilation, as well as economic infrastructure, all helped to turn 'peasants into Frenchmen', in Eugene Weber's well-known formulation. But there was one field, in particular, which helped to create the imagined community of *la France*: history, or more especially, history teaching. It was during this period that a single history textbook, the Lavisse history, was formulated in different editions for successive age groups and school levels, and pre-scribed for all pupils in every French school, both within France and in its colonies. Thus African and Vietnamese schoolchildren were all set on the path of grasping and identifying with the imagined community of France by repetition of the catechism, *nos ancêtres les Gaulois*, and by recitation of the history of France from Clovis to Louis XIV, Napoleon and the Third Republic.[4]

Now the standardization of history through a canonical textbook is only one, albeit a particularly important, way of forging an imagined com-munity. There are others. The creation of a canonical literature represents another popular strategy: Shakespeare, Milton and Wordsworth; Racine, Molière and Balzac; Pushkin, Tolstoy and Lermontov, become icons of the new imagined community, creating in their reading publics a communion of devotees and providing the national image with a textual fabric. Music can also serve this collective purpose; a Sibelius or Chopin has done as much for the image of Finland and Poland and the cultural communion of Poles and Finns as has a Runeberg or Mickiewicz. And here lies the point: these artefacts have created an image of the nation for compatriots and outsiders alike, and in doing so have forged the nation itself. Signifier and signified have been fused. Image and reality have become identical; ultimately, the nation has no existence outside its imagery and its representations.[5]

Let me give another European illustration. Recent Swiss historians have devoted some attention to the 700th anniversary of the Swiss *Eidgenoss-enschaft*. Their researches have revealed that both the official date for the foundation of the Confederation (1291) and the interpretation of it as a foundation myth were inventions of the nineteenth century. Indeed, it was only the 600th anniversary celebrations of 1891 that consecrated the Oath of the Rütli in its present form, and turned it into the foundation document of the nation. From this, it is a short step to claiming that the Swiss nation was really a product of the settlements of 1848 and 1874, rather than a gradual growth from the late thirteenth century foundation myth. The myth is revealed as a fiction, if not a fabrication, of the modern nation-alists; and the Swiss nation becomes a recently imagined community propagated, and re-presented, by those same nationalists.[6]

The position becomes even plainer when we turn to the recently formed states of Africa and Asia. In most of these cases, the nation cannot be any-thing but an imagined, and very recent, community, one that is being quite deliberately engineered in often polyethnic societies. In sub-Saharan Africa, for example, the boundaries of several new states were drawn artificially by the colonial powers in the 1880s, sometimes across ethnic categories and communities like the Ewe, Somali and Bakongo. In what sense, apart from the imaginations of nationalists, are these new states 'nations'? Even in their own eyes, they are no more than 'nations-to-be', 'nations of intent', in Robert Rotberg's phrase. Nigeria, Ghana, Kenya, Uganda, Zaire, Chad: deeply cross-cut by ethnic communities and regions, these territorial states are being used by their élites as the framework for inventing nations. They are territorial 'nations of design', a *mélange* of ethnic groups thrown together in a cauldron, as it were, by the colonial powers—as opposed to the 'old, continuous nations' of Western Europe. To this end, national histories, symbols, mythologies and rituals are being fabricated to implant a spurious unity and fraternity in their heterogeneous and divided populations.[7]

The very novelty of these new states in Africa and Asia carries with it a sense of the fragility and invented quality of the nation-to-be. It takes much art and design to construct nations from such diverse ingredients. These nations of intent are novel cultural artefacts, of very recent vintage. Their presumed need for roots in history is the product of their lack of such roots. This is why charismatic leaders like Nkrumah, Nasser, Nehru, and Sukarno in the 1960s sought to create 'political religions' after independence, in order to mobilize their often divided populations and instil in them a spirit of self-sacrifice for the tasks of development. The representations and symbols of a political religion aimed to evoke a sense of unitary culture in societies which lacked even a semblance of unity and whose peoples had not only different cuisine and costume, but also diverse religions, customs and languages. Clearly, more than a nostalgic 'ploughman's lunch' was required if the state was not to disintegrate.[8]

What all this amounts to is a rejection of the orthodox 'modernist' theories of the nation and 'nation-building' of Karl Deutsch, J. H. Kautsky, Peter Worsley, Elie Kedourie, Ernest Gellner, Charles Tilly, and Tom Nairn, in favour of a critical anti-foundational stance that questions the unity of the nation and deconstructs the power of nationalism into its component images and fictions. This essentially 'post-modernist' reading turns the nation into a 'narrative' to be recited, a 'discourse' to be interpreted and a 'text' to be deconstructed. Constructing the nation is more a matter of disseminating symbolic representations than forging cultural institutions or social networks. We grasp the meanings of the nation through the images it casts, the symbols it uses and the fictions it evokes, in the novels, plays, poems, operas, ballads, pamphlets, and newspapers which a literate reading public eagerly devours. It is in these symbolic and artistic creations that we may discern the lineaments of the nation. For the post-modernists, the nation has become a cultural artefact of modernity, a system of collective imaginings and symbolic representations, which resembles a pastiche of many hues and forms, a composite patchwork of all the cultural elements included in its boundaries.[9]

It is an image that could well apply to an emergent nation like Israel. According to this account, modern Israel represents an imagined community incorporating a medley of ethnic groups and cultures of widely differing provenance. Christian and Muslim Arabs, Druse, Ashkenazi and Sephardic Jews comprise its main components; but the latter include religious and secular Jews from many lands and times, from America and Yemen, from India and Romania, from Ethiopia and Russia. The ingathering of the exiles is a perfect reflection and precise symbol of the Israeli nation as an imagined and an invented community. What is taking place in modern Israel is the cultural construction of a new nation, which we witness daily in the work of cultural representation in Israeli 'texts'—in its newspapers, novels, plays, poetry, film, broadcasts, television, and the like. It is a nation culturally far removed from any other, including the Jews of the diaspora, not only by virtue of its official language, Hebrew, but even more by the cultural contexts and assumptions of its symbolic representations. In and through concepts like *sabra, kibbutz, aliya, yored, zionut,* used in official pronouncements and everyday life, the work of symbolic construction permeates the fabric of social life and creates a community of shared assumptions and cultural practices out of ethnically and socially heterogeneous populations; in other words, a nation.[10]

MODERNIST AND POST-MODERNIST ACCOUNTS

At this point let me summarize the 'post-modernist' theory of nationality and contrast it with the hitherto fashionable 'modernist' accounts.

For 'modernists' like Deutsch, Lerner, Kedourie, Gellner, J. H. Kautsky, Tilly, and Tom Nairn, the nation is a modern category, emerging into history in Western Europe and America in the late eighteenth century, along with the ideology of nationalism. The modern nation is a product of nationalist conceptions, but nationalism itself is a force generated by the needs of modernity, that is, of modern societies. Hence, nationalism and nations are intrinsic components of a modern capitalist, industrial and bureaucratic world. They are an integral part of its fabric. Though the fires of nationalism may burn less fiercely with the advance of affluence, nations and national states will remain the basic forms and elements of modern society. Hence every society and population must forge a viable large-scale community, and 'build a nation' where none had existed, because the nation is the only tested framework for economic and social development. In other words, nationalism was both the result of the need for growth and its motivation and dynamic, while the nation provided the only reliable basis and framework for that growth.[11]

This is an optimistic, activist account. It sees the nation as a community of participants sharing common values and purposes, appropriate to a modern era of economic growth and political emancipation. In this account, nationalism may be a regrettable, even destructive, force in a plural world, but the nation is the only really viable unit of political organization and community today. This is because for modernists the nation is socially and politically determined. Its foundations lie deep in the economic, social and political processes of modernization since the French Revolution, if not earlier, and the nation partakes of the social and political benefits of modernity. It follows that for a modernist the interesting questions concern not the nature of nations and national states, but their historical origins and sociological bases.[12]

Now all this appears quite *passé* and uninteresting to a 'post modernist'. For one thing, it appears to reify the nation, to treat it as a 'thing' out there, with a dynamic of its own. For another, the modernist account fails to grasp the elusive, shifting character of all communities, including the nation. And third, for all their commitment to the idea that nationalism creates nations and not vice versa, the modernists shy away from the implication that the nation is ultimately a text, or set of texts, that must be 'read' and 'narrated', a particular historical discourse with its peculiar set of practices and beliefs, which must first be 'deconstructed' for their power and character to be grasped.

But there is something even more fundamental that divides postmodernist approaches from all their predecessors. This is their emphasis on cultural construction, as opposed to social and political determination. Here there has been a twofold shift: first, from structure to culture as the locus of analysis, and second, from determination to construction and representation. What this means is the abandonment of any notion of social structure and the constraints that it operates over social and political phenomena. Nations (or anything else) are no longer the products of social processes like urbanization or mass education or uneven capitalism, though uneven capitalism may still be lurking somewhere in the background. There is no need to search for origins or causal patterns. If you want to understand the meaning of national, ethnic or racial phenomena, you have only to unmask their cultural representations, the images through which some people represent to others the lineaments of national identity. For only in these images or cultural constructs does the nation possess any meaning or life. The nation is a communion of imagery, nothing more nor less.

It follows from this that 'post-modernist' accounts lack that optimism or activism that distinguishes modernist approaches to nationalism. There is, in fact, something weary and cynical, if not playful, about their conceptions of the nation, for all their recognition of its explosive power. Anderson, for example, certainly underlines the mass death that nationalism can inspire, but there is an air of fatality in his stress on human mortality, linguistic diversity, and the onward march of chronological, empty time. It seems there is little hope for the inhabitants of Babel.[13]

Little hope, and less light. For what does this radical re-think of the problems of nations and nationalism illuminate? What insights can it reveal that earlier approaches prevented us from seeing? Is there anything new in the assertion that nations are imagined communities, composed of engineered and invented traditions? Couldn't most nationalists themselves have told us as much? Wasn't—isn't—that the business of nationalism—inventing national traditions, representing images of the nation to sceptical compatriots, imagining a community that as yet exists only in their dreams? Are we then to conclude that 'post-modernist' approaches to the nation are no more than the theory of nationalist practices?

There seems to be no other conclusion, and it suggests that the recent radical rethinking of the problem of nationalism has abandoned the attempt to understand it causally and has substituted a series of descriptive metaphors. To those who may affect disdain, but in reality are perplexed and repelled by nationalism and its often unpredictable manifestations, these culinary and artistic metaphors have an undoubted attraction. But their charm is in inverse proportion to their theoretical penetration and rigour. Probe behind their colourful exterior, and we shall be unable to discover any real clue to the origins, power and ubiquity of nations and nationalisms in the modern world. Compared to the older 'modernist' accounts, their 'post-modernist' successors seem historically shallow and sociologically implausible.

But have the 'modernist' accounts of Deutsch and Gellner, Nairn and Kedourie, J. H. Kautsky and Tilly, fared any better? Have they been able to escape these charges? Have their activism and optimism enabled them to render a more plausible account of the rise of nations and the diffusion of nationalism? In many ways they have; but this has not been a consequence of their 'modernism'. Their relative success has been the result of their insistence on social determination: the belief that nations and nationalisms are causally determined by a variety of social and political factors. What has made their various analyses less plausible is their concomitant belief that these are all factors of 'modernity', that nations are products of factors operating in the last two or three centuries, which together constitute a revolution of modernity. In this vital respect, 'post-modernist' accounts concur. They too insist on the modernity, as well as the artificiality, of nations. They too see modern conditions like print-capitalism and political mobilization spawning nationalisms that invent and imagine nations. And they too fail to see the ways in which these conditions operate, not on some *tabula rasa* population, but on varying degrees and kinds of pre-formed populations. The images and traditions that go into the making of nations are not the artificial creations of intelligentsias, cultural chefs or engineers, but the product of a complex interplay between these creators, their social conditions and the ethnic heritages of their chosen populations.[14]

THE NATION AS HISTORIC DEPOSIT

It is at this point that a quite different concept of the nation suggests itself. This is the idea of the nation as a deposit of the ages, a stratified or layered structure of social, political and cultural experiences and traditions laid down by successive generations of an identifiable community. In this view, the contemporary situation of the nation is explained as the outcome, the precipitate, of all its members' past experiences and expressions. For this 'geological' standpoint, the ethnic past explains the national present. This is in stark contrast to recent anthropological approaches that emphasise how the present—its concerns, interests and needs—shapes and filters out the ethnic past.[15]

Let me illustrate with two examples. The first comes from early twentieth-century India. In the 1905 agitation over the British partition of Bengal, the radical Indian nationalist Tilak turned to the Hindu past for inspiration in his campaign against the British authorities. He had already appealed to the local cult of the Marathi hero, Shivaji, in Maharashtra; now he extended the scope of his appeal by invoking the Hindu cult of the dread goddess of destruction, Kali. Even more interestingly, he turned to passages from the Hindu classic, the *Bhagavad Gita*, and used its essentially devotional poetry on behalf of a political objective, the fight against British domination. The advice of the great Lord Krishna to the hero, Arjuna, became, in Tilak's hands, no longer simply the advice of a god to the hero in a family feud, but an invocation to courage, heroism and resistance against aliens. In this way, Tilak selected from the manifold past of the sub-continent of India certain specifically Hindu traditions and symbols, because he wished to extend the social composition of the Indian nation-alist movement to the lower classes; and he also reinterpreted those selected aspects to fit a new, essentially political and national purpose which the original experiences and texts did not bear.[16]

Now, according to the 'gastronomic' theory, Tilak and his followers were like culinary artists devising a new recipe for the reimagined Indian nation, a hot and explosive Hindu recipe. As social engineers they devised a new political strategy for the mobilization of the Hindu masses. From the standpoint of the 'geological' theory, however, all Tilak and his fol-lowers did was to rediscover layers of the ethnic Hindu past, deposits that had lain dormant for millennia in the Hindu consciousness, and allow these materials to dictate the shape of a reconstructed Hindu Indian nation. Indeed, modern India in this approach is largely another layering upon a pre-existing series of strata, without which it would be impossible to recon-struct, or indeed grasp, the modern Indian nation. To understand the ideas and activities of Tilak, of Indian nationalists, and of the modern Indian nation as a whole, we must trace its origins through the successive strata of its history back to the initial formation of a Hindu Indian ethnic com-munity in the Vedic era.[17]

Modern Israel affords a second example. The heroic self-sacrifice of 960 Jewish men and women on the fortress of Masada in 73 CE was not an event of major significance in the shaping of subsequent Jewish history. Compared to the defence, fall, and destruction of Jerusalem and its Temple, it was insignificant. Masada, in fact, was barely remembered, despite the accounts in Josephus and later Jossipon, preserved by the Church; it was not commemorated by Jews or Judaism, nor mentioned in the Talmud or Midrash. Only in the early twentieth century was interest in Masada kindled—first in a Masada Society in London, and then in Yitzhak Lam-dan's poem of 1927, entitled *Masada*, written in and for the Palestinian Yishuv. In that earlier period, the image of Masada as set down in Lamdan's poem answered to feelings of despair and defeat, as many Jews left Palestine, unable to face its hardships. Later, after 1948, Masada came to symbolize the spiritual victory of the Jewish people over a perennially hostile envir-onment, a heroic affirmation of national will and dignity in the face of superior external forces besieging the infant state, an image reinforced by the vivid discoveries of Yigal Yadin's excavations.[18]

Now, for the 'gastronomic' theory, the recent Israeli selection of Masada, while in no way opportunist like the Englishman's 'ploughman's lunch', was determined by the needs of modern Israeli generations for whom it has become a symbol of siege and victorious self-sacrifice over all odds. It has become an important ingredient in the Zionist image of modern Israel, one with a special appeal and use for the nationalist imagination. For the 'geological' theory, on the other hand, Masada represents, like the rock itself, one of the foundations of the Jewish people and hence of modern Israel, an undergirding of national will and aspiration in the face of tyranny and servitude. Ancient Zealot resistance represents a bedrock of the nation in its ancestral homeland, an historical prototype as well as an explanatory principle. Masada itself may have been of only symbolic importance, but the resistance of Maccabees and Zealots was crucial for grasping the later survival of the Jewish people, the necessary foundation on which later generations of diaspora Jewry could rest and build.[19]

As these two examples suggest, the 'geological' theory introduces a deep explanatory principle, namely, that modern developments cannot be understood without grasping the contours of much earlier social formations. Communities are, on this theory, built up in stages, each stratum lying on top of earlier ones, as in the ancient tells that punctuate the Middle Eastern landscape. The new ethnic layer or stratum has its own specific qualities, but it cannot be understood without thorough knowledge of the one beneath, and so on right back to the moment of ethnogenesis. Similarly, the later deposits or strata are to varying degrees shaped by earlier layers, at least in terms of their location and main features. Just as earlier deposits set limits to all the later strata, so the experiences of our ancestors limit and shape our own experiences. On this theory, the modern nation as an enduring descent group is in large part a precipitate of all the deposits of earlier generations of the community. The ethnic heritage determines the character of the modern nation.

We can take this theory a stage further. The modern nation becomes not just the collective precipitate of earlier deposits but a summation, and a new form, of those deposits. On this reading, the contemporary nation is simply the modern form of an age-old biological nation. According to this view, nations have always existed in one form or another. Human beings are recorded in the earliest surviving documents as belonging to nations; and nations are recorded from earliest antiquity as engaging in trade, diplomacy and war. Nations are ubiquitous. They are also immemorial. Like the family, the nation is a perennial feature of human history and society.

This is the perspective on the nation that I have described elsewhere as 'perennialism'. It was very popular, also in academic circles, before the Second World War. It remains popular in the world at large, even if most scholars today no longer accept its premises. Actually, it is only a radical form of the 'geological' theory of nations. It postulates an unchanging essence of the nation beneath different forms. Hence, each form adds a new layer of meaning and colour to the underlying principle of the nation. But it is the same nation, as it is the same rock or tell.[20]

But is it the same nation? Is the nation like a rock or tell? Does it have strata and layers like geological deposits? Is ancient Israel one form of an unchanging essence of Israel, and modern Israel another (modernized) form? Are ancient Hindu India and modern India different forms of the self-same India beneath? What about all those modern nations whose ancient national pasts are unknown or dimly remembered? Was the shamanistic culture of ancient Finland, recalled in the *Kalevala*, simply another form of an unchanging Finland and Finnish culture? Was the Zoroastrian religious culture of Sassanid Persia just another form of an underlying Persia and its Farsi culture? Or did the introduction of Christianity into Finland and Islam to Iran change more than the outer form of an underlying national substance? If they did, has not the revolution of modernity changed much more than the outer form of these communities?[21]

These are not just rhetorical questions. Merely to pose them is to highlight the implausibility of a 'perennialist' perspective. Clearly, modern India, Israel, Finland, and Iran are not simply modern forms of an unchanging communal essence. They are quite different societies and polities from what we understand of ancient India, Israel, Finland, and Iran, and not just in economics and politics, demography and social structure, where vast changes can be expected, but also in the more slowly changing realms of culture, language, religion, and historical consciousness. Though we can detect some elements of continuity, the revolutions of modernity have created a radical break in the cultural realms too, a break that can at times amount to a displacement, a break in continuity and memory—as if lightning had struck and split the communal rock, and a destructive fire had ravaged several cultural layers of the ancient tell.

THE NATIONALIST AS ARCHAEOLOGIST

Yet the fact that such questions about the identity of ancient and modern communities can be, and have been, posed suggests that the 'geological' metaphor is not wholly misleading. The nation is not a purely modern creation *ex nihilo*, much less a *mélange* of materials constantly reinvented to suit the changing tastes and needs of different élites and generations. The nation may be a modern social formation, but it is in some sense based on pre-existing cultures, identities and heritages.

The questions are: how shall we understand the relationship between modern nation and pre-modern culture? Does the modern nation lie like another layer on top of pre-existing ethnic traditions? Or does it simply emerge and grow out of earlier ethnic communities?

Neither of these alternatives captures the essential processes at work in the formation of nations. Nations cannot be likened to recent strata inertly covering much older ethnic cultures, even if they are related to earlier cultures. A geological metaphor fails to convey the active dynamism, the transformative power, which is characteristic of what we call 'nation-building'. It has no room for popular participation, for interaction with other nations, for projects of reconstruction or for the influence of different ideologies and myths. It presents a closed, static image of the nation, one far removed from the powerful currents of modern national will and aspiration.

Nor can we convincingly claim that modern nations simply 'grew' out of earlier ethnic communities and cultures. There is nothing immanent or cumulative about the nation. An evolutionary metaphor minimizes the discontinuity, the dislocation and struggle with outside forces which has so often accompanied the rise of modern nations. Nations cannot be regarded as part of some natural social order, as a necessary and irreversible process of growth, as nationalists themselves like to claim. Once again, this is to omit the unpredictable event, the conflict of interests, the influence of participants and the impact of external structures and forces. The rise of nations must be placed in the context of specific modern conditions, even where these are shaped by past experiences and ethnic heritages. How then shall we understand this complex process?

Let us return for a moment to the question raised by the episode of the rediscovery of Masada. Why was this ancient and obscure act of heroism raised to such symbolic heights? It was not simply an ingredient in the Zionist imagination of modern Israel; in fact, it hardly figured in early Zionist imagery. Nor can we regard it as a fundamental base or foundation on which modern Israel rests. The fact is that 'Masada' was both literally and symbolically rediscovered by particular groups at a specific moment in Jewish experience. Its cult was actively propagated, and it struck a deep chord in the hearts and minds of many Jews, both inside Israel and in the diaspora. There is an obvious explanation: in the popular modern Jewish consciousness

Masada echoed the heroic resistance of the Warsaw Ghetto fighters and more broadly the martyrdom of the Holocaust. This is what gave a relatively unknown episode of ancient Jewish history its great resonance. That, and the excitement of Yadin's discoveries on the fortress itself.[22]

This example suggests a different perspective on our problem of the relationship of the ethnic past to the modern nation, one that accords an important role to the nationalist as archaeologist. We commonly think of the archaeologist as an excavator of the material remains of past ages. But this is to omit the underlying purpose of the discipline of archaeology, which is to reconstruct a past era or civilization and relate it to later periods, including the present. This is done, of course, pre-eminently by dating. Chronology is the expression of a linear worldview that relates the past to the present and the future. Hence, in dating relics of past epochs, the archaeologist locates a community in its historic time, and in that sense provides a symbolic and cognitive basis or foundation for that community. In doing so, the archaeologist reconstructs the modern community by altering its temporal perspective and self-view.

But the archaeologist also fixes communal location in space. Excavations determine the where as well as the when. 'We', the present generation of the community, are located in specific places on the map. We are told of 'our origins' in space as well as time. Archaeology suggests the stages of 'our development', as well as those of earlier peoples who have not survived, in the land of our origins, the cradle of 'our civilization'. It also reveals and preserves the different achievements of those past stages in the homeland and hence the possibilities for future developments. And archaeologists do all this in the name of, and through the use of, modern science.[23]

What I am arguing is not that the archaeologist is a prototypical nationalist—though he or she may well be—but that we should regard the nationalist as a kind of archaeologist. This is not because archaeology has been central to the formation of modern nations, though it often has been, but because nationalism is a form of archaeology and the nationalist is a kind of social and political archaeologist.

What does it mean to say that nationalism is a form of political archaeology? And how does this suggest a new perspective on our problem? We may start by observing that all nations require, and every nationalist seeks to provide, a suitable and dignified past. This is true even of revolutionary nationalists, who seek out a distant, pristine past, an era of primitive communism. An ancient or primordial past is essential to the enterprise of forming nations for a number of reasons. It lends dignity and authority to the community and bolsters self-esteem. It suggests precedents for all kinds of innovation. This helps to make often painful changes more accept-able to the people. Moreover, the past provides *exempla virtutis*, models of nobility and virtue for emulation. The French revolutionaries, for example, modelled the France of their dreams on ancient republican Rome and looked to the likes of Cincinnatus, Scipio and Brutus the con-sul for moral and political guidance. Modern Greeks looked back to the age of Periclean Athens, modern Irishmen to a pagan Celtic era, modern Indians to the heroes of the *Ramayana* and *Mahabarata*, and modern Jews to Moses, David and Judah the Maccabee. All these ancient heroes and golden ages now entered the pantheon of the modern nation.[24]

But there is a deeper reason for the drive to rediscover an ethnic past, or 'ethno-history'. This is the need to reconstruct the modern nation and locate it in time and space on firm and authentic foundations. The role of nationalist intellectuals and professionals is to rediscover and rein-terpret the indigenous ethnic past as the key to an understanding of the present epoch and the modern community, much as archaeologists recon-struct the past in order to locate a culture, community or civilization in history, and thereby also relate it to the present era. Both are animated by the belief that the ethnic past explains the present, an understanding that is quite different from the modernist and post-modernist belief that the past is a construct of the present or simply a quarry of materials for its needs.

There is, however, still something missing from this historicist under-standing. It is the element of active intervention by nationalists and oth-ers in the construction of the nation. This is not the social engineering or culinary art of post-modernist approaches, nor even the Herculean social and political labours of 'nation-builders' (or better 'state-building') beloved of the modernists, important though these are. The active role of nation-alism, and of nationalists, is threefold: rediscovery, reinterpretation, and regeneration of the community. Let me take these in turn.

Rediscovery is fairly straightforward. It involves a quest for authentic communal 'ethno-history', the recording of memories, the collection of indigenous myths and traditions, the researching of fresh dimensions and the location of new sources, like the ballads of the Finnish *Kalevala* or the Irish sagas of the Ulster cycle of epic poetry. This is the role *par excellence* of the nationalist historian, philologist, anthropologist and archaeologist, the starting point of cultural nationalism.[26]

Reinterpretation is more complicated. Weighing the sources, sifting the traditions, fixing the canon of ethno-history, selecting from myths and mem-ories, so as to locate the community in a significant context, raises all kinds of questions of evidence and verification. But in this case the ethnic past is reinterpreted to make the national aspirations of the present appear authentic, natural and comprehensible. Forming part of a single unfolding drama of national salvation, that past must be selected and interpreted in a specifically national light. But the present too is selectively appropriated and interpreted, in accordance with the ideology of national authenticity. And nationalism postulates the need for a dignified, vernacular and preferably glorious, past. Hence, the nationalist actively intervenes in both history and the present, to provide particular interpretations of the communal past, according to the nationalist criterion that accords primacy to explanations in terms of an authentic past.[26]

This view accords considerable importance to the transformations wrought by nationalist activity but sees its role as rather more limited than that envisaged by both modernists and post-modernists. The latter regard the nation as the conceptual product of nationalism. As Gellner put it: 'Nationalism invents nations where they do not exist', though he added that it needs some pre-existing cultural materials to work on. Hobsbawm agrees: 'Nations do not make states and nationalisms but the other way round'. All this leaves out the role of the ethnic past, and hence of nationalism as a form of archaeology.[27]

We see this particularly clearly in the third activity of the nationalist: that of collective regeneration. Regeneration involves a summons to the people, mobilizing the members of the community, tapping their collective emotions, inspiring them with moral fervour, activating their energies for national goals, so as to reform and renew the community. Here the nationalist-archaeologist is revealed as a missionary romantic, drawing political conclusions from the cultural work of rediscovery and reinterpretation: 'if this is how we were, and that is how we must understand things, then this is what we now must do'.[28]

Such an approach suggests a more subtle view of the relationship of the ethnic past to the present than that presented by modernists or post-modernists, but also one which is more dynamic and active than that embodied in the geological metaphor. The past is not some brew of random ingredients put together by artistic inclination, nor a quarry of cultural materials out of which nation-builders invent nations, nor yet a succession of epochs on whose foundations the modern nation securely rests. The ethnic past is composed of a series of traditions and memories which are the subject of constant reinterpretation.

Several factors influence such reinterpretations. One, the impact of nationalist ideology, I have already discussed. A second is the scientific evidence at any given moment in time. Interpretations of 'our' ethnic past will depend, not only on nationalist ideology, but also on what historians currently tell us about past events or epochs. Historical research can change our evaluation of heroes or events of the community's past, just as it can explode myths. A third influence is social and political: whether the interpretation has popular resonance. Does it mean anything to a wider audience? Can it take root among the people at large? Thus the tale of Joan of Arc took root among the French people in the nineteenth century, as historians and Catholic apologists began more detailed and sympathetic enquiries into her trial and fate and as a more religious and popular nationalism swept the country.[29]

The final influence is less tangible. It is the patterning of a particular ethno-history and its symbolism, the relationship over time between certain key components that recur in that community's history. For example, the dominance of the state in Russia, the relative weakness of Russian civil society and Russian liberalism, and the consequent alternation between periods of strong, cruel leadership and factional anarchy, set limits to all subsequent developments in Russia. These patterns are also expressed in peculiarly Russian institutions, language and symbolism: in concepts of tsar, zemlya, narod and the like, in the role of the Kremlin, in the diffusion of bureaucracy, in conceptions of space and territory, chosenness and mission. Such concepts, institutions and symbols impose limits on the way subsequent generations grasp the experiences of their communal forebears. As a result, not only is Russian history utterly unlike French, German, or any other history, but it also sets clear limits to subsequent interpretations of itself, irrespective of the ideology of the interpreter.[30]

The upshot of all this is to confine the role of nationalism to that of discovery and interpretation of the past for the mobilization of the present. The nationalist finds that there are clear limits to the way in which his or her chosen nation can be reconstructed. These are the limits of particular ethno-histories, as determined by scientific, popular-political and cultural-symbolic criteria. Thus Masada could be woven into the drama of the rebirth of Israel and given its due, because the scientific evidence of Yadin's excavations coincided with a popular sense of siege and determination bred by the Holocaust and Arab encirclement; and because Masada, though itself a lesser episode, echoed many similar acts of Jewish heroism and martyrdom through the ages *al Kiddush HaShem.* It fitted well into a dominant pattern and symbolism of Jewish experience over the centuries. In rediscovering and reinterpreting the siege and martyrdom of Masada, Jewish nationalism was able to add another regenerative

motif to its understanding of Jewish history, and thereby inspire and mobilize many Israelis and Jews to greater heroism and self-sacrifice.[31]

CONCLUSION

Perhaps the central question in our understanding of nationalism is the
role of the past in the creation of the present. This is certainly the area in
which there have been the sharpest divisions between theorists of nationalism. Nationalists, perennialists, modernists, and post-modernists have
presented us with very different interpretations of that role. The manner
in which they have viewed the place of ethnic history has largely determined their understanding of nations and nationalism today.

For nationalists themselves, the role of the past is clear and unproblematic.
The nation was always there, indeed it is part of the natural order, even
when it was submerged in the hearts of its members. The task of the nationalist is simply to remind his or her compatriots of their glorious past, so
that they can recreate and relive those glories.

For perennialists, too, the nation is immemorial. National forms may
change and particular nations may dissolve, but the identity of a nation
is unchanging. Yet the nation is not part of any natural order, so one can
choose one's nation, and later generations can build something new on
their ancient ethnic foundations. The task of nationalism is to rediscover
and appropriate a submerged past in order the better to build on it.

For the modernist, in contrast, the past is largely irrelevant. The nation
is a modern phenomenon, the product of nationalist ideologies, which themselves are the expression of modern, industrial society. The nationalist is
free to use ethnic heritages, but nation-building can proceed without the
aid of an ethnic past. Hence, nations are phenomena of a particular stage
of history, and embedded in purely modern conditions.

For the post-modernist, the past is more problematic. Though nations
are modern and the product of modern cultural conditions, nationalists
who want to disseminate the concept of the nation will make liberal use
of elements from the ethnic past, where they appear to answer to present
needs and preoccupations. The present creates the past in its own image.
So modern nationalist intellectuals will freely select, invent and mix traditions in their quest for the imagined political community.

None of these formulations seems to be satisfactory. History is no
sweet shop in which its children may 'pick and mix'; but neither is it an
unchanging essence or succession of superimposed strata. Nor can history

be simply disregarded, as more than one nationalism has found to its cost. The challenge for scholars as well as nations is to represent the relationship of ethnic past to modern nation more accurately and convincingly.

Here I have suggested an approach that balances the influence of the ethnic past and the impact of nationalist activity. It does not pretend to offer a comprehensive theory of the role of nationalism. There are many other factors that need to be considered. But nationalists have a vital role to play in the construction of nations, not as culinary artists or social engineers, but as political archaeologists rediscovering and reinterpreting the communal past in order to regenerate the community. Their task is indeed selective—they forget as well as remember the past—but to succeed in their task they must meet certain criteria. Their interpretations must be consonant not only with the ideological demands of nationalism, but also with the scientific evidence, popular resonance and patterning of particular ethno-histories. Episodes like the recovery of Hatsor and Masada, of the tomb of Tutankhamun, the legends of the *Kalevala,* and the ruins of Teotihuacan, have met these criteria and in different ways have come to underpin and define the sense of modern nationality in Israel, Egypt, Finland and Mexico. Yigal Yadin, Howard Carter, Elias Lonnrot, and Manuel Gamio form essential links in the complex relationship between an active national present and an often ancient ethnic heritage, between the defining ethnic past and its modern nationalist authenticators and appropriators. In this continually renewed two-way relationship between ethnic past and nationalist present lies the secret of the nation's explosive energy and the awful power it exerts over its members.

Notes

1. For the kilt, see Hugh Trevor-Roper: 'The Invention of Tradition: The Highland Tradition of Scotland', in Hobsbawm and Ranger (1983), 15–42. For the English rural landscape, see Alun Howkins: 'The Discovery of Rural England', in Colls and Dodd (1986), 62–88.
2. E. Hobsbawm: 'Introduction: Inventing Traditions', in Hobsbawm and Ranger (1983, 13). For Kedourie's much earlier formulation, see Kedourie (1960, 1 and passim). What is new here is the stress on artifice and representation.
3. See Breuilly (1982, Conclusion) for the idea of the nation as a pseudo-solution to the modern split between the state and civil society. For the analysis of literary devices, see Anderson (1983, ch. 2); see also Samuel (1989, vol. III).

4. History textbooks in the Third Republic and thereafter are carefully analysed in Citron (1988); cf. also Weber (1979). For Hobsbawm's recent analysis, which is particularly critical of ethnic and linguistic nationalism, see Hobsbawm (1990).

5. For musical nationalism and Chopin, see Einstein (1947, ch. 17). For the influence of Sibelius' tone-poems of the *Kalevala*, see Layton (1985). On the role of literary intellectuals in Europe, see Smith (1981, ch. 5) and Anderson (1983, ch. 5).

6. See for example Fahrni (1987) and the critique in Im Hof (1991). Though the date and celebration of the Oath may be the products of nineteenth-century Swiss nationalism, its memory and significance were preserved as early as the White Book of Sarnen in the 1470s and then by Aegidius Tschudi's Chronicle of the sixteenth century, from which Schiller took the materials for his play, *Wilhelm Tell* of 1802. The position is more complex than 'post-nationalist' scholarship suggests.

7. See Rotberg (1967) for this phrase. For Nash (1989), ethnic relations are best viewed as a cauldron, but also as a refuge, one that often preserves and enhances the power and ties of ethnicity.

8. See Apter (1963) for the classic statement; also Binder (1964). For a penetrating recent survey of ethnicity and nationalism in Nigeria, see Igwara (1993).

9. For an application of the idea of 'imagined community' to modern Greek nationalism, see Kitromilides (1989). For the use of this type of discourse, see the essays in Samuel (1989, notably vol. III).

10. For earlier analyses stressing ethnic differences in modern Israel, see Friedmann (1967) and Smooha (1978).

11. 'Modernist' accounts include Deutsch (1966), Kautsky (1962), Kedourie (1971, Introduction), Tilly (1975, Introduction), Nairn (1977, chs. 2, 9) and Gellner (1964, ch. 7 and 1983).

12. A detailed discussion of some of these 'modernist' approaches can be found in Smith (1983).

13. For Anderson, nationalism is here to stay. It is like kinship and culture, not ideology. A more sceptical mood is conveyed in some of the essays in Samuel (1989) and in Tonkin, McDonald and Chapman (1989). See also Elshtain (1991) on cultural representations of collective sacrifice.

14. For a more detailed critique of the concepts of 'invention' and 'imagination' in relation to nations and nationalism, see Smith (1991b); for a critique of the 'modernist' standpoint, see Smith (1988). Cf. also the discussion of the case of ancient Sri Lanka in relation to these theories in Roberts (1993).

15. See the introduction and essays by Ardener, Just and Collard in Tonkin, McDonald and Chapman (1989). In the same volume, however, Peel criticizes what he calls the 'blocking presentism' of some of these contributions. Cf. also Kapferer (1988).

16. See M. Adenwalla: 'Hindu Concepts and the *Gita* in Early Indian National Thought', and R. I. Crane: 'Problems of divergent developments in Indian

nationalism, 1895–1905', both in Sakai (1961). The problem of what we may term ethnic Hinduism, i.e. the ethnicization of a Hindu religious community, has become a burning issue today.

17. For the modern Indian nationalist rediscovery of the Hindu past, see McCulley (1966) and Kedourie (1971, Introduction). Tilak was only one of a series of Indian nationalists, including Pal, Banerjea and Aurobindo, who sought in a glorious Aryan Hindu past the roots and inspiration for nation-building.

18. Lamdan's poem and the adverse circumstances of the Palestinian Yishuv in the 1920s are discussed in Schwartz, Zerubavel and Barnett (1986). For the Jewish resistance on Masada, see Josephus: *Jewish War* VII, 323–33.

19. For the Zealot resistance movement, and its religious dimensions, see Brandon (1967, ch. 2); for the role of Masada, and the excavations, see Yadin (1966).

20. See for example Walek-Czernecki (1929) and Koht (1947); for fuller discussion of 'perennialism', see Smith (1984b).

21. For discussions of the culture and historicity of the *Kalevala* sagas, see Branch (1985) and Honko (1985). For the demise of Zoroastrianism in Iran after the invasion of Islam, see Frye (1966).

22. See for example Elon (1972) on the influence of the Holocaust on modern Israel, and its cult of heroism and military resistance.

23. For the nationalist uses of archaeology, see Chamberlin (1979); also Horne (1984). See also the discussions in Smith (1986, chs. 7–8) and Renfrew (1987).

24. See Mary Matossian: 'Ideologies of "delayed industrialisation": some tensions and ambiguities', in Kautsky (1962). For classical *exempla virtutis*, especially in the French Revolution, see Rosenblum (1967) and Herbert (1972).

25. For an analysis of the nature of cultural nationalism, and its interplay with political nationalism, see Hutchinson (1987) and also Lyons (1979), both of whom discuss the Gaelic revival in late nineteenth century Ireland.

26. For the ideal of cultural authenticity in Herder, see Berlin (1976). For applications of this ideal in the appropriation of the ethnic past, and for nationalist intervention in history, see also Hobsbawm (1990, ch. 4) and Smith (1991a, ch. 4).

27. Gellner (1964, ch. 7); and Hobsbawm (1990, ch. 1), for whom 'invention' is an exposure of nationalist delusions.

28. It is particularly among 'vertical' demotic *ethnies* that we find this process of 'vernacular mobilization'; cf. Anderson (1983, ch. 5) and Smith (1989).

29. For Joan of Arc and her 'rediscovery' in nineteenth-century France, see Warner (1983). On the question of the popular resonance of nationalist interpretations and ethnic myths, see Kedourie (1971, Introduction) and Smith (1984a).

30. On tsarist Russian ethnic concepts and institutions, see M. Cherniavsky: 'Russia', in Ranum (1975) and for the patterns of Russian history, see Pipes (1977).

31. On the Zionist revolution and its connections with earlier Jewish conceptions, see Yerushalmi (1983) and Almog (1987); cf. also Smith (1992).

References

ALMOG, S. 1987 *Zionism and History*. Jerusalem: Magnes Press.

ANDERSON, B. 1983 *Imagined Communities: Reflections on the Origin and Spread of Nationalism*. London: Verso Books.

APTER, D. 1963 'Political religion in the new nations', in C. Geertz (ed.), *Old Societies and New States*. New York: Free Press.

ARMSTRONG, J. 1982 *Nations before Nationalism*. Chapel Hill: University of North Carolina Press.

BERLIN, I. 1976 *Vico and Herder*. London: Hogarth Press.

BINDER, L. 1964 *The Ideological Revolution in the Middle East*. New York: John Wiley.

BRANCH, M. (ed.) 1985 *Kalevala, the Land of Heroes*, trans. W. F. Kirby. London: The Athlone Press, and New Hampshire: Dover.

BRANDON, S. G. F. 1967 *Jesus and the Zealots*. Manchester: Manchester University Press.

BREUILLY, J. 1982 *Nationalism and the State*. Manchester: Manchester University Press.

CHAMBERLIN, E. R. 1979 *Preserving the Past*. London: J. M. Dent and Sons.

CITRON, S. 1988 *Le Myth National* Paris: Presses Ouvriers.

COLLS, R. and DODD, P. (eds.) 1986 *Englishness: Politics and Culture*, 1880–1920. London: Croom Helm.

DEUTSCH, K. W. 1966 *Nationalism and Social Communication*. New York: MIT Press.

EINSTEIN, A. 1947 *Music in the Romantic Era*. London: J. M. Dent and Sons.

ELON, A. 1972 *The Israelis: Founders and Sons*. London: Weidenfeld and Nicolson.

ELSHTAIN, J. B. 1991 'Sovereignty, identity, sacrifice', *Millennium, Journal of International Studies* 20, 3: 395–406.

FAHRNI, D. 1987 *An Outline History of Switzerland*. Zurich: Pro Helvetia, Arts Council of Switzerland.

FRIEDMANN, G. 1967 *The End of the Jewish People?* London: Hutchinson.

FRYE, R. 1966 *The Heritage of Persia*. New York: Mentor.

GELLNER, E. 1964 *Thought and Change*. London: Weidenfeld and Nicolson.

—— 1983 *Nations and Nationalism*. Oxford: Blackwell.

HERBERT, R. 1972 *David, Voltaire, Brutus and the French Revolution*. London: Allen Lane.

HOBSBAWM, E. 1990 *Nations and Nationalism since 1780*. Cambridge: Cambridge University Press.

HOBSBAWM, E. and RANGER, T. (eds.) 1983 *The Invention of Tradition*. Cam-bridge: Cambridge University Press.

HONKO, L. 1985 'The Kalevala process', *Books from Finland* 19, 1: 16–23.

HORNE, D. 1984 *The Great Museum*. London and Sydney: Pluto Press.

HUTCHINSON, J. 1987 *The Dynamics of Cultural Nationalism; The Gaelic Revival and the Creation of the Irish Nation State.* London: Allen and Unwin.

IGWARA, O. 1993 'Ethnicity, nationalism and nation-building in Nigeria, 1970–1990'. Unpublished Ph.D., University of London.

IM HOF, U. 1991 *Mythos Schweiz.* Zürich: Neue Zürcher Zeitung.

KAPFERER, B. 1988 *Legends of People, Myths of State.* Washington and London: Smithsonian-Institution Press.

KAUTSKY, J. H. (ed.) 1962 *Political Change* in *Underdeveloped Countries.* New York: John Wiley.

KEDOURIE, E. 1960 *Nationalism.* London: Hutchinson.

—— (ed.) 1971 *Nationalism in Asia and Africa.* London: Weidenfeld and Nicolson.

KITROMILIDES, P. 1989 '"Imagined Communities" and the origins of the national question in the Balkans', *European History Quarterly* 19, 2: 14–92.

KOHT, H. 1947 'The dawn of nationalism in Europe', *American Historical Review* 52: 26–80.

LAYTON, R. 1985 'The Kalevala and music', *Books from Finland* 19, 1: 56–59.

LYONS, F. S. 1979 *Culture and Anarchy in Ireland,* 1890–1930. London: Oxford University Press.

McCULLEY, B. T. 1966 *English Education and the Origins of Indian Nationalism.* 2nd edn, Gloucester, MA: Smith.

NAIRN, T. 1977 *The Breakup of Britain.* London: New Left Books.

NASH, M. 1989 *The Cauldron of Ethnicity in the Modern World.* Chicago: The University of Chicago Press.

PIPES, R. 1977 *Russia under the Old Regime.* London: Peregrine Books.

RANUM, O. (ed.) 1975 *National Consciousness, History and Political Culture in Early-Modern Europe.* Baltimore and London: Johns Hopkins University Press.

RENFREW, C. 1987 *Archaeology and Language.* London: Jonathan Cape.

ROBERTS, M. 1993 'Nationalism, the past and the present: the case of Sri Lanka', *Ethnic and Racial Studies* 16, 1: 13–16.

ROSENBLUM, R. 1967 *Transformations in Late Eighteenth Century Art.* Princeton: Princeton University Press.

ROTBERG, R. 1967 'African nationalism: concept or confusion?', *Journal of Modern African Studies* 4, 1: 33–6.

SAKAI, R. A. (ed.), *Studies on Asia,* Vol. II. Lincoln: University of Nebraska Press.

SAMUEL, R. (ed.), *Patriotism, the Making and Unmaking of British National Identity.* 3 vols. London: Routledge.

SCHWARTZ, B., ZERUBAVEL, Y. and BARNETT, B. M. 1986 'The recovery of Masada: a study in collective memory', *The Sociological Quarterly* 27, 2: 147–64.

SMITH, A. D. 1981 *The Ethnic Revival in the Modern World.* Cambridge: Cambridge University Press.

—— 1983 *Theories of Nationalism.* 2nd edn, London: Duckworth and New York: Holmes and Meier.

SMITH, A. D. 1984a 'National identity and myths of ethnic descent', *Research in Social Movements, Conflict and Change* 7: 95–130.

—— 1984b 'Ethnic persistence and national transformation', *British Journal of Sociology* 35: 452–61.

—— 1986 *The Ethnic Origins of Nations*. Oxford: Blackwell.

—— 1988 'The myth of the "modern nation" and the myths of nations', *Ethnic and Racial Studies* 11, 1: 1–26.

—— 1989 'The origins of nations', *Ethnic and Racial Studies* 12, 3: 340–67.

—— 1991a *National Identity*. Harmondsworth: Penguin.

—— 1991b 'The nation: invented, imagined, reconstructed?', *Millennium, Journal of International Studies* 20, 3: 353–68.

—— 1992 'The question of Jewish identity', *Studies in Contemporary Jewry* 8: 219–33.

SMOOHA, S. 1978 *Israel: Pluralism and Conflict*. London: Routledge and Kegan Paul.

TILLY, C. (ed.) 1975 *The Formation of National States in Western Europe*. Princeton: Princeton University Press.

TONKIN, E., McDONALD, M. and CHAPMAN, M. (eds.) 1989 *History and Ethnicity*. ASA Monographs 27. London: Routledge.

WALEK-CZERNECKI, M. T. 1929 '*Le rôle de la nationalité*' dans l'histoire de l'antiquité', *Bulletin of the International Committee of the Historical Sciences* 2: 305–20.

WARNER, M. 1983 *Joan of Arc*. Harmondsworth: Penguin.

WEBER, E. 1979 *Peasants into Frenchmen: The Modernisation of Rural France, 1870–1914*. London: Chatto and Windus.

YADIN, Y. 1966 *Masada*. London: Weidenfeld and Nicolson.

YERUSHALMI, Y. H. 1983 *Zakhor: Jewish History and Jewish Memory*. Seattle and London: University of Washington Press.

7

Ethnic Nationalism and the Plight of Minorities*

ABSTRACT

Ethnic nationalism is one of the main causes of the present plight of min-orities and the increasing flow of refugees around the world. This kind of nationalism emerges from demotic 'vertical' *ethnies* which are forged by intelligentsias into ethnic nations through vernacular mobilization of the masses. By redefining, re-educating and regenerating the *ethnie* and its mem-bers, ethnic nationalists politicize its culture and are drawn into purifying the community of 'alien' elements, which in turn may lead to the expulsion and even the extermination of minorities, the 'outsider within'. Only by some attenuation of ethnic nationalism, can minorities be protected.

Nationalism remains in the closing decade of the second millennium one of the most powerful social and political forces in the modern world. Not only does it continue to shape the relations between national states, even where they seek to form ever closer unions, it has proliferated in every part of the globe as a movement of collective protest and self-assertion against the existing distribution of power within and between states. As such, it constitutes the most dangerous, because unpredictable, threat to the present world order, while at the same time paradoxically guarantee-ing the pluralist shape of that order. At one and the same time, national-ism insures humanity against imperial tyrannies, while lending its name and sometimes its power to the creation of local tyrannies.

It is therefore fitting that those concerned with the problems of refugees should take time to consider one of the fundamental long-term, recurrent causes of both the category and the plight of refugees. Ethnic conflicts within states, and national conflicts between states regularly, if sometimes unpre-dictably, fill the reservoirs of refugees and asylum-seekers across the globe,

* *Journal of Refugee Studies* Vol. 7. No. 2/3 1994.

as human beings are uprooted by the ferocity of the nationalisms that help to generate such conflicts and are thrown onto the mercies of states that are currently less strife-torn by ethnic and national antagonisms. In the Balkans and the former Soviet Union, in the Middle East and the Indian sub-continent, in southeast Asia, in the Horn of Africa, central and southern Africa, not to mention the lapping tides of those seeking refuge in Western Europe and North America, the same inexorable process can be found: the rise of new movements of collective self-assertion, conflict with established states and other ethnic communities, displacement of men, women and children in their thousands from their ancestral homes, and the consequent ever tighter restrictions on entry into more fortunate states fearful of creating ethnic strife within their own borders and of a possible nationalist backlash against asylum-seekers.

Of course, not all ethnic conflicts produce vast numbers of refugees; nor do nationalist conflicts exhaust the many causes of refuge-seeking in the modern world, let alone in pre-modern eras. But it can be shown that many of the largest tides of refuge-seeking, certainly since the Second World War, have been the direct outcome of nationalist conflict, in the areas that I have just enumerated. Ethnic nationalisms, in particular, have helped to create the climate of fear, suspicion and resentment that make it so much easier to erect barriers to entry into more fortunate, wealthier states; and these in turn influence popular reactions to economic migrants and *Gastarbeiter* who make up so many of the numbers of non-nationals in the states of Western and Central Europe.

ETHNIC AND TERRITORIAL NATIONALISMS

But why should nationalism, and more particularly ethnic nationalism, figure so prominently and recurrently among the causes of refuge-seeking in the modern world?

To answer this question, we must briefly consider the *doctrine* and *movement* of nationalism, as well as the main features of its chief varieties.

There are, of course, as many descriptions and definitions of nationalism as there are students in the field. But we can isolate the main propositions of a '*core doctrine*' of nationalism, if we look at the goals and activities of nationalists in every part of the globe. We can list these propositions as follows:

1. The world is divided into nations, each with its peculiar character and destiny;

2. The nation is the sole source of political power;
3. Loyalty to the nation overrides all other loyalties;
4. Real freedom for individuals can only be realized in and through the nation;
5. Global peace and security can only be based on free nations.

Of course, these are only the basic tenets. Specific nationalisms elaborate on them with other, more contextual, and particularist, notions; and many of these are fairly florid and rhetorical notions like Ataturk's Sun Language theory of Turkish origins, or the Vedic Hindu vision of Indian destiny (Lewis 1968, ch. 10; McCulley 1966).

The *movement* that embraces these propositions strives for several goals. But certain themes recur. The nation must have a distinctive identity, a definite 'national character'. The nation must be unified. It cannot tolerate internal divisions, territorial or social. It must exemplify *fraternité* and appear like a vast family, a family of many families. Finally, the nation must be truly free, that is, autonomous, living according to its own inner laws, without external compulsion. That may include autarchy, economic self-sufficiency. It may also lead to expansion and conflict; but such outcomes are by no means a necessary consequence of the doctrine and movement *per se*. They depend on political circumstances and historical memories (Smith 1973, section 2; 1991, ch. 4).

On this basis, I would define *nationalism*, not as a general sentiment, but as

a definite ideological movement for attaining and maintaining autonomy, identity and unity of a social group, some of whose members deem it to be an actual or potential 'nation'.

The *nation* in turn I would define as

a named social group, with common historical memories and mass culture, occupying an historic territory or homeland, and possessing a single division of labour and common legal rights and duties for all members.

Once again, the definition here is based on a reading of the main goals and activities of nationalists in every country, as they try to mould autonomous, united and culturally distinctive nations out of the pre-existing cultures and ethnic ties of chosen populations (Deutsch 1966, ch. 1; Gellner 1983, ch. 5; and Smith 1983, ch. 7).

Nationalism is a doctrine and movement on behalf of the chosen nation. The *state* is not an intrinsic part of the doctrine or movement. Nevertheless, nationalism conceives the nation in different ways, and in some of these the state plays a greater conceptual role than in others. This has definite consequences for both the nature and consequences of particular nationalisms.

For our purposes, it is necessary to distinguish two kinds of nationalism. The first is territorial, the second ethnic. Territorial nationalisms regard the nation as a form of rational association. In this version, the individual must belong to a nation, but can choose which to join. Four features define the territorial nation: a definite, compact territorial homeland; common legal codes and the equality of all members before the law; the social and political rights of citizenship; and a shared 'civic religion' and mass, public culture.

Ethnic nationalisms, on the other hand, conceive of the nation as a community of culture and history, with a bond of solidarity that resembles the familial bond. Here a myth of common ancestry replaces residence in an historic homeland as the criterion of national membership; genealogy rather than territory defines the ethnic nation. Similarly, vernacular cultures, notably language and customs, are more highly prized than legal equality, and popular mobilization than citizenship. Finally, in place of a civic, mass culture, ethnic nationalisms extol native history and a more circumscribed ethnic culture.

As we shall see, both kinds of nationalism (which, in any case, are not mutually exclusive) may breed homogenizing policies and exclusive attitudes. But these are, for reasons that will shortly become apparent, more marked in the case of ethnic nationalisms. Since the latter are in any case much more common today than their territorial counterparts, the paper concentrates on the features, processes and consequences of ethnic nationalisms, and returns only at the end to their impact on more territorial forms of nationalism.

ETHNIES AND NATIONS

What are the ethnic bases of modern nations and nationalisms?

It is fashionable today to characterize modern nations as socially constructed units, or as imagined communities, in Anderson's well-known definition (Anderson 1983, ch. 1). It is true that many nationalisms seek to create nations where none existed, and some of today's nations are recent constructions in their present form. Nevertheless, those nations with the most durable solidarity and most distinctive cultural heritage have emerged on the basis of strong pre-existing ethnic ties. These ties may characterize only a 'core' region or group in the total population, be it central France, or Piedmont and Tuscany, or Castile; yet historically they have formed the crucible of state-formation or cultural standardization. Put differently, those nations that have a strong 'ethno-history' at their core, with resonant myths, memories, values and symbols, are more likely to endure and become viable political communities (Smith 1988).

There are three reasons for this. The first is historical. Many nations have grown out of a combination of pre-existing ethnic ties and state activities, over long periods. Second, the concept of the nation is sociologically related to that of the ethnic community, or what the French term an *ethnie*. In certain ways, the concept of the nation modifies and extends some of the features of an *ethnie* into the territorial, educational, economic and legal domains. The third reason is political. More and more nationalists conceive of the nation in ethnic terms, and use an ethnic model in their attempts to create nations where they have not existed. And this is where the problems begin.

What do I mean by an 'ethnic model' of the nation? What are the features of an *ethnie* that nationalists seek to appropriate for their new nations? These features include myths of common origins, shared ethno-histories, elements of shared culture and links with an historic territory. This means that we can tentatively define an *ethnie* as

a named unit of population with myths of common ancestry, shared memories and culture, an association with a homeland and sentiments of social solidarity (Horowitz 1985, chs. 1–2; Smith 1986, ch. 2).

Now, the forging of a new nation in the image of an older *ethnie* is fraught with problems. Modern nations are in a number of respects quite different from pre-modern *ethnies*. They are more compact and territorially more sharply demarcated; they are characterized by a mass, public culture; they manifest a single division of labour throughout, with concomitant mobility; and their members are subject to a single code of laws, with common rights and duties. In all these respects, they offer a contrast with the looser, vaguer but also more familial bonds of *ethnies* (Geilner 1983, chs. 3–5; Smith 1991, chs. 1–2).

At the same time, nationalists are concerned to incorporate into the modern nation certain features associated with earlier *ethnies*. In particular, they feel a need to endow the nation of their dreams with a common history, based on shared ethnic memories; as well as a sense of common destiny, emanating from those shared memories. They also wish to strengthen the distinctive cultural profile of the nation; here too they hark back to those shared components of culture, such as language or religion and customs, that characterize older *ethnies*.

But, whereas territorial nationalisms are content to endow their nation with a common history and mass culture, such that people of different origin can join and participate in both, *ethnic* nationalisms predicate shared history and culture on a myth of common ancestry, i.e. on ethnicity in the narrowest sense. Only people of a particular presumed descent can be members of the ethnic nation. Only such people can belong to the intimate family circle of the ethnic nation. Here lie the seeds of a collective exclusiveness that so frequently begets persecution and homelessness.

THE RISE OF DEMOTIC ETHNO-NATIONALISMS

We can trace the process of exclusion by comparing two kinds of premodern *ethnies* (Smith 1986, ch. 4).

The first of these is 'lateral' and aristocratic. Its boundaries are widely-drawn and ragged, often spanning considerable areas. Socially, lateral *ethnies* are confined to the upper strata, the monarch and his court, the nobles, priests and officials, sometimes the richer merchants. Typically, they evince no interest in disseminating their ethnic culture to outlying groups or lower strata; for their particular culture is part and parcel of their exclusive social status.

In contrast, 'vertical' *ethnies* are more compact and they have higher barriers to entry. They tend to be confined to much smaller areas, but often have more clear-cut boundaries. Socially, the ethnic culture is more widely diffused through the social scale; we find artisans and urban traders, and even some peasants, drawn into a more sharply defined ethnic community, especially where religious movements reinforce the sense of community.

The fundamental point about the 'vertical' *ethnie* is its demotic or popular nature. The ethnic community, in this case, consists of 'the people', and is regularly mobilized as a whole by religious or political leaders. These demotic *ethnies* often manifest a sense of popular mission, and are prone to social and religious movements with charismatic leaders. Such popular sentiments and mass movements bring an element of political instability which may lend their ethnic exclusiveness a dangerous and unpredictable character.

Now, many demotic *ethnies* have found themselves subjected to aristocratic ethnic polities and incorporated into unwieldy, but often oppressive empires. For longer or shorter periods, oppression nurtured the sense of collective mission and destiny, and kept alive popular sentiments of ethnic election. For Irish, Basques, Finns, Poles, Greeks, Armenians, Kurds, Druse, Sikhs, and many others, the loss of statehood and/or incorporation in large empires helped both to preserve their sense of ethnic identity over long periods and to feed their defensive zeal.

It is in the decline of empire from the eighteenth to the twentieth centuries that the roots of the present ethno-national crises lie. As their economies broke down under the impact of increasingly inefficient land tenure systems and trade rivalries, and their political systems failed to cope with the competing demands of social classes and ethnic communities, these empires revealed their inherent political weakness and cultural heterogeneity. In these circumstances, the various component groupings, social and ethnic, became the most probable bases for new political alignments. This is hardly surprising. But what matters is the manner in which this was brought about.

The break-up of modern empires was hastened by the twin processes of politicization of culture and vernacular mobilization. In pre-modern periods, culture rarely assumed any political significance. There were instances when religious communities like the Jews and Armenians came under attack for their religious culture, and felt it necessary to mobilize in its defence. But, on the whole, neither religion nor language became the object of political struggle as such, until the Reformation.

But, with the decline of empires went a new desire on the part of the rulers to legitimate their position through attempts to homogenize their populations. Such attempts could include linguistic standardization and/or conversion, as with the example of Russification under the last Tsars. This in turn provoked resistance on the part of hitherto quiescent and accommodated demotic ethnies. Since these attempts to homogenize ethnic minorities were often accompanied by social and cultural discrimination, they soon incited disaffection, notably by the small intelligentsias of each *ethnie* (Kedourie 1971, Introduction).

What these intellectuals and professionals sought was to mobilize their ethnic kinsmen of other classes against the incursions of the imperial state, by a process of rediscovering and renewing pre-existing ethnic ties and cultures. Through the promotion of vernacular languages, folklore and native customs, ethnic rituals and traditions, and the like, they hoped to secure a political base, but also to build a culture-community which could withstand imperialist interventions that threatened the foundations of their culture. By appealing to 'the people' in their native tongues, dress and customs, by evoking the mythological past and the shared memories and symbols of earlier generations of the mass of the chosen population, the intelligentsia brought a popular ethnic culture into the political arena, and made it the subject of political aspirations and struggles. Czech, Finn, Irish,

Kurdish, and Sikh intelligentsias, to name but a few, did not 'invent' a nation where none existed; they went back to the elements of an older ethnic culture and gave them a new social and political meaning, forging the lineaments of a political nation out of older demotic *ethnies*, by rediscovery and selective appropriation of popular myths, symbols, values, memories, and traditions (Hobsbawm and Ranger 1983; Hobsbawm 1990, ch. 2).

THE POLITICS OF ETHNO-NATIONALISM

Let us examine a little more closely the content and political consequences of this process of 'vernacular mobilization'.

Essentially, we are dealing with processes of re-definition, re-education and regeneration. The first step is perhaps the crucial one: the minuscule coterie of intellectuals redefine a loose ethnic community and its traditions as a potential nation, with compact social and territorial boundaries, common laws and institutions and a single, prescribed political culture. In the ethnic version of the nation with which I am concerned, they do all these things on the basis of a criterion of alleged common descent; we, the members of the future ethnic nation, are all descended from a named mythical ancestor and hence form a single family. 'We' had a definite origin in time and space, be it in the Central Asian steppes in the early first millennium, or the north German forests, or the Arabian deserts. Those who can lay claim to such ancestry and origins are true members of the nation-to-be; others who reside among us are guests or strangers.

The process of redefinition is one that sharpens the boundaries between 'us' and 'them'. Typically, ethnic communities in antiquity and the middle ages, for all their ethnocentrism and myths of ethnic election, were fairly open and accessible. There was in practice a good deal of intermarriage between members of different *ethnies*, even of the demotic variety, and even more cultural borrowing; witness all those biblical injunctions against idolatry and heathen ways, which clearly proved so perennially attractive to ancient Israelites and Jews (Zeitlin 1984).

But the process of redefining the community as a nation-to-be lays down a trajectory and sets up a boundary that is exclusive and potentially divisive. It locks out all those who cannot prove their membership credentials through the criterion of alleged ancestry.

The second step in the process of vernacular mobilization is to re-educate the genuine membership in the true culture, the pristine culture of their ancestors, unsullied by contact with modern civilization. This true culture is to be found in the authentic products of the people, their songs and ballads, their dances and games, their customs and folklore, their poetry, music, arts and crafts. Inspired by the researches and praises of Herder and his followers, folklorists, philologists, historians, archaeologists, anthropologists and other social science intellectuals, as well as poets, composers and painters, began to unearth the medieval cultures of eastern European and Asian *ethnies*, hitherto neglected by scholars and officials.

The Hungarian millennial celebrations of 1896 are a case in point. They produced a vast array of scholarly historical research into Magyar origins and history, as well as an efflorescence of Hungarian cultural artefacts, from grandiose buildings and monuments to history paintings and craft objects that embodied styles and genres deemed to retrieve and reproduce the primitive and medieval splendour of the Hungarian past (Eri and Jobbagyi 1989).

In this example, the nationalist intelligentsia have already assumed power in a semi-independent national state. But the process of re-education may take place outside the state framework, through a nationalist movement, a national reformist school system, a nationalist guerrilla campaign, or a national-religious upsurge. In all these cases, the genuine folk, the chosen people of the nation-to-be, must be nurtured in the authentic culture of their forebears.

The third step is to regenerate and politicize the culture itself. This means rediscovering its primordial elements, selecting the genuine components and rejecting extraneous accretions. Only by excluding foreign elements can the original culture emerge and be reborn. Thus, Eliezer ben-Yehuda went to Palestine to revive what he took to be an original biblical Hebrew on its own soil, excluding all those medieval accretions which the wandering Jewish communities had acquired in their long sojourn in the diaspora (Hertzberg 1960).

It is of course but a further step to the idea of purifying the nation itself. Not only the culture, but the people too, must become worthy scions of an original culture-community, one whose 'irreplaceable culture-values', in Max Weber's phrase, must be preserved and safeguarded. So must their bearers and guardians, lest both values and people be lost to the world. But the process of national purification which begins with a desire to recover a partly submerged ethnic past, can so easily end in the exclusion of other, non-national values and ultimately their bearers, lest they defile the rediscovered and regenerated original culture. Thus the more fervent Finnish nationalists began to exclude alien cultural influences and ground their native culture on the heroic myths of the *Kalevala*; their German counterparts ended by excluding the bearers of values they considered alien, even before the advent of National Socialist racism (Branch 1985; Mosse 1964).

The drive for national purification in demotic ethno-nationalisms, tends to elevate the people as the repository of truth and virtue, and the embodiment of true national values. This is an extension of the quest for popular sovereignty, which originated in the West, but took on an increasingly populist form among the demotic nationalisms of eastern Europe and Asia. Democratization may give birth to a mass nationalism, which defines the community that will exercise sovereignty; but it also raises the values and culture of the populace to become the touchstone of national purity and national identity. The nation and the people have been fused, and identified with the *ethnie*.

At this point, we may begin to speak of the creation of an ethnic nation, and a national identity whose point of reference is a myth of ancestry and shared ethnic memories. In the ethnic model of the nation, citizenship becomes coextensive with the membership of the dominant ethnic community, while territory and culture are defined in terms of the community and treated as its exclusive property. So, the homeland and its cultural heritage become expressions of an enduring kinship bond, one that is unable to accommodate those who do not share that bond.

What are the typical political consequences of creating ethnic nations? One effect is to hasten, as we saw, the break-up of empires. But not only of empires; also of multi-national states of all kinds, of Yugoslavia and Czechoslovakia as well as the former Soviet Union and Ethiopia. Circumstances permitting, ethnic secession is the normal outcome of the creation of ethnic nations, a process encouraged and guided by ethnic intelligentsias eager for economic rewards and status denied them in the larger multi-national states into which they had been incorporated. By mobilizing the people and purifying its vernacular culture, the intelligentsia set in motion an exclusionary trend whose long-term outcome inevitably leads to separation from other *ethnies* and from the incorporating state.

Because such separations, however, are rarely without problems, the process of vernacular mobilization tends to breed ethnic tensions and conflicts. Separatist Czechs came into competition and conflict with urban Sudeten Germans, Slovaks with Czechs, Lithuanians with Russians, Sikhs with Punjabi Hindus, Tamils with Buddhist Sinhalese, and Kurds with Sunni Iraqis and Turks. In these and many more cases, the very process of reappropriating an authentic heritage and mobilizing the masses in their vernacular culture ruptures the old interethnic relations and turns passive communities into active political nations. By locating these communities in their historic landscapes, and evoking the heroic legends of their golden ages, the myth-making intelligentsias strike a popular chord that separates as it inspires the popular masses (Smith 1986, ch. 8).

THE PLIGHT OF MINORITIES

The second political consequence is internal. It involves the categorization of 'outsiders' within, of those who cannot and do not form part of the chosen, and who therefore sully the community's ideal purity. This is a process found in earlier periods of religious conflict, when schismatic sects sought to bind their members together more securely by persecuting any deviants and heretics within. In a more secular era, we find similar processes at work in mobilized demotic *ethnies*; only in these cases the deviants and heretics are replaced by 'outsiders' within, members of ethnic minorities who happen to reside on the historic territory claimed or possessed by a dominant *ethnie*.

There are a number of stages involved in the creation of alien minorities. Many of them may already have suffered from exclusion and alienation, as with the Jews, Armenians and Chinese. But in the early modern era, the drive to unify absolutist states, followed by the even stronger homogenization programmes of national states, provoked resistance among the larger and more resilient *ethnies* and their intelligentsias. Where the new national state was dominated by a single *ethnie*, intent on self-purification and vernacular mobilization, the opportunities for accommodation or assimilation by members of other ethnic groups and categories were substantially reduced.

The process of homogenization is not itself a product of nationalism. In fact, it antedates the rise of nationalism. Apart from attempts to create religious uniformity in earlier periods, linguistic and cultural standardization and uniformity were policies of absolutist monarchs from the Tudors and Bourbons on; and were partly reproduced in the French colonies, at least for indigenous élites. Nevertheless, the rise of ethnic nationalism has significantly reinforced these trends, with corresponding pressures on ethnic minorities.

The key point here is the tendency of ethnic nationalisms to single out and categorize minorities within as 'alien' to the historic culture-community. Since the latter is seen as pure and authentic, non-members within are inevitably cast as counter-types and become targets of suspicion and hostility. Where there is also significant ethnic competition in labour markets, housing and education opportunities, the process of targeting is intensified and rationalized. Not only are jobs and houses reserved for members of the dominant *ethnie* and its authentic culture, aliens within become politically suspect and vulnerable. In these circumstances, they may be discriminated against, harassed, segregated and finally expelled, or even exterminated.

Genocide, however, is generally confined to those cases where ethnic nationalism mingles with biological racism to produce a determined policy of dehumanization and victimization. In these instances, 'race' in the sense of allegedly immutable physical characteristics defining group identity, entirely excludes and negates the rights and humanity of aliens within. They are pushed outside the human family and denied a human face (Van den Berghe 1967; Poliakov 1974; Kuper 1981).

More often, however, ethnic nationalism does not involve a specifically racist component, but manages to exclude non-members within and deny their rights, while preserving their essential humanity. Instead of being exterminated, they are rendered homeless. As indigestible minorities in their own homes, they suddenly find themselves deprived of a homeland. They are felt to constitute a threat to the continued existence, and purity, of the emergent ethnic nation. They must therefore be denied citizenship in their own land, rendered defenceless and homeless and ultimately driven out. Of course, not all political refugees are the victims of radical ethnic nationalism and its homogenizing drive. Some are the human cost of local and global wars. Yet here too, aggressive ethnic nationalisms play a pivotal role. Many local wars today are the product of ethnic antagonisms, such as those between Armenians and Azeris, Palestinians and Israelis, Somali and Amhara, Tamils and Sinhalese, Hutus and Tutsis, and Serbs, Muslims and Croats, as well as the conflict in northern Ireland. In each of these cases, we have witnessed the plight of helpless minorities and the flight of families in the path of war, an image only magnified a hundredfold in the last global war.

The study of ethnic nationalism's political impact also casts a fresh light on the old controversy about economic and political refugees. From 1881 to 1914, over five million Jews left the Russian Pale of Settlement and sought refuge in the West, mainly America. Many left because of bleak economic prospects, others because they feared call-up for twenty five years in the Tsarist armies, others still because of virulent pogroms and festering religious anti-Semitism. Whatever the immediate reasons, their migration was structured by prior classifications, sentiments and policies: confinement to the Pale as Jews, aliens within, barely tolerated as a 'pariah people'. Ethnic nationalisms in such a structured situation could only exacerbate and intensify ethnic and religious antagonisms, rendering alien minorities entirely unassimilable (Greenberg 1976).

From this standpoint, the attempt to separate purely economic from political or ethnic refugees, on the basis of subjective assessments and information, is a flawed exercise; it omits the overall ethno-national framework within which the more specific grounds for seeking refuge and asylum operate.

CONCLUSION: DE-ETHNICIZING THE NATION?

What conclusions can be drawn from this general analysis of the processes of ethnic nationalism?

The first is clear enough. As long as ethnic nationalisms proliferate across the globe, we may expect the flow of refugees and asylum-seekers to continue. While it is not possible to establish any exact correlations between intensities of ethnic nationalisms and rates of refuge-seeking, we may hazard the generalization that the more protracted and bitter the conflicts engendered by ethnic nationalisms, the more likely are we to witness large-scale refugee problems, as in Sri Lanka, Palestine, Kurdistan, Bosnia, Ethiopia, and central and southern Africa.

A second conclusion is also fairly obvious. As long as the purely ethnic model of nationalism prevails, we can expect to find new groups being categorized as outsiders within and treated as second-class citizens in their own lands, if not harassed and expelled. The mobilization of the people and the purification of their culture soon spills over into the political and economic spheres, bringing in their wake ethnic citizenship and ethnic job reservation. For all those ethnic minorities that cannot hope to convince their neighbours and the world of their right to national self-determination in a state of their own, the outlook is grim; smouldering resentments are likely to produce periodic uprisings—and waves of refugees, when the revolts are crushed.

Third, as long as most national states and most of the, new 'state-nations' of Africa and Asia remain wedded to a model of ethnic integration, if not assimilation, in which the dominant *ethnie* and its culture takes pride of place in political and economic terms, the chances of reducing the periodic flow of ethnic refugees are slim. Perhaps the single most important programme needed to stem these unpredictable tides, apart from initiatives to overcome chronic poverty, malnutrition and ecological disaster, would be to try to 'de-ethnicize' the nation and the state-nation (that is, the state which strives to become a nation, where several *ethnies* now compete). Such a programme involves redefining the nation in more territorial, legal, cultural and educational terms, employing a more polyethnic and pluralist perspective on nationalism. In this way, it may become possible to relax the more ethnic components of this bond and lay more emphasis upon a public, mass culture, a shared homeland and common legal codes.

There are two major problems here. The first, as always, is the role of 'history' and 'destiny' in the fabric of de-ethnicized nations. It is the problem of shared memories. Whose past and whose future does the concept of the nation encompass? Who can be said to belong to this community of history and destiny? And what is the cultural heritage and 'ethno-history' that can include, rather than exclude, the different ethnic communities within its territorial boundaries? The second problem is the need for solidarity. Every society and polity requires some principle of solidarity, and this is especially true of a modern era in which states and their citizens must compete against each other for finite resources in a very unequal division of international labour. Presumed ethnic ancestry provides a clear and salient principle. As long as members of the nation believe that they are related through a myth of common origins and descent, and this is reinforced by shared memories and culture, the likelihood of their relinquishing ethnicity for some other, more fluid and flexible, principle of solidarity is remote.

There are no easy solutions to such problems. All we can say is that upon those solutions, as much as upon economic and ecological conditions, will depend not only the present fate of so many of the world's refugees, but also the prospects for reducing the chronic problems of refuge-seeking in the future.

For the pressures of refugees themselves exert a further profound impact, this time upon the host countries in the West that have to date operated with more territorial national self-definitions. Increasingly we may be witnessing the 're-ethnicization' of territorial nations, their adoption of more exclusive ethno-national self-definitions and a corresponding stress on the culture and heritage of the dominant *ethnie*. This can be construed on an immediate, individual level, as an ethnic backlash against the multicultural uses to which territorial definitions of national identity have been put. But on a longer-term, more collective level, such 're-ethnicization' must be seen as one more step in the process of territorial hardening and ethnic impermeability, which can only compound the bitter tragedies of so many refugees, whether in France or Italy, Britain or Hong Kong.

Creating polyethnic nations, on the Swiss model, is a difficult and complex task. In Switzerland, it took some six hundred years, several bloody conflicts and considerable national exclusiveness in times of crisis. The world cannot wait even sixty years, before massive population growth, profound economic inequalities and ethnic wars combine to produce vast tides of refugees with hardly any sanctuaries. The ethnic aspect of this complex set of problems needs to be tackled at both ends of the refugee chain: in the originating areas and in the destination states. In both, purely ethnic models of the nation and predominantly ethnic varieties of nationalism would need to be attenuated, in favour of more inclusive, cultural, territorial and political concepts and movements (though 'civic' models may turn out to be just as severe to minorities, or rather their communal culture). As the case of Catalonia demonstrates, it may even prove possible to combine linguistic-cultural with territorial concepts of the nation and generate an inclusive, assimilative cultural nationalism (Conversi 1990).

Nationalism is not a unitary, fixed set of tenets and ideals. As doctrine, movement and symbolism, it has proved chameleon-like, capable of almost infinite adaptation and reformulation, while preserving its underlying purposes. The regenerated nation can be seen in many different ways, only some of which have those adverse political consequences of conflict, terror and endemic instability which nationalism's many detractors so frequently denounce. What I would contend is that, even if we cannot begin to move beyond a world of nations—and that may remain a dream for some time to come—we may perhaps be able to construct a series of more polyethnic nations held together by cultural, territorial, economic and legal bonds, which can accommodate many of the world's refugees and asylum-seekers—with adequate safeguards for ethnic minorities. If this turns out to be a vain hope, then we shall be witnessing many more refugee tragedies in the next millennium.

References

ANDERSON, B. 1993 *Imagined Communities: Reflections on the Origins and Spread of Nationalism*. London: Verso Books.

BRANCH, M. (ed.) 1985 *Kalevala: the Land of Heroes*. trans. W. F. Kirby, London: The Athlone Press, and New Hampshire: Dover.

CONVERSI, D. 1990 'Language or Race? The Choice of Core Values in the Development of Catalan and Basque Nationalisms', *Ethnic and Racial Studies* 13(1): 50–70.

DEUTSCH, K. W. 1966 *Nationalism and Social Communication*. 2nd edn, New York: M.I.T. Press.

ERI, G. and JOBBAGYI, Z. (eds.) 1989 *Art and Society in Hungary 1896–1914*. London: Barbican Art Gallery, Corvina.

GELLNER, E. 1983 *Nations and Nationalism*. Oxford: Blackwell.

GREENBERG, L. 1976 *The Jews in Russia, 2 vols*. New York: Schocken Books.

HERTZBERG, A. (ed.) 1960 *The Zionist Idea: A Reader*. New York: Meridian Books.

HOBSBAWM, E. 1990 *Nations and Nationalism since 1780*, Cambridge: Cambridge University Press.

HOBSBAWM, E. and RANGER, T. (eds.) 1983 *The Invention of Tradftion*. Cambridge: Cambridge University Press.

HOROWITZ, D. 1985 *Ethnic Groups in Conflict*. Berkeley, Los Angeles and London: University of California Press.

KEDOURIE, E. (ed.) 1971 *Nationalism in Asia and Africa*. London: Weidenfeld and Nicolson.

KUPER, L. 1981 *Genocide*. Harmondsworth: Penguin.

LEWIS, B. 1968 *The Emergence of Modern Turkey*. London: Oxford University Press.

McCULLEY, B. T. 1966 *English Education and the Origins of Indian Nationalism*. Gloucester, Mass: Smith.

MOSSE, G. 1964 *The Crisis of German Ideology*. New York: Grosset and Dunlap.

POLIAKOV, L. 1974 *The Aryan Myth*. New York: Basic Books.

SMITH, A. D. 1973 'Nationalism, A Trend Report and Annotated Bibliography', *Current Sociology* 21, no. 3.

—— 1983 *Theories of Nationalism*. 2nd edn, London: Duckworth.

—— 1986 *The Ethnic Origins of Nations*. Oxford: Blackwell.

—— 1988 'The Myth of the "Modern Nation" and the Myths of Nations', *Ethnic and Racial Studies* 11, no. 1, 1–26.

—— 1991 *National Identity*. Harmondsworth: Penguin.

VAN DEN BERGHE, P. 1967 *Race and Racism*. New York: John Wiley.

ZEITLIN, I. 1984 *Ancient Judaism*. Cambridge: Polity Press.

Zionism and Diaspora Nationalism*

There are two main views of Zionism. The first regards it as a unique phenomenon, the second as yet another of the many ethnic nationalisms of small peoples. The first view is internal: it proceeds from the specifics of the Jewish historical experience. The second view is largely external: it locates and explains Jewish nationalism, and Zionism, within the broader European experience of nationalism. Neither approach has much to commend it. The first fails to consider the different kinds of Jewish nationalism and the changes within Zionism in response to a changing world. The second is unable to deal with the many continuities between Jewish nationalism and Jewish traditions and experiences through the ages, except in a very superficial manner. Even more serious, while the first, or uniqueness, view is unable to see any parallels between Jewish and other ethnic experiences, the second, or similarity, perspective can never grasp the subjective Jewish meanings of the Zionist ideals for the participants or appreciate the special features of Jewish nationalism. What we need instead, and what I shall be arguing for, is a perspective that does justice to both the external and internal aspects of Zionism and Jewish nationalism, and which locates them in that special sub-type of nationalisms, ethno-religious diaspora nationalism. By placing Zionism within this category of ethnic nationalisms, I think we can clarify a number of features that have puzzled observers of Jewish nationalism.

UNIQUENESS AND SIMILARITY

Let me start with the external, or similarity, approach. It was well argued by Hugh Trevor-Roper over thirty years ago. For Trevor-Roper, Jewish nationalism was a 'secondary' nationalism like the neighbouring Czech, Slovak or Croat examples, all of which emerged in the latter half of the nineteenth century within the confines of the Habsburg Empire. These

* *Israel Affairs*, Vol. 2, No. 2 (Winter 1995).

nationalisms were secondary or derivative because they succeeded and responded to the earlier 'primary' nationalisms of the Italians, Germans and Hungarians. These were the original and exemplary nationalisms, from which the later nationalisms derived most of their ideas and methods. They were also unifying, whereas the later, derivative nationalisms were divisive. While the German, Italian and to a lesser extent the Hungarian movements aimed to unite adjacent principalities and areas on the basis of assumed linguistic homogeneity, the movements of small peoples like the Czechs, Slovaks and Jews aimed to divide and fragment larger political units along cultural and linguistic lines.[1]

This is a view shared more recently by Eric Hobsbawm, who discerns two kinds of nationalism, the first civic, political and democratic, stemming from the French Revolution, the second ethnic, linguistic and cultural, deriving from the ideas of the German Romantics. The earlier kind of nationalism which flourished in Europe in the period 1830–70, tended to unify and homogenize populations in powerful states and create large territorial markets for an expanding economy. The ethno-linguistic types of nationalism, on the other hand, flourished in the period 1870–1914, and tended to split larger political units along cultural lines, thereby impeding the movement of history, which is always to create larger units of population and territory to accommodate the new forces of production and technology characteristic of an expanding global capitalism.

For Hobsbawm, indeed, the flight into ethno-linguistic nationalism is always a reaction of anxiety and disappointment: popular fear of the vast economic and social transformations of global capitalism, and disappointment after the failure of international ideological projects to harness the potential created by those changes, notably the project of international socialism.[2]

There is a further similarity between Hobsbawm and Trevor-Roper. Both see secondary, or ethno-linguistic, nationalism as the special preserve of intellectuals or intelligentsia, what Hobsbawm refers to as the 'lower examination passing classes'. Trevor-Roper, like Elie Kedourie, regards the intellectuals as the conduit for the spread of nationalism. They both imitate the major nationalisms of their larger neighbours and react against them. While he does not embrace this 'imitation-reaction' mechanism, Hobsbawm too lays at the feet of the intelligentsia the main responsibility for the shift towards a reactionary ethnic and linguistic nationalism. However, it is not clear from his account why the intelligentsia should embrace cultural mini-nationalisms, nor why language and culture are now elevated as principles of national differentiation.[3]

Interestingly, neither historian allows any role to the past in their accounts of nationalism. Both are strictly 'modernist'. That is, they view nationalism as a quintessentially modern movement, being both chronologically recent (since the French Revolution) and qualitatively unprecedented and novel. They also look to specifically modern developments for an explanation of nationalism, the one in the rise and role of intellectuals, excluded from power, the other in the tendency of capitalism and state power to create larger units of resource and population, and the subsequent popular reactions against such tendencies expressed and orchestrated by petit-bourgeois intelligentsia. Modernism is assumed in Trevor-Roper's, as in Kedourie's, account: the story starts in the nineteenth century, and there is no need, or place, for the past, except in the sense that the 'peoples' for whom the movements strive are already present on stage. In Hobsbawm's case, the removal of the past is explicit. He devotes a whole chapter to what he calls 'proto-nationalism'. One might expect from his introduction of this concept that he was about to demonstrate the often subtle interweaving of past with present in nationalisms of all kinds; but not a bit of it. Hobsbawm resolutely refuses to relate pre-modern communities of sentiment, based on religion, region or language, to modern civic-political nationalism, or, it seems, to ethno-linguistic nationalisms. This comes out particularly sharply in the case of Zionism, where he argues that the modern territorial ingathering of Jewish exiles into Palestine has no connection with the age-old religious yearning for Zion among diaspora Jews. Only in the case of Russia, where state and church so clearly created a proto-national community which formed the basis of the modern Russian nation, is Hobsbawm prepared to allow any connection between ethnic past and secular present.[4]

For historians like Kedourie, Trevor-Roper or Hobsbawm, Zionism like other nationalisms is simply a creation of frustrated intellectuals and professionals. Hobsbawm uses the idea of 'invented traditions' to suggest how much of nationalist symbolism, history and mythology is specifically engineered and tailored for the needs of the present and the interests of ruling classes to which the intellectuals cater with their inventions. Thus Zionist symbolism, history and mythology was the work of modern intellectuals from Max Nordau to Ben-Zion Dinur, who supplied their leaders and movements with resonant materials culled from a rich heritage to suit present preoccupations and needs.[5]

In stressing the role of construction, invention and diffusion, modern historians of all ideological hues are reacting against an older generation of historians for whom nations were part of the human, if not the natural, order, and could be found in all periods of time and every continent. For such 'perennialists', the Jews provided powerful ammunition. Have not the Jews survived at least from the time of Ezra, have they not been associated with their own sacred land, have they not through all their wanderings preserved their ancient faith and sacred tongue? And do not Jews everywhere respond to the ancient symbols of their people, the Torah scrolls and menorot, the fasts and feasts, the Kaddish and Shema, the Shabbat candles and Kashrut, even when they do not observe all or even most of the *mitzvot*? Are not the Jews truly a perennial, even a 'primordial' people?[6]

More important, the singular history of the Jews demonstrated that every perennial nation is, after all, a unique phenomenon, incommensurable and *sui generis*. It is therefore vain to search for common antecedent causes for what are quite disparate phenomena with no more than a loose family resemblance which attracts the catch-all term of 'nationalism'. One cannot treat nations and their nationalisms like the phenomena of the natural world, which can be subsumed under general laws with efficient causes. The reason is that the very idea of 'nationness' defies the logic of cause and effect; it operates only at the level of intelligibility and meaning, the meaning or meanings with which the members of that nation endow it. Thus the Jewish nation is only to be grasped through a thorough knowledge and understanding of the meanings and sentiments of its members through the ages; and it is enough for those members to aver that they are 'Jews', rather than anything else, for us to have to accept the existence of the Jewish nation in each epoch of its history.[7]

From an internal standpoint, therefore, each nation is necessarily unique and perennial. It is the members who view the nation in this light, and their view is privileged. We as outsiders are in no position to challenge that view. We can have only a superficial, schematic and distorted understanding of each nation, since we do not share in its history or culture, and are debarred from true understanding which comes from membership in a common fate. This is especially true of the Jewish people, where persecution and genocide have sharpened the cleavage with non-Jews and forced the Jews to rely on their own inner resources; and where the return to the homeland is predicated on the whole idea of Galut and its messianic resolution.

But are the Jews perennial and unique? And is their national movement, Zionism, to be understood as the working out of their unique and immemorial destiny? Certainly, some of the heroic founders of Israel thought in these terms, and saw the return to the land as recreating the nation on its own soil. But, even here, there is the awkward problem of the nearly 2000-year long diaspora slumber. How can we explain this long-standing refusal to be reawakened and regenerated? If auto-emancipation was acceptable in the 1880s, why not in the 1780s or earlier?[8]

Then there is the problem of continuity. Even if we trace the history of the Jewish people no further back than the return of the exiles from Babylon, in what sense can we speak of continuity between the followers of Ezra and Nehemiah and the Jews of, say, medieval Spain or Poland or Yemen, let alone modern Israelis or American Jews? Are we not simply imposing a modern, perhaps Zionist, pattern on Jewish history, by which Jewish nationalism is seen as the logical fulfilment of the millennial Jewish destiny? Have not the bifurcations and transformations of Jewish history sundered later generations from any identity with their ancient Palestinian forefathers?[9]

Finally, there is the fact of the modernity of nationalism. The Jews are no exception to the rule that pre-modern ages have no need or room for nationalism, while the modern epoch is saturated with nationalisms. For the Jews of medieval Spain or seventeenth-century Eastern Europe, there was no real possibility of collective restoration, despite the settlement of religious devotees in Safed, and the later messianic outburst occasioned by Sabbatai Zvi. It was only in the context of state competition in Europe, and the proliferation of nationalisms in the eastern half of that continent, that the concept of a Jewish national state in its ancient homeland could gain acceptance and have any chance of political success.[10]

ZIONISM AND COLLECTIVE MEMORY

We seem to have arrived at an impasse. If the modernists failed to grasp the inner life and understanding of the Jewish or any other people, the perennialists overstated the identity of a Jewish or any other nation across the ages. If modernists were debarred from paying attention to the unique features of each people, including the Jews, perennialists mistook these features for the whole phenomenon and thereby precluded any comparison, let alone causal explanation, of Jewish with other nationalisms. Carried through to their logical conclusions, perennialism and modernism provide us with rather superficial, partial and implausible accounts of Jewish nationalism.

I believe we can do better. To provide more convincing accounts of Jewish, and indeed other nationalisms, we need to look more closely at the specific Jewish and contextual features of Zionism, but also consider whether and how far they have parallels elsewhere and may therefore be part of a more general account.

Let me start with a general proposition. An essential element, perhaps the essential element, in any kind of human identity is memory. In other words, human identity is not simply a matter of sameness through time, of persistence through change, but also of reflective consciousness of personal connection with the past. In the case of collective cultural identities, such as *ethnies* and nations, later generations carry shared memories of what they consider to be 'their' past, of the experiences of earlier generations of the same collectivity, and so of a distinctive ethno-history. Indeed, their ethnicity is defined, first of all, by a collective belief in common origins and descent, however fictive, and thereafter by shared historical memories associated with a specific territory which they regard as their 'homeland'. On this basis arises a shared culture, often a common language or customs or religion, the product of the common historical experiences that give rise to shared memories.[11]

How are these collective memories transmitted? Very often, through oral traditions of the family, clan or community and its religious specialists. In other cases, oral traditions are supplemented, sometimes overshadowed, by canonical texts—epics, chronicles, hymns, prophecies, law-codes, treatises, songs, and the like—as well as by various forms of art, crafts, architecture, music, and dance. All of these—tales and legends, documents, objects—embody and crystallize popular memories and myths—local, regional and pan-ethnic. Sometimes, as with the traditions of the twelve Israelite tribes, they may be welded together and edited into a single canon; in other cases, such as the Karelian traditions of the *Kalevala*, they remain localized and are later adapted by nationalists to fulfil a national function.[12]

Collective memories, and encoded memories, are central to the Jewish experience and to the rise of Zionism. In the Jewish case, religion has been both the source and the vehicle of shared memories. These memories have been both local and popular—memories peculiar first of all to the various Israelite tribes and later to each of the scattered Ashkenazi and Sephardi communities—and pan-ethnic and canonical, that is, carried by the basic tenets and practices of Judaism. This duality is evident in the celebration of the festivals. Each diaspora community, for example, evolved its own customs and practices for Passover, but they operated within the framework of the commandments and statutes set down in the Bible and Talmud, and within the basic format of the recital (Haggadah) of the Seder set down in the Mishnah.[13]

In the Jewish case, scriptures and their commentaries occupy a central place. They have, of course, several purposes and roles, but one of them is the recording of collective experiences to be memorized by later

generations. This is never a neutral function. The commandment to remember, to remember Horeb and the days of old and what was done to
your forefathers, is an exhortation to emulation and fulfilment of the
mitzvot. These are not simply records, they are part of the moral framework of the Covenant of God with His chosen people. They require action,
both individual and communal. Hence they are intimately linked to the
central myth of ethnic election at the heart of Judaism and Jewish experience. In each generation and each community, what is to be remembered
is located in the framework of meaning and couched in the language of
this election myth.[14]

Jewish nationalism, then, when it emerged in the third quarter of the
nineteenth century in central and eastern Europe, could and did draw on
a vast reservoir of collective memories, set down in an ever expanding
corpus of religious documents—scriptures, commentaries, law-codes,
and the like—which together recorded the collective experiences of the scattered Jewish communities in many epochs as well as their origins in the
Middle East. As a result, modern Jewry had particularly full and well recorded
ethno-histories, replete with rich symbolisms, mythologies, values and
traditions, which were widely disseminated to all strata in the many
communities of the diaspora, but especially in the Pale of Settlement,
the largest concentration of Jews in the nineteenth century.

In this respect, the Jewish experience is unusual. Few other peoples could
boast so rich a variety and continuity of shared memories and traditions
over so many centuries. Even fewer could display so many varied documents
recording those memories and traditions—documents which, though
they emanated from priestly, rabbinic and scribal circles, were nevertheless concerned with the people as a whole, the community of practising
believers, and which were therefore accorded a primary role as the pur-
veyors of collective memory as well as legal ordinance. Among this
restricted circle, few peoples could display such a tenacity of belief and
practice as a result of the peculiar covenantal myth of ethnic election which
formed the bedrock of Jewish identity and community, and which endowed
the Jewish people with a sacred trust as a people of priests. More than
anything else, the sacred and covenantal character of ancient Israelite
memories, myths and symbols ensured their retention in the collective
consciousness of generations of the Jewish people through successive
commentaries and interpretations of the original holy scriptures, the Torah
and Talmud. Similarly, the sacred character of these memories, symbols
and traditions constituted a major resource, parameter and problem for
a secular Zionism at the turn of the century.[15]

ZIONISM AND THE DIASPORA

A second major characteristic of the Jewish experience was its trans-position from a homeland to a diaspora mode of existence. This was, of course, a gradual process, begun with the Babylonian Captivity and Egyptian settlement. But by the seventh century CE, after the completion of the Babylonian Talmud, during the ascendancy of Sura, Pumbeditha and other academies in Mesopotamia, the phenomenon of shifting centres of Jewish communal life had begun. The result was a rich variety of eth-nic traditions, each of them combining Jewish rituals and beliefs with the customs and mores of the host society through the ages—in Egypt, Babylonia and Persia, Spain, France and Germany, Poland and Russia, as well as communities further afield. After the sixth century, no single centre of Jewish existence defined the Jewish experience; the *diaspora* as a whole constituted that experience, conceived as a status of exile from the Holy Land, and no one centre outside Palestine could claim legitimate pre-eminence. On the contrary, each congregation, its customs and its particular rite, was both autonomous and of equal standing, provided it accorded with the Halachah of Rabbinic Judaism, and each community contributed in its own way to the whole diaspora.[16]

In these respects—the richness of its encoded memories and traditions and the number and autonomous status of its diaspora communities—the Jewish experience is in marked contrast to those of many other com-munities and peoples. Among the latter, as we saw, few can match the Jews in sheer volume, variety and recording of shared memories, let alone their sacred quality. Among other peoples, too, rootedness in a specific terrain or homeland has become the hallmark of identity and authenticity: their people can habitually claim to have been the physical possessors of the land for centuries, with few co-ethnics residing for long outside the 'homeland' ethnic community or ethnic state. In the Jewish case, the bulk of the Jewish population came to reside outside Palestine for one-and-a-half millennia, and the link with the homeland became largely symbolic, despite a continuing small Jewish presence in Palestine after the Crusades. That link continued to exercise an appeal and provide the setting for the ideal of restoration, but it ceased to play an active role for the Jewish people as a whole. In the case of many non-Jewish peoples, there was no exile and therefore no need for a dream of restoration, only a desire for liberation from the oppression of others in their own homelands. Among Italians, Poles, Serbs, Czechs, Ukrainians, Georgians, Arabs, Indians, Vietnamese, and Africans, intelligentsias emerged who pressed for the realization of popular aspirations for de-colonization and liberation within their long-occupied and often recognized homelands. In the case of the Jews, no such claim or aspiration was possible. As the classic and fully realized diaspora, Jewish national liberation could only take the forms of diaspora autonomism, colonization elsewhere, or restoration to the homeland.[17]

Jewish nationalism, therefore, was primarily conditioned by the peculiar diaspora situation of the Jewish people that it claimed to represent and regenerate. Its outlook, especially that of Zionism, was permeated by problems that stemmed from that condition. These included the occupational imbalance and economic deformity suffered by diaspora Jewry as a result of economic competition, persecution, and ecclesiastical regulation, which only a return to the land could allegedly cure; the political powerlessness and inexperience of the Jewish people forced to enter a world of competing national states, which only the wresting and exercise of sovereignty could counteract; and the cultural variety of Jewry's constituent communities and traditions—mainly Western and Eastern Ashkenazic, and North African, Balkan and Middle Eastern Sephardic—which only integration in a sovereign Israeli nation would overcome.

Implicit in the very conception of a diaspora is the contrast with an ancestral homeland and the possibility of returning to it. In the Jewish case, the homeland was a sacred territory and the return was part of a religious drama, enacted by God as part of the salvation of His people and the world. Hence, the conception of Galut as the antithesis of restoration to the Holy Land was an intrinsic component of the inner world of Jewry on the eve of Jewish emancipation; and it remained so, among all those Jewish communities, especially in the Pale of Settlement, which adhered to traditional religious conceptions of the fate of the Jewish people, until the advent of political Zionism.

That is why, even among many secular Jewish intellectuals who had embraced socialism and whose conception of restoration was a return to agrarian labour, Palestine retained its hold: only in the land of the forefathers, where Jews had once been free and their own masters, far from the superstition, deformities and degradation created by shtetl culture in a Europe of Christian persecution and economic prejudice, could the Jews regain their self-respect and dignity through auto-emancipation. In the debate about the British offer of a homeland for the Jewish people in Uganda at the 1903 Zionist Congress, some Western Jewish intellectuals and professionals like Herzl were prepared to envisage a territorial nationalism that would secure the Jews against persecution at the cost of inner rupture with

Judaism and its covenantal drama. But many of the secular Russian Zionist intelligentsia rejected the offer to ensure the continuity within the secular domain of the old religious ideal of restoration to Eretz Israel. Here, the inner world of Jewish myth and memory was translated into collective political choices under the impact of external events.[18]

GREEKS, ARMENIANS, AND JEWS

The Jewish experience, then, has features that set it apart from those of other peoples. But, is the trajectory of the Jewish people in the modern era unique? Can we find other peoples with a rich sacred history and shared memories distilled in canonical texts and other writings; and who have similarly endured a millennial fate of dispersion in the hope of restoration?

There are a number of peoples who can boast a rich sacred history and memories enshrined in canonical texts and liturgies. They include the Orthodox Russians, the Ulster-Scots, the Afrikaners, the Muslim Arabs, the Monophysite Amhara and the Catholic Irish. Here we have not only chosen peoples, but peoples with a highly developed and sacred documentary record of their ideals and experiences. Only within the monotheistic traditions can we find that exclusive and strong conception of chosenness, whereby a people of clear ancestral descent is covenanted with its God in a sacred homeland for the fulfilment of its moral duties and hence the salvation of the world.[19]

Yet even here all these peoples have remained rooted in their sacred homelands for centuries. Though oppressed and colonized by outsiders, they have never been expelled *en masse*, and so the theme of restoration to the homeland has played little part in the conceptions of these peoples. There are, however, two peoples, apart from the Jews, for whom restoration of the homeland and commonwealth have been central: the Greeks and the Armenians, and together with the Jews, they constitute the archetypal diaspora peoples, or what John Armstrong has called 'mobilized diasporas'.[20]

Unlike diasporas composed of recent immigrant workers—Indians, Chinese and others in Southeast Asia, East Africa and the Caribbean— mobilized diasporas are of considerable antiquity, are generally polyglot and multi-skilled trading communities and have ancient, portable religious traditions. Greeks, Jews, and Armenians claimed an ancient homeland and kingdom, looked back nostalgically to a golden age or ages of great kings, saints, sages and poets, yearned to return to ancient capitals with sacred sites and buildings, took with them wherever they went their ancient

scriptures, sacred scripts and separate liturgies, founded in every city congregations with churches, clergy and religious schools, traded across the Middle
East and Europe using the networks of enclaves of their co-religionists to
compete with other ethnic trading networks, and used their wealth, education and economic skills to offset their political powerlessness.[21]

But the parallels go further. Greeks, Jews, and Armenians after their subordination to others and emigration or expulsion from their original
homelands, became diaspora ethno-religious communities cultivating
the particular virtues and aptitudes of their traditions. These included a
respect for scholarship and learning, derived from constant study of
sacred texts (and in the Greek case some of their ancient secular texts seen
through religious filters); and hence a generally high status accorded to
religious scholars and clergy within each enclave. Allied to this was a marked
aptitude for literary expression—poetic, philosophical, legal, liturgical,
linguistic, and historical.

The resulting fund of documentary records encoding shared memories
and interpretations increased in practically every generation, enriching
the ethno-heritage of these communities. The rise of diaspora communities in many lands further augmented that heritage through the growing
emphasis on the autonomy of each community within a common ethno-
religious framework. Institutionally, that autonomy was greatest in the Jewish
case, where it was reinforced by the autonomy accorded to each rabbi and
congregation: in the Armenian case, there was a greater hierarchy of
priests; while in the Greek case, the Patriarchate in Constantinople and
the higher clergy exercised a tighter supervision over the lower clergy in
each congregation, at least in theory.[22]

There were also more specific links between the three ethno-religious
diaspora communities. In Greek Orthodoxy, the Church became the new
Israel, and the Emperor a Priest-King after the manner of Melchizedek,
King of Salem. His capital, imperial Constantinople, was the new Jerusalem,
with its 'temple' in Hagia Sophia, while Greek, the language of the New
Testament, became the sacred language of a holy Orthodox community,
in place of Hebrew and the Jews. At the same time, Greeks emigrated
to many cities throughout Europe and the Levant, especially after the fall
of Constantinople, becoming as polyglot and culturally adaptable as the
Armenians and Jews. In many Mediterranean and European cities, Greek
Phanariot merchants and traders dominated the commerce of the Ottoman empire, utilizing their kinship networks and social and religious
institutions to maximize not only their business and assets, but also their
cultural capital. Diaspora Greeks became especially prominent from the

eighteenth century in the development of printing and the press, and experienced a major intellectual revival in cities as far afield as Vienna, Venice, Odessa, Paris, and Amsterdam.[23]

Armenians had even closer links with the Jews. The Armenian royal family had converted early to Christianity, claiming thenceforth to be the first Christian nation and the true heir of Israel. Armenians came to regard themselves as a chosen people, their kings and Bagratid nobles claimed Jewish descent, and their models of heroism were drawn from the Jews, notably Joshua and Judas Maccabeus. Like the Jews, Armenians lost their ancient kingdom on the field of battle (Avarayr, 451 CE) and were increasingly persecuted under the late Byzantine emperors after the final split with Greek Orthodoxy at the second Council of Dvin in 554 CE; many Armenians began to emigrate in this period and subsequently under the Muslim Arabs, some as far afield as Russia and India. Like the Jews, they yearned to return to their idealized mountain homeland with its revered sacred centre, Echmiadzin, and its holy mountain, Ararat; but more and more of them made their fortunes in distant communities as traders and artisans, and experienced both an economic and intellectual revival in the early modern period.[24]

In each case, the concept of chosenness played a central role. For Greeks and Armenians, the myth of ethnic election was both direct and transmitted. It was an act of God who had singled out a special community of His faithful to live according to His holy laws and receive His special blessings, the blessings being conditional on the holding of correct beliefs and the performance of sacred obligations. As with the Jews, the overriding purpose was to become a holy people beloved of God, a people of priests worthy of the status and location which God had bestowed on the community. But, unlike the Jews, Armenians and Greeks saw their election as a reward for receiving the true faith rejected by the Jews. They were therefore required to supplant the Jews as the chosen people, and become the heirs of a people who had fallen from grace. In this sense, the chosen status of Greeks and Armenians was a legacy from the Jewish people, and only much later did the Orthodox community of true believers become imbued with Greek culture and a sense of Greek-speaking community. Though Orthodoxy never relinquished its religious universalism, by the late Byzantine empire the ideal of true faith and the myth of chosenness was increasingly vested in the Greek-speaking community, and to the outside world Orthodoxy became synonymous with Greek culture and origins. In the Armenian case, Gregorian Christianity was soon regarded as the peculiar possession of the Armenian kingdom and people, despite attempts to convert others to Gregorianism, with the result that the status of a chosen people was automatically conferred on the Armenian nation.[25]

TRAUMA AND THE 'GOLDEN AGE'

But there was also another myth that provided the ground for the revolution of diaspora nationalism: the myth of a 'golden age'. Myths of this kind can be found among many peoples, and sometimes they merge with recorded historical memories. For the classical authors, the golden age was set among the legendary Hyperboreans beyond the confines of the known world, at its outermost northern rim. For Confucian Chinese and Hindu Indians, it was set in the classical era of warring city-states, the age of saints and sages and warrior kings in the sixth and fifth centuries BCE. Similarly, the Book of Kings (the *Shahnameh*) of Firdausi looked back to the golden age of Chosroes and the Sassanid Persian emperors. In each case, an epoch is idealized through a mixture of fact and fantasy. Great personalities and events which have a foundation in documented fact are brought together and their stories are embellished and exaggerated, while the darker elements of the age are glossed over or purged away. In Jewish memory, the Davidic and Solomonic kingdom possessed a similar appeal; its heroes were magnified, their exploits continually recounted, its temple held up as the religious ideal, its literature treated as canonical. The religious interpretation and popular imagination have excised the hardships, corruption and exploitation of the united Israelite kingdom, though the original texts themselves are unsparing in their condemnations. Alternatively, the era of the great rabbis and Sanhedrin of Palestinian Galilee in the second and third centuries has come to possess all the elements of a golden age, its wisdom, virtue, heroism and autonomy. For Greeks and Armenians, the golden ages were located in their independent empire and kingdom: in the great ages of Byzantium, under Justinian, Heraclius, Basil, and others, ruling a mighty empire from the sacred city of Constantine; or in the great epochs of the Armenian kingdom, under Tigranes the Great (95–55 BCE), the Arsacid kings in the third and fourth centuries, and later under the Bagratids in the ninth century.[26]

The myth of the golden age long antedates the modern era. It is part of the shared memories of the community and may function as its *mythomoteur*, the myth that is constitutive of its polity. This was very much the case for the later Greek and Armenian *millets* under Ottoman rule. However, even when it becomes part of the constitutive myth, other myths and memories may be equally important. In the Jewish case, and this marks it out from the two other cases, another myth is more central: the Exodus from Egypt and the revelation on Mount Sinai. The link between the Jewish liberation myth and the memories of a golden age is twofold: on the one hand, through the belief in a chosen people covenanted to its God, and on the other hand, in the location of myths and memories within or in relation to the Holy Land. The Abrahamic and Mosaic election myth sets out God's promise of fulfilment in the holy land, the liberation Exodus myth points the way towards the holy land, and the Davidic golden age kingdom becomes its first fulfilment in the holy land. Enter the orbit of just one of those myths, share in only one of these collective memories, and the logic of their relationship points forward, under propitious circumstances, to a second fulfilment.[27]

What are those circumstances? There are two kinds of fertilizing conditions for the working out of the inner springs of communal memory and myth. The first is negative, the experience of catastrophe and trauma, sudden or prolonged or both. The second is positive, the provision of channels and vehicles of collective action. The modern epoch provided both, but did so in the case of diaspora peoples within a received framework of meaning which 'made sense' of the new conditions.

Let me start with the Greeks and their sense of trauma. For the Greek Orthodox community, the catastrophe came in 1453. The fall of Constantinople spelt the end of the universal Byzantine empire and the leading role of Orthodox Greek-speakers and Greek culture in the eastern Mediterranean. It also entailed a sense of Greek Orthodox captivity, the *Tourkokratia*, which weighed down the Greek spirit and enchained the true faith. Reduced to one of several millets in the Ottoman empire, the Greek-speaking Orthodox community under its Patriarch yearned for the end of Muslim rule and the restoration of the Byzantine empire. Yet, though they might call themselves *Romaioi*, the educated Greek-speaking Orthodox classes were increasingly imbued with Greek culture (including classical secular culture) and with hostility to Ottoman Muslims (and Latin Christians). In the Greek War of Independence, a majority of rebels fought (insofar as they fought for any ideal) for the restoration of the Orthodox Byzantine empire and the return to Constantinople, but an articulate minority of intellectuals and traders looked further back to Periclean Athens for their inspiration in creating a modern westernized national state. Here too it was a case of restoration. But the restoration in question was also a regeneration from social and economic backwardness through a moral revolution of secular education in enlightened classicism. This was the message of Katartzis, Rhigos Pheraios, Adamantios Korais and other diaspora Greek intellectuals, though it took until 1922, the year of further disaster at the hands of a militant Turkish state, to translate that message into the dominant policy of the Greek state.[28]

In the Armenian case, the disaster was more generalized. It took the form of dispossession of the homeland, first on the battlefield of Avarayr when the Arsacid kingdom was destroyed—commemorated annually (on 2 June) to this day, along with the Armenian commander, Vardan Mamikonian—then through the loss of the Bagratuni kingdom and the principality of Cilicia and the resulting expulsions of Armenians, through the Ottoman conquest to the great massacres of 1895–96 in Constantinople under Sultan Abdul Hamid and finally the attempted genocide of the Armenians in the Ottoman Empire engineered by the Young Turk regime in 1915. The ensuing division of Armenia, with only one part obtaining independence, and the current struggle over Nagorno-Karabakh, suggests the achievement of only a partial restoration, one that would hardly satisfy the various Armenian nationalist parties of the late nineteenth century, or fully assuage the sense of both recent and millennial trauma.[29]

That sense of trauma is particularly acute and well-documented among the Jews. Indeed, history as martyrology became a common mode of presentation of the Jewish experience, according well with the way in which each new disaster was placed within a religious framework of meaning which could be traced back to the ancient prophetic responses to national catastrophe. The idea that collective disaster is the direct outcome of collective sin, of the violation by the people of the covenant, of their failure to live up to the obligations which that covenant required, continued to explain and legitimize God's harsh judgements, at least until the Emancipation led to an increasing rejection of the religious framework itself. Even then the sense of guilt lingered on to undermine the secular confidence of Jewish enlighteners (*Maskilim*), as each hammer-blow of religious and racial persecution destroyed the initial messianic optimism with which they greeted the age of assimilation. The pogroms of 1881, which are usually taken to mark the birth of Zionism in the shape of the First Aliyah, the publication of Leo Pinsker's seminal booklet, *Auto-emancipation* (1882), and the foundation of the *Hovevei Zion* movement, were really only one of a series of increasingly severe reminders of the failure of non-Jewish society to accept the Jews socially, while according them legal equality and political freedoms.[30]

In fact, the first stirrings of Jewish nationalism and Zionism occurred some years earlier, in the writings of Rabbis Alkalai and Kalischer, Moses

Hess and Peretz Smolenskin during the 1850s–70s. They were moved both by specific catastrophes, such as the Damascus Blood Libel of 1840 and the new political anti-semitism in Central Europe, as well as by the new channels, resources and examples all around them. Of these, the most important was the ideology and movement of nationalism itself. From at least the 1810s the ideology and language of nationalism was disseminated across Europe, and in 1848 nationalist movements began to demonstrate their potential. The unification of Italy and Germany by 1870 further revealed the power inherent in the national ideal. Yet it would be a mistake to see the rise of Greek, Armenian, and Jewish nationalisms from the 1800s to the 1880s as mere reactions to these threats or as somehow deriving from the nationalisms of the great powers. Certainly, diaspora nationalists learned from them strategies and methods of resistance and drew comfort and inspiration from their success. But the growth of diaspora nationalisms does not simply follow on from these pressures or from other, better-known movements. Externally, one must rather look to the factors of urbanization, commerce and secular education to supply the social basis of diaspora, as of other nationalisms, and to imperial attempts to modernize their domains and divide their subject peoples, to account for the timing of these nationalist movements. Among Jews, growing alienation of the urbanized intelligentsia at the failure of Alexander II's reforms in the Romanov Empire, coupled with considerable expansion of secular education and assimilation among Russian Jews, prepared the ground for the reception of both the diaspora autonomism of Simon Dubnow, and the Zionism of *Hovevei Zion*.[31]

Trauma involves not only a sense of loss and dispossession, but also of betrayal. The Greeks and Armenians felt not only a sense of collective bereavement, of reduction to passive subject status, but also betrayed by their own Christian kinsmen, who failed to deliver them from Islam, the Ottoman yoke and captivity or genocide. In the case of the Jews, these feelings of exile, bereavement and impotence which had been assimilated into the religious framework and given ritual expression, were subsequently inflamed by the betrayal by the civilized West which had promised the Jews legal equality, only to render it hollow by social and cultural prejudice and finally by the silence of indifference in the hour of extermination. This is what the Russian Jewish intellectuals felt when confronted by the relative indifference of their Russian counterparts to the horrors of the pogroms of 1881; and this of course is what the great mass of Jews came to feel when they grasped the full extent of the Holocaust and the failure of the West to undertake preventive action.[32]

Yet it would be a mistake to imagine that either trauma or socio-economic changes or political penetration, let alone the example of other nationalisms, dictated the course of modern Jewish nationalisms. We know all too well the genuine differences in goals and means between cultural and political Zionists, revisionists and minimalists, let alone between Zionism and its rivals, territorial nationalism and diaspora autonomism (or even Bundism). All of these, except perhaps Bundism, derived their concepts and ideals from the diaspora situation of the Jewish people, and from the variety and powerlessness of its separate enclave communities. But Zionism was able to draw on something more. To the comparative, sociological and political analysis of the others, it could add a much deeper understanding, in historical and cultural-religious terms, of the experience of the Jewish people. In this respect, territorial nationalism was at a disadvantage. True, it accorded with the spirit of the modern era in grasping the centrality of the national state, and arguing that the Jews must become like any nation and so acquire both a territory of their own and a sovereign state. But what was 'their own'? The territorialists forgot that nationalism is also a doctrine of authenticity. Nationalists do not seek to acquire any territory. They want their 'homeland', that is, an historic territory which their people can feel is theirs by virtue of a convincing claim of possession and efflorescence sometime in the past. In the case of the Jews, this conviction was provided, and accepted by the vast majority of the people, by the documentary title-deed of the Bible. In an opposite way, diaspora autonomism was also always at a disadvantage. In a world of compact, exclusive and competing national states, minority autonomy was ultimately a matter of sufferance, not right. Dubnow was correct in claiming that the Jews had in the medieval past enjoyed communal autonomy and had fashioned vital cultures in their many diaspora centres. Unfortunately, the modern world of national states was unable to tolerate millets. His hope that the Jewish diaspora enclaves could now combine autonomy with equality within a concert of civilized national states was always likely to be utopian even for well-intentioned regimes in stable and democratic states.[33]

Dubnow may have been politically naive in the context of mid-twentieth century Europe but he was right about the culture-bearing potential of diaspora *ethnies*. The question is whether such cultures can flourish in the modern epoch without a national centre in a homeland. In the absence of a sovereign homeland, can a diaspora long survive and bear cultural fruit? Blacks, Chinese, Indians, Irish, Lebanese have felt the need for sovereign homelands in a world of nation-states, even when they proved unable to provide material assistance. So have the Greeks, Armenians, and

Jews. Their diasporas continue to prove culturally fertile in a triangular relationship with the national centre and the host society. But in each case, the necessary condition was the acquisition of a national centre in the homeland, and preferably a sovereign one, and this was one reason for the triumph of Zionism.

CONCLUSION

There were also other, deeper reasons. Unlike territorialism and diaspora autonomism, Zionism could present a longer, millennial continuity of the Jewish people as the stage for its own drama. It could thereby harness the religious framework of meaning for new ends and present them as consonant with the old covenantal myths and the ancient memories of liberation, the holy land and the golden ages. In this way, it could tap the religious energies in the myths of ethnic election and liberation, and could offer a promise of collective restoration which was tinged with messianism and religious redemption, even if its own premises, in tune with the spirit of modernity, were secular and political in content.[34]

In the second place, it could present as immemorial what was in fact relatively novel, without any need of manipulation. The 'old-new land' of Herzl resonated with the fulfilment of an age-old dream, even though the enterprise of collective return to a homeland in Palestine and the creation there of a national homeland was unprecedented in Jewish history. In this respect, Zionism chimed with other nationalisms that used apparently 'primordial' ideals of chosenness and return for new political ends. But Zionism's success was, in large measure, due exactly to the fact that the ancient conceptions of the holy land and chosen people had retained their popular resonance through encoded collective memories, symbolism and ritual, and the generational repetition of collective aspirations.

Third, Zionism was able to reinterpret the diaspora situation of the Jews as reaching its fulfilment through restoration. Zionism was a successful example of diaspora nationalism, not simply in the political sense which was often outside its control, but in the psychological sense of turning a psychic deficit into a spiritual victory. Even more than other diaspora nationalisms because of its far larger proportion of exiles and the odds against political success, Zionism was able to utilize the heterogeneity and sense of powerlessness of the scattered Jewish communities to create a new sense of unity and power through rootedness. The metaphor of the 'ingathering of the exiles' sums up perfectly the diaspora basis of Zionist restoration, integrating it with far older religious myths and prophetic memories and enabling otherwise disparate Jewish communities to work together in the task of rebuilding the land.

Finally, the inner and outer worlds of Jewish experience, its basis in both modernity and the *longue durée*, are brought into dramatic fusion by the Zionist revolution. On the one hand, Zionism fits the modern world of nationalisms seeking to mobilize the masses and establish independent home-lands for their peoples in a world of nations, using whatever cultural and historical materials are available to create a sense of continuity with a relevant past. On the other hand, Zionism translates into secular terminology the shared memories and myths and the inner religious yearnings of Jews everywhere for a return to Zion in a sovereign state 'as in the days of old', thereby fulfilling the myths of liberation and the covenant through a renewal of the former golden age in the holy land. In this fusion, the myth of collective restoration plays a central role. It links Zionism to both the past Jewish experience over three millennia and to the diaspora condition which formed its character and goals. In this respect, Zionism is perhaps the most dramatic and vivid of the ethno-religious diaspora nationalisms. It has carried to its logical conclusions the potentialities inherent in this special variety of nationalism and through its relative success has demonstrated not only the power of nationalism in the face of huge obstacles, but also the continuing hold exerted on masses of people in the modern age by the collective memories and myths of their pasts.

Notes

1. Hugh Trevor-Roper, *Jewish and Other Nationalisms*, London, 1961.
2. Eric Hobsbawm, *Nations and Nationalism since 1780*, Cambridge, 1990, chs. 3, 6.
3. For the central role of intellectuals in nationalist movements, see Elie Kedourie (ed.), *Nationalism in Asia and Africa*, London, 1971, Introduction; for their role in Eastern European nationalist movements, see Miroslav Hroch, *Social Preconditions of National Revival in Europe*, Cambridge, 1985.
4. The relevant quotation runs: 'Again, while the Jews, scattered throughout the world for some millennia, never ceased to identify themselves, wherever they were, as members of a special people quite distinct from the various brands of non-believers among whom they lived, at no stage, at least since the return from the Babylonian captivity, does this seem to have implied a serious desire

for a Jewish political state, let alone a territorial state, until a Jewish nationalism was invented at the very end of the nineteenth century by analogy with the newfangled western nationalism. It is entirely illegitimate to identify the Jewish links with the ancestral land of Israel, the merit deriving from pilgrimages there, or the hope of return there when the Messiah came—as he so obviously had *not* come in the view of the Jews—with the desire to gather all Jews into a modern territorial state situated on the ancient Holy Land. One might as well argue that good Muslims, whose highest ambition is to make the pilgrimage to Mecca, in doing so really intend to declare themselves citizens of what has now become Saudi Arabia.' Hobsbawm, *Nations and Nationalism since 1780*, pp. 47–48 (italics in original). This view is both historically questionable and at odds with the thrust of a chapter on popular 'proto-nationalism'. For a general critique, see Anthony D. Smith, *Nations and Nationalism in a Global Era*, Cambridge, 1995, ch. 1. See also Elie Kedourie, *Nationalism*, London, 1960.

5. Eric Hobsbawm and Terence Ranger (eds.), *The Invention of Tradition*, Cambridge, 1983. For these Zionist intellectuals, see Arthur Hertzberg (ed.), *The Zionist Idea, A Reader*, New York, 1960; Shlomo Avineri, *The Making of Modern Zionism*, New York, 1981; and Avineri, *Moses Hess*, New York and London, 1985. For the concept of 'invented traditions', see Hobsbawm and Ranger, *The Invention of Tradition*, chs. 1, 7.

6. On the debate between 'perennialism' and 'modernism', see Anthony D. Smith, 'The Myth of the "Modern Nation" and the Myths of Nations', *Ethnic and Racial Studies* vol. 2, No. 1 (1988), pp. 1–26; Anthony D. Smith, 'Gastronomy or Geology? The Role of Nationalism in the Construction of Nations', *Nations and Nationalism* vol. 1, no. 1 (1995), pp. 3–23.

7. This view is close to Weber's *verstehende Soziologie* and to the interpretation in Peter Winch, *The Idea of a Social Science*, London, 1958. But Weber, in fact, insisted on the need to back up 'intelligibility' with 'adequate causation'; see Raymond Avon, *German Sociology*, Westport, 1978.

8. For such 'determined slumberers', see Ernest Gellner, *Nations and Nationalism*, Oxford, 1983, ch. 5. This is part of Gellner's critique of nationalist self-images. One such Jewish nationalist who did awaken was Eliezer Ben-Yehudah, who insisted on renewing the nation on its own soil. See Hertzberg, *The Zionist Idea*.

9. A view that comes through in the closing pages of Edmond Fleg's *Why I am a Jew*, London, 1943; and more systematically in Ben-Zion Dinur, *Israel and the Diaspora*, Philadelphia, 1969.

10. For this general view of nationalism, see Gellner, *Nations and Nationalism*, ch. 2; see also David Vital, *The Origins of Zionism*, Oxford, 1975.

11. For definitions of *ethnic, ethnos* and *ethnicity*, see Elisabeth Tonkin, Maryon McDonald, and Malcolm Chapman (eds.), *History and Ethnicity*, London, 1989, Introduction; Anthony D. Smith, *The Ethnic Origins of Nations*, Oxford, 1986, ch. 2; and Smith, *National Identity*, Harmondsworth, 1991, ch. 2.

12. See Steven Grosby, 'Religion and Nationality in Antiquity', *European Journal of Sociology*, vol. 32 (1991), pp. 229–65: Michael Branch (ed.), *Kalevala: The Land of Heroes* (trans. W. F. Kirby), London, 1985, Introduction.

13. For the various Passover traditions of different *minhagim*, see Chaim Raphael, *A Feast of History*, London, 1972; and Philip Goodman (ed.), *A Passover Anthology*, Philadelphia, 1993.

14. Anthony D. Smith, 'Chosen Peoples: Why Ethnic Groups Survive', *Ethnic and Racial Studies*, vol. 15, no. 3 (1992), pp. 436–56.

15. Donald Akenson, *God's Peoples*, Ithaca, 1992, Part I; Smith, 'Chosen Peoples'.

16. Robert M. Seltzer, *Jewish People, Jewish Thought*, New York, 1980.

17. Daniel Elazar, 'The Concept of the Jewish Diaspora', in Gabriel Sheffer (ed.), *International Diasporas in Historical Perspective*, London and Sydney, 1986. Zionism is an example of the 'diaspora' sub-variety of ethnic nationalisms, whereas the ethnic nationalisms of resident and rooted peoples represent the far more numerous 'secession' sub-variety; see Anthony D. Smith, *Theories of Nationalism*, Second Edition, London, 1983, ch. 9.

18. Ben Halpern, *The Idea of the Jewish State*, Cambridge, Mass., 1961, ch. 5.

19. There are parallels outside the monotheistic traditions—notably the Persian Shi'ites, the Buddhist Sinhalese and the Punjabi Sikhs—but they lack the strenuous covenantal character of the monotheistic cases; cf. Akenson, *God's Peoples*.

20. John Armstrong, *Nations before Nationalism*, 1982. Partial exceptions are furnished by the Irish diaspora, occasioned by the great potato famine of 1845, and the Afrikaner trekkers who escaped British rule by moving into Natal and the Orange Free State after 1835.

21. Armstrong, *Nations before Nationalism*; Hugh Seton-Watson, *Nations and States*, London, 1977, ch. 10.

22. Armstrong, *Nations before Nationalism*, ch. 7; K. V. Sarkissian, 'The Armenian Church', in A. J. Arberry (ed.): *Religion in the Middle East: Three Religions in Concord and Conflict*, vol. 1: Judaism and Christianity, Cambridge, 1969; C. A. Frazee, *The Orthodox Church and Independent Greece, 1821–52*, Cambridge, 1969.

23. N. H. Baynes, and H. St. L. B. Moss (eds.), *Byzantium: an Introduction to East Roman Civilization*, Oxford, 1969, pp. 119–27; Cyril Mango, 'The Phanariots and Byzantine Tradition', in Richard Clogg (ed.), *The Greek Struggle for Independence*, London, 1973; Paschalis Kitromilides, 'The Dialectic of Intolerance: Ideological Dimensions of Ethnic Conflict', *Journal of the Hellenic Diaspora*, vol. 6, no. 4 (1979), pp. 5–30; Armstrong, *Nations before Nationalism*, pp. 176–81.

24. K. S. Atiyah, *A History of Eastern Christianity*, London, 1968, pp. 315–56; David Lang, *Armenia, Cradle of Civilization*, London, 1980, ch. 8; Armstrong, *Nations before Nationalism*, ch. 7.

25. Of course, there are many differences between the three ethno-religious diaspora peoples, notably the number of co-ethnics residing inside the homeland

for most of the period of exile and the geopolitical location of those home-lands in relation to powerful overlords and neighbours. But for our purposes these are secondary to the factors that have made the popular ideal of spiritual redemption and political restoration so central to their destinies. Cf. Philip Sherrard, *The Greek East and the Latin West*, London, 1959; Atiyah, *A History of Eastern Christianity*, pp. 315–28; Lang, *Armenia*; Armstrong, *Nations before Nationalism*, ch. 7.

26. For the ideals of Jewish golden ages, see Hertzberg, *The Zionist Idea*, Intro-duction; and I. Eisenstein-Barzilay, 'National and Anti-National Trends in the Berlin Haskalah', *Jewish Social Studies*, vol. 21 (1959), pp. 165–92. For Greek Byzantinism, see John Campbell and Philip Sherrard, *Modern Greece*, London, 1968, ch. 1. For Armenian golden ages, see David Lang, *The Armen-ians, A People in Exile*, London, 1982.

27. Irving Zeitlin, *Ancient Judaism*, Cambridge, 1984, ch. 3; Grosby, 'Religion and Nationality'; Akenson, *God's Peoples*, Part I.

28. See Campbell and Sherrard, *Modern Greece*, ch. 1; Baynes and Moss, *Byzantium*, pp. 43–4, 119–27; C. Koumarianou, 'The Contribution of the Greek Intelligentsia towards the Greek Independence Movement', in Richard Clogg (ed.), *The Struggle for Greek Independence*, London, 1973; Paschalis Kitromilides, '"Imagined Communities" and the Origins of the National Question in the Balkans', *European History Quarterly*, vol. 19, no. 2 (1989), pp. 149–92.

29. Louise Nalbandian, *The Armenian Revolutionary Movement: the Develop-ment of Armenian Political Parties through the Nineteenth Century*, Berkeley 1963, Richard Hovannisian, *Armenia: The Road to Independence*, Berkeley, 1967; Christopher Walker, *Armenia: The Survival of a Nation*, London, 1980; Lang, *Armenia*, chs. 7–8 and his *The Armenians*.

30. Leo Pinsker, *Auto-Emancipation*, New York, 1948; Hertzberg, *The Zionist Idea*, Introduction; Vital, *The Origins of Zionism*.

31. Salo Baron, *The Russian Jew under Czars and Soviets*, New York, 1964, espe-cially Chs. 9–10; Louis Greenberg, *The Jews of Russia*, 2 vol., New York, 1976.

32. Hertzberg, *The Zionist Idea*, Introduction; David Aberbach, *Trauma, Loss and Bereavement*, London, 1993; Tony Kushner, *The Holocaust and the Liberal Imagination*, Oxford, 1994.

33. On Dubnow and his diaspora nationalism, see his essays edited and intro-duced in Koppel Pinson, *Nationalism and History*, Philadelphia, 1958.

34. S. Z. Klausner, 'Why They Chose Israel', *Archives de Sociologie des Religions*, vol. 9 (1960), pp. 119–44.

9

National Identity and the Idea of European Unity*

ABSTRACT

Since the project of European integration began, at issue has always been whether a European political identity could develop to underpin political unification. Is a genuine European identity possible? Anthony Smith takes up the question from the standpoint of his work on nationalism. Why is it that we are witnessing a revival of nationalism even as the globalizing trends of post-industrial society become clearer? Established cultures are essentially antithetical to the development of a cosmopolitan culture, he writes, which poses problems for a European identity. If this is to do more than coexist weakly alongside national and subnational identities, it may come at a dangerous price—only if Europe defines itself exclusively against other world actors.

There is nothing new about the idea of European unity. It can be traced back to Sully, Podiebrad, perhaps even Charlemagne and the Holy Roman Empire. Nor is there anything new about national identity. Even if not as old as nationalists would have us believe, national consciousness can be traced back to the later Middle Ages, to the wars of the Scots, English and French in the fourteenth century, to Joan of Arc, to Spanish unification under the Catholic monarchs, and certainly to the Elizabethans and the age of Shakespeare; though not until the next century, in the Puritan Netherlands and England, can one discern the first flowerings of popular (albeit religious) *nationalism*, and not until the American and French Revolutions does nationalism appear as a fully fledged secular ideology.[1]

So why should there be such interest now in the European idea and its relationship to national identities? Is it simply the fact that European unification, in whatever form, is for the first time a distinct possibility—that

* *International Affairs* 68: i (1992), pp. 55–76.

we can 'make Europe' where previous generations could only dream about it? Or is it rather that the sheer pace of social and political change has forced us to reassess rooted structures like the nation-state, and hallowed values like national identity?[2]

Clearly, modern technologies and communications have led many people to question the old certainties. They grope in some confusion towards a new type of social order, yet are afraid to let go of the old. They wonder whether the new structures and identities that may be forged will answer to their needs and interests as well as the habitual and familiar ones. What exactly will a vast, overarching 'Europe' mean for individuals and families? Will the seat of authority become still more impersonal and remote? Will it be less sensitive to local problems and needs? What does growing European unification mean for the values, heritages and cultures of Europe's many ethnic communities, regions and nations?

There is a more fundamental reason for the current interest in the cultural impact of European unification. It lies in the problem of 'identity' itself, one that has played a major part in European debates over the past 30–40 years. At issue has been the possibility and the legitimacy of a 'European identity', as opposed to the existing national identities. For nationalists, the nation is the sole criterion of legitimate government and of political community. Does this exclude the possibility of a European identity and political community? Or can, and must, a unified Europe be designated a 'super-nation'? Alternatively, should we regard a United States of Europe as a new type of 'supranational' identity and community? What exactly does that mean? These issues are central to the continuing debates between pro- and anti-Europeans, between federalists, Gaullists, and today's Bruges Group.

I hope to show that some of these debates are exaggerated in their assumptions and scope. It is true that at the practical level of policy the claims of these competing identities—the European and the national—may come into conflict. This appears to have been the case recently, when the states of Europe, responsive to national public opinion, were in disarray over foreign policy over the Gulf War and then over Yugoslav conflicts. A common European cultural identity, if such there be, does not yet have its counterpart on the political level; to date, each state of the European Community has placed its perceived national interests and self-images above a concerted European policy based on a single presumed European interest and self-image.

At the conceptual level, however, the contradiction between a European identity and existing national identities may be more apparent than real. It rather depends on the version of nationalist doctrine held. If we hold to a Romantic doctrine and view the nation as a seamless, organic cultural unit, then the contradiction becomes acute. If, on the other hand, we accept a more voluntaristic and pluralistic conception and regard the nation as a rational association of common laws and culture within a defined territory, then the contradiction is minimized. For in this version—which is the one generally accepted in Western countries—individuals may choose to which nation they wish to belong, and there is, as we shall see, room for competing focuses of identity. So the conflict between the claims of the nation and those of a looser European identity becomes more situational and pragmatic, even if in a political crisis it could never be eliminated. I shall return to this key question below.

FIRST CONSIDERATION: METHOD

Though there have been many studies of the economic organizations and political institutions of the European Community, relatively little attention has been devoted to the cultural and psychological issues associated with European unification—to questions of meaning, value and symbolism. What research there has been in this area has suffered from a lack of theoretical sophistication and tends to be somewhat impressionistic and superficial. This is especially true of attitude studies, in which generalizations over time are derived from surveys of particular groups or strata at particular moments. In few areas is the attitude questionnaire of such doubtful utility as in the domain of cultural values and meanings.[3]

Clearly, what is needed in this field is a series of case-studies over time of *changes* in collective perceptions and values, as recorded in literature and the arts, in political traditions and symbolism, in national mythologies and historical memories, and as relayed in educational texts and the mass media. Such studies rarely focus on the European dimension as such. Rather, they address changes in the content of *national* symbolism and mythology, ethno-history and collective values and traditions, which may or may not include an opening towards a wider, European dimension, but whose central focus is the continuing process of reconstructing or re-imagining the nation.[4]

Such studies form a useful point of departure for investigations into the complex relationships between national identities and the processes of European unification in the sphere of culture and values. Here I shall concentrate specifically on the cultural domain and its links with politics, leaving on one side the processes of economic and political integration that form the main concern of European studies. I shall focus on five interrelated areas.

1. The impact and uses of the pre-modern 'past' or 'pasts' of ethnic communities and nations in the continent of Europe, and the ways in which pre-modern structures and images continue to condition modern processes and outlooks.
2. The origins and nature of collective, cultural identities, and more specifically of national identities, and their consequences for social and political action.
3. The growth of globalizing tendencies in communications, education, the media and the arts, which transcend national and even continental boundaries, bringing a truly cosmopolitan character to society that surpasses internationalism.
4. Allied to these tendencies, fundamental geopolitical and ecological changes in the world at large often of an unpredictable nature, like the dangers of a shrinking Soviet Union or a Middle Eastern vortex, or of pollution and epidemic disease—which affect changing values.
5. The processes of regional or continental unification, of which Europeanization is only the most explicit and advanced example. Here the question is not just the history of an idea or process, but the changing contents and boundaries of 'Europe' in the context of a rapidly evolving world.

MULTIPLE IDENTITIES

A comparative method using case-studies of national identity and culture needs some kind of theoretical framework; and given the nature of our problem, a logical starting-point is the concept of collective cultural identity. This would refer not to some fixed pattern or uniformity of elements over time, but rather to a sense of shared *continuity* on the part of successive generations of a given unit of population, and to shared *memories* of earlier periods, events and personages in the history of the unit. From these two components we can derive a third: the collective belief in a common *destiny* of that unit and its culture. From a subjective standpoint, there can be no collective cultural identity without shared memories or a sense of continuity on the part of those who feel they belong to that collectivity. So the subjective perception and understanding of the communal past by each generation of a given cultural unit of population—the 'ethno-history' of that collectivity, as opposed to a historian's judgement of that past—is a defining element in the concept of cultural identity, and hence of more specific national and European identities.[5]

From this starting-point we might go on to characterize the cultural history of humanity as a successive differentiation (but also enlargement) of processes of identification. In the simplest and earliest societies, the number and scale of such identities were relatively limited; but as populations organized themselves into more complex agrarian societies in a variety of political formations, the number and scale of such identifications multiplied. Where once gender, age, clan and tribe had provided the chief units of identity, now there were also village communities, regions, city-states, religious communities and even empires. With the growing stratification of such societies, classes and status groups (castes, estates, ethnic communities) also took on vital roles as focuses of identification in many societies.

In the modern era of industrial capitalism and bureaucracy, the number and in particular the scale of possible cultural identities have increased yet again. Gender and age retain their vitality; class and religious loyalties continue to exercise their influence; but today, professional, civic and ethnic allegiances have proliferated, involving ever larger populations across the globe. Above all, *national* identification has become the cultural and political norm, transcending other loyalties in scope and power.

Yet however dominant the nation and its national identification, human beings retain a multiplicity of allegiances in the contemporary world. They have *multiple* identities. These identifications may reinforce national identities or cross-cut them. The gendered perceptions of the male population may reinforce their sense of national identity, whereas those of the female part of the same collectivity may detract from it. The class allegiances of upper and middle classes may subjectively fuse with their sense of national identification, whereas the class solidarities of workers may conflict with their national loyalties. Similarly, some collective religious sentiments can reinforce a sense of national identity, as we witness today in Ireland, Poland and Israel; whereas some other kinds of religious loyalty transcend and thereby diminish purely national identities, as in the case of Roman Catholicism and Islam.[6]

Under normal circumstances, most human beings can live happily with multiple identifications and enjoy moving between them as the situation requires. Sometimes, however, one or other of these identities will come under pressure from external circumstances, or come into conflict with one of the individual's or family's other identities. Conflicts between loyalty to a national state and solidarity with an ethnic community, within or outside the boundaries of that state, may lead to accusations of 'dual loyalties', and families may find themselves torn between the claims of competing communities and identities. There is in fact always the potential for such identity conflicts. That they occur less often than one might expect is the result of a certain fluidity in all processes of individual identification.

At this point it becomes important to observe the distinction between individual and collective identification. For the individual, or at any rate for most individuals, identity is usually 'situational', if not always optional. That is to say, individuals identify themselves and are identified by others in different ways according to the situations in which they find themselves; as when one goes abroad, one tends to classify oneself (and be classified by others) differently from one's categorization at home.[7]

Collective identities, however, tend to be pervasive and persistent. They are less subject to rapid changes and tend to be more intense and durable, even when quite large numbers of individuals no longer feel their power. This is especially true of religious and ethnic identities, which even in pre-modern eras often became politicized. It is particularly true of national identities today, when the power of mass political fervour reinforces the technological instruments of mass political organization, so that national identities can outlast the defection or apathy of quite large numbers of individual members. So we need to bear this distinction between the collective and the individual levels of identity in mind and to exercise caution in making inferences about collective sentiments and communal identifications on the basis of individual attitudes and behaviour.[8]

NATIONAL IDENTITY: SOME BASES AND LEGACIES

This preliminary survey of the types and levels of *cultural* identity provides a general framework for analysing specifically *national* identities. Here it may be useful to take together the first two areas of analysis—the impact of the pre-modern past and the nature and consequences of national identity—since in Europe at any rate it is mainly through such identities that these 'pasts' have been retained and mediated.

The concept of national identity is both complex and highly abstract. Indeed the multiplicity of cultural identities, both now and in the past, is mirrored in the multiple dimensions of our conceptions of nationhood. To grasp this, we need only enumerate of few of these dimensions. They include:

1. the territorial boundedness of separate cultural populations in their own 'homelands';

2. the shared nature of myths of origin and historical memories of the community;
3. the common bond of a mass, standardized culture;
4. a common territorial division of labour, with mobility for all members and ownership of resources by all members in the homeland;
5. the possession by all members of a unified system of common legal rights and duties under common laws and institutions.

These are some of the main assumptions and beliefs common to all nationalists everywhere. Drawing on these, we may define a nation as a named human population sharing a historical territory, common memories and myths of origin, a mass, standardized public culture, a common economy and territorial mobility, and common legal rights and duties for all members of the collectivity.[9]

This definition is just one of many that have been proffered for the concept of the 'nation'. But, like most others, it reveals the highly complex and abstract nature of the concept, one which draws on dimensions of other types of cultural identity, and so permits it to become attached to many other kinds of collective identification—of class, gender, region and religion. National identifications are fundamentally multidimensional. But though they are composed of analytically separable components—ethnic, legal, territorial, economic, and political—they are united by the nationalist ideology into a potent vision of human identity and community.

The ideology of nationalism which emerged in Western Europe and America in the late eighteenth century was premised on the belief in a world of exclusive nations. The basic goals of nationalists everywhere were identical: they sought to unify the nation, to endow it with a distinctive individuality, and to make it free and autonomous. For nationalists, the nation was the supreme object of loyalty and the sole criterion of government. There was no legitimate exercise of political power which did not emanate expressly from the nation, for this was the only source of political power and individual freedom.[10]

Yet there were also important differences between nationalists in their conceptions of the nation. In fact we can usefully distinguish two main models of the nation, which emerged out of different historical contexts and which retain a certain importance even in our era. The first, or 'Western', model of the nation arose out of the Western absolutist states whose rulers inadvertently helped to create the conditions for a peculiarly territorial concept of the nation. The second, or 'Eastern', model emerged out of the situation of incorporated ethnic communities or *ethnies* (from the French), whose intelligentsias sought to liberate them from the shackles of various empires.

The Western model of the nation tended to emphasize the centrality of a national territory or homeland, a common system of laws and institutions, the legal equality of citizens in a political community, and the importance of a mass, civic culture binding the citizens together. The Eastern model, by contrast, was more preoccupied with ethnic descent and cultural ties. Apart from genealogy, it emphasized the popular or folk element, the role of vernacular mobilization, and the activation of the people through a revival of their native folk culture—their languages, customs, religions and rituals, rediscovered by urban intellectuals such as philologists, historians, folklorists, ethnographers, and lexicographers.[11]

The contrast between these two concepts of the nation should not be overdrawn, as we find elements of both at various times in several nationalisms in both Eastern and Western Europe. And it is perhaps more important for our purposes to underline the distinction between the concepts of the nation and of the state. The latter is a legal and institutional concept. It refers to autonomous public institutions which are differentiated from other, social institutions by their exercise of a monopoly of coercion and extraction within a given territory.[12] The idea of the nation, by contrast, is fundamentally cultural and social. It refers to a cultural and political bond which unites in a community of prestige all those who share the same myths, memories, symbols and traditions. Despite the obvious overlap between the concepts of state and nation in terms of common territory and citizenship, the idea of the nation defines and legitimates politics in cultural terms, because the nation is a political community only in so far as it embodies a common culture and a common social will. This is why today no state possesses legitimacy which does not also claim to represent the will of the 'nation', even where there is as yet patently no nation for it to represent. Though the vast majority of contemporary states are 'plural' in character—that is, they have more than one ethnic community within their borders and so cannot claim to be true 'nation-states' in the strict sense—they aspire to become at least 'national states' with a common public culture open to all citizens. Their claim to legitimacy, in other words, is based on the aspiration of a heterogeneous population to unity in terms of public culture and political community, as well as popular sovereignty.[13]

This reiterated reference to a community of common public culture reveals the continuing influence of ethnicity and its common myths, symbols and memories in the life of modern European nations. On the one hand, these nations seek to transcend their ethnic origins, which are usually the myths and memories of the dominant ethnic community (the English, the northern French, the Castilians); on the other hand, in a world of growing interdependence, they very often feel the need to revert to them to sustain community as well as to justify their differences. The link with the distinctive pre-modern past serves to dignify the nation as well as to explain its mores and character. More important, it serves to 'remake the collective personality' of the nation in each generation. Through rituals and ceremonies, political myths and symbols, the arts and history textbooks—through these the links with a community of origin, continually reshaped as popular 'ethno-history', are reforged and disseminated.

In this respect, national identifications possess distinct advantages over the idea of a unified European identity. They are vivid, accessible, well established, long popularized, and still widely believed, in broad outline at least. In each of these respects, 'Europe' is deficient both as idea and as process. Above all, it lacks a pre-modern past—a 'prehistory' which can provide it with emotional sustenance and historical depth. In these terms it singularly fails to combine, in the words of Daniel Bell *à propos* ethnicity, 'affect with interest', resembling rather Shelley's bright reason, 'like the sun from a wintry sky'.[14]

Recently it has been suggested that nationalism's halcyon days are drawing to a close, and that the current spate of fissiparous ethnic nationalism runs counter to the 'major trends' of world history, which are towards ever-larger economic and political units. In other words, that substance is belied by appearance—that today's ethnic nationalisms are divisive and have lost the breadth and power of the former mass democratic and civic nationalisms of Western Europe.[15]

Others take the view that the current renewal of ethnic nationalism represents the shape of the future 'post-industrial' society, one whose economy is based increasingly on the service sector and on the social and cultural needs of consumers. They argue that in such societies the means of communication and information become much more important than mass production of commodities; that the mass media, telecommunications and computerized information spawn smaller but dense networks for those who share the same ethno-linguistic networks of language, symbols and culture. This, they argue, is the reason why we are witnessing the proliferation of ethnic nationalisms; they are intrinsic to a post-industrial 'service society'.[16]

There are in fact a number of reasons why we are witnessing an ethnic revival today, and why it is challenging the accepted frameworks of the national state. For one thing, the state itself has become immensely more powerful, both as an international actor and *vis-à-vis* society within its boundaries. Its powers, scope and capacity for intervention in every sphere of social life and will to do so have increased profoundly since 1945 (helped, no doubt, by the powers conferred on it by the exigencies of two world wars). Second, the spread of literacy and the mass media to the remotest hinterlands of European and other states has raised the level of consciousness and expectations of minority peoples, who witness national protests and movements in neighbouring territories almost as soon as they occur. Third, the impact of public, mass education systems, while on the face of it uniting a given national population into a single civic culture, also creates divisions along pre-existing ethnic lines. By forcing all its different peoples to employ a single civic language and by preaching allegiance to national symbols and historical myths, the state's élites may actually stir up resentment and bitterness at the neglect of minority cultures and the suppression of minority peoples' histories. The latter have not been entirely forgotten among the relevant peoples themselves; they remain embedded in separate folklore, customs, myths and symbols. State intervention, literacy and civic culture, and mass education and the mass media tend to rekindle these memories and regenerate these ancient cultures in new forms.

So recent political developments in Western as well as Eastern Europe, not to mention the Third World, offer few grounds for hope of an early end to the proliferation of ethnic nationalisms, even if their intensity periodically diminishes. What we are currently witnessing is no more than the latest of the periodic waves of ethnic nationalism that have swept different parts of the world since the early nineteenth century, and such demotic ethnic nationalisms have always accompanied the more territorial state-based nationalisms of ethnic majorities since the first stirrings of Serb, Greek, and Irish nationalisms. There is therefore little warrant for regarding recent ethnic nationalisms as inimical or irrelevant to the 'major trends' of economic development or world history, as long as most of the world's trade, production and consumption is still organized in terms of relations between sovereign (if increasingly interdependent) national states.[17]

If we disregard the evolutionary undertones of these recent interpretations of nationalism, we are left with the problem of determining the relative strength and influence of European nations, their cultures and their myths from their ethnic pasts at the turn of the second millennium. Anthropologists have begun to explore some of the cultural aspects of the ethnic identity of such European nations as the Basque, the Breton and the Greek, but much research still needs to be conducted into the continuing impact of ethno-histories, of ethnic myths and symbols, and of the different value systems embodied in various popular traditions, ceremonies and rituals. There is also much work to be done on the recent revival of cultural heritages and political traditions in the wake of new concepts of multiculturalism, which have gained ground following demographic shifts and population migrations.

Given the multiplicity of language groups and ethnic heritages in Europe, it is reasonable to expect the persistence of strong ethnic sentiments in many parts of the continent, as well as the continuity or periodic revival of national identities, fuelled by the quest for ethnic traditions and cultural heritages of distinctive myths, memories and symbols.

A GLOBALIZING CULTURE?

Against these predictions must be set the 'major trends' of world history that so many have discerned and welcomed. These include:

1. the rapid growth of vast transnational companies, with budgets, technologies, communications networks and skill levels far outstripping those of all but the largest and most powerful of contemporary national states;
2. the rise and fall of large power blocs based on one or other military 'superpower', and forming a military-political network of client-states in an increasingly interdependent international system of states; and
3. the vast increase in the scale, efficiency, density and power of the means of communication, from transport to the mass media, from telecommunications to computerized information and transmission.

What this means, in the most general terms, is an accelerating process of globalization: of trends and processes that transcend the boundaries of national states and ethnic communities, and that serve to bind together into common economic, political and cultural patterns the various populations into which the globe is at present divided.[18]

That such trends and processes can be observed is not in question. It is not difficult to point to processes that transcend national boundaries, and appear to unite different populations in those respects. This is as true of patterns of world trade, nuclear proliferation and diplomatic language as it is of styles in modern art, fashion and television serials. The question is whether there is anything new in such boundary-transcending activities and processes, and whether they serve to unite distinctive populations in more than superficial respects. Do they, in other words, portend that global cosmopolitanism of which Marx and Engels, as well as so many liberals, dreamed?

We should perhaps recall in this context the many imperial cultures that sought to integrate, even homogenize, ethnically different populations, from the Hellenizing policies of Alexander and his successors right up to the Russification policies of the later Romanovs. Here, too, the conscious intention to overleap local boundaries was evident, as was also the case with the 'world religions' of Buddhism, Islam and Christianity. It is true that today the English language and American cultural styles can reach an even wider audience and penetrate much more of the globe. But do they, can they, have as profound an effect? Can there be a truly cosmopolitan culture, one that is genuinely 'post-national' in form and content? The answer to such a question may have a profound bearing on the possibility of a European cultural identity.

It is undeniable that we are witnessing an immense and rapid growth of communications and information technology, spanning the globe; and with it a slower but definite, albeit uneven, increase in literacy and mass education in many countries. There is also considerable convergence in parts of each state's education system: an emphasis on technology, a concern with mathematics and science, an interest in at least one other lingua franca, and so on. In other parts of each education system, however, there is a conscious retention of national difference: in literature, in history, in the arts. In so far as the state can control and use the instruments of mass education effectively, this policy of national self-maintenance is not to be underestimated.[19]

This is not to deny the possibility that governments may actively intervene to try to change popular perceptions of their identity. One could cite here not only the recent efforts of the British government to change the content of the history curriculum to accord with its perceived 'national interests', but also the efforts of France and Germany to change earlier perceptions of each other, through the use of symbols, through massive youth exchange programmes, and by subsidizing academic studies of common history, all of which have after 25 years had a significant effect. (Whether the efforts of the Council of Europe to encourage changes in national histories, on both the academic and the official levels, have been effective is open to doubt.)

At the same time, there are clear limits to what governments can achieve. Thus the recent uneasy position of the German government during the Gulf War shows up clearly the constraints on governments which are at all responsive to public opinion. The same is true for other governments in such recent foreign policy crises as Yugoslavia or the Lebanese hostage situation.

There is another side to the question of cultural globalization—what will a truly cosmopolitan culture involve? Will it resemble the imperial prototype, on this occasion various versions of Americanization? Or will it be something genuinely new? The evidence to date suggests neither alternative. What a 'post-modernist' global culture is more likely to resemble is the eclectic patchwork we are witnessing in America and Western Europe today—a mixture of ethnic elements, streamlined and united by a veneer of modernism on a base of scientific and quantitative discourse and computerized technology.[20]

This is not to deny the global diffusion of some aspects of modern Euro-American culture, especially popular music, films, videos, dress and some foods. The worldwide spread of consumer commodities, of art styles in furnishing, of architecture and the visual arts, not to mention the mass media and tourism, is evidence of a global nexus of markets for similar products and the ability of consumer industries to mould shared tastes, in some degree at least. But even here, ethnic and class factors intrude. The appreciation and assimilation of Western styles and cultural products is generally adaptive: the audiences in Third World countries tend to interpret these products and experiences in ways that are specific to the perceptions and understanding of their own peoples.[21]

Side by side with this adaptive Westernization, there is also a more or less conscious rediscovery of and return to indigenous styles and values. This process was stimulated by political nationalism or by a vaguer consciousness of and pride in the past of particular peoples and cultural areas, and has been continuing since the early nineteenth century—first in Central and Eastern Europe, then in the Middle East and India, then in the Americas, and finally in Africa and Eastern Asia. In each case, myths and memories of an ancient ethnic past (not necessarily strictly that of the revivalists themselves) have been reappropriated, often through a process of vernacular mobilization in which the peasant masses are treated as a repository of truth, wisdom and culture.

The revival of ethnic myths, memories and traditions, both within and outside a globalizing but eclectic culture, reminds us of the fundamentally memoryless nature of any cosmopolitan culture created today. Such a culture must be consciously, even artificially, constructed out of the elements of existing national cultures. But existing cultures are time-bound, particular and expressive. They are tied to specific peoples, places and periods. They are bound up with definite historical identities. These features are essentially antithetical to the very nature of a truly cosmopolitan culture. Herein lies the paradox of any project for a global culture: it must work with materials destined for the very projects which it seeks to supersede—the national identities which are ultimately to be eradicated.

THE EUROPEAN 'FAMILY OF CULTURES'

This, then, is where the European project must be located: between national revival and global cultural aspirations. Thus expressed, it makes the old debate between pan-Europeans and anti-Europeans seem faintly antiquated.

That debate centred on the possibility and desirability of creating a unified Europe 'from above', through economic and political institutions, perhaps on the model of German unification in the nineteenth century. Pan-Europeans conceded that there would be local delays and problems, but believed that European unity was imperative to prevent a recurrence of any European 'civil war', to create a third power between East and West and to secure a prosperous future for Europe's peoples. They also argued that the route of 'state-making' from above through bureaucratic incorporation and the building of institutions was the only way forward. Just as in the past dynastic states had moulded the first nations in the West, so today the framework of a United States of Europe and swift political union, based firmly in the Western heartlands, would forge a European consciousness in place of the obsolete national identities.

Anti-Europeans countered by pointing to the 'unevenness' of Europe's peoples and states, to the difficulties of deciding the boundaries of 'Europe', to the continuing strength of several European national states and to the linguistic and ethnic pluralism of Europe's mixed areas. But at the root of their opposition to pan-Europeanism, whether unitary or federal in character, was their belief in the overriding importance of existing national identities and the ethnic histories and cultures they enshrined. Behind the economic facade and the agonizing over subsidies and monetary union, the embattled camps of Brussels and Bruges agreed on the mutual incompatibility of 'Europe' and 'national' identity.[22]

But is there any warrant for this dichotomous view of cultural identities and for the battle cries on either side? We have already seen that, sociologically, human beings have multiple identities, that they can move between them according to context and situation, and that such identities may be concentric rather than conflictual. None of this is to deny the cultural reality and vivid meanings of these identities, which, transmitted through successive generations, are not exhausted by the often fickle volitions and changing perceptions of individuals. At the same time, there is plenty of historical evidence for the coexistence of concentric circles of allegiance.[23] In the ancient world it was possible to be Athenian, Ionion and Greek all at the same time; in the medieval world, to be Bernese, Swiss and Protestant; in the modern Third World to be Ibo, Nigerian and African simultaneously. Similarly, one could feel simultaneously Catalan, Spanish and European; even, dare one say it?—Scottish or English, British and European.

But if the possibility of being intensely French or British and intensely European exists, what does it mean to feel and be European? Is 'Europe' merely the sum total of its various national identities and communities? If so, is there not something quite arbitrary about aggregating such identities simply because certain otherwise unrelated communities happen to reside in a geographical area which is conventionally designated as the continent of Europe?—Which raises further questions about the eastern and southern boundaries of Europe, as well as about important internal geographical and historical divisions within that continent.

On the other hand, if 'Europe' and 'European' signify something more than the sum total of the populations and cultures that happen to inhabit a conventionally demarcated geographical space, what exactly are those characteristics and qualities that distinguish Europe from anything or anyone else? Can we find in the history and cultures of this continent something or things that are not replicated elsewhere, and that shaped what might be called specifically 'European experiences'?

There are a number of areas in which one might seek for specifically European characteristics, qualities and experiences. The first is linguistic. Though not all the languages of Europe belong to the Indo-European family, the vast majority do, and though there are important linguistic fault-lines between Latin, Germanic and Slav subfamilies, there has been sufficient movement across these lines to speak of at least a tenuous interrelationship which is modern as well as prehistoric. At the same time, the disastrous political consequences of drawing ethnic inferences from purely linguistic relationships suggests serious limitations in this area for any support for the European idea in ethno-linguistic terms.[24]

A second area of enquiry is that of cultural geography and territorial symbolism. The recent idea of a European 'home' from the Urals to the Atlantic is supported by the lack of any serious geographical barriers (apart from the Alps and Pyrenees, and perhaps the Carpathians and the Rhine and the Channel?), and by the protected geopolitical space between the Atlantic and the Mediterranean into which successive 'barbarian' ethnic communities poured and in which they found permanent shelter and adjacent homes. But what may be true in the north and west has no counterpart in the south and east. The Mediterranean forms a unifying internal (Roman?) lake—*mare nostrum*—rather than an impermeable boundary, while to the east the rolling plains, as the terrified populations found in the face of Hun and Mongol onslaughts and as the shifting boundaries of Poland–Lithuania and Russia–Ukraine bear witness, afford neither defence nor borderland. Besides, where is the geographical centre of the European homeland? In Burgundy or along the Rhine? In Berlin or Prague, or Budapest? In the Benelux countries, or in Provence or northern Italy? All these are historical claims, not geographical 'facts'.[25]

Third, there is the old issue of religious cleavages. Might this not provide a test of European inclusion and exclusion? There is a clear sense, going back at least to the Crusades and probably even to Charles Martel, in which Europeans see themselves as not-Muslims or as not-Jews. The history of resistance to Arab and Turkish Muslim encroachment provides potent memories, though there is the great exception of Spain and its Moorish and Jewish conduits for the enormous legacy of Arab Islam to Christian European culture.'

What of the inter-Christian divides? The most potent is still that between 'Western' Christendom (Catholic and Protestant) and Eastern Orthodoxy. Hungarians, for example, emphasize their Western connections through their historic 'choice for the West' over 1,000 years ago, in contrast to the Russians, for example, who chose Greek Byzantine Orthodoxy. But this brings problems of its own, not least for the position of Greece and potentially Serbia in the European Community. If religion is a real criterion of identity, should not Poland, rather than Greece, be a member of the new Europe? And what of that other great division, between the Protestant and Catholic states of Europe? Politically, Catholic–Protestant divisions may have declined, but how far, again, does this extend to the vast majority of Europeans in small towns and villages? This is another aspect of the wider question of the gulf between urban élites and rural masses in Europe over perceptions of and attitudes to Europe and European unification.

Fourth, there is the more inchoate sense of the 'outsider', which has recently found expression in various European countries, directed at immigrants and guest-workers. Might not the older nationalistic exclusive attitudes to foreigners now become 'Euro-nationalist' exclusion of blacks, Asians, and other non-Europeans? There is some evidence for this. But it is difficult to disentangle it from the older attitudes. If it is the case, it supports the idea that there is a continuum between collective cultural identities, as I have argued. This may well be reinforced after 1992, when common passports and European frontiers will help to 'create' an element of perceived common identity for those who travel beyond the European frontiers—and for those who seek to enter (or return to) them. The effect of such frontiers on creating an *out-group*, so vital to the formation of identity, depends of course on the degree of unity of perceptions and sentiments among the Europeans themselves, and on the degree of common political action, especially in the field of defence and foreign policy, which a more united Europe can evolve. The evidence in these fields to date has not been encouraging.

We are thrown back on history, and specifically on political and legal traditions and cultural heritages and symbolisms. Here, if anywhere, we may hope to find experiences and collective memories that differentiate the communities of Europe from other communities, and which, in some degree at least, provide common reference points for the peoples of Europe.

This is an area which, of its nature, is not amenable to rigorous positivistic criteria. We are dealing with shared memories, traditions, myths, symbols and values, which may possess subtly different meanings and significance for different communities in the area conventionally designated as Europe. The Roman heritage, for example, penetrated certain areas more than others, and some not at all. Christianity embraced most of the continent eventually, but it did so unevenly and split early into separate cultural and ethnic traditions. The various attempts to recreate the Roman Empire foundered, but they left their imprint on some areas of Europe more than others. Even such 'event-processes' as the Crusades, the Renaissance, the Reformation, and the Enlightenment affected some areas, peoples and states more than others, and a few hardly at all.

So what is common to all Europeans? What can they be said to share and in what respects can they be said to differ from non-Europeans? To these kinds of questions there can never be satisfactory answers. Europeans differ among themselves as much as from non-Europeans in respect of language (Basques, Finns, Hungarians), territory (Russians, Greeks, Armenians), law (Roman, Germanic), religion (Catholic, Orthodox, Protestant) and economic and political system (democracy, communism, unitary state, federalism, etc.)—*as well as* in terms of ethnicity and culture.

On the other hand, there *are* shared traditions, legal and political, and shared heritages, religious and cultural. Not all Europeans share in all of them; some share in particular traditions and heritages only minimally.

But at one time or another all Europe's communities have participated in at least *some* of these traditions and heritages, in some degree.

What are these partially shared traditions and heritages? They include traditions like Roman law, political democracy, parliamentary institutions, and Judeo-Christian ethics, and cultural heritages like Renaissance humanism, rationalism and empiricism, and romanticism and classicism. Together they constitute not a 'unity in diversity '—the official European cultural formula—but a 'family of cultures' made up of a syndrome of partially shared historical traditions and cultural heritages.

The idea of a 'family of cultures' resembles Wittgenstein's concepts of 'family resemblances' and of the 'language game', which features several elements, not all of which figure in each particular example of the game. What we have instead is a 'family' of elements which overlap and figure in a number of (but not all) examples. So, for example, the Italian Renaissance and its humanism found its way into many, but not all, parts of Europe, as did the spirit and methods of the French Enlightenment. 'Europe' here represents a field favourable to diffusion and cross-fertilization of cultural traditions, but one of uneven receptivity. Specific European states or communities may reveal only certain of the above traditions or heritages, or only to a limited extent. But the sum total of all Europe's states and communities has historically revealed a gamut of overlapping and boundary-transcending political traditions and cultural heritages, which together make up what we may call the European experience and the European family of cultures.

There has always been such cultural cross-fertilization in various parts of Europe. What now needs to be established is how far those shared traditions and heritages have become part of each of Europe's national identities, how far each national tradition has embraced and assimilated these 'trans-European' cultural heritages; how far Romanticism, Roman law or parliamentary democracy has taken on a peculiar national form, or conversely the extent to which French, or German, classicism and humanism partake of some shared trans-European tradition.

It is important here to distinguish between families of culture and political or economic unions. The latter are usually deliberate creations; they are consciously willed unities, rationally constructed sets of institutions, the kind of frameworks that some European states are trying to hasten and others to delay. Families of culture, like a lingua franca, tend to come into being over long time-spans and are the product of particular historical circumstances, often unanticipated and unintentional. Such cultural realities are no less potent for being so often inchoate and uninstitutionalized. Thus the sentiments and identities that underpin the Islamic *umma* or community of Muslims are no less significant than any official Islamic social and political institutions.[26]

But this very lack of institutionalization poses severe difficulties for the researcher. One of them is the problem of interpreting recent trends and developments as, in some sense, European manifestations. Can the growth of mass tourism, for example, be interpreted as a contribution to a more European identity? The fact that many more Europeans can and do travel abroad is open to several interpretations. When the British working classes took package holidays to Spanish beaches, were they even exposed to Spanish, let alone European, culture? Has the long-standing German love affair with Italy made any difference to the intensity of German nationalism, in this or the last century? Or shall we rather agree with Karl Kautsky that the railways are the greatest breeder of national hatreds (and by implication the most potent force for anti-Europeanism)?[27]

Or take the astonishing growth of large-scale 'European' music festivals and travelling art exhibitions. Do these great events testify to a new 'European spirit'? Can they not equally be seen as expressions of local pride, be it in Edinburgh or Spoleto, Moscow or Leeds, in the Royal Academy or the Louvre or the Prado? By their nature such artistic events are all-inclusive; great artistic events are as likely to be shown in America or Japan and include contributions from all parts of the world. Europe may well have become a 'great museum' for the heritage industry, but only its greater openness and capitalist spirit have given it the edge over other tourist centres and 'great museums' in the Middle East or Asia.[28]

Given these problems, where may we look for signs of a possible European identification—and among whom? It is one thing for élites in Brussels, Strasbourg and some European capitals to identify with and work for a united Europe, quite another to attribute such sentiments and beliefs to the great mass of the middle and working classes, let alone the surviving peasantries of Southern and Eastern Europe. Whence will *they* derive a sense of European identity?

One answer often given suggests the mass, standardized, public education system. The problem here is that there is no pan-European system, only *national* systems; and what they teach, or omit to teach, is determined by *national*, not European, priorities. In other words, education systems are run by and for national states. Until there is a single, centralized, unitary European state, we cannot expect too much from the national education systems of each European state. This can be confirmed by a glance at schoolroom texts in history, civics and literature. Even when they include positive reference to contemporary Europe, the bulk of such texts are national in content and intent. The recent study of French school history textbooks by Suzanne Citron is a striking case in point.[29]

What about the mass media? Are they equally tied to purely national criteria of choice and content? Here there is clearly more variety as between different European national states. Yet even here, national priorities are very much in evidence: news stories tend to be relayed or at least interpreted from a national standpoint, drama, comedy shows, children's tales, even the weather reports accord the national state and its literature and outlook first place. Given the linguistic and historical barriers and the national frameworks of most mass media institutions, this is only to be expected.

Some changes are occurring in these areas, and given the political will of the élites, more rapid changes may soon take place. But the question still remains: how will the new 'European message' be received? Will it be reinterpreted by audiences and pupils in ethnic and national terms, as with so many cultural products? For until the great majority of Europeans, the great mass of the middle and lower classes, are ready to imbibe these European messages in a similar manner and to feel inspired by them to common action and community, the edifice of 'Europe' at the political level will remain shaky. This is all too clear today in respect of foreign policy and defence, where we are witnessing the need for European governments to respond to their national public opinion and the failure of Europeans to agree on a common policy. Once again, the usual divisions of public opinion between European states have been exposed, and with them the tortuous and divided actions of Europe's governments. Once again, too, the division between Britain and the Continent has become plain, and with it the crucial relationship of all European states to American political leadership. The 'European failure' only underlines the distance between the European ideal and its rootedness in the popular consciousness of Europe's national populations—and hence the distance between European unification at the political and cultural levels and the realities of divergent national identities, perceptions and interests within Europe.

Clearly these are areas for detailed and intensive research, which would focus not on ephemeral attitudes but on what is taught and portrayed and how it is received by the majority of Europe's populations. In more concrete terms, this means examining the ways in which news and documentaries are purveyed; how far a European dimension is added to, and received in, matters of art, music and literature; how far education systems are harmonized and teachers and taught acculturated to the different values, goals and forms of education and training, and how far history textbooks are rewritten to accommodate a European standpoint.[30]

If this were not problematic enough, there is the deeper question of popular myths and symbols, and historical memories and traditions. Here we are placed firmly back in the pre-modern past of each national state. There is no European analogue to Bastille or Armistice Day, no European ceremony for the fallen in battle, no European shrine of kings or saints. When it comes to the ritual and ceremony of collective identification, there is no European equivalent of national or religious community. Any research into the question of forging, or even discovering, a possible European identity cannot afford to overlook these central issues.[31]

We encounter similar problems when it comes to the question of a genuinely European political mythology. The founding fathers of the European movements, such as Coudenhove-Kalergi, recognized the problem. They tended to look back to the imperial myths of the Carolingian and Ottonian Holy Roman Empire and to the medieval urban civilization centred on the Rhine as their models of a 'golden age' of European Christendom. But as a modern political *mythomoteur*, these models are deeply flawed. Secularism has made deep inroads into the political consciousness of most classes in several European states, too deep for any genuine religious revival to be less than divisive. Besides, the imperial format of such myths is profoundly inimical to the spirit of democracy which the West espouses and Eastern Europe so ardently seeks. There is also the persistent unease over locating one's guiding myth in a particular part of Europe at the expense of the rest. Once again, these models assert the primacy of 'the West' as the home of innovation and progress, traceable to that early spirit of capitalism in the free cities of late medieval Europe.[32]

It is clear that such historical *mythomoteurs* are inappropriate for the modern European project. But where else can one look for the necessary political mythology? Is it possible for the new Europe to arise without 'myth' and 'memory'? Have we not seen that these are indispensable elements in the construction of any durable and resonant collective cultural identity?

Here lies the new Europe's true dilemma: a choice between unacceptable historical myths and memories on the one hand, and on the other a patchwork, memoryless scientific 'culture' held together solely by the political will and economic interest that are so often subject to change. In between, there lies the hope of discovering that 'family of cultures' briefly outlined above, through which over several generations some loose, overarching political identity and community might gradually be forged.

EUROPE IN A WIDER WORLD

At present the tide is running for the idea of European unification as it has never done before. This is probably the result of dramatic geopolitical and geocultural changes, which remind us that the future of 'Europe', as indeed of every national state today, will be largely determined by wider regional, or global, currents and trends. The most immediate of these, of course, has been the dramatic shift in world power resulting from the adoption of perestroika in the Soviet Union and the liberation of the states of Eastern Europe and the republics of the former Soviet Union to determine their own political future. But this same current may serve simultaneously as a model and a warning: what may flow so suddenly and vigorously in one direction may equally swiftly change course, for reasons that have nothing to do with intra-European developments, and in so doing reverse the climate that seemed so conducive to the project of European unification.

There are many other currents and trends affecting the chances of fulfilling a European project. We may cite several:

1. dramatic regional developments, like the vortex of conflict in the Middle East, into which European states may be drawn, severally or together;
2. the dangers of ethnic conflict, separatism and large-scale wars in other parts of the world such as the Indian subcontinent or Africa, which may again involve one or more European states and so divide the interests of those states and even threaten, by example, their stability and cohesion;
3. the impact of waves of migrants and guest-workers on the economies and societies of European states, which may differentially affect their attitudes and priorities;
4. larger problems of environmental pollution and ecological disaster, as well as epidemic disease, which may require both individual action by each European state and wider, perhaps global, responses which may pre-empt the integration of Europe; and
5. problems of large-scale crime and terrorism, which may again call for immediate action by individual states, or by bodies larger and more powerful than any European organization.

The point of this list, which could be extended, is simply to underline the dramatic pace and scope of change within which the project of European unification must locate itself. Unification is in fact one of several possible responses to wider changes; but these trends do not all work in the same direction, and they may be reversed. Hence the importance of basing any European project on firm and deep cultural and social foundations that are to some extent independent of economic and political fluctuations, even of the much vaunted trends of mass democracy and popular capitalism.

There is another and equally important issue raised by the project of European unification and its relationship with nations and nationalism. Identities are forged out of shared experiences, memories and myths, in relation to those of other collective identities. They are in fact often forged through opposition to the identities of significant others, as the history of paired conflict so often demonstrates. Who or what then, are Europe's significant others? Until now, the obvious answers were the protagonists of the ideological Cold War. In this context Europe was often seen as a third force *between* the respective superpower blocs, though there was always something unreal about such a posture. Now, however, the problem of relationship to other identities has become more perplexing. To whom shall Europe be likened, against whom shall it measure itself? Today's geo-political uncertainty makes a direct comparison and relationship with the United States ambiguous; Europe is increasingly wholeheartedly a part of the 'capitalist' and 'democratic' camp of which the United States is likely to remain the military leader. Shall Europe look to Japan as its *alter ego*? But Japan is an ethnically almost homogeneous society, it poses no military or political threat, and its economic rivalry is still mainly directed at the United States.

There is another, a less pleasing, possibility: the relationship of a unifying Europe to a disaggregated Third World. There is the prospect of an increasingly affluent, stable, conservative but democratic European federation, facing, and protecting itself from, the demands and needs of groupings of states in Africa, Asia and Latin America. To some extent this prospect is still mitigated by the remaining ex-colonial ties between certain European and certain African or Asian states. But were the European project to achieve its political goals, it would also entail, not just economic exclusion, but also cultural differentiation and with it the possibility of cultural and racial exclusion. The forging of a deep continental cultural identity to support political unification may well require an ideology of European cultural exclusiveness.

These dangers are well known in respect of the maintenance of national identities by individual European states. In many respects, it is European institutions that are leading the struggle against racial discrimination, ethnic antagonism and anti-Semitism, though with mixed success. The deeper question remains. Is not the logic of cultural exclusion built into the process of pan-European identity formation? Will not a unified Europe magnify the virtues and the defects of each of Europe's national identities, precisely because it has been built in their images? And might a European 'super-nation' resemble, in its external as well as its internal policies and relations, this national model?[33]

This is a fear that has been often expressed. It is one that still haunts the European political arena, as each of Europe's national states seeks to influence the future shape of a European union along the lines of its own self-image. In its relations with minorities inside Europe, as well as with states and peoples outside the continent, these images have not been appealing ones. Here too lies an agenda for policy-oriented research, one beset by sensitive issues and thorny problems.

Facing and understanding these problems is a precondition for forging a pan-European identity that will eschew these undesirable and self-defeating images and features. Shaping a cultural identity that will be both distinctive and inclusive, differentiating yet assimilative, may yet constitute the supreme challenge for a Europe that seeks to create itself out of its ancient family of ethnic cultures.

Notes

1. On the forerunners of the idea of European unity, see Denis de Rougemont, *The meaning of Europe* (London: Sidgwick & Jackson, 1965).

2. This article was prepared for a seminar series on 'Europe in the 1990s: forces for change', held at the RIIA in 1991 and funded by the Economic and Social Research Council.

3. Studies of European economic and political integration go back to Karl Deutsch *et al.*, *Political community and the North Atlantic area* (Princeton, NJ: Princeton University Press, 1957) and Ernest B. Haas, *Beyond the nation state* (Stanford University Press, 1964). Cf. William Wallace, *The transformation of Western Europe* (London: Pinter/RIIA, 1990), ch. 4.

4. See, for example, the essays in Eric Hobsbawm and Terence Ranger, eds., *The Invention of Tradition* (Cambridge: Cambridge University Press, 1983), and also in Elisabeth Tonkin, Maryon McDonald, and Malcolm Chapman, eds., *History and ethnicity* (London: Routledge, 1989).

5. For studies of ethnic identity, see George de Vos and Lola Romanucci-Rossi, eds., *Ethnic identity: cultural continuities and change* (Chicago, Ill.: University of Chicago Press, 1975), and A. L. Epstein, *Ethos and identity* (London: Tavistock, 1978).

6. On the relationships between religion and nationalism, see Donald E. Smith, eds., *Religion and political modernisation* (New Haven, Ct.: Yale University Press, 1974), and Pedro Ramet, ed., *Religion and nationalism in Soviet and East European politics* (Durham, NC.: Duke University Press, 1989). For some case-studies of the relationships between gender and nationality, see Floya Anthias and Nira Yuval-Davis, eds., *Woman–nation–state* (London: Macmillan, 1989).

7. For the concept of 'situational ethnicity' see J. Y. Okamura, 'Situational ethnicity', *Ethnic and Racial Studies* 4: 4 (1981), pp. 452–65.

8. On the 'individualist fallacy' see E. K. Scheuch, 'Cross-national comparisons with aggregate data', in Richard L. Merritt and Stein Rokkan, eds., *Comparing nations: the use of quantitative data in cross-national research* (New Haven, Ct.: Yale University Press, 1956).

9. This definition summarizes long and complex discussions of the many definitions of 'nation'. See, *inter alia*, Karl Deutsch, *Nationalism and social communication* (2nd edn, New York: MIT Press, 1966), ch. I; and Walker Connor, 'A nation is a nation, is a state, is an ethnic group, is . . .', *Ethnic and Racial Studies* 1: 4 (1978), pp. 377–400.

10. For fuller discussions of nationalist ideologies, see Elie Kedourie, *Nationalism* (London: Hutchinson, 1960); Elie Kedourie, ed., *Nationalism in Asia and Africa* (London: Weidenfeld & Nicolson, 1971); and A. D. Smith, *Theories of nationalism* (2nd edn., London: Duckworth, 1983). On the multidimensionality of national identity, see A. D. Smith, *National identity* (London: Penguin, 1991), ch. I.

11. On the distinction between these types of nationalism, see Hans Kohn, *The idea of nationalism* (2nd edn, New York: Macmillan, 1967), and A. D. Smith, *The ethnic origins of nations* (Oxford: Blackwell, 1986), ch. 6.

12. I have adapted the definitions given in the introductions to Charles Tilly, ed., *The formation of national states in Western Europe* (Princeton, NJ: Princeton University Press, 1975), and Leonard Tivey, ed., *The nation-state* (Oxford: Martin Robertson, 1980).

13. See Walker Connor's seminal article, 'Nation-building or nation-destroying?', *World Politics* 24 (1972), pp. 319–55; and Ernest Gellner, *Nations and nationalism* (Oxford: Blackwell, 1983).

14. See Daniel Bell, 'Ethnicity and social change', in Nathan Glazer and Daniel P. Moynihan, eds., *Ethnicity: theory and experience* (Cambridge, Mass.: Harvard University Press, 1975).

15. This argument is presented in the last chapter of Eric Hobsbawm, *Nations and nationalism since 1780* (Cambridge: Cambridge University Press, 1990).

16. This argument is presented with force and clarity by Anthony Richmond in 'Ethnic nationalism and post-industrialism', *Ethnic and Racial Studies* 7: 1 (1984), pp. 4–18; it is also implicit in Benedict Anderson, *Imagined communities: reflections on the origin and spread of nationalism* (London: Verso, 1983).

17. The ethnic revival in the West in the 1970s suggests the difficulty of 'reading' any 'major trends' of world history. Regions and ethnic communities are being revitalized *alongside* a strengthened national state and an overarching European Community. On ethnic nationalisms in the West see Milton Esman, ed., *Ethnic conflict in the Western world* (Ithaca, NY: Cornell University Press, 1977), and A. D. Smith, *The ethnic revival in the modern world* (Cambridge: Cambridge University Press, 1981).
18. For a discussion of globalization, see Mike Featherstone, ed., *Global culture: nationalism, globalization and modernity* (London: Sage, 1990).
19. For a searching analysis of the role of mass, public education systems in shaping national identities, see Gellner, *Nations and nationalism*.
20. The argument is presented fully in A. D. Smith, 'Towards a global culture?', *Theory, Culture and Society* 7 (1990), pp. 171–91.
21. This point is documented in Philip Schlesinger, 'On national identity: some conceptions and misconceptions criticised', *Social Science Information* 26: 2 (1987), pp. 219–64.
22. For the early debates between pan-Europeans and anti-Europeans, see Miriam Camps, *What kind of Europe? The Community since de Gaulle's veto* (London: Oxford University Press, 1965), and Wallace, *The transformation of Western Europe*, ch. 4.
23. On the idea of concentric circles of allegiance see James Coleman, *Nigeria: background to nationalism* (Berkeley, CA: University of California Press, 1958), appendix.
24. On Europe's linguistic divisions, see Andrew Orridge, 'Separatist and autonomist nationalisms: the structure of regional loyalties in the modern state', in C. Williams, ed., *National separatism* (Cardiff: University of Wales Press, 1982), and John Armstrong, *Nations before nationalism* (Chapel Hill, NC: University of North Carolina Press, 1982), ch. 8.
25. On Europe's protected geopolitical position, see introduction, Tilly, ed., *The formation of national states*; for Europe's problematic eastern boundaries, see Raymond Pearson, *National minorities in Eastern Europe, 1848–1945* (London: Macmillan, 1983), and Roger Portal, *The Slavs* (London: Weidenfeld & Nicolson, 1969).
26. On the Islamic *umma* and the Muslim states, see Erwin Rosenthal, *Islam in the modern national state* (Cambridge: Cambridge University Press, 1965). Pan-Europeans have sometimes tried to construct culture areas through the deliberate manufacture of myths, symbols and traditions: see Lord Gladwyn, *The European idea* (London: New English Library, 1967).
27. On Karl Kautsky's argument, see Horace Davis, *Nationalism and socialism: Marxist and labor theories of nationalism* (London, New York: Monthly Review Press,1967). There is evidence that mass tourism among the younger generations of Western Europe, which grew up in an era of peace, has confirmed their lack of national antagonisms.

28. European élites, going back to feudal nobility and clergy, have always been more cosmopolitan and open to outside influences than the middle and lower classes: see Armstrong, *Nations before nationalism*, ch. 3, and Smith, *The ethnic origins of nations*, ch. 4.

29. Suzanne Citron, *Le mythe national* (Paris: Presses Ouvriers, 1988), analyses the strongly nationalistic content and framework of French school history textbooks based on Lavisse, which came into use during the late nineteenth century under the Third Republic. The continuing debate in Britain over the place of British, even English, history, as opposed to European and world history illustrates the same issues; see Raphael Samuel, ed., *Patriotism: the making and unmaking of British national identity* (London: Routledge, 1989), vol. 1, and Juliet Gardiner, ed., *The history debate* (London: Collins & Brown, 1990).

30. Even this does not take us to the heart of the problem. We need also to explore people's attachments to national landscapes, or myths thereof; to certain events and heroes from the national past; to certain kinds of social institutions and mores, food, family life and village community; and how far all these are felt to override, conflict with or deny a more overarching European identity that is inevitably more abstract, intellectual and political.

31. The centrality of such rites and ceremonies for creating and maintaining collective cultural identities is only now receiving the attention it deserves. See, e.g., John Breuilly, *Nationalism and the state* (Manchester: Manchester University Press, 1982), ch. 16; Hobsbawm and Ranger, eds., *The invention of tradition*.

32. The primacy of Western Europe as a 'core' to the northern, southern and especially eastern peripheries (which in medieval times were sparsely inhabited) was seized on by the myth-makers of the European idea; see Gladwyn, *The European idea*, and de Rougemont, *The meaning of Europe*.

33. A fear summed up in Johan Galtung, *The European Community: a superpower in the making* (London: Allen & Unwin, 1973), but with recent events taking on a new meaning: namely, the fear that Germany's economic domination might influence the political shape of a future Europe, and the chances of greater cultural and racial exclusiveness, at the expense mainly of Third World migrants but stirring all too vivid memories of the Nazi past. Fears, like memories, are no less real for being intangible and difficult to research.

10

The Resurgence of Nationalism? Myth and Memory in the Renewal of Nations*

ABSTRACT

Contrary to liberal evolutionary expectations, the world has witnessed a resurgence of ethnic conflicts and nationalist movements since the end of the Cold War. Though it calls into question theories of the demise of nations and nationalism, this revival should not be interpreted as a throwback to earlier nationalisms or a passing phenomenon. Rather, it is one of many resurgences since the French Revolution and it demonstrates once again the power of the resources and trends which reproduce a world of nations and nationalism. These resources include: the uneven distribution of ethno-history and memories of golden ages; the politicization of myths of ethnic election and covenant which inspire peoples with a sense of renewal and glorious destiny; and the power of territorial attachments to ancestral homelands and sacred sites. Even ethnic categories and communities that lack some of these 'deep resources' are stimulated to rediscover or acquire them by the example of influential neighbours. Though the timing of the current ethnic revival is a function of social and geopolitical changes, their contents and intensities are largely determined by pre-existing ethno-symbolic resources.

The world of the 1990s is a bewildering place. Gone are the old certainties. The division of the world into competing blocs, the familiar ideologies and propaganda, the games of political chess played by the superpowers in Africa, Asia and Latin America, the Cold War patterns of trade, aid and defence, all of these guaranteed a predictable, if tense, global order in which the arts of espionage and political double dealing served to reinforce the moral verities on both sides.

Today these simple verities have been replaced by the complex moral and political judgements of a multi-polar world. This is a world in which

* *British Journal of Sociology*, Volume no. 47, Issue no. 4, December 1996.

superpowers have shrunk or disintegrated, economic giants have so far failed to acquire political power or military muscle, the state itself has been outflanked by the new international division of labour and mass communications, and the old ethical norms have been replaced by moral ambivalence and political ambiguity.

In this turmoil of power and ideas, one familiar face has reappeared: that of nationalism. For many it is as unwelcome as it is unbidden and unexpected. For others its reappearance is regrettable but comes as no surprise. For still others, it represents the only sure way forward after the sudden ruptures created by totalitarianism in the developmental paths of so many societies. For all, nationalism represents a stage in the evolution of humanity to 'higher forms' of society, one that must be endured or embraced, but is surely destined to pass after a few turbulent decades (Smith 1990; Gellner 1994).

None of these scenarios seems to accord with the historical facts or sociological realities of ethnicity and nationalism. Instead of treating ethnicity and nationalism as phenomena in their own right, they insist on evaluating them by the yardstick of a liberal evolutionary scheme, explicit or tacit, one that is inherently problematic and demonstrably irrelevant to the dynamics of nations, nationalism and ethnic conflict. For liberals and socialists, committed to the view that humanity progresses in stages to greater units of inclusiveness and higher values, the nation and nationalism can only represent a halfway house to the goal of a cosmopolitan culture and a global polity. On the one hand, the nation can be commended for superseding all those local, ascriptive ties and communities that have restricted innovation and opportunity and enchained the human spirit. Its wider horizons have brought together all kinds of peoples with varying origins, religions, occupations and class backgrounds and turned them into citizens of the territorial, civic nation. On the other hand, the nation today has become a barrier to progress, seeking vainly to control the flow of information and the channels of mass communication, and to impede and regulate the great economic institutions—transnational companies, world banks and trade organizations—and the global financial and commodities markets. But the great forces of globalization, economic, political and cultural, have already undermined the power of the nation-state and are fast making all national boundaries and sentiments obsolete (Smelser 1968; Arnason 1990; Hobsbawm 1990: ch. 6).

Unfortunately, contemporary facts as well as theoretical weaknesses belie these confident predictions. As Walker Connor pointed out over twenty years ago, the ethnic revival in the West, not to mention continuing ethnic struggles in Africa and Asia, highlighted grave problems for Western states as well as Western scholars of nationalism. These problems have only been aggravated by the demise of the Soviet Union and events in the former Yugoslavia. They suggest that, far from withering away with the advance of modernity and mass communications, ethnic and national conflicts have been exacerbated by just those forces that were supposed to dissolve the ties that engendered these conflicts. In other words, contrary to the expectations of liberals and socialists, a progressive modernity and all its works have actually increased ethnic conflict and nationalism; and as modernization bites deeper, we can only expect an intensification of such conflicts (Connor 1973; Smith 1995).

The inevitable result of this signal failure to grasp the nature and consequences of ethnicity and nationalisms, is widespread disappointment and exasperation at their apparent resilience and explosive unpredictability.

In fact, there is little that is new about the recent wave of nationalism. It represents one more wave in a series of upsurges of ethnic conflict and nationalism in various parts of the world since the French Revolution. Perhaps its most salient effect is to redraw the inter-state map of different regions, but the more profound consequences of nationalism permeate the organization of modern societies and the nature of modern cultures. For, underlying the global system of states is a cultural division of the world into nations based on distinctive ethnic histories, ethnic myths and territorial associations stemming in many cases from deep-rooted pre-modern cultural and ethnicities.

A RESURGENCE OF NATIONALISM?

Let me begin by considering in more detail the flaws in the conventional views of contemporary nationalism. The most common view is that nationalism is once again rampant, and that we are witnessing its sudden and dramatic resurgence now that the Cold War is over and the last empires have disintegrated. As a result, some fifteen new states have been created on the ruins of the Soviet and Ethiopian empires, and four (perhaps five) more have arisen out of the failures of two federal states, Yugoslavia and Czechoslovakia. This is surely dramatic evidence of the power of nationalism at the end of the second millennium.

The assumption behind this view is that nationalism had been suppressed by the former empires and can now resume its interrupted course. This may be true in some cases such as the Baltic states or Georgia, but it would be hard to find a pre-imperial Eritrean, Kazakh or Kirghiz nationalism—unless of course we were to regard nations as primordial and nationalism as natural to the human condition, albeit often in latent form.[1]

There is a more important objection to this resurgence view. Can we legitimately generalize from the contingencies of the end of the Cold War? Since the fall of the Soviet and Ethiopian empires is a once-for-all event, it would be foolhardy to make deductions about the future impact of nationalism on their basis alone. The other two instances of ethnic secession from modern federal states—the Slovak, and the Croat and Slovene—are certainly more ominous for state stability, but they too constitute too small a population to allow us to predict, with any degree of confidence, a wider resurgence of nationalism.

On the other hand, there are a number of potential separatisms such as Quebec, Kurdistan and Tamilnad, which suggest a wider movement of nationalism in the last decades of the second millennium, one that may yet break the bounds of the inter-state system. It could, of course, be objected that these nationalisms have been struggling for several decades for independence, without much success, and that the national state system is therefore quite capable of containing the centrifugal forces of ethnic nationalism which inter-state competition and state expansion have unleashed.

However, in a multipolar, and therefore less predictable, global environment, where the international community is somewhat more favourably inclined to the partial redrawing of the inter-state map, the chances of ethnic separatisms gaining international or at least regional support may have been enhanced and the probability of consensual separations increased (Mayall 1990: ch. 4; Heraclides 1991).

But these arguments tell us only part of the story. They relate largely to the immediate post-cold War era, and they fail to locate the contemporary manifestations of ethnic conflict and nationalism in a broader historical and sociological context. Let me briefly recall some salient aspects of that broader context.

As I indicated, 'nationalism', defined here as *an ideological movement for attaining and maintaining autonomy, unity and identity for a human population deemed by some of its members to constitute an actual or potential 'nation'*, has been with us for two centuries, since the French Revolution at least, and in that period has spread from western Europe and the Americas to every continent.[2]

Second, the pattern of appearance of nationalisms has been serial and wave-like. Groups of nationalisms have emerged at different times and places, after periods of warfare or the demise of *ancien régimes,* only to subside and give way to other waves of nationalisms elsewhere, which have harked back to the earlier examples for some of their inspiration. As Anderson and Orridge have demonstrated, the types of nationalisms varied according to the features of each culture area and period, but they drew on the same underlying ideals and motifs (Orridge 1980; Anderson 1983).

Third, the state has become a 'national' state. Though often ethnically heterogenous, it has sought to become unitary by adopting the ideological postulates of nationalism as its legitimation and attempting to mould, homogenize and create 'the nation' out of the various ethnic communities and ethnic categories that had been incorporated, usually accidentally, by and into the domains of the state—often at the expense of minority ethnic communities (Connor 1972).

Fourth, as a result, 'national identity' has become a primary criterion of social solidarity and individual affiliation. The concept of national identity has come to represent the ideal of collective cultural distinctiveness and social cohesion to which citizens and governments aspire or at least pay lip service. A state that cannot boast some kind of national identity for its citizens is deemed to have failed in one of its primary functions, the creation of a distinctive collective loyalty based on consent (see Grodzins 1956; Doob 1964).

Finally, the global system of states is today justified primarily in terms of the postulates of nationalism and national self-determination. The political pluralism of its inter-state systems is underpinned by a radical cultural pluralism, which combines a respect for cultural diversity and individuality with a commitment to popular participation. (Smith 1995: chs. 4, 6).

It follows from these considerations that there is nothing remarkable about the present wave of nationalisms in certain parts of the world, and that, on past experience, we can expect the present upsurge to recede after the period of post-Cold War turmoil has subsided, to be followed in the near future by other waves of ethnic nationalisms elsewhere—of which there is never a shortage of aspirants. In other words, while the timing of the appearance of nationalisms depends on a variety of contingent forces—including the reactions of dominant state élites, the balance of local and regional forces, and the general climate of international opinion—nationalism itself as ideology, symbolism and movement has become endemic. The potential for nationalist movements is always with us.

This is not to claim that nationalism is the only, or even necessarily the most powerful, force in the modern world. What we can say is that nationalism has become the most ubiquitous and enduring phenomenon in the modern world, the ideological movement and symbolic structure with the greatest staying power, one that always appears, as it were, to be waiting in the wings for its opportunity to emerge, in the chaos of conflict and disintegration that attends the fall of states and empires.

THE DECLINE OF NATIONALISM?

So far I have concentrated on arguments that emphasize and generalize from the present upsurge of nationalism. These fears stand in sharp contrast to all those prophecies of the imminent demise of the nation-state and the decline of nationalism, which have become the standard coin of international statesmen and 'post-modernist' scholarship alike. For these theorists the current proliferation of contemporary mini-nationalisms is merely the product of a passing phase of turmoil in the aftermath of the Cold War. Broadly speaking, three kinds of argument are usually advanced to back this contention: arguments about economic globalization, social hybridization and cultural standardization.

1. The first set of arguments is usually addressed to the state, or the so-called 'nation-state'.[3] The new international division of labour of advanced capitalism knows no frontiers and its operations take no account of the national interest or national state policies. The operations of the transnational companies, of the great financial institutions, of the major money and commodities markets, as well as the flows of trade and production, have simply by-passed the restrictive confines of the 'nation-state', with the result that in these and other areas, the national state has lost its former independence. We live in a global economy and an increasingly global polity.

Few would wish to quarrel with the positive assertions of this argument, but questions can be raised about its deductions for the present position of the so-called 'nation-state'. One might start by asking whether the comparison with former times was historically accurate, whether there was ever a time when 'the state' or 'the nation-state' was economically and financially independent. Great empires have always depended for their continued prosperity on the goods and labour of their colonies and smaller states operated under the economic hegemony of larger ones. It was really only under the influence of mercantilism and later of the economic nationalist theories of List that the ideal of a self-sufficient national state became more prevalent (see Johnson 1968; Tivey 1980).

One might wish to question the zero-sum assumption of the globalization argument. If the greater part of trade flows, markets, investment, financial speculations and production are directed by institutions and groups outside the domain of the nation-state, it does not follow that the state has become obsolete and increasingly irrelevant, even assuming it did once possess economic and financial independence. For many people and in many areas of the world, the national state remains the main regulator of economic practices and formulator of economic policies, even if its room for manoeuvre is more restricted. Through its control over legislation, administration and adjudication, state élites retain considerable powers in the economic sphere. In the social domain, these powers have, if anything, been vastly increased both by the state's capacity to penetrate society and by the welfare planning that resulted from the two World Wars. In terms of popular perceptions, too, the national state, not the global economy, remains the chief source of benefits and sanctions for the individual citizen (Mann 1984).

Besides, national states have always had other primary tasks and governments are periodically judged by the way in which they fulfil these tasks. Foremost among these, of course, has been the protection of the citizen, both internally in the form of maintaining 'law and order' and externally through defence of the national territory. But, in addition, the state has been increasingly charged with the protection and enhancement of the health, education and culture of the nation and its citizens. This has come to include attempts to safeguard through control of the media and a national curriculum the special character of the national community from being undermined by what have been perceived as culturally alien concerns or debased standards or subversive movements (see Tilly 1975; Tomlinson 1990: ch. 3).

2. If the state is still resilient and functional even in a globalizing economy, what of the nation? The second, or 'social hybridization' argument, suggests that the concepts of the nation and national identity need to be redefined in a 'post-modern' world. The recent massive influx of immigrants, ex-colonials, asylum-seekers and guest workers has eroded the old traditions and beliefs in an homogenous national identity and turned the unified nation into a series of culturally discrete segments. The old pedagogical and homogenizing narratives of the people and the nation have given way to split and doubled perceptions of identity, history and community, where the self is defined by its relationship to the other. We live today in fragmented and precarious nations housed in anxious states (Anderson 1983; Bhabha 1990: ch. 16).

If we define the 'nation' as *a named human population with shared myths and memories occupying an historic territory or homeland, and possessing a common public culture, a single unified economy and common legal rights and duties*, we can see that the concept of the nation presupposes shared experiences, cultural unity and a degree of commonality among its citizens. On the other hand, however much the ideologues of a romantic ethnic nationalism may have desired a seamless national unity and genuine homogeneity, most actual national states were culturally and ethnically plural and even the unitary nation represented only an ideal to which the nationalists aspired. Here again, we may ask: was there ever a unified national identity, except in the dreams of ethnic nationalists and the official propaganda of nationalist state regimes? Have not, and do not, most nations possess dominant and minority traditions of ethnic identification and incorporation? And is not even the official version of national identity subject to modification and change through debate and reinterpretation (McNeill 1986: chs. 2–3)?[4]

On the other hand, there are definite limits to these processes of reinterpretation. Modern states require a principle of political solidarity. This is often furnished by some form of civic, territorial nationalism which legitimates the common, public culture and the equal legal rights and duties of its citizens. This is what the *patriots* preached during the French Revolution, and the vision was put into practice by the leaders of the Third Republic in France. Civic nationalism operates on a territorial principle, by which all residents are citizens. But civic nationalism may not suffice. In a world of massive population movements, it may give way to, or be combined with, a more ethnically based principle of national solidarity, in which only those born of grandparents of the dominant ethnic group are members and hence citizens of the nation. In the many plural (polyethnic) states around the world this can prove both unifyng and divisive. Genealogical citizenship may help to unite co-nationals and give them a sense of intimacy and solidarity, but it is apt to be much more exclusive and restrictive, expressive of a drive to purify the community of alien elements which are seen to be corroding the moral fabric and cultural individuality of the nation. Such a criterion has surfaced periodically in France, notably at the time of the Dreyfus Affair and during the Vichy years, but its role in Germany and Eastern Europe has been to this day much more fundamental.[5]

3. National identity therefore remains a most important, if contested, criterion and ideal of political solidarity. Its importance is, if anything, enhanced by the third set of debates around the issues of cultural standardization. The claim here is that globalization is producing a standardized consumerist culture everywhere as a result of mass communications based on electronic media and information technology. This is not the place

to rehearse these arguments in detail. Suffice it to say that in so far as it is something new and other than old-style cultural imperialism or simply the cross-fertilization of cultures, both of which have been with us for centuries, a 'global culture' represents a contradiction in terms. Being by definition timeless, placeless, neutral and technical, a global culture would be essentially memoryless and presentist, or simply a *mélange* and pastiche of other rooted and specific cultures. But no culture that we have ever encountered can flourish without collective memories and traditions, neither can cultural identities and communities exist without their distinctive symbolic codes. As for a pastiche culture, how long could it withstand its own disintegrative tendencies?[6]

In fact, specific cultures, as distinctive symbolic codes, can only be seen as the historical product of the collective experiences, memories and traditions of different categories and groupings of human beings—be they ethnic, regional, class or religious—whose sense of identity and community they tend to express and symbolize. Hence cultures are essentially reflective and distinctive. They require human beings to draw on, and interpret, each other's experiences over generations and they express the separate patterns of those experiences in artefacts, rituals, behaviour and symbols that are peculiar to that community—an observation that suggests a very different perspective on the bases of ethnic conflict and nationalism today than those we have been considering. It is a perspective that requires us to place the present upsurge of ethnic nationalisms in a different and broader context, and to replace the conventional emphasis on the timing of these movements, with more fundamental questions about the nature, character and intensity of these ethnic nationalisms.

ETHNO-HISTORY AND THE 'GOLDEN AGE'

The real question raised by the present spate of ethnic nationalisms is not, why they have re-emerged now, or why they proliferate in an era of globalization, but how we can explain both the continuing power and the diversity of expression of ethnic nationalisms.

The usual account of the power and variety of nationalism is some version of modernization theory. Its basic proposition is that modernity in one of its many guises requires the formation of nations. Some regard nationalism as a response to incipient industrialization and the nation as a necessary and functional element of industrial modernity (Gellner 1983). Others seek to derive the nation and nationalism from the modern rational state and its self-reflexive capacities, or from the interests of sub-élites who use national arguments to wrest control of the state (Breuilly 1982; Giddens 1985). Still others regard nationalism, and nations, as ideological constructs of intellectuals and professionals seeking to undermine *ancien régimes* and establish modernized states in societies committed to the ideal of progress, or to control the mass mobilization of a democratic era (Kedourie 1960 and 1971; Kautsky 1962; cf. also Hobsbawm 1990).

Now, in general terms it may be true that the processes of modernization, variously defined, create the conditions for the formation of national states and the spread of 'nationalism–in–general'; and in this respect each of the above modernization perspectives undoubtedly captures an important aspect of the phenomenon of nations and nationalism. At the same time, they are incapable of explaining the paradox of variety and persistence in nationalism, of why nations and nationalisms have such staying power in the modern epoch, yet manifest such vast differences in their content and style of expression.

This is because they fail to take seriously three sets of components, or resources, that underlie all nationalisms: the uneven distribution of ethno-history, the varying impact of religious ideals, and the differential nature and location of the 'homeland' or ancestral territory. By exploring the nature and influence of these sets of ethnic-symbolic resources, we are able, I believe, to give a more convincing account of the power and variety of modern nationalisms.

Let me start with uneven ethno-history and a general proposition. As I intimated, any identity is based on memory conceived of as an active principle of recall of earlier states of activity and experience of that person. By analogy, collective cultural identities are based on the shared memories of experiences and activities of successive generations of a group distinguished by one or more shared cultural elements. Ethnic identity in turn may be seen as the product of shared memories of collective experiences and activities of successive generations of a group claiming a common origin and ancestry. Ethnicity in turn may be defined as *the sense of collective belonging to a named community of common myths of origin and shared memories, associated with an historic homeland.*[7]

Ernest Renan had long ago, of course, recognized the significance of shared memories of great sacrifices and battle experiences for the formation of nations. But collective memories range more widely. They include recollections not only of wars and their heroes, but of religious movements and their leaders, migrations, discoveries and colonizations, foundations of cities and states, dynasties and their kings, lawcodes and their legislators, great buildings and their architects, painters, sculptors, poets, musicians and their immortal works. Above all, the idealized memories of a *'golden age'*, or golden ages, of virtue, heroism, beauty, learning, holiness, power and wealth, an era distinguished for its collective dignity and external prestige (Renan 1882; cf. Armstrong 1982, ch. 2).

It is notoriously difficult to disentangle the elements of genuine shared memory from those of exaggeration, idealization and heroization which we associate with myth and legend, since there is usually more than a kernel of truth in the latter. But we can say that the more faithfully recorded, better documented and more comprehensive a golden age, the more impact it can exert over later generations and epochs of that community (or in some cases other communities). In this respect, Periclean Athens can have a greater and more varied impact for modern Greeks and others than, say, Kievan 'Rus can have for modern Ukrainians.

Now there is nothing fixed or immutable about a golden age or the principle of its selection. Successive generations of the community may differ as to which epoch is to be regarded as a golden age, depending on the criteria in fashion at the time. For some it will be a golden age because it boasted religious virtuosi, saints and sages; for others because great art, drama, music and philosophy flourished; for still others because the community enjoyed its greatest territorial extent and military power; or pioneered great moral and legal codes and institutions. Thus the ethnohistory of a community may boast more than one golden age from which to choose, and different sections of the latterday community may look back to quite different golden ages, as with modern Jews who look back nostalgically to the Davidic and Solomonic kingdom, or revere the era of the Talmudic sages or dream of the Golden Age of Spain with its many poets and philosophers (Eisenstein-Barzilay 1959; Seltzer 1980).

The ideal of a golden age is not simply a form of escapism or consolation for present tribulations. For later generations, the standards of golden ages come to define the normative character of the evolving community. They define what is and what is not to be admired and emulated. They define what is, and what is not, distinctive about that community. They define an ideal, which is not so much to be resurrected (few nationalists want actually to return to the past, even a golden past) as to be recreated in modern terms. Even the Jacobin leaders who dreamt of emulating Brutus the Consul, Cincinnatus and Leonidas had no intention of founding an agrarian city-republic in France, only of transposing the ethos and heroism of republican Rome and Sparta to French soil (see Rosenblum 1967, ch. 2; Herbert 1972).

A second function of the ideal of a golden age is the sense of regeneration which it stimulates. Just as 'our ancestors' created a great culture or civilization, so surely can 'we', runs the leitmotif. This is important, exactly because most nationalisms, viewed from inside, start out from a sense of decline, alienation and inner exile, and go on to promise renewal, reintegration and restoration to a former glorious state. The nationalist mythology into which the memory of the golden age is inserted is one of humble, if special, origins, miraculous liberation, glorious efflorescence, divisive conflict, inner decay, even exile—and then national rebirth (see Smith 1984).

A third function of the golden age is its suggestion of potential through filiation. The emphasis is always on the descendants of heroes, sages, saints and poets having within themselves, in virtue of their blood relationship, the inner resources to become like their glorious forefathers and foremothers; and hence the inherent capacity of grandsons and granddaughters and their descendants to give birth to a civilization and culture worthy of the golden age. So the community will be purified of alien accretions, and by returning to its former faith and purity will be renewed and restored 'as in the days of old'. In this respect, the golden age reveals to the latterday community its 'authentic' (usually pre-industrial and rural) self and bids it rediscover and realize that self under quite different conditions (see Thaden 1964; Mosse 1964).

Finally, the memory of a golden age is closely linked to a sense of collective destiny. The road that the community expects to take in each generation is inspired and shaped by its memories of former heroic ages. Their values and symbols form the basis and spur to heroic feats of communal self-sacrifice in the future, a future that can become as glorious and fulfilling as the days of old. Memories of Irish golden ages, pagan and Christian, endowed Irish men and women with a vision of a resurrected Ireland and inspired Irish nationalists to heroic self-sacrifice on its behalf. In early twentieth-century Egypt, two visions of a resurgent Egypt, the one strictly Egyptian and territorial, the other Arab and ethnic, competed for the loyalty of Egyptians; the secular, territorial vision drew on the memories of Pharaonic grandeur to underpin a separate Egyptian destiny, whereas the more religious, ethnic vision harked back to Islam and the Fatimids for the Arab destiny which it sought. In other words, the ideal of self-renewal and the vision of collective destiny are built into the collective memory of a golden age and justify all the sacrifices that citizens may be asked to make (Lyons 1979; Hutchinson 1987; Gershoni and Jankowski 1987).

So much for the concept and general functions of the golden age. In concrete historical instances, golden ages, like the ethno-histories of which they form the high points, are unevenly distributed across the globe. Just as some communities can boast full, rich and well-documented ethno-histories with more than one golden age, others must be content with only shadowy memories of a collective past and its heroes. Slovaks, for example, had great difficulty disentangling their ancient past of 'greater Moravia' with ninth-century heroes like Svatopluk from the better-known and fuller records of the Bohemian kingdom of the Czechs. To this day, Ukrainians seek to disentangle their closely related culture yet separate past with its golden ages in Kievan 'Rus and the Cossack hetmanates from the much more all-embracing culture and better documented Muscovite and 'Great Russian' golden ages. One must add that it is not only large and powerful nations with long-independent states like Russia, China, Japan, France and Spain that can boast rich, well-documented ethno-histories with more than one golden age to emulate. Smaller, but ancient communities like the Irish, Armenians and Jews can also point to several golden ages in their long and well-recorded ethno-histories (Brock 1976; Portal 1969; Armstrong 1982: ch. 7).

On the whole, those communities with rich ethno-histories possess 'deep resources' on which to draw, and so can sustain themselves over long periods and maintain an extended struggle for recognition or parity. Even where they lack political and military security, their successive layers of cultural resources underpin their political claims as well as their sense of common ethnicity. This is not to say that ethnic nationalisms will only emerge in communities able to boast rich ethno-histories, but simply that such communities are unlikely to disappear or be submerged and, once aroused, can continue their struggle for long periods under adverse circumstances. Communities that lack these well-documented ethno-historical resources may well rise up in protest, as have the Moro and Eritreans. Some of them may even succeed in gaining independence after a long struggle, but whether, in the absence of such cultural resources, they will be able to sustain their new-found sense of community forged in battle, remains an open question. If they cannot create out of their prolonged struggle an ethno-history and even a golden age of heroic resistance to be recalled and emulated in times of crisis, they will not have those 'deep' cultural resources to fall back upon when internal conflicts and dissensions break out. In these as in other cases, history must be turned into ethnic myths and shared memories must become the basis of an ethno-heritage.

On the other hand, their very lack of rich ethno-histories relative to other better endowed neighbours stimulates these culturally peripheral and politically disprivileged communities to remedy this deficiency in a world where power stems from culture, in the same way as relative economic deprivation often spurs resentment and political emulation. Thus analysts would do well to focus on the comparative politics of uneven ethno-history, and more especially of golden ages, if they wish to understand both the power and variety of ethnic nationalisms.

ETHNIC ELECTION

The second major set of 'deep resources' on which different nationalisms can draw relates to religious belief, and more particularly to myths of ethnic election.

The general proposition here concerns the relationship between popular mobilization and sanctification. In order to mobilize large numbers of people, leaders and movements need to appeal to either material and status interests or promise individual salvation, or both. For many, status interests at least are served by a promise of individual and collective salvation. Now salvation in turn requires men and women to sanctify their lives and situations through correct belief and practice on the part of each member of a community of believers, and through the periodic ritual and moral renewal of that community.

Where a population is defined through processes of sanctification as a community of shared faith or belief, such a community tends to underpin and redefine populations united by shared memories and myths of origin, and thereby impede their politicization. To memory and myth are added collective beliefs and rituals; yet these selfsame beliefs and rituals may prevent the population in question from conceiving itself in any other way than as a 'faith community' or acting outside the limits of traditional orthopraxy, as occurred for some time with both Arabs and Jews (see Klausner 1960; Smith 1973).

One of the most important and influential of these collective beliefs is the *myth of ethnic election*. This singles out the community as a 'chosen people' entrusted with a sacred mission to proselytize or crusade or act as standard-bearer of the true faith. The mission sanctifies the community and the world and its fulfilment brings closer the salvation of the community and the world of which it forms the epicentre.

This is the general form of election myths that we encounter among so many peoples and communities in history from the Neo-Sumerian revival under the Third Dynasty of Ur and the ancient Egyptians of the New Kingdom to medieval Catholic France and early modern Protestant America and modern Afrikanerdom. In all these cases, election myths attach redemption through sanctification to a community of shared memories and myths of origin, turning it into a chosen people entrusted with a sacred task in the world's moral economy and thereby helping to purify and set that community apart from outsiders. Here we have a potent source of the moral exclusiveness of so many *ethnies,* their belief that by being entrusted with a sacred mission they stand in a position of superiority at the moral centre of the universe (Smith 1992).

Among some communities, a stronger form of election myth has emerged. This is the idea of '*the covenant*', the belief in a once-for-all contract between the community and its god, which requires the members of the community to fulfil certain ritual and moral obligations which define their sacred mission in return for which the deity will accord the community a special status, protection and privileges. The covenantal scheme was pioneered in ancient Israel, but it has been adopted elsewhere by such communities as the Armenians, Ulster Irish and Afrikaners. The ideal of a covenant as the source of their ethnic election has given these communities of shared memory and origin myths a durability and self-renewing capacity which forms one of the bedrocks of their contemporary political struggles (Akenson 1992).

Covenanted peoples manifest a particular intensity and persistence in their sense of ethnic election which validates their orthodoxy and sustains their communal practice through continual acts of sanctification. These in turn strengthen their belief in collective salvation through the periodic mobilization of a sacred community. In this way, the community's shared memories and origin myths are drawn into the covenantal scheme and are reinterpreted as sacred events in the formation and mission of a holy people.

There are a number of important consequences of such myths. Ethnic election myths, and particularly covenantal schemes, confer on the communities that evolve such beliefs an extraordinary sense of rectitude and *moral superiority.* This contrasts starkly, and indeed often compensates for, the many hardships and tribulations endured by the ethnic elect. These myths endow the persecuted, exiled or subject community with a determination and moral fibre which enables the community (if not all its members) to withstand a harsh fate, thereby providing the people with what Herder would have regarded as a deep well-spring of energy (*Kraft*) (see Berlin 1976).

Second, myths of ethnic election offer the members of a community a chronological scheme of *status reversal*. The elect may be persecuted now and subjects today; but in time their sufferings will be recognized and their virtue rewarded. They will, in the end, triumph over their enemies and attain the goal of their journey in history. This is particularly vividly expressed in covenantal schemes of which the Israelite Exodus from Egypt stands as the prototype, but it also applies to peoples without a clear covenantal scheme like the Catholic Irish or the Welsh who nevertheless regard themselves as an elect community. Conversely, the triumphant elect, those communities that are regnal and dominant like the Castilian, French or Amhara, credit their high status and privilege to the fulfilment of their sacred mission and the virtue of their members (see Armstrong 1982; Smith 1986: ch. 3 and 1992; Ullendorff 1973).

Linked to the ideas of mission and status reversal is the broader ideal of collective destiny which draws on the concept of chosenness to chart a unique path for the elect community. Reinforced in its mission by a sense of election, the nation can look forward confidently to a unique and glorious future commensurate with its true status. This sense of a distinctive and peculiar destiny has become, in secular form, part of the rhetoric of party politicians and statesmen; but it also has important morale-boosting and unifying functions in times of crisis and danger, as in Churchill's or de Gaulle's speeches to the British and French during the Second World War (Marwick 1974; Smith 1981c).

Fourth, ethnic election myths and especially covenantal schemes draw a strict *boundary* between the members of the elect and outsiders who cannot be redeemed. It is because they have accepted the obligations of their sacred mission that they have in turn been sanctified and chosen as a community. Conversely, it is because the outsiders have rejected those obligations and that mission that they have become profane and excluded, even damned. Such a sharp boundary demarcation appears to justify the ethnic elect in programmes of self-purification through exclusion and segregation of outsiders.

Finally, ethnic election myths are demotic. The energy they tap is that of the people, the whole community and not a particular segment; similarly, it is only through the mobilization of the people, the whole community, that the sacred mission can be achieved. The mission in turn requires every member to fulfil their sacred duties and regards every member as being equally eligible to enjoy the privileges of ethnic election—something that is particularly clear in covenantal schemes which are always contracts between whole peoples and their gods (see Zeitlin 1984).

SACRED TERRITORIES

The third set of 'deep resources' relates to historic territories and more specifically an *'ancestral homeland'*.

In general, a specific geographical area or space becomes associated with a particular collectivity, in the eyes of its members and of those around, in so far as it provides the location and arena for, and is felt to contribute uniquely to, key moments or turning points in the past experiences of the collectivity. The mountains, rivers, lakes and forests of a particular geographical space have afforded a special place and provided the scene for historic events—battles, treaties, revelations, oaths, shrines, migrations and so on—associated with a given community, and in subsequent lore have become an indispensable part of the shared memories and mythology of that community.

For *ethnies* a particular geographical area has become associated with a given community either as the traditional place of origin (in the origin myth) or as the locus of its liberation, settlement and golden ages. The association is threefold: first, as the unique and indispensable setting of events and experiences that moulded the community; second, in so far as the ethnic landscape is felt to have influenced and contributed to the course of events and the efflorescence of the community; and third, and perhaps most important, as the final resting-place of our forefathers and foremothers. These shrines underline the way in which a special space has come to belong to a particular community and, reciprocally, the community has become part of a specific land and particular ethnic landscapes. So, the land becomes 'our' territory and the 'eternal home' of our ancestors, an *ancestral homeland*, a motif that figures prominently, along with the paeans to ethnic landscapes, in the folklore and cultural heritage of ethnic communities (see Mosse 1994: ch. 2).

This relationship between people and land is the product over the *longue durée* of continual myth-making and the recitation of shared memories. Through the elaboration of folktales and legends and the performance of rituals and ceremonies, successive generations are reminded of various periods of their ethnic histories, and above all, of their golden ages.

In this way, a particular territory and specific landscapes are historicized. They become essential elements of the community's history, and the land becomes an historic homeland (Smith 1981b and 1986: ch. 8).

The association is even stronger where the *ethnie* is also a community of believers, animated by a unifying faith and cult. In these circumstances, the ancestral and historic homeland becomes also a *'sacred territory'*. A holy people must be located in an equally sanctified land, a land conferred by the deity on a sanctified people as a reward for correct belief and conduct in the execution of their sacred mission. The terms of the covenant between the community and its god requires a sacred arena set aside for the fulfilment of the spiritual mission, a 'promised land'. When the community is sundered from it, it is said to be in a state of spiritual exile; spiritual redemption therefore requires its restoration to the 'promised land'.

Interestingly enough, the sanctification of the land came later, as a result of the community's sense of election, of being set apart from its neighbours in the pursuit of the sacred mission with which God had entrusted the people. Thus the land of Canaan, though it figured prominently in the early formulations of the Covenant between God and Abraham as a reward for its fulfilment, did not become sacred in the eyes of the ancient Israelites and Jews till the late eighth century B.C., although it was long revered as the site of burial of the patriarchs and other holy figures (Zeitlin 1984; Grosby 1991).

There is an alternative scenario. Here the elect must search for, and discover, a promised land, a territory that a community of believers will sanctify through the performance of moral and ritual actions in building an ideal ethnic and civic community. It is the believer-pioneers themselves who, in creating their New Jerusalem whether on the African veldt or the American prairie, will realize the promise of a land whose features are integral to the utopia which they hope to build in fulfilment of their sacred mission (Tuveson 1968; Akenson 1992: ch. 3).

In both cases, the historic homeland becomes sacred partly through the same processes of myth-making and shared remembering as occurs in all ethnic communities, but also through the special heroic acts of moral and ritual conduct of a community of believers and its religious heroes. It is the memory of their example in moments of revelation and crisis that creates a special bond of holiness between the community and its homeland, as well as the piety and awe which surrounds the tombs of prophets, poets and holy men and the sepulchres of righteous kings and warriors, laid to rest in the land of their people.

The ancestral land also links memory to destiny. For it is in the reborn land, the homeland which is renewed, that national regeneration takes place. The sacred land of our ancestors is also the promised land of our descendants and posterity. It is only on our 'native soil' that we can realize ourselves, that the nation can become truly free and authentic again. Hence the liberation of the land from oppressors is not simply a political or economic necessity; it is demanded by a unique history that requires fulfilment in a glorious destiny through the rebirth of a community on its own terrain (see Hertzberg 1960; Mosse 1964).

The 'deep resource' which an ancestral, even a sacred, homeland offers, is not isolated from the other deep resources. Usually the three sets of resources are combined. Shared memories of golden ages are always associated with attachments to ancestral homelands, even where these are not sacred territories; and myths of ethnic election require both ancestral homelands for their execution, and usually a standard or model of inspiration for future generations, the memory of a golden age in which the sacred mission was heroically fulfilled. Hence the tendency for the three sets of deep resources—ancestral homelands, golden ages and myths of ethnic election—to combine and recombine in varying forms and degrees, thereby endowing many *ethnies* with great resilience and staying power down the ages.

VARIETY AND SELF-RENEWAL OF NATIONALISMS

Here, then, we have the main components in our analysis of the durability of modern nationalisms. Shared memories of a rich ethno-history, and especially of golden ages; religious beliefs in ethnic election, and especially sacred covenants; and sentiments of belonging to ancestral homelands, especially sacred territories; these provide the sure foundations for nationalist movements aiming to regenerate the community or cultural category and form it into a modern nation in its ancestral homeland, preferably with its own protective state in a comity of national states. The memories, myths, symbols and values of which these 'deep' ethno-symbolic resources are composed furnish a distinctive and varied repertoire from which different élites can select those elements which can mobilize and motivate large numbers of their designated population, providing that they adhere to the cultural patterns and remain within the cultural parameters laid down by successive generations of a particular ethno-history. It is not difficult to see how the elements of these 'deep resources' can be drawn upon to renew the community, form it into a modern territorial 'nation' and point the way to a glorious destiny for the chosen people.

Similarly, the sheer diversity and variety of these resources, and of the particular ethno-symbolic elements of which they are composed, goes a long way to explaining the variety and diversity of nationalist expression and the individuality of each nation. Much of the answer to questions such as 'who is the nation?' and 'what is the character of this nationalism?', lies in the distinctive patterning of elements drawn from each of these ethno-symbolic resource repertoires—the memories of golden ages, the beliefs in ethnic election and the attachments to ancestral homelands. Hence the uniqueness of nations is not absolute. It is a consequence of the many permutations of myths, symbols, memories and values that compose the three sets of ethno-symbolic resources, as well as of any special features that mark out that community, such as its geopolitical and ecological position, its class composition and its ethnic and religious complexity.

Moreover, the uneven distribution of ethno-histories, ethno-religious beliefs and territorial attachments goes some way towards explaining another important aspect of nationalism: its variable intensity, not only between different communities but at different times within the same community. One might, for example, seek to explain the durability and intensity of Serb and Croat nationalisms in terms of their collective memories of former golden ages, vivid beliefs in ethnic election and powerful attachments to ancestral homelands. Conversely, the persistent but less intense nationalism of the Slovenes is explained, not only by their different political demography, but also by their relative lack, compared to their neighbours, of such vivid ethno-religious beliefs. Similarly, Basques and Catalans share equally vivid memories of former golden ages; but the greater intensity and exclusiveness of Basque nationalism is also related to their strong attachment to a relatively isolated homeland and their belief in ethnic election through nobility of blood (Schöpflin 1980; Greenwood 1977).

There is, however, a further complication. Cultural categories that are in the process of acquiring ethnic myths of origin and descent and attachments to ancestral homelands, may well feel at a cultural and historical disadvantage in relation to neighbours that have richer and better documented memories of golden ages and stronger beliefs in ethnic election. In other words, if they lack one or more of the ethno-symbolic 'deep resources' found among successful nations and more powerful nationalisms, they may seek to compensate for these deficiencies by a more violent display of territorial attachments and the rediscovery, even invention, of a suitable ethno-history. This may even be supplemented by a zealous return to a religious tradition that exalts their community above the belief-systems of their neighbours, as has to some extent occurred among Bosnian Muslims who till recently had been defined only in terms of *having once been Muslim*, a badge without content, but who are now engaged in a Muslim revivalism (Gellner 1983).

This goes some way to explaining why we witness so many intense and violent nationalisms among poorer, less educated peoples in fairly backward regions. It is not simply that they and their habitats are economically and educationally less advanced, in their own eyes no less than those of others; they are also less well-endowed with the deep resources of ethno-history, ethnic election and ancestral homeland than some of their neighbours. Both Eritreans and Slovaks fit into this category. Slovaks in the early twentieth century and Eritreans after the 1960s felt at a disadvantage in terms of cultural distinctiveness and cohesion in relation to their neighbours, and compensated for this by either forging a community through conflict, or by stressing attachments to a homeland and its separate history and, in the Slovak case, the differential nature of its shared Catholic beliefs (see Horowitz 1985: ch. 6; Cliffe 1989; Pynsent 1994).

Analysis of the ethno-symbolic components of the three sets of 'deep resources' can help us, then, to assess the likelihood of persistence and self-renewal of nationalism, and the durability and variety of nations. For example, the more an *ethnie* is also a faith community harking back to a religious golden age, and the stronger its links with a particular, especially a sanctified, territory, the more intense and persistent is likely to be its nationalism and the ensuing nation. This is clearly the case with such diaspora communities as the Armenians, Greeks and Jews. In each of these ancient communities the ideal of collective restoration in their ancestral homelands emerged from a sense of exile of an ethnic elect whose members looked back nostalgically to the glorious epochs of its ethno-history (Klausner 1960; Campbell and Sherrard 1968: ch. 1; Atiyah 1968; Vital 1975; Armstrong 1982: ch. 7; Almog 1987: ch. 1).

In the case of the Afrikaners, a heightened form of ethnic election myth, of the strict covenantal variety, coupled with shared memories of the golden age of the Great Trek to a 'promised land' outside British domination, has produced a singularly intense and racially exclusive nationalism. The long series of conflicts of the ethnic elect with white oppressors and native unbelievers, notably in the era of Kruger, further consolidated the exclusive sense of Afrikanerdom and underpinned an extraordinarily resilient and durable Afrikaner ethnic nationalism (Thompson 1985; Akenson 1992).

Similar deep resources are drawn upon by an Ulster Scots nationalism which since the seventeenth century has grown more intense and pervasive in north-eastern Ireland. Here vivid shared memories of the vicissitudes of the first settlements, and memories of earlier golden ages after the battle of the Boyne and the siege of Londonderry, are coupled with a deep-rooted belief in ethnic election as God's covenanted people to produce a powerful attachment to Ulster as the ancestral and promised homeland of the Protestant settlers (see Lyons 1979; Akenson 1992: ch. 4).

SELF-RENEWAL IN THE 1990s

Of course none of these components can tell us *when* nationalisms are likely to emerge. The *timing* of nationalist resistance depends largely on material and geopolitical trends, including:

1. the rise of an intelligentsia, able to translate ethno-historical traditions, ethnic beliefs and territorial attachments into the language of modern nationalism, the language and symbolism that have become common currency in the contemporary world;
2. the socio-economic development and cultural infrastructure (schools, universities, books, newspapers, modernized language, film and TV, the arts) of the community designated by the intelligentsia and other élites as the nation-to-be, and hence its ability to form a durable nationalist movement and wage an often protracted struggle against alien oppressors;
3. the reactions of state élites of the polity in which the community is incorporated and the nationalism located, whether such élites be indigenous or foreign;
4. the general geopolitical situation, including changing international attitudes to ethnic separatism and irredentism and the regional location of the mooted nation.

On the geopolitical level, indeed, the 1990s has witnessed a cautious relaxation of the rigid and hitherto almost frozen inter-state system. The possibility of some limited redrawing of territorial boundaries has been admitted, albeit only in a few select cases. The greater fluidity of a multipolar era after the end of the Cold War has encouraged new attitudes in this respect, but the emphasis throughout has been on orderly and limited change. While Eritrea and the ex-Soviet republics could be seen as the inevitable consequences of dismantling the last vestiges of imperialism and colonialism (in which case the UN Charter sanctions separatism), the ethnic secessions of Slovakia, Croatia, Bosnia and Slovenia have opened up vistas of more radical ethnic territorial changes which the West has not welcomed, nor the UN Charter allowed (see Wiberg 1983; Mayall 1990: ch. 4).

State élites too have been cautious. Most have remained firmly committed to the political *status quo*, often violently so, as in Turkey, the Caucasus and Sri Lanka; and the superpowers, themselves composed of a variety of ethnic communities, have been loathe to consider, let alone encourage, separatism. Nevertheless a few state élites have been reluctantly prepared to concede peaceful secessions, as in Czechoslovakia and possibly in Quebec at some future date.

At the same time, many of the nationalisms of the 1990s operate on behalf of ethnic communities and cultural categories that possess considerable socio-cultural resources and have produced intelligentsias who can mobilize their ethnic kinsmen. Many of these movements, too, are heirs to other waves of ethnic nationalisms which appeared in earlier decades or centuries. Some of these earlier movements were arrested or emasculated, and their intelligentsias silenced or deported. This is what happened under Stalinism in the former Soviet Union from the 1920s and in Eastern Europe from the 1940s; some of the current movements have openly taken up their cause where it was so rudely interrupted after the Bolshevik Revolution. In other cases, in Africa and Asia, ethnic nationalisms have been smouldering since the 1950s and 1960s—in Eritrea, among the Shan and Karen in Burma, the Moro in the Philippines, the southern Sudanese, the Palestinians, Tamils, Sikhs and Nagas, reappearing with renewed vigour in successive situations. In yet other instances, the origins of the ethno-nationalist movements can be traced back to the early twentieth century— among Kurds and Bretons, Arabs and Turks, Indonesians and Burmese —or even into the nineteenth century—among Basques and Catalans, Scots, Welsh and Irish, Finns, Latvians and Lithuanians, Czechs and Slovaks, Serbs and Croats, and many others. In the later twentieth century, many of these nationalisms have changed direction, acquired a new social and economic programme and appealed to new strata of the population. But they remained firmly within the parameters of their ethno-historical traditions, drawing on the same shared memories, ethnic myths and territorial attachments, even if the language had become secular and political, and the symbolism reflected the needs of modern communities rather than those of their pre-modern ethno-religious forebears.[8]

Though these nationalisms were modern and the nations they helped to create relatively new, their cultural and social bases, the ethno-symbolic elements that made each nation, and nationalism individual and distinctive and gave to each its persistent character, derived from specific repertoires and resources of ethno-history, religious myth and ancestral territory. This is true of nationalisms in every continent and all economic backgrounds. Thus in the advanced industrial capitalism of North America we have witnessed a relatively recent nationalist upsurge among the Québecois, which started in the 1950s with the silent revolution of the francophone intelligentsia. But the deeper well-springs of that movement derive from the peculiarities of the Québecois ethno-history of subordination to British domination, from earlier defensive Catholic beliefs in ethnic superiority and from powerful territorial attachments to the province, all of which sustained the community in its long period of relative agrarian isolation and which now undergird its modern secular expressions (Pinard and Hamilton 1984).

CONCLUSION

In the history of ethnicity and nationalism, then, there is nothing peculiar about the upsurge of ethnic nationalism in the 1990s in the aftermath of the Cold War, beyond a very partial and perhaps temporary relaxation of habitual inter-state norms and attitudes to ethnic claims and national aspirations. As I said at the outset, ethnic nationalisms surface in all kinds of crisis situation and every type of social and political change. The real questions concern not the timing of the surges and resurgences, but the character and intensity of the ethnic nationalisms, and the durability and variety of the nations they aim, and sometimes succeed, in creating. These are 'who' and 'what', rather than 'when' and 'where', questions. We need to know why some nations arise rather than others, why these nations and nationalisms possess a particular character, and why some nationalisms are more intense and exclusive than others.

My suggestion is that, to answer these questions, we should look not only at the specific economic and political circumstances in which given nationalisms emerge, but also at the 'deep' ethno-symbolic resources that they command. In particular the durability and character of a given nationalism can be in large part explained by analysing the ethno-historical, religious and territorial heritages that its proponents can draw upon. These ethno-heritages set the limits and provide the patterns within which modern élites, religious or secular, must operate if they are to be successful in mobilizing large numbers of their designated co-nationals. They also furnish the models and inspiration for the regenerative and purificatory drives of modern nationalism. Above all, the light of shared memories, religious convictions and ancestral attachments sustains ethnic communities and nationalist movements in their long hours of darkness through an historically-based faith in a glorious collective destiny.

Notes

1. There is a long debate among scholars about the origins and dating of nationalist ideology. For most, the late eighteenth century marks the moment of origin, the period of the Partitions of Poland and the American and French

Revolutions. See *inter alia* Kohn (1967), Cobban (1969) and Mosse (1994). For the problems of definition, see Smith (1983: ch. 7) and, for the present definition (1991: ch. 4).

2. There are several types of 'primordialism'. In addition to the naturalist variant of many nationalists, a sociobiological version is represented by Van den Berghe (1979). A more modest 'participants' primordialism' can be found in Geertz (1963) and Shils (1995). See the rejoinder by Grosby (1994) to the critique by Eller and Coughlan (1993).

3. The misleading nature of this term, in the light of the ethnic pluralism of the majority of the world's states, is underlined by Connor (1972). Thus Tilly's term, the 'national state' (Tilly 1975) seems preferable; this is a state that seeks broader national unity on the basis of nationalist ideals.

4. For the problems of defining the concept of 'the nation', see Deutsch (1966: ch. 1) and Connor (1978). For the definition adopted here, see Smith (1991: ch. 1).

5. There is a keen debate on the merits and demerits of ethnic and civic nationalisms. See especially Plamenatz (1976), Breton (1988), Ignatieff (1993) and Smith (1994b); for French and German criteria of citizenship, and their different forms of nationalism, see Brubaker (1992) and Llobera (1994).

6. For a much fuller exposition of these arguments, see Smith (1995: ch. 1). For various assessments of global culture and nationalism, see Featherstone (1990).

7. There is a vast literature on ethnicity and identity. For attempts to relate them, see Barth (1969); Epstein (1978); Armstrong (1982); and Eriksen (1993). For a discussion of ethnic and national identity in pre-modern epochs, see Smith (1994a).

8. On the 'ethnic revival' in the West, see Esman (1977) and Smith (1981a). For a more general analysis of ethnic separatism in Africa and Asia, see Horowitz (1985). For the background to national separatism in the former Soviet Union, see G. Smith (1990).

References

AKENSON, D. 1992 *God's Peoples*. Ithaca: Cornell University Press.

ALMOG, S. 1987 *Zionism and History*. Jerusalem: Magnes Press.

ANDERSON, B. 1983 *Imagined Communities: Reflections on the Origins and Spread of Nationalism*. London: Verso.

ARMSTRONG, J. 1982 *Nations before Nationalism*. Chapel Hill: University of North Carolina Press.

ARNASON, J. 1990 'Nationalism, globalism and modernity', in Mike Featherstone (ed.) *Global Culture: Nationalism, Globalisation and Modernity*. London, Newbury Park and New Delhi: Sage Publications.

ATIYAH, A. S. 1968 *A History of Eastern Christianity*. London: Methuen.

BARTH, F. (ed.) 1969 *Ethnic Groups and Boundaries*. Boston: Little, Brown and Co.

BERLIN, I. 1976 *Vico and Herder*. London: Hogarth Press.

BHABHA, H. (ed.) 1990 *Nation and Narration*. London and Boston: Routledge.

BRETON, R. 1988 'From ethnic to civic nationalism: the case of Canada', *Ethnic and Racial Studies* 11(1): 91–112.

BREUILLY, J. 1982 *Nationalism and the State*. Manchester: Manchester University Press.

BROCK, P. 1976 *The Slovak National Awakening*. Toronto: Toronto University Press.

BRUBAKER, R. 1992 *Citizenship and Nationhood in France and Germany*. Cambridge, Mass. and London: Harvard University Press.

CAMPBELL, J. and SHERRARD, P. 1968 *Modern Greece*. London: Benn.

CLIFFE, L. 1989 'Forging a Nation: the Eritrean experience', *Third World Quarterly* 11(4): 131–47.

COBBAN, A. 1969 *The Nation-State and National Self Determination*. rev. edn, London: Collins, Fontana.

CONNOR, W. 1972 'Nation-building or nation-destroying?', *World Politics* 24: 319–55.

—— 1973 'The politics of ethno-nationalism', *Journal of International Affairs* 27(1): 1–21.

—— 1978 'A nation is a nation, is a state, is an ethnic group, is a . . .', *Ethnic and Racial Studies* 1(4): 378–400.

DEUTSCH, K. 1966 *Nationalism and Social Communication*, 2nd edn, New York: MIT Press.

DOOB, L. 1964 *Nationalism and Patriotism: Their psychological foundations*. New Haven: Yale University Press.

EISENSTEIN-BARZILAY, I. 1959 'National and anti-national trends in the Berlin Haskalah', *Jewish Social Studies* 21: 16–92.

ELLER, J. and COUGHLAN, R. 1993 'The poverty of primordialism: the demystification of ethnic attachments', *Ethnic and Racial Studies* 16(2): 18–202.

EPSTEIN, A. L. 1978 *Ethos and Identity*. London: Tavistock Publications Ltd.

ERIKSEN, T. 1993 *Ethnicity and Nationalism*. London: Pluto Press.

ESMAN, M. (ed.) 1977 *Ethnic Conflict in the Western World*. Ithaca: Cornell University Press.

FEATHERSTONE, M. (ed.) 1990 *Global Culture: Nationalism, Globalisation and Modernity*. London, Newbury Park and New Delhi: Sage Publications.

GEERTZ, C. 1963 'The Integrative Revolution', in Clifford Geertz (ed.) *Old Societies and New States*. New York: Free Press.

GELLNER, E. 1983 *Nations and Nationalism*. Oxford: Blackwell.

—— 1994 *Encounters with Nationalism*. Oxford: Blackwell.

GERSHONI, I. and JANKOWSKI, J. 1987 *Egypt, Islam and the Arabs: The Search for Nationhood, 1900–1930*, New York and Oxford: Oxford University Press.

GIDDENS, A. 1985 *The Nation-State and Violence*. Cambridge: Polity Press.

GREENWOOD, D. 1977 'Continuity in change: Spanish Basque ethnicity as an historical process', in Esman (1977: 81–102).

GRODZINS, M. 1956 *The Loyal and the Disloyal: Social Boundaries of Patriotism and Treason*. Cleveland and New York: Meridian Books.

GROSBY, S. 1991 'Religion and Nationality in Antiquity', *European Journal of Sociology* XXXII: 229–65.

—— 1994 'The verdict of history: the inexpungeable tie of primordiality—a response to Eller and Coughlan', *Ethnic and Racial Studies* 17(1): 164–71.

HERACLIDES, A. 1991 *The self-determination of Minorities in International Politics*. London: Frank Cass.

HERBERT, R. 1972 *David, Voltaire, Brutus and the French Revolution*. London: Allen Lane.

HERTZBERG, A. (ed.) 1960 *The Zionist Idea, A Reader*. New York: Meridian Books.

HOBSBAWM, E. 1990 *Nations and Nationalism since 1780*. Cambridge: Cambridge University Press.

HOROWITZ, D. 1985 *Ethnic Groups in Conflict*. Berkeley and Los Angeles: University of California Press.

HUTCHINSON, J. 1987 *The Dynamics of Cultural Nationalism: The Gaelic Revival and the Creation of the Irish Nation State*. London: Allen and Unwin.

IGNATIEFF, M. 1993 *Blood and Belonging: Journeys into the New Nationalisms*. London: Chatto and Windus.

JOHNSON, H. (ed.) 1968 *Economic Nationalism in Old and New States*. London: Allen and Unwin.

KAUTSKY, J. (ed.) 1962 *Political Change in Underdeveloped Countries*. New York: John Wiley.

KEDOURIE, E. 1960 *Nationalism*. London: Hutchinson. (ed.).

—— 1971 *Nationalism in Asia and Africa*. London: Weidenfeld and Nicolson.

KLAUSNER, S. 1960 'Why they chose Israel', *Archives de Sociologie des Religions* 9: 129–44.

KOHN, H. 1967 *The Idea of Nationalism*. 2nd edn, New York: Collier-Macmillan.

LLOBERA, J. 1994 *The God of Modernity: The Development of Nationalism in Western Europe*. Oxford: Providence, USA: Berg.

LYONS, F. S. L. 1979 *Culture and Anarchy in Ireland, 1890–1930*. London: Oxford University Press.

MANN, M. 1984 'The autonomous power of the state: its origins, mechanisms and results', *European Journal of Sociology* XXV: 185–213.

MARWICK, A. 1974 *War and Social Change in the Twentieth Century*. London: Methuen.

MAYALL, J. 1990 *Nationalism and International Society*. Cambridge: Cambridge University Press.

McNEILL, W. 1986 *Polyethnicity and National Unity in World History*. Toronto: University of Toronto Press.

MOSSE, G. 1964 *The Crisis of German Ideology*. New York: Grosset and Dunlap.

Mosse, G. 1994 *Confronting the Nation: Jewish and Western Nationalism*, Hanover and London: Brandeis University Press.

Orridge, A. 1980 'Varieties of nationalism', in L. Tivey (ed.), *The Nation State*. Oxford: Martin Robertson.

Pinard, M. and Hamilton, R. 1984 'The class bases of the Quebec Independence movement: conjectures and evidence', *Ethnic and Racial Studies* 7(1): 19–54.

Plamenatz, J. 1976 'Two types of nationalism', in Eugene Kamenka (ed.) *Nationalism: The Nature and Evolution of an Idea*. London: Edward Arnold.

Portal, R. 1969 *The Slavs: A Cultural Historical Survey of the Slavonic Peoples*. trans. Patrick Evans, London: Weidenfeld and Nicolson.

Pynsent, R. 1994 *Questions of Identity: Czech and Slovak Ideas of Nationality and Personality*. London: Central European University Press.

Renan, E. 1882 *Qu'est-ce que'une nation?*, Paris: Calmann-Levy.

Rosenblum, R. 1967 *Transformations in late Eighteenth Century Art*. Princeton: Princeton University Press.

Seltzer, R. 1980 *Jewish People, Jewish Thought*. New York: Macmillan.

Schöpflin, G. 1980 'Nationality in the fabric of Yugoslav politics', *Survey* 25: 1–19.

Shils, E. 1995 'Nation, Nationality, Nationalism and Civil Society', *Nations and Nationalism* 1(1): 93–118.

Smelser, N. 1968 *Essays in Sociological Explanation*. Englewood Cliffs: Prentice Hall.

Smith, A. D. 1973 *Nationalism, A Trend Report and Annotated Bibliography*, a Special Issue of *Current Socioloy* 21(3), The Hague: Mouton.

—— 1981a *The Ethnic Revival in the Modern World*. Cambridge: Cambridge University Press.

—— 1981b 'States and homelands: the social and geopolitical implications of national territory', *Millennium, Journal of International Studies* 10(3): 187–202.

—— 1981c 'War and ethnicity: the role of warfare in the formation, self-images and cohesion of ethnic communities', *Ethnic and Racial Studies* 4(4): 375–97.

—— 1983 *Theories of Nationalism*. 2nd edn, London: Duckworth and New York: Holmes and Meier.

—— 1984 'Ethnic myths and ethnic revivals', *European Journal of Sociology* XXV: 28–305.

—— 1986 *The Ethnic Origins of Nations*. Oxford: Blackwell.

—— 1990 'The supersession of nationalism?', *International Journal of Comparative Sociology* XXXI(1–2): 1–31.

—— 1991 *National Identity*. Harmondsworth: Penguin.

—— 1992 'Chosen peoples: why ethnic groups survive', *Ethnic and Racial Studies* 15(3): 436–56.

—— 1994a 'The problem of national identity: ancient, medieval and modern?', *Ethnic and Racial Studies* 17(3): 375–99.

—— 1994b 'Three concepts of the nation', *Revista del Occidente* 161: 7–23.

—— 1995 *Nations and Nationalism in a Global Era*. Cambridge: Polity Press.

SMITH, G. (ed.) 1990 *The Nationalities Question in the Soviet Union*. London and New York: Longman.

THADEN, E. 1964 *Conservative Nationalism in Nineteenth Century Russia*. Seattle: University of Washington Press.

THOMPSON, L. 1985 *The Political Mythology of Apartheid*. New Haven and London: Yale University Press.

TILLY, C. (ed.) 1975 *The Formation of National States in Western Europe*. Princeton: Princeton University Press.

TIVEY, L. (ed.) 1980 *The Nation State*. Oxford: Martin Robertson.

TOMLINSON, J. 1990 *Cultural Imperialism*. London: Pinter Publishers.

TUVESON, E. L. 1968 *Redeemer Nation: The Idea of America's Millennial Role*. Chicago and London: University of Chicago Press.

ULLENDORFF, E. 1973 *The Ethiopians, An Introduction to Country and People*. 3rd edn, London: Oxford University Press.

VAN DEN BERGHE, P. 1979 *The Ethnic Phenomenon*. New York: Elsevier.

VITAL, D. 1975 *The Origins of Zionism*. Oxford: Clarendon Press.

WILBERG, H. 1983 'Self-determination as an international issue', in Ioann Lewis (ed.): *Nationalism and Self-determination In the Horn of Africa*. London: Ithaca Press.

ZEITLIN, I. 1984 *Ancient Judaism*. Cambridge: Polity Press.

INDEX